Corporate Social Responsibility Approaches to Ethical AI in Business

Erum Shaikh
Shaheed Benazir Bhutto University, Sanghar, Pakistan

IGI Global
Scientific Publishing
Publishing Tomorrow's Research Today

Vice President of Editorial	Melissa Wagner
Managing Editor of Acquisitions	Mikaela Felty
Managing Editor of Book Development	Jocelynn Hessler
Production Manager	Mike Brehm
Cover Design	Phillip Shickler

Published in the United States of America by
IGI Global Scientific Publishing
701 East Chocolate Avenue
Hershey, PA, 17033, USA
Tel: 717-533-8845
Fax: 717-533-8661
E-mail: cust@igi-global.com
Website: https://www.igi-global.com

Library of Congress Cataloging-in-Publication Data

Names: Shaikh, Erum, 1988- editor.
Title: Corporate social responsibility approaches to ethical AI in business / Erum Shaikh.
Description: Hershey, PA : IGI Global, [2025] | Includes bibliographical references and index. | Summary: "This book delves into the intricate interplay between technology, organizational dynamics, and societal expectations. It employs the Technology-Organization-Environment (TOE) framework to dissect the factors influencing AI implementation. By synthesizing cutting-edge research with theoretical insights, this volume equips professionals across industries with the tools to navigate the ethical complexities of AI"-- Provided by publisher.
Identifiers: LCCN 2024038201 (print) | LCCN 2024038202 (ebook) | ISBN 9798369334782 (hardcover) | ISBN 9798369349120 (paperback) | ISBN 9798369334799 (ebook)
Subjects: LCSH: Social responsibility of business. | Business enterprises--Technological innovations.
Classification: LCC HD60 .C67317 2024 (print) | LCC HD60 (ebook) | DDC 658.4/080285--dc23/eng/20240913
LC record available at https://lccn.loc.gov/2024038201
LC ebook record available at https://lccn.loc.gov/2024038202
ISBN:979-8-3693-3478-2
eISBN:979-8-3693-3479-9

British Cataloguing in Publication Data
A Cataloguing in Publication record for this book is available from the British Library.

I devote this project and all of my efforts to my loving parents, caring husband and dear sisters who truly supported me to complete this book.

Their support and encouragement have consistently demonstrated to me that:

"PATH TOWARDS SUCCESS"

Table of Contents

Detailed Table of Contents

With the advent of artificial intelligence (AI), there arises a new frontier in CSR practices, as AI-powered solutions also have the ability to promote innovation; increase stakeholder involvement; improve the efficacy, efficiency, and scalability of corporate social responsibility (CSR) endeavours; and make evidence-based decisions in CSR efforts easier. But incorporating AI into CSR initiatives also brings up difficult moral, legal, and societal issues. The purpose of this chapter is to provide insights into the ways in which artificial intelligence (AI) is changing corporate social responsibility (CSR) and how AI can encourage transparency, drive innovation in CSR programs, and involve stakeholders to produce significant social, environmental, and economic results. This study also explores the current trends in CSR and AI. This may help businesses allocate their resources more effectively, spot new trends, and improve impact measurement at large.

This chapter analyzes the impact of AI in CSR through a bibliometric analysis using the Web of Science. A general overview and a lay of the land of studies that connect AI and CSR are presented, as well as a specific analysis showing the evolution of publications merging both topics, a description of the most relevant publications in the field, the most cited authors, the countries in which most articles have originated, key words, and sponsors, among others. Bibliometric maps that show co-authorship, bibliographic coupling, co-citations, and keywords that allow the analysis of emerging clusters and future trends are done with the software VOS Viewer.

Over the past few years, there has been an apparent surge in the application of corporate social responsibility (CSR) advertising by companies to convey their dedication to social and environmental causes. However, this trend has also sparked increasing doubt among consumers about the credibility and impact of CSR advertisements. This study seeks to explore the impact of content and delivery on consumer skepticism towards CSR advertisements. This study identifies key components of CSR communication (content and delivery) and specific variables within each (company-CSR fit, consumer-CSR fit for content, self-promotional tone, inauthentic information for delivery). It confirms the significant impact of these variables on consumer skepticism towards CSR communications, suggesting that aligning company-CSR fit can mitigate skepticism. Consumers are skeptical of CSR motives when there's a gap between company claims and actions. By focusing on content and delivery, practitioners can mitigate skepticism and shape perceptions of corporate responsibility.

Finding strategies to maintain employee well-being is becoming more and more important to a variety of stakeholders, both within and beyond the context of the workplace, in today's rapidly evolving and fast-paced global workplace where preserving competitive edge is essential to success. The research design of study is descriptive in nature. Data was collected from secondary sources to study the importance of sustainable HR practices and wellbeing in a changing environment. Evidence demonstrates that a direct connection between HRM practices, well-being, and performance—possibly more significantly for organizations—can give practitioners the knowledge they need to motivate them to spend their resources. The findings of the research are relevant to a broad range of company sectors involved with innovative HRM, greening, and sustainability practices as well as corporate strategies that support well-being.

This chapter provides a comprehensive analysis of digital infrastructure and connectivity as foundational elements for fostering digital technologies and economic development. It defines the role and significance of digital infrastructure and examines the history and technological progression of connectivity projects. Key components such as broadband networks, telecom structures, and data centers are analyzed for their importance in supporting modern communication and information exchange. The chapter also reviews the impact of laws and policies on digital infrastructure, focusing on financing, rural access, and security. A case study on Zorez Telecom's expansion project highlights the challenges organizations may face when implementing digital infrastructure, covering regulatory and economic issues, while offering practical approaches for students and professionals to address these challenges.

This research aims to explore the influence of corporate social responsibility (CSR) on the development and adoption of ethical AI practices in businesses through a quantitative approach. The study investigates how CSR initiatives drive responsible AI governance, focusing on transparency, accountability, and fairness. By analyzing data from a cross-sectional survey of companies across various industries, key metrics such as CSR expenditure, ethical AI adoption rates, and regulatory compliance are examined. Statistical methods, including regression analysis and correlation testing, are employed to assess the impact of CSR on ethical AI outcomes. The findings are expected to provide data-driven insights into how CSR investments align with the development of ethical AI frameworks, contributing to sustainable business practices. This study also highlights the role of CSR in fostering trust, improving corporate reputation, and mitigating risks associated with AI technologies. The results could guide policymakers and business leaders in shaping future CSR and AI strategies.

The integration of artificial intelligence (AI) in the hotel industry has brought about significant advancements in customer service, operational efficiency, and personalized experiences. However, the ethical implications of AI usage in this sector raise critical concerns that necessitate a proactive approach to corporate social responsibility (CSR). This chapter explores the various CSR strategies adopted by hotel businesses to ensure the ethical implementation of AI technologies. It discusses the importance of transparency, fairness, and accountability in AI applications, and the role of CSR in addressing issues such as data privacy, bias, and the impact on employment. By adopting ethical AI practices, hotels can not only enhance their reputation but also contribute to sustainable business models that prioritize the well-being of all stakeholders.

Preface

In the fast-evolving landscape of technology, the integration of artificial intelligence (AI) into business practices has introduced profound ethical dilemmas. These challenges demand careful consideration of the impacts on societal values and corporate responsibilities. *Corporate Social Responsibility Approaches to Ethical AI in Business* addresses these pressing issues, offering a comprehensive exploration of AI adoption within organizations.

This book delves into the intricate interplay between technology, organizational dynamics, and societal expectations. It employs the Technology-Organization-Environment (TOE) framework to dissect the factors influencing AI implementation. By synthesizing cutting-edge research with theoretical insights, this volume equips professionals across industries with the tools to navigate the ethical complexities of AI.

The audience for this book spans corporate leaders, academics, and policymakers alike. It serves as a guiding compass for organizations and policymakers navigating the evolving landscape of corporate social responsibility (CSR) and ethics in the AI era. By fostering a nuanced understanding of trust and responsibility, it empowers stakeholders to embrace AI-driven innovation while upholding ethical principles and promoting societal well-being.

This publication covers a wide array of academic disciplines, including Artificial Intelligence, Business Ethics, Corporate Social Responsibility, Emotional Intelligence, Ethical Challenges, Human Intelligence, Machine Ethics, Moral Values within Corporations, Social Wellbeing, and Technology Ethics. It invites readers to join the discourse and embark on a journey toward responsible AI adoption—a journey where ethics and innovation converge to forge a sustainable future for all.

ORGANIZATION OF THE BOOK

Chapter 1: Ethical AI Entrepreneurial Strategies for Business Intelligence and Blockchain

This chapter explores the multifaceted applications of Blockchain Technology (BT) beyond cryptocurrencies. It provides a comprehensive overview of BT's impact across diverse sectors such as Real Estate, Finance, Healthcare, and Manufacturing. Titled "Blockchain Beyond Cryptocurrencies," the chapter elucidates the transformative potential of decentralized technologies in reshaping business intelligence and entrepreneurial strategies. It delves into Smart Contracts, Decentralized Finance apps (DeFi), and Non-Fungible Tokens (NFTs), emphasizing their role in fostering innovation and ethical practices in modern business environments.

Chapter 2: Navigating the Digital Workforce Shift: Social Implications of AI on Employment and CSR Strategies for Reskilling

This chapter tackle the social implications of AI-driven workforce shifts in this chapter. They advocate for Corporate Social Responsibility (CSR) strategies aimed at reskilling employees amidst technological advancements. Titled "Navigating the Digital Workforce Shift," the chapter examines how CSR initiatives can mitigate job displacement risks while harnessing the transformative potential of AI in enhancing human development. It provides a roadmap for organizations to navigate these changes responsibly, ensuring sustainable and inclusive growth in the digital era.

Chapter 3: Challenges Obstructing the Effective Usage of Artificial Intelligence in Psychotherapy and Feasible Remedies: A Reflective Discussion

This chapter addresses the underutilization of AI in psychotherapeutic practices. It identifies barriers hindering AI adoption in mental health care and proposes innovative AI techniques to enhance therapeutic outcomes. Titled "Challenges in AI in Psychotherapy," the chapter advocates for ethical and responsible integration of AI to improve the quality of life for individuals, underscoring the potential of technology to augment mental health services while respecting ethical boundaries.

Chapter 4: Navigating the Role of Artificial Intelligence (AI) in Transforming Corporate Social Responsibility (CSR) Strategies

This chapter examine the evolving role of AI in Corporate Social Responsibility (CSR) practices. This chapter, titled "AI in CSR Strategies," explores how AI-powered solutions can drive innovation, enhance transparency, and scale CSR efforts effectively. It discusses the ethical implications and societal benefits of integrating AI into CSR initiatives, offering insights into current trends and future possibilities for leveraging technology to achieve meaningful social, environmental, and economic outcomes.

Chapter 5: Impact of Artificial Intelligence in Corporate Social Responsibility: A Bibliometric Analysis and Literature Review from the Web of Science (WoS)

The authors conduct a bibliometric analysis in this chapter to explore the intersection of AI and CSR. Titled "AI in CSR: Bibliometric Analysis," the chapter provides a comprehensive overview of research trends and key publications linking AI and CSR. It utilizes data from The Web of Science to identify emerging clusters, influential authors, and thematic trends, offering a scholarly perspective on the evolving landscape of AI-driven CSR practices.

Chapter 6: Managing the AI Period's Confluence of Security and Morality

This chapter delves into the ethical implications of AI in this chapter, titled "AI Security and Morality." It examines the complex interplay between technological advancement, ethical considerations, and privacy concerns in AI-driven systems. The chapter highlights the need for robust ethical frameworks to balance innovation with societal values, providing insights into safeguarding privacy and upholding moral standards amidst rapid technological progress.

Chapter 7: The Intersection of Climate Change and Global Health Security

This chapter explores the nexus between climate change and global health security. Titled "Climate Change and Health Security," it examines the direct and indirect health impacts of climate change, emphasizing the urgent need for global collaboration and sustainable practices to mitigate environmental risks and safeguard human health.

Chapter 8: Consumer Skepticism Towards CSR Communication: Role of Content and Delivery

This chapter analyze consumer skepticism towards CSR communications in this chapter. Titled "Consumer Skepticism and CSR Communication," it investigates how content and delivery strategies influence public perceptions of corporate responsibility. The chapter identifies key factors such as company-CSR fit and authenticity in messaging, offering insights to help organizations enhance trust and credibility in their CSR initiatives amidst growing consumer scrutiny.

Chapter 9: Corporate Social Responsibility in the Age of Artificial Intelligence: A Critique

This chapter critique the integration of Artificial Intelligence (AI) in Corporate Social Responsibility (CSR) practices. Titled "CSR in the Age of AI," the chapter examines ethical considerations and societal impacts associated with AI adoption in business operations. It evaluates current CSR guidelines and proposes strategies for businesses to adopt responsible AI practices, ensuring alignment with ethical standards and societal expectations.

Chapter 10: Ethical Geospatial Analytics Balancing Business Interests and Social Responsibility

This chapter explores ethical considerations in geospatial analytics in this chapter. Titled "Ethical Geospatial Analytics," it underscores the importance of ethical practices and stakeholder engagement in leveraging geospatial data for business and societal benefits. The chapter discusses challenges such as algorithmic bias and privacy concerns, advocating for ethical leadership and interdisciplinary collaboration to promote responsible decision-making in geospatial analytics.

Chapter 11: The Magnitude of Sustainable HRM Practices and Wellbeing in a Changing Environment

This study examines the importance of sustainable HR practices and employee well-being in the evolving global workplace. Using descriptive research design and secondary data, the study highlights a direct relationship between HRM practices, employee well-being, and organizational performance. These findings emphasize the role of HR strategies in fostering well-being, offering valuable insights for organizations aiming to integrate innovative, sustainable, and well-being-focused practices into their corporate strategies.

Chapter 12: Digital Infrastructure and Connectivity: The Backbone of Modern Civilization

This chapter explores digital infrastructure and connectivity as crucial drivers of digital technologies and economic growth. It delves into the evolution of connectivity projects and examines key components like broadband networks, telecom structures, and data centers. The chapter also discusses the influence of laws and policies on infrastructure development, addressing financing, rural access, and security. A case study on Zorez Telecom's expansion illustrates regulatory and economic challenges and provides practical solutions for students and professionals.

Chapter 13: Data-Driven Insights into CSR Influence on Ethical AI Development: A Quantitative Approach

This study examines how Corporate Social Responsibility (CSR) influences the adoption of ethical AI practices in businesses. Using a quantitative approach, it analyzes data from cross-industry surveys to assess the relationship between CSR initiatives and responsible AI governance, focusing on transparency, accountability, and fairness. Statistical analysis reveals how CSR investments impact ethical AI adoption, regulatory compliance, and corporate reputation. The findings offer insights for policymakers and business leaders on aligning CSR with ethical AI frameworks to promote trust, mitigate risks, and support sustainable business practices.

Chapter 14: Corporate Social Responsibility Approaches to Ethical AI in Hotel Industry Business

This chapter explores the use of AI in the hotel industry that has improved customer service, efficiency, and personalization, but it also raises ethical concerns. This paper examines how hotels use Corporate Social Responsibility (CSR) strategies to ensure ethical AI implementation. Key issues addressed include transparency, fairness, accountability, data privacy, bias, and employment impacts. Ethical AI practices guided by CSR can enhance hotel reputations and support sustainable business models that prioritize stakeholder well-being.

Chapter 15: AI-Driven Sustainable Business in CSR Reporting Regime: A Systematic Literature Review

This paper explores the integration of AI-driven technologies in Corporate Social Responsibility (CSR) reporting and its impact on sustainable business practices. As global emphasis on sustainability grows, AI technologies like machine learning and natural language processing are enhancing the efficiency, accuracy, and transparency of CSR reports. This systematic literature review synthesizes findings from 63 studies, highlighting how AI optimizes data management, predicts sustainability trends, and addresses ethical challenges in CSR. The study offers insights into the strategic and ethical implications of AI adoption in CSR reporting, emphasizing the potential of AI to transform sustainable business models.

Each chapter offers a unique perspective on the ethical implications and strategic considerations related to AI, CSR, and emerging technologies, contributing to a comprehensive understanding of their impact on business, society, and the environment.

In Conclusion

I conclude this edited reference book, *Corporate Social Responsibility Approaches to Ethical AI in Business*, it becomes evident that the integration of artificial intelligence (AI) into business practices presents both immense opportunities and profound ethical challenges. Throughout the chapters authored by esteemed researchers and practitioners, have explored the diverse applications of AI—from blockchain technologies and digital workforce transformations to mental health interventions and geospatial analytics.

Each chapter has underscored the critical importance of ethical considerations in leveraging AI for societal benefit. I have seen how AI can enhance transparency, innovation, and stakeholder engagement in Corporate Social Responsibility (CSR) initiatives, while also necessitating careful navigation of issues such as privacy, bias, and accountability.

Moreover, this book has provided a scholarly foundation for understanding the intersection of AI and CSR through bibliometric analyses, theoretical frameworks, and practical case studies. It has served as a roadmap for policymakers, corporate leaders, and academics alike, guiding them towards responsible AI adoption and fostering a culture of ethical innovation.

I look ahead, the discourse initiated by this book encourages ongoing dialogue and collaboration across disciplines. By aligning technological advancements with ethical principles, I can pave the way for a more sustainable and inclusive future—one where AI-driven innovation serves as a catalyst for positive societal change.

I invite you to engage with the insights presented in this volume, join the conversation on ethical AI adoption, and together, shape a future where technology and humanity thrive in harmony.

Warmest regards.

Erum Shaikh
Shaheed Benazir Bhutto University, Sanghar Campus, Pakistan

Acknowledgment

I give thanks to Almighty for granting us the capacity to think, act, and accomplish our goals.

Without the collaborative efforts and support of the many team members, this project would not have been possible to finish. I am grateful to the IGI Global team for their exceptional assistance and cooperation throughout the project.

The hard work and feedback provided by the reviewers and members of the Editorial Advisory Board during this process was important in choosing the best articles to publish.

Introduction

In an era of rapid technological advancement, integrating artificial intelligence (AI) into various facets of society has raised profound ethical and social concerns. Businesses, in particular, grapple with the ethical implications of AI adoption, navigating the complex terrain of business ethics (BE) and corporate social responsibility (CSR). The divergent perspectives on AI's impact further complicate efforts to harness its potential for positive societal change. Addressing these challenges necessitates a holistic understanding of the intricate interplay between technology, organizational dynamics, and the broader societal landscape.

Corporate Social Responsibility Approaches to Ethical AI in Business emerges as a timely solution, offering a comprehensive exploration of the factors influencing AI adoption within organizations through the lens of the Technology-Organization-Environment (TOE) framework. Synthesizing cutting-edge research findings with relevant theoretical frameworks equips professionals across industries with the insights needed to navigate the ethical complexities of AI integration.

A diverse audience, spanning the corporate sector, academia, and policymaking spheres, will make use of this book as a roadmap for organizations and policymakers to navigate the evolving landscape of CSR and ethics in the AI era. Fostering a nuanced understanding of the strategic role of trust and responsibility empowers stakeholders to embrace AI-driven innovation while safeguarding ethical principles and societal well-being. Join the discourse and embark on a journey toward responsible AI adoption, where ethics and innovation converge to shape a more sustainable future for all.

The importance of this research lies in its ability to provide a roadmap for organizations and policymakers to navigate the evolving landscape of CSR and ethics in the AI era. By fostering a nuanced understanding of the strategic role of trust and responsibility, this book empowers stakeholders to embrace AI-driven innovation while safeguarding ethical principles and societal well-being.

The chapters within this volume address key areas of concern, such as the ethical challenges of AI in psychotherapy, the impact of AI on employment and reskilling strategies, and the role of AI in transforming CSR practices. Each chapter contributes to a deeper understanding of how AI can be integrated responsibly into various sectors, ensuring that technological advancements do not come at the expense of ethical considerations.

Coverage

The many academic areas covered in this publication include, but are not limited to, artificial intelligence, business ethics, corporate social responsibility, emotional intelligence, ethical challenges, human intelligence, machine ethics, moral values within corporations, social wellbeing, and technology ethics.

The research presented in this book is of paramount importance as it bridges the gap between technological innovation and ethical responsibility. By addressing the multifaceted implications of AI, this book not only guides current practices but also paves the way for future developments that align with the principles of CSR. We invite you to engage with the profound insights and innovative approaches presented in this book, and to join us in fostering a future where AI and ethics coalesce to drive positive change.

Chapter 1
Ethical AI Entrepreneurial Strategies for Business Intelligence and Blockchain

Kathirvel Ayyaswamy
https://orcid.org/0000-0002-5347-9110
Tagore Engineering College, Chennai, India

Naren Kathirvel
Anand Institute of Higher Technology, India

Maheswaran C. P.
https://orcid.org/0000-0001-5985-2564
Sri Krishna College of Technology, Coimbatore, India

ABSTRACT

The development of numerous cryptocurrencies, dApp monetization, smart personal contracts, decentralized finance apps (Defi), and non-fungible tokens (NFTs) preceded general adoption of the blockchain concept. Blockchain technology (BT) is digital money that increases in value every hour by a factor of bigger than its previous worth. Even though blockchain's widespread appeal has been confined to its role in the development of Bitcoin and other cryptocurrencies, a number of other applications are currently being developed steadily. This demonstrates the promise of decentralized technology and the undeniable influence of blockchain on business across many industries. Because of these built-in characteristics, blockchain is now used in a number of sectors, including real estate, finance, agriculture field, healthcare sector, education institutions, design and manufacturing unit, and

DOI: 10.4018/979-8-3693-3478-2.ch001

retail shopping. The chapter provides a thorough explanation of the various use cases and areas of BT.

1. INTRODUCTION

We are aware that BT extends beyond transactions and cryptocurrencies, let's examine the technologies that serve as the foundation for blockchain technology and how it advances technological advancement. The Four Elements of Blockchain Technology's Foundation

A. ICO

Initial Coin Offerings (ICO) are a type of fundraising used by businesses and startups that incorporate Blockchain technology into their operations. This is how it functions:

Prior to Announcement making the necessary preparations for the ICO is the first step in the process. At this point, digital advertising promotions are launched on Internet that ICO investors frequently visit, and the white paper—which contains the project's details—is being produced.

Supplying: It consists of the written policy terms and environments of the agreement that are given to potential investors are given in the Figure 1.

Figure 1. ICO token system

Shareholders are offered an investment vehicle known as a cryptocoin in exchange for their capital. Each cryptocoin has a unique toe given to it.

Strategy for Advertising: This is the phase in which the real work is done. The target audience for the campaign is small investors and institutions, and it usually lasts up to one month. The demand is far more than that of the other well-liked fundraising strategy. Venture Finance

B. Smart Contact

Smart Contracts are the other technology that has become well-known in the realm of blockchain-powered businesses, after ICOs.

With BT based Smart Contracts as shown in the Figure 2, you can accomplish the same goals as their equivalents in the physical world: no party may violate the terms of the agreement.

When using BT based smart contracts, party is required to contribute a guaranteed amount to a separate account that is outside of their mechanism and is only free when the contract's terms and situations are met. Many essential features are promised by the design of smart contracts, including inherent trust, high transactional speed, accuracy, and zero conflicts.

Figure 2. Smart contracts

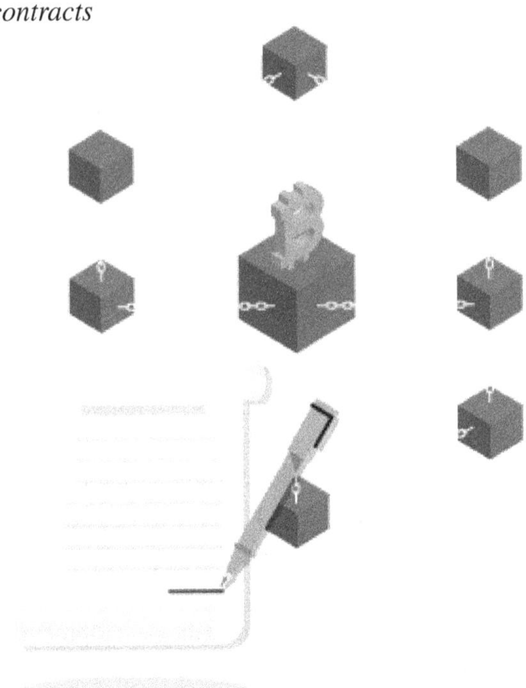

C. Cryptocurrency Wallets

Figure 3. Cryptocurrency wallet

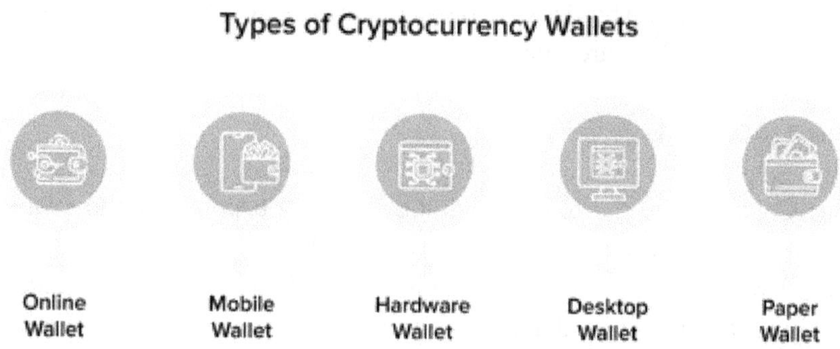

The second Blockchain component we'll examine is cryptocurrency wallet apps as shown in the Figure 3, which are what got the decentralization movement started. In the state that Bitcoin has made for itself, there are currently over 1,600 cryptocurrencies in circulation worldwide, and more are being introduced practically every day.

No matter what use you choose to give your cryptocurrency wallet, you have a lot of alternatives, especially in terms of development. Options include hardware wallets, paper wallets, hot/cold wallets, mobile banking wallets, Internet web online wallets, and personal desktop computer wallets.

D. Blockchain NFTs

NFTs are the most widely used investing method in 2022 and are a relatively new addition to the Blockchain family. What makes NFTs so unique? To begin with, they aren't tradable. For instance, Bitcoin may be exchanged for other bitcoins with no loss in value because it is fungible. NFTs, however, cannot be traded.

Fundamentally, everything digital that is original to you—like music, drawings, pictures, etc.—can be considered an NFT. They are most likely trending on all social media platforms now a days everyone wants to secure digital moneys.

NFTs are a component of powered moneys on the Ethereum Blockchain that are enabled by smart contracts. You should look into the development if this is something that interests you for your startup or established company.

2. APPLICATIONS IN VARIOUS INDUSTRIES

There are countless uses and applications for blockchain as a service across different industrial areas. Now let's examine the leading sectors that have integrated decentralization into their everyday operations.

2.1 Blockchain in Healthcare

The fact that blockchain is transforming the medical field and ready to solve many of the problems that impede effective care and medical across the world, despite the numerous debates surrounding the impact of BT on the healthcare sector and whether or not it is a realistic possibility. The decentralized spaces left by blockchain are those where healthcare is lacking. Blockchain facilitates:

Fast Data Access: Dispersed and safe access to patient health data is made possible by the distributed ledger that is included in the Blockchain and Healthcare Mix package. Real-time changes are also made to the patient's shared data.

System Interoperability: Cryptocurrency provides an international decentralized computer network and internet.

Security of Data: Only those who require access to the patient's data can access it, as it is entirely decentralized and unchangeable.

Blockchain technology in healthcare enables the centralization of user-generated IoT data and medical organization data in one location.

2.2 Blockchain in FinTech

Figure 4. Blockchain in finance sector

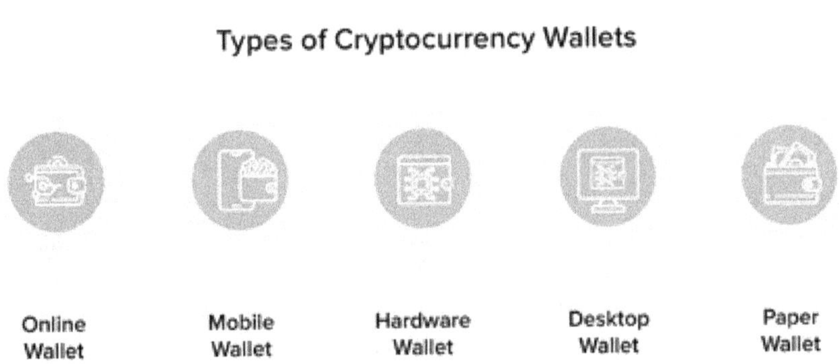

Technological innovation entered the globe through the merger of FinTech (refer Figure 3) and Blockchain. Blockchain will undoubtedly bring about a digital revolution in the banking sector overall, affecting all other financial areas as well. This includes KYC procedure, credit and debit transactions, and reduced costs. Take a look at how Asian Bank used Appinventiv's assistance to adopt a blockchain-based, cryptocurrency-focused banking solution through its app.

The customer recognition system, electronic payment methods, insurance, loans, and credits are the monetary services that will begin to exhibit symbols of simplification and speedier, reliable procedures.

2.3 Blockchain in Real Estate

Probably the only real estate industry has successfully proposed and use BT in real estate is the industry real estate sector. The industry's very definition is made up of procedures that Blockchain for Real Estate may simplify and decentralize as shown in the Figure 4.

Figure 5. BT in real estate sector

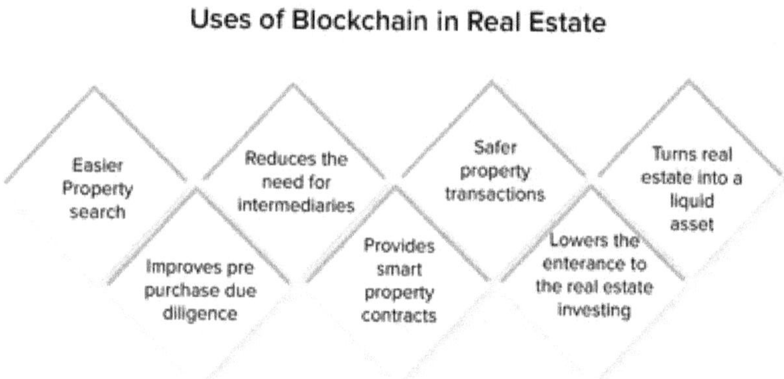

If you examine the current state of adoption of BT in real estate, you will discover that governments in multiple countries are utilizing decentralization and BT to promote more efficient real estate practices in their respective countries, in addition to individual property developers, real estate brokers, and insurance providers.

2.4 Blockchain in Manufacturing

The Internet of Things is present in every technological trend that you look at. BT and IIoT (Industrial IoT), two technological phenomena, it is combined to save industrial and supply chain companies from using manual labor.

Figure 6. Supply chain and manufacturing industry

Blockchain technology can assist in tracking the history of all linked devices for manufacturing and operations problems if it is directly connected to IoT devices. The global decentralized ledger in the supply chain can prevent collusion and tampering with any machinery data, hence eliminating a single source of error in the world of IoT. In order to prevent risks, IoT and BT can also offer harmony and contract models in digital bonds.

By serving as a safe, scalable, and transparent energy transaction ecosystem, blockchain technology is completely changing the energy industry. For a detailed understanding of blockchain's influence, read our blog post on How It's Disrupting the Energy Sector.

3. BT IN RECENT STARTUPS AND INITIATIVES

There's no denying that the efficiency and profitability generated by incorporating blockchain technology into their processes makes it too important for BT companies to ignore. However, the majority of organizations that have implemented blockchain for business are still outweighed by those who haven't.

3.1 Blockchain in Enterprises

The presence of legacy technologies that have greatly improved a business is a contributing factor to the challenge of implementing any new technology. It's time for businesses to release their worries, but still proceed with caution. They should start using enterprise blockchain solutions in certain areas of their operations and only scale up if they see tangible benefits from the technology (refer Figure 5.1).

Figure 7. Enterprises BT

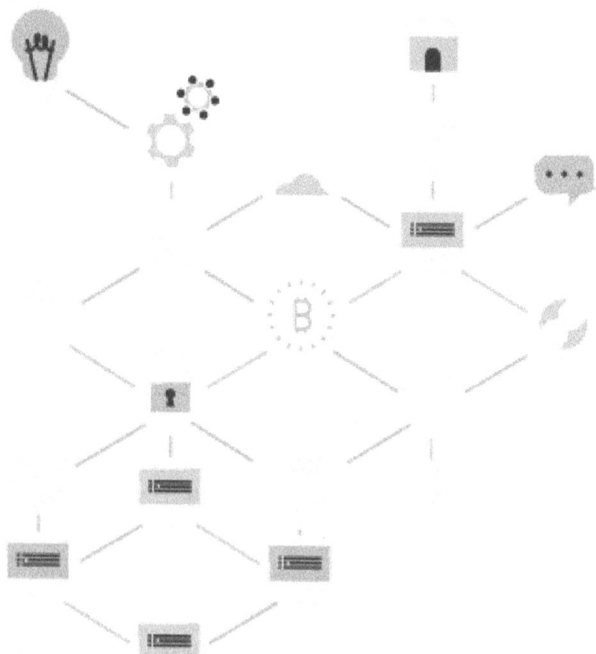

You too can join the ranks of businesses benefiting from decentralized technology by using platforms like Ethereum, Hyperledger Fabric, R3 Corda, Ripple, and Quorum.

3.2 Blockchain in Startups

Like Businesses, Startups do not face legacy system issues that could delay the integration of BT into their daily operations. Therefore, when you are a startup, you've got an advantage over established players in the market by using technology that addresses nearly all of the issues that prevent businesses from providing genuine value to both internal and external stakeholders.

With all of its parts, Blockchain for New companies can do more than just build a fence around all of the processes that a startup needs to handle more frequently than an established organization, such as managing a decentralized team and creating contracts between various stakeholders given in Figure 6.

There is seldom a procedure that is not affected by decentralization when discussing the integration of BT inside a startup ecosystem. This is a great opportunity for entrepreneurs who want to attract capital or just make a name for themselves as industry innovators.

Figure 8. BT startup

3.3 Blockchain Solutions to Digital Business

The business world is entering the most revolutionary era thanks to BT, as forward-thinking companies, inventors, and investors embrace blockchain solutions to promote transparency and trust. Let us determine which Blockchain solution is most suitable for your organization, ranging from developing mobile applications to facilitating international transactions.

3.3.1 Blockchain in Business Transactions

Transactions are at the heart of every industry you examine because they are the most fundamental business operation. In addition to its widespread use, the problems with transactions are also industry-wide: a lack of safety, a lack of clearness, and a lack of subsidiarity. For each of these problems, BT offers a standard solution.

These are the various ways that Blockchain for Transactions can make a difference, regardless of the industry that is being closely examined.

A. Enhanced Openness and Security of Data

Virtual distributed ledgers, or blockchains, are devoid of all these drawbacks. Transactions are kept in a structured manner, encrypted, and unchangeable. All nodes can access them, but they cannot be changed.

B. Getting Rid of Middlemen

Miners work tirelessly to solve mathematical puzzles and confirm blockchain transactions, with no involvement from third parties for mediation or verification. Once the calculations are finished, the transaction is validated and then added to the distributed ledger.

C. Effectiveness in Communities

One of the biggest advantages of BT is the speed at which settlements can be finalized.

3.3.2 Blockchain in Mobile Business Apps

BT mobile application manufacturing is changing and being disrupted in many ways as a result of new technologies and use cases, but there are still a number of areas where the sector is still behind, including high advertising costs, inconsistent in-app purchase procedures, and the app approval process. Let's shed a little illumination about the way BT is applied in apps to address these enduring problems facing the mobile app market.

3.3. App Approval Process

By putting approval policies and apps on a public ledger that is accessible for public scrutiny, the integration of BT into app creation breaks the dominance of the Play Store and App Store.

3.3.1 In-App Acquisition

When it comes to in-app purchases, consumers are initially charged by the app store for permitting in-app transactions on their platform. After that, they incur additional costs from the debit or credit card they use to make the purchase, such as transaction fees and processing fees.

All of these reductions in a user's in-app purchases typically total more than thirty percent; this is something that can be easily averted by using cryptocurrency payments with no transaction costs.

3.3.2 Expensiveness of Advertising

Decentralizing the ad platforms allows one to cut out the middlemen and lower transaction costs by increasing transparency throughout the entire process. These are just a few instances of how Blockchain technology can be used to further streamline the mobile app market.

4. BLOCKCHAIN SECURITY SOLUTIONS

Blockchain security can protect and render tamper-proof a variety of corporate operations because to its decentralization, encryption, and immutability features. The combination of blockchain technology with security will significantly influence and contribute to the protection of data protection, data transparency, infrastructure security, and the password-free economy. This is just a summary of the various ways blockchain technology may help secure your company; to learn more about how blockchain can protect your mobile app company.

All in all, what matters most is how much it will cost you to use Blockchain technology, which has the potential to make you a disruptive force in the industry. Services related to the development of Blockchain are most frequently obtained by startups and large companies from reputable development firms, whose staff of professionals may assist in connecting your company with a decentralized ecosystem.

4.1 Factors Affecting Blockchain App Development

The following factors affecting the BT app development Cost are

Blockchain App Category

A. Cryptocurrency Based Solution
B. Non-Cryptocurrency Based Solutions

4.2 App Services for Blockchain

4.2.1 Digital-Wallet

A distributed decentralized ledger capable of removing a single point of failure in the Internet of Things ecosystem and safeguarding all device data against manipulation and collusion ICO Development of Smart Contracts Distributed Ledger Technology

4.2.2. Crypto-Market

These thus are the variables that affect the price of developing a blockchain app. As promised, let us now introduce you to the Blockchain App Development Cost Estimate's numerical values. The sort of Blockchain service you use will also affect the cost factor.

5. CASE STUDIES: 3D BIOPRINTING

By making it possible to create biological tissues and organs that function, 3D bioprinting, a rapidly developing technology, has the potential to transform the field of tissue engineering. (Chen et al., 2021) Living cells and biomaterials are layer-by-layer deposited during the procedure to produce intricate 3D structures that resemble the architecture of natural tissue. It is essential for tissue regeneration and organ transplantation to be able to accurately control the spatial distribution of cells and extracellular matrix (ECM) elements to create structures with certain mechanical and biological qualities.

5.1 3D Bioprinting

The bioprinter itself, the bio-inks (materials used to print the cells and ECM), and the living cells are three important elements in the 3D bioprinting process. Inkjet-based and extrusion-based bioprinters are the two primary categories into which they can be divided. Although extrusion-based printers utilize pneumatic or mechanical pressure to extrude bio-ink through a tiny nozzle, ink jet-based printers use thermal or piezoelectric technologies to expel droplets of bio-ink onto a substrate. Depending on the application, both types of printers offer advantages and disadvantages (Ozbolat & Hospodiuk, 2015).

Natural polymers like collagen and hyaluronic acid, synthetic polymers like polycaprolactone and polyethylene glycol, and mixtures of these materials can all be used to create bio-inks. (Kang et al., 2016) The final tissue construct's desirable mechanical and biological qualities, as well as the bio ink's suitability for printing with living cells, all influence the choice of bio-ink.

Living cells are essential to the 3D bioprinting process because they give the tissue construct its useful qualities. Stem cells, primary cells, immortalized cell lines, and other sources can all be used to create new cells. Because different cell types have varied qualities and functions, the selection of cell type relies on the particular application. For instance, (Barron et al., 2004) stem cells are valuable in regenerative medicine applications because they can develop into many cell types. Primary cells, which are separated straight from tissues, are more faithful to the original tissue and are capable of producing physiological responses that are more precise. Although immortalized cell lines, which are produced from cancer cells, are frequently employed in research, they may not be acceptable for use in therapeutic settings because of tumorigenic potential

Cell separation and preparation, bio-ink preparation, the printing of the tissue construct, and post-printing processing are typical processes in the 3D bioprinting process. Incubation, which encourages cell division and tissue growth, as well as mechanical and/or chemical treatments to enhance the construct's mechanical qualities, are all examples of post-printing processing. (Marga & Jakab, 2012)

While 3D bioprinting technology has made significant progress in recent years, there are still many challenges that need to be addressed before it can be widely adopted for clinical applications. These include improving the resolution and speed of printing, optimizing the choice and composition of bio-inks, and ensuring the viability and functionality of printed cells. Additionally, ethical and regulatory considerations must be taken into account when developing 3D bio-printed tissues and organs for transplantation.

5.2 Techniques and Materials Used in 3D Bioprinting

Due to its potential to completely change tissue engineering and regenerative medicine, the topic of 3D bioprinting is s still in its infancy but has recently attracted a lot of interest. By layer-by-layer depositing cells, biomaterials, and growth factors, this method produces intricate three-dimensional (3D) structures that closely resemble the structure and functionality of natural tissues and organs. Here are the various methods and supplies utilized in 3D bioprinting.

5.2.1 Techniques

A. Inkjet bioprinting: This method uses a customized inkjet printer to precisely deposit cells and biomaterials onto a substrate. To produce a 3D structure, the printer produces cell and biomaterial droplets that are ejected onto the substrate layer by layer. Because of its capacity to generate high-resolution structures with exact control over cell arrangement, this approach is widely employed (Coggiola et al., 2020)

B. Extrusion-based bioprinting: This method extrudes a bio-ink made of cells, a hydrogel, or another biomaterial through a nozzle to create a three-dimensional structure. To build complicated structures, the nozzle has three-dimensional movement capabilities. This method is frequently employed because it can print substantial structures with high cell densities (Vu et al., 2022)

Bioprinting with a laser concentrates energy into a small area of a substrate that has been covered in cells and biomaterials. A 3D structure is produced as a result of the energy fusing and solidifying the cells and biomaterials. This method is very helpful for printing highly cell-viable, high-resolution structures (Chung et al., 2020) (see Figure 1).

5.2.2 Materials

5.2.2.1 Hydrogels: Due to their capacity to offer cells a 3D environment in which to grow and develop, hydrogels are frequently employed as bio-inks in 3D bioprinting. Hydrogels can be made to support particular cell types and can imitate the mechanical characteristics of natural tissues (Wang et al., 2020)

5.2.2.2 Decellularized extracellular matrix (dECM): is produced by eliminating cells from tissues and organs and leaving the extracellular matrix in its place (ECM). To provide a scaffold for cells to grow and differentiate, this ECM can be employed as a bio-ink. Cell attachment, proliferation, and differentiation have all been demonstrated to be supported by ECM (Wang et al., 2021)

5.2.2.3 Synthetic polymers: In 3D bioprinting, synthetic polymers like poly(lactic-co-glycolic acid) (PLGA) and polycaprolactone (PCL) are frequently utilized as biomaterials. To construct hybrid scaffolds, these materials can be mixed with different biomaterials and tailored to imitate the mechanical characteristics of native tissues (Liu et al., 2022)

3D bioprinting is an intriguing field that is fast developing and has exciting potential in a wide range of applications, including regenerative medicine, drug screening, and disease modeling. The functionality, accuracy, and resolution of 3D bioprinted structures are being actively improved by researchers through the development of novel materials and methods. With further development, 3D bioprinting might be essential in solving some of the biggest problems in biology and medicine.

5.3 Current Applications of 3D Bioprinting

The creation of tailored medicine is a promising area for 3D bioprinting. Patient-specific tissues and organs that can be utilized for drug testing and other medical procedures can be made via 3D bioprinting. Researchers showed the possibility of 3D bio-printing for producing liver and heart tissue models that may be used to assess drug toxicity and efficacy (Liu et al., 2022).

In the area of regenerative medicine, 3D bioprinting has vital uses as well. Researchers can produce intricate tissues and organs using 3D bioprinting that can be utilized to treat or replace diseased or damaged tissues. Researchers created a 3D bio-printed scaffold that could support the development of cartilage tissue (Advincula et al., 2021). The potential for treating a wide range of medical diseases with the ability to build such sophisticated tissues is great.

Personalized medicine, regenerative medicine, and 3D bio-printing have all been applied to the planning and practice of surgical procedures. Surgeons can plan surgeries and create plans for reducing risks and maximizing outcomes using 3D-printed replicas of patient-specific organs. Researchers showed the value of 3D bio-printed models for preoperative planning in heart surgery (Xu et al., 2020).

3D bioprinting offers a lot of potential for the future of medicine as its applications continue to grow. 3D bioprinting has the potential to completely alter how we approach medical care and treatment with further research and development.

Figure 9. 3D bioprinting

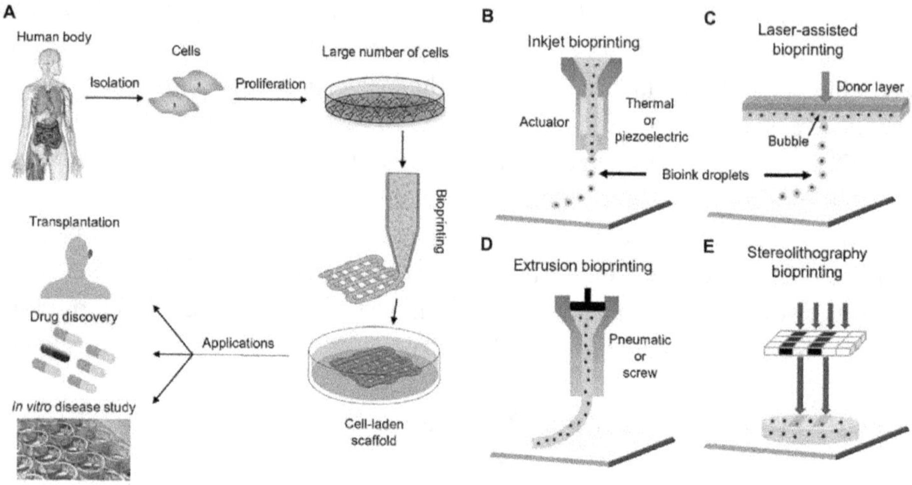

5.4 Quality Control in 3D Bioprinting

A crucial component of 3D bioprinting is quality control, which makes sure that the printed tissues or organs have the appropriate structural and functional characteristics. The difficulties of quality control in 3D bioprinting have been addressed in recent years using a variety of strategies, from improved imaging techniques to machine learning algorithms explained in Figure 7.

The requirement to maintain high printing accuracy and precision are one of the fundamental problems in 3D bioprinting. To do this, several researchers have looked into the use of real-time monitoring and feedback systems to change the printing parametrial- time based on the results seen. For instance, [19] suggested a vision-based monitoring system in a recent study that employs machine learning algorithms to analyze the printed structures in real time and modify the printing parameters as necessary. To achieve high printing accuracy and precision, (Alimian et al., 2020) presented an intelligent quality control system that combines computer vision, machine learning, and robots.

The requirement to guarantee the biological functionality of the printed tissues or organs is a crucial component of quality control in 3D bioprinting. This necessitates evaluating the printed cells' and tissues' vitality, morphology, and functionality. A non-invasive imaging method based on multi-photon microscopy was suggested (Shukla et al., 2022) in recent work to evaluate the extracellular matrix and cellular components of printed tissues. According to the study, the method could accurately determine whether printed cells and tissues were viable and what shape they took.

Several studies have looked into the use of quality control standards and guidelines for 3D bioprinting in addition to these methods. For instance, (Yu & Jiang, 2020) emphasized the necessity for standardized protocols and guidelines for 3D bioprinting to ensure uniform and trustworthy results in a recent study. The assessment put up a set of criteria, including structural integrity, cellular organization, and biological functionality, that may be used to gauge the quality of printed tissues and organs.

To ensure that the printed tissues and organs satisfy the required standards in terms of structural and functional features, quality control is an essential component of 3D bioprinting. The accuracy, precision, and functioning of tissues and organs created by 3D bioprinting have recently increased because of developments in imaging methods, machine learning algorithms, and quality control standards.

Figure 10. Flowchart of 3D bioprinting

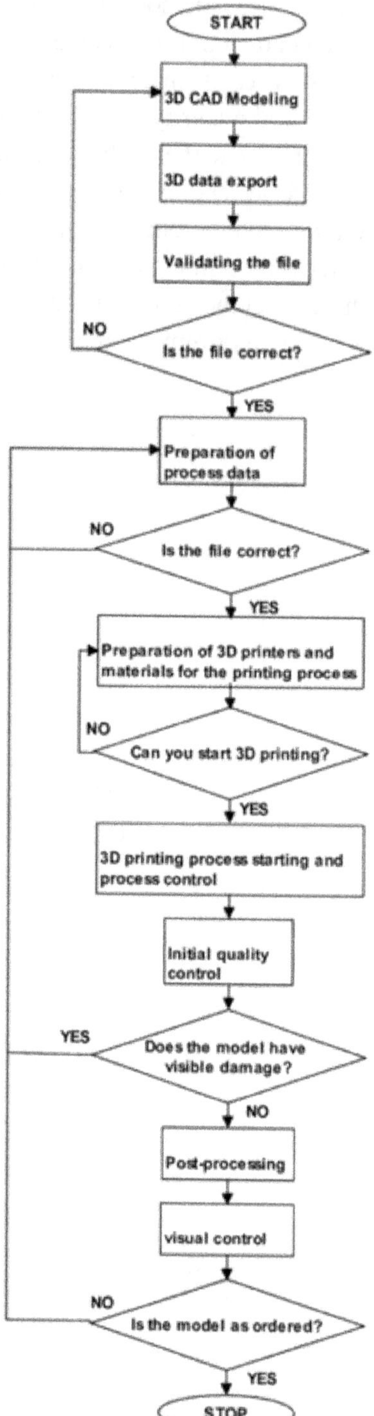

6. ADVANTAGES OF BT USING STARTUPS

Blockchain technology has been a game-changer for entrepreneurship, offering several advantages to startups and small businesses:

Decentralization: Blockchain enables decentralized systems, removing the need for intermediaries. This allows entrepreneurs to create innovative business models without relying on centralized authorities.

Transparency and Security: The immutable nature of blockchain ensures transparency and security in transactions. This fosters trust among customers and partners, which is crucial for startups aiming to establish credibility.

Smart Contracts: These self-executing contracts automate and enforce agreements without intermediaries, reducing costs and potential disputes for entrepreneurs.

Funding through ICOs and STOs: Initial Coin Offerings (ICOs) and Security Token Offerings (STOs) provide alternative fundraising methods for startups, allowing them to access global investment opportunities.

Supply Chain Management: Blockchain enhances traceability, reducing fraud and ensuring the authenticity of products, which is especially beneficial for startups dealing with supply chains.

Tokenization and Asset Management: Entrepreneurs can tokenize assets, enabling fractional ownership and making traditionally illiquid assets more accessible to investors.

Data Security and Privacy: Blockchain offers enhanced data security and privacy controls, enabling entrepreneurs to protect sensitive information effectively.

Despite these benefits, entrepreneurs should consider challenges such as scalability, regulatory uncertainties, and the need for technical expertise when implementing blockchain solutions. However, when integrated thoughtfully, blockchain can offer tremendous opportunities for entrepreneurial ventures.

Importance of Customer Engagement in Modern Marketing

Customer engagement is a crucial aspect of modern marketing strategies, as it helps build brand loyalty, drive sales, and foster long-term customer relationships. In today's competitive marketplace, businesses must go beyond traditional advertising to connect with their audience on a deeper level. Customer engagement is directly linked to brand loyalty and advocacy, as engaged customers develop a strong affinity for a brand, leading to repeat purchases and positive word-of-mouth referrals. By cultivating meaningful interactions, businesses can create brand ambassadors who champion their products or services, amplifying their reach and influence. Customer engagement is also closely tied to customer satisfaction and retention, as when customers feel valued and appreciated, they are more likely to remain loyal and continue doing business with the brand(George et al., 2024).

Customer engagement is a crucial tool for businesses to improve their products, services, and customer experience. Engaged customers provide valuable feedback through surveys, reviews, and social media interactions, which can inform strategic decision-making and product development. By listening to their audience and acting on their feedback, businesses can demonstrate commitment to continuous improvement and customer-centricity, strengthening their competitive position. Additionally, customer engagement drives sales and revenue growth, as engaged customers are more likely to make purchases, upgrade to premium offerings, and participate in upsell and cross-sell opportunities(Khan & Iqbal, 2020).

Gap Analysis Objectives

A gap analysis is vital for identifying opportunities and enhancing a company's customer engagement efforts, with important objectives outlining specific areas to focus on.

- Evaluate existing engagement metrics, such as social media interactions, email open rates, and customer satisfaction scores, to understand the current state of customer engagement.
- Compare engagement metrics against industry benchmarks and competitors to identify areas of strength and weakness.
- Conduct market research and customer surveys to gain insights into the preferences, behaviors, and expectations of the target audience regarding engagement strategies and channels.
- Assess the effectiveness of existing technology and tools for customer engagement, such as CRM systems, marketing automation platforms, and social media management tools, to identify gaps and opportunities for improvement.
- Analyze the effectiveness of current content strategies in driving engagement, including the type, format, and distribution channels of content, to identify areas for optimization and refinement.
- Evaluate the quality and responsiveness of customer service and support channels, such as live chat, phone support, and self-service portals, to ensure they meet customer expectations for engagement and satisfaction.
- Assess the level of employee engagement and empowerment in delivering exceptional customer experiences, as engaged employees are more likely to drive positive customer interactions and outcomes.

- Explore emerging trends and technologies in customer engagement, such as artificial intelligence, chatbots, and personalized experiences, to identify opportunities for innovation and differentiation.

A gap analysis helps businesses understand their customer engagement state, identify improvement opportunities, and develop targeted strategies to enhance engagement and drive business growth in the modern marketing landscape. This comprehensive understanding informs the development of effective marketing initiatives.

CONCLUSION

Blockchain is a distributed database that is shared by multiple system nodes. The reason it is named Blockchain is that it gathers data in encrypted blocks that are connected to other sets of blocks to create a virtual chain. These days, businesses use blockchain technology and its various features, like as ICOs and smart contracts, for a variety of objectives that are related to their daily operations. Because of these built-in characteristics, blockchain is now used in a number of sectors, including Real Estate, Finance, Agriculture field, Healthcare sector, Education Institutions, Design and Manufacturing unit, and Retail shopping, etc. The article titled Blockchain Beyond Cryptocurrencies provides a thorough explanation of the various use cases and areas of BT. A promising innovation, 3D bioprinting has the potential to completely change the landscape of regenerative medicine. Yet, there are possible concerns linked with its use, such as problems with quality control, just like with any technology. Artificial intelligence (AI) has become a potent tool for enhancing 3D bioprinting quality control in recent years. To guarantee the security and effectiveness of produced tissues and organs, AI quality control plays a crucial role in 3D bioprinting. AI is going to play an increasingly significant role in advancing the caliber and dependability of 3D bioprinting technology as the field of regenerative medicine develops.

REFERENCES

Advincula, R. C., Dizon, J. R. C., Caldona, E. B., Viers, R. A., Siacor, F. D. C., Maalihan, R. D., & Espera, A. H.Jr. (2021). On the progress of 3D-printed hydrogels for tissue engineering. *MRS Communications*, 11(5), 539–553. DOI: 10.1557/s43579-021-00069-1 PMID: 34367725

Alimian, M., Ghezavati, V., & Reza, T.-M. (2020). New integration of preventive maintenance and production planning with cell formation and group scheduling for dynamic cellular manufacturing systems. *Journal of Manufacturing Systems*, 56, 341–358. Advance online publication. DOI: 10.1016/j.jmsy.2020.06.011

Andreas, I. (2022). Tooulias,Three-dimensional bioprinting in medical surgery, 3D Printing: Applications in Medicine and Surgery. https://science.sciencemag.org/content/338/6109/921

Ayyaswamy, K. (2024). Enhancing Digital Technology Planning, Leadership, and Management to Transform Education. In Bhatia, M., & Mushtaq, M. T. (Eds.), *Navigating Innovative Technologies and Intelligent Systems in Modern Education* (pp. 1–9). IGI Global. DOI: 10.4018/979-8-3693-5370-7.ch001

Barron, J. A., Wu, P., Ladouceur, H. D., & Ringeisen, B. R. (2004). Biological laser printing: a novel technique for creating heterogeneous 3-dimensional cell patterns. Biomed Microdevices. https://pubmed.ncbi.nlm.nih.gov/15320636/

Chung, J. J., Im, H., Kim, S. H., Park, J. W., & Jung, Y. (2020). Toward Biomimetic Scaffolds for Tissue Engineering: 3D Printing Techniques in Regenerative Medicine. Front. Bioeng. Biotechnol. https://www.frontiersin.org/articles/10.3389/fbioe.2020.586406/full

Cyrus, W. (2021). A fluid-supported 3D hydrogel bioprinting method. *Biomaterials*, 276, 121034. Advance online publication. DOI: 10.1016/j.biomaterials.2021.121034

Earnest, P. (2021). 3D Bioprinting of Vascularized Tissues for in vitro and in vivo Applications. Front Bioeng Biotechnol. https://www.ncbi.nlm.nih.gov/pmc/articles/PMC8158943/

Fang, Guo, Liu, Xu, Mao, Mo, Zhang, Ouyang, Xiong, & Sun. (2022). Advances in 3D Bioprinting. Chinese Journal of Mechanical Engineering: Additive Manufacturing Frontiers. DOI: 10.1016/j.cjmeam.2022.100011

Gao, Q., Liu, Z., Lin, Z., Qiu, J., Liu, Y., Liu, A., Wang, Y., Xiang, M., Chen, B., Fu, J., & He, Y. (2017). 3D Bioprinting of Vessel-like Structures with Multilevel Fluidic. *ACS Biomaterials Science & Engineering*, 3(3), 399–408. Advance online publication. DOI: 10.1021/acsbiomaterials.6b00643 PMID: 33465937

Gobinath, V., Ayyaswamy, K., & Kathirvel, N. (2024). Information Communication Technology and Intelligent Manufacturing Industries Perspective: An Insight. *Asian Science Bulletin*, 2(1), 36–45. DOI: 10.3923/asb.2024.36.45

Gobinath, V. M., Kathirvel, A., Rajesh Kanna, S. K., & Annamalai, K. (2024). Smart Technology in Management Industries: A Useful Perspective. Artificial Intelligence Applied to Industry 4.0. Wiley. https://www.wiley.com/en-us/Topics+in+Artificial+Intelligence+Applied+to+Industry+4+0-p-9781394216116DOI: 10.1002/9781394216147.ch5

Kang, H. W., Lee, S., Ko, I., Kengla, C., Yoo, J. J., & Atala, A. (2016). A 3D bio-printing system to produce human-scale tissue constructs with structural integrity. *Nature Biotechnology*, 34(3), 312–319. Advance online publication. DOI: 10.1038/nbt.3413 PMID: 26878319

Kathirvel, A. (2024). Applications of Serverless Computing: Systematic Overview. In Aluvalu, R., & Maheswari, U. (Eds.), *Serverless Computing Concepts, Technology and Architecture*. IGI Global. DOI: 10.4018/979-8-3693-1682-5.ch014

Kathirvel, A. (2024). Innovation and Industry Application: IoT-Based Robotics Frontier of Automation in Industry Application. In Satishkumar, D., & Sivaraja, M. (Eds.), *Internet of Things and AI for Natural Disaster Management and Prediction* (pp. 83–105). IGI Global. DOI: 10.4018/979-8-3693-4284-8.ch004

Kathirvel, A., & Gobinath, V. M. (2004). A Review on Additive Manufactuing in Industrial. Modern Hybird Machince and Super Finishing Process: Technology and Application. CRC. https://books.google.co.in/books/about/Modern_Hybrid_Machining_and_Super_Finish.html?id=I_VW0AEACAAJ&source=kp_book_description&redir_esc=y

Kathirvel, A., Gopinath, V. M., Naren, K., Nithyanand, D., & Nirmaladevi, K. (2024). Manufacturing Smart Industry Perspective an Overview. *American Journal of Engineering and Applied Sciences*, 17(1), 33–39. DOI: 10.3844/ajeassp.2024.33.39

Kathirvel, A., & Maheswaran, C. P. (2023). Enhanced AI-Based Intrusion Detection and Response System for WSN. Artificial Intelligence for Intrusion Detection Systems. CRC. https://www.taylorfrancis.com/chapters/edit/10.1201/9781003346340-8/enhanced-ai-based-intrusion-detection-response-system-wsn-kathirvel-maheswaranDOI: 10.1201/9781003346340-8

Kathirvel, A., Maheswaran, C. P., Subramaniam, M., & Naren, A. K. (2023). Quantum Computers Based on Distributed Computing Systems for the Next Generation: Overview and Applications. Quantum Computers Based on Distributed Computing Systems for the Next Generation, Handbook of Research on Quantum Computing for Smart Environments. IGI Global. DOI: 10.4018/978-1-6684-6697-1.ch025

Kathirvel, A., & Naren, A. K. (2024). Critical Approaches to Data Engineering Systems Innovation and Industry Application Using IoT. In *Critical Approaches to Data Engineering Systems and Analysis*. IGI Global. DOI: 10.4018/979-8-3693-2260-4.ch005

Kathirvel, A., & Naren, A. K. (2024). Diabetes and Pre-Diabetes Prediction by AI Using Tuned XGB Classifier. In Khang, A. (Ed.), *Medical Robotics and AI-Assisted Diagnostics for a High-Tech Healthcare Industry* (pp. 52–64). IGI Global. DOI: 10.4018/979-8-3693-2105-8.ch004

Kathirvel, A., Naren, K., Nithyanand, D., & Santhoshi, B. (2024). Overview of 5G Technology: Streamlined Virtual Event Experiences. *Advances of Robotic Technology*, 2(1), 1–8. DOI: 10.23880/art-16000109

Kathirvel, A., Rithik, G., & Naren, A. K. (2024). Automation of IOT Robotics. In *Predicting Natural Disasters With AI and Machine Learning*. IGI Global. DOI: 10.4018/979-8-3693-2280-2.ch011

Kathirvel, A., Subramaniam, M., Navaneethan, S., & Sabarinath, C. (2021). Improved IDR Response System for Sensor Network. Journal of Web Engineering, 20(1), 53–88. DOI: 10.13052/jwe1540-9589.2013

Kathirvel, A., Sudha, D., Naveneethan, S., Subramaniam, M., Das, D. & Kirubakaran, S. (2022). AI Based Mobile Bill Payment System using Biometric Fingerprint. American Journal of Engineering and Applied Sciences, 15(1), 23-31. DOI: 10.3844/ajeassp.2022.23.31

Khalaf, A. T., Wei, Y., Wan, J., Zhu, J., Peng, Y., Abdul Kadir, S. Y., Zainol, J., Oglah, Z., Cheng, L., & Shi, Z. (2022). Bone Tissue Engineering through 3D Bioprinting of Bioceramic Scaffolds: A Review and Update. *Life (Chicago, Ill.)*, 12(6), 903. Advance online publication. DOI: 10.3390/life12060903 PMID: 35743934

Liu, P., Zhao, R., Li, H., Zhu, T., Li, Y., Wang, H., & Zhang, X.-D. (2022). Near-infrared-II deep tissue fluorescence microscopy and application. Nano Research. https://www.ncbi.nlm.nih.gov/pmc/articles/PMC8126817/

Liu, P., Zhao, R., Li, H., Zhu, T., Li, Y., Wang, H., & Zhang, X.-D. (2022). Near-infrared-II deep tissue fluorescence microscopy and application. Nano Research. DOI: 10.1007/s12274-022-4836-y

Michael, Pramanik, Basak, Prakash, & Shankar. (2022). Progress and challenges on extrusion based three dimensional (3D) printing of biomaterials. DOI: 10.1016/j.bprint.2022.e00223

Murphy, S., & Atala, A. (2014). 3D bioprinting of tissues and organs. *Nature Biotechnology*, 32(8), 773–785. DOI: 10.1038/nbt.2958 PMID: 25093879

Naveneethan, S., Madhan, E.S., & Kathirvel, A. (2022). Identifying and Eliminating the Misbehavior Nodes in the Wireless Sensor Network. In Soft Computing and Signal Processing. ICSCSP 2021. Advances in Intelligent Systems and Computing, vol 1413. Springer International Publishing. DOI: 10.1007/978-981-16-7088-6_36

Shukla, A. K., Gao, G., & Kim, B. S. (2022). Applications of 3D Bioprinting Technology in Induced Pluripotent Stem Cells-Based Tissue Engineering. Micromachines. https://www.ncbi.nlm.nih.gov/pmc/articles/PMC8876961/

Subramaniam, M., Kathirvel, A., Sabitha, E., & Anwar Basha, H. (2021). Modified Firefly Algorithm and Fuzzy C-Mean Clustering Based Semantic Information Retrieval. Journal of Web Engineering, 20(1), 33–52. DOI: 10.13052/jwe1540-9589.2012

Sudha, D., & Kathirvel, A. (2022). The effect of ETUS in various generic attacks in mobile ad hoc networks to improve the performance of Aodv protocol. International Journal of Humanities, Law, and Social Sciences, 9(1), 467-476.

Sudha, D., & Kathirvel, A. (2022). An Intrusion Detection System to Detect and Mitigating Attacks Using Hidden Markov Model (HMM) Energy Monitoring Technique. Stochastic Modeling an Applications, 26(3), 467-476.

Sudha, D., & Kathirvel, A. (2022). The Effect of ETUS in Various Generic Attacks in Mobile Ad hoc Networks to Improve the Performance of AODV Protocol. International Journal of Humanities. *Law and Social Sciences*, 9(1), 23–31.

Sudha, D., & Kathirvel, A. (2023). The performance enhancement of Aodv protocol using GETUS. International Journal of Early Childhood Special Education, 15(2), 115-125. DOI:DOI: 10.48047/INTJECSE/V15I2.11

Wang, C., Zhang, L., Qin, T., Xi, Z., Sun, L., Wu, H., & Li, D. (2020). 3D printing in adult cardiovascular surgery and interventions: a systematic review. J Thorac Dis. https://www.ncbi.nlm.nih.gov/pmc/articles/PMC7330795/

Wang, K. (2021). Unified distributed robust regression and variable selection framework for massive data. *Expert Systems with Applications*, 186, 115701. Advance online publication. DOI: 10.1016/j.eswa.2021.115701

Wang, Y., Deng, L., Zheng, L., & Robert, X. (2021). Gao, Temporal convolutional network with soft thresholding and attention mechanism for machinery prognostics. *Journal of Manufacturing Systems*, 60, 512–526. Advance online publication. DOI: 10.1016/j.jmsy.2021.07.008

Xu, S., Jiang, M., Lu, Q., Gao, S., Feng, J., Wang, X., He, X., Chen, K., Li, Y., & Ouyang, P. (2020). Properties of Polyvinyl Alcohol Films Composited With Hemicellulose and Nanocellulose Extracted From Artemisia selengensis Straw. *Frontiers in Bioengineering and Biotechnology*, 8, 980. Advance online publication. DOI: 10.3389/fbioe.2020.00980 PMID: 32984277

Xue, Z., Jin, T., Xu, S., Bai, K., He, Q., Zhang, F., Cheng, X., Ji, Z., Pang, W., Shen, Z., Song, H., Shuai, Y., & Zhang, Y. (2022). Assembly of complex 3D structures and electronics on curved surfaces. *Science Advances*, 8(32), 32. DOI: 10.1126/sciadv.abm6922 PMID: 35947653

Yu. (2020). A Perspective on Using Machine Learning in 3D Bioprinting. *International Journal of Bioprinting*, 253. https://www.ncbi.nlm.nih.gov/pmc/articles/PMC7415853/

Zhou, W., Li, X., Duan, H., & Pengyu, L. (2021). Multi-Material Integrated Three-Dimensional Printing of Cylindrical Li-Ion Battery. Journal of Manufacturing Science and Engineering. https://www.sciencedirect.com/science/article/pii/S1226086X17301559

Chapter 2
Navigating the Digital Workforce Shifts:
Social Implications of AI on Employment and CSR Strategies for Reskilling

Aarti Chopra
https://orcid.org/0000-0002-9068-0155
Poornima University, Jaipur, India

Pradeep Singh Soni
http://orcid.org/0009-0000-8600-4253
St. Xavier's College, Jaipur, India

ABSTRACT

The advent of artificial intelligence has opened many opportunities across industries. However, there are chances of job displacement that have occurred as a part of this modification. As a remedy to the changing landscape of digital workforce generation, appropriate strategies be designed as a part of the corporate social responsibility (CSR) initiatives which can lead to harnessing the role of technology in human development. The chapter dives further into the ways in which the two aspects can be integrated and provides a method through which CSR activities can lead to navigating AI powered workforce shifts and its social implications. This study looks into the previous literature dealing with the use of CSR strategies for reskilling of individuals. The challenges and ways of overcoming them have been discussed here for future outlook.

DOI: 10.4018/979-8-3693-3478-2.ch002

INTRODUCTION

With the role of digital transformation, the methods of working across different sectors have drastically changed in recent times. The optimization of digital methods has led to stakeholders enjoying a number of benefits in the process (Bloomberg, 2018; Bouwman et al., 2019). It can be stated that the digital revolution has led to a number of advantages that have helped industries to shape themselves to derive better efficiency (Torres & Augusto, 2020). One of the most crucial innovations that have emerged as a result of digital transformations include the development of artificial intelligence or popularly known as AI. The role of AI in the digital spectrum have been quite innovative and effective and has led to transformations which seemed impossible ten years ago (Haenlein & Kaplan, 2019; Li, 2019). Listing out some of the major changes brought about with the implementation of AI include real-time data monitoring, using chatbot instead of human labor, investing in quick decision-making through data driven analytics etc (Y. Chen & Feng, 2021; Nadimpalli, 2017; Shinde et al., 2021). In this process one of the noteworthy shapes that have occurred as a result of this AI driven working situation is the generation of a digital workforce. It has led to changes that have occurred in the employment generation landscape. The methods of employment have seen changes in recent times due to the digital workforce being propagated thoroughly (J. Lee et al., 2018; Pantano & Pizzi, 2020). However, it can be stated that the use of AI in the employment landscape not only comes with restrictions but can offer a number of benefits as well. It can act as a tool for providing skill development to the employees followed by generating dynamic nature to adopt the ongoing changes (Sari et al., 2020).

The discussion on AI and its application is an ongoing topic and requires further contribution in various aspects (Atwal & Bryson, 2021). This chapter is an attempt to understand the role of AI with respect to the changing job employment landscape while investigating its pros and cons. The chapter here attempts to integrate to meet your societal implications that emerge out of businesses. The first one refers to understanding how AI can be used as an effective tool in changing the job scenario after its emergence. The second concern that would be undertaken in the chapter includes understanding the corporate social responsibility (CSR) driven initiatives and the role of AI in shaping them. By collaborating both of these aspects in line with the AI mechanism, the chapter would deal with framing the understanding of the CSR activities that act in order to address the social implications of AI on employment. The CSR activities among companies include the well-being of its employees as a prime concern (Jamali et al., 2015). These activities include promoting a good life for its employees while trying to upskill or reskill their set of abilities. The companies are of the belief that investing in the well-being of its employees would contribute to its long-term profits as well as provide a satisfactory life for its employees (Kim

& Kim, 2020). It would provide the employees ability to sustain in the increasing competitiveness of the job market. The provisions include designing an optimum plan for mentorship programs, providing a collaboration between industry and academia for better understanding and providing personalized paths for their overall development (Adu-Gyamfi et al., 2021; Bapat & Upadhyay, 2021). These methods of uplifting the employee skills have seen a number of changes due to the emergence of AI. There are several aspects across the industries that have been overtaken by AI and are driven by such developments. This has created psychological distress among the employees due to their concerns about their future job prospects (Loor-Zambrano et al., 2022). The emotional troll that has occurred on the employees due to the threatening discourse of AI should not be taken lightly.

As a remedy to the changing landscape of digital workforce generation, appropriate strategies can be designed as a part of the CSR initiatives which can lead to harnessing the role of technology in human development. The chapter here would dive further into the ways in which the two aspects can be integrated and provide a method through which CSR activities can lead to navigating AI powered workforce shifts and its social implications.

THE CHANGING LANDSCAPE OF EMPLOYMENT

The changing landscape of employment in the technological era, particularly in the last five years, has been characterized by a significant impact of artificial intelligence (AI) (Mor & Gupta, 2021; Pallathadka et al., 2021). This has led to an increasing impact on job displacement and marking the evolution of job roles. As per (Thormundsson, 2024), the AI market is about to grow into one trillion U.S dollars by the year 2028. As AI continue to advance surge through its updated versions, they are immensely contributing towards reshaping various industries and professions, leading to the generation of both opportunities and challenges for the workforce.

(Thormundsson, 2024) also mentioned that with the use of AI there is a need for around 20% or even more employees to be reskilled. It goes into the understanding that everyone out of five employees will have to undergo the reskilling which would take up a sufficient amount of company's time and money. The adoption of AI technologies in workplaces has been accelerated and the prime areas where these are employed include using AI for tasks such as data analysis, customer service, and automation of routine tasks (Mhlanga, 2020). This has led to increased efficiency and productivity across sectors, and has resulted in job displacement for certain roles that can be automated. The examples that can be considered here include the cases of industries such as manufacturing, retail, and transportation have seen a significant shift towards automation, leading to a reduction in the demand for manual labor jobs (J. Lee et al., 2018; Talwar et al., 2021). Moreover, AI-powered algorithms have been increasingly used in recruitment processes, leading to concerns about potential biases and discrimination in hiring practices. It is also seen that the evolution of job roles has been quite evident, with the emergence of new positions that require skills in AI, data analytics, and machine learning. It leads to the requirement of more skilled personnel and has limited the need for individuals who are not equipped with such capabilities (Königstorfer & Thalmann, 2020). While these roles offer opportunities for individuals with the necessary expertise, they also highlight the growing demand for continuous learning and upskilling in the workforce. The impact of AI on job displacement has not only economic implications but also societal and psychological effects (Gruetzemacher et al., 2020). The world today undergoes massive psychological distress and when it comes to the professional lives, job loss leading to financial instability can further lead to increased stress, and a sense of uncertainty about the future (Patrawala, 2019). Moreover, it can generate existing inequalities, as those with lower levels of education and skills may be more vulnerable to job displacement.

Additionally, job displacement can have broader societal effects, such as changes in community dynamics and social cohesion. In regions heavily reliant on industries affected by automation, there may be a decline in local economies and an increase in social isolation and mental health issues (N. Chen et al., 2022). From a psychological perspective, job displacement can have a profound impact on individuals' sense of identity and self-worth. Many people derive a significant portion of their identity from their work, and losing a job can lead to feelings of inadequacy, shame, and depression (Plikas et al., 2024). Moreover, the process of retraining or transitioning to a new career can be challenging and stressful, further exacerbating these psychological effects (Rawashdeh, 2023). In response to these challenges, policymakers, businesses, and educational institutions must collaborate to mitigate the negative effects of AI on employment. This includes investing in education and training programs to equip workers with the skills needed for the jobs of the future, implementing policies that support job creation and economic resilience, and fostering a culture of lifelong learning and adaptability in the workforce.

Overall, the changing landscape of employment especially in the post-ChatGPT era is characterized by the dual forces of job displacement and the evolution of job roles driven by AI technologies (Ngo, 2024; Zhao & Jakkampudi, 2023). While these changes offer opportunities for innovation and growth, they also pose significant challenges that require proactive and collaborative responses from all stakeholders. The need to address certain remedies to overcome these tense situations is essential. It would not only help in generating better opportunities for the employees but can also promote a sound and positive work culture across organisations.

CSR AND THE RESKILLING IMPERATIVE: EXPLORATION OF EXISTING LITERATURE THROUGH

The above sections in the chapter have shown the changing landscape of employment and the role of AI in driving it towards the next level. The use of CSR activities in the process can be quite beneficial as stated in the previous discussions. There are a number of researchers who have attempted to investigate the role of CSR in terms of reskilling the employees in their organisation. In order to understand the existing studies and their focus along it, an exploration in the current body of knowledge is done. The systematic investigation of the exploration has been utilized using the method of PRISMA. This would ensure the proper depiction of the facts in the topic. A stage approach as suggested by (Moher et al., 2009) has been considered to include the final list of studies in the chapter. The four-stage approach taken here includes identification, screening, eligibility and inclusion.

The identification process is used for searching the appropriate articles in the relevant databases. The review process described above involves an overall scanning of the existing literature. The databases to be considered when undergoing the extensive search for relevant research articles include SCOPUS, Web Science, ScienceDirect and taking Google Scholar databases for sources. As the Web of Science database is a part of the SCOPUS database, it would be here that the majority of the articles would be taken. The condition for considering the mentioned databases is to source the articles which are of high quality. The identification of the required literature within these databases is done with the use of specific keywords like "CSR", "Digital Workforce Shift", "Employment", and "Reskilling." The subsequent section outlines the detailed process followed to select the research papers under consideration. The period of searching of the articles is for a duration of 5 years which is from 2018 to 2023 to mark the emergence of AI in the scope. A total of 1409 articles have been located under the stage.

The second stage in the process is that of screening which begins with the articles having been investigated through the reading of its title and working upon the presence of the inclusion criteria. The criteria being considered include the presence of CSR strategies as an element for the understanding of employee reskilling. In the screening stage by including the criteria, a total of 33 articles have been found relevant. The articles which are found redundant have been removed along with those which do not fulfil all the required criteria for the study. Next in the eligibility stage, the presence of the inclusion criteria is reassured and the final list of articles to be reviewed have been scrutinized. Finally, through a detailed content analysis, the 33 articles in the study are being reviewed to get the answers to the set research questions.

Figure 1. The PRISMA framework following the above four stages are being provided in the graphical representation below.

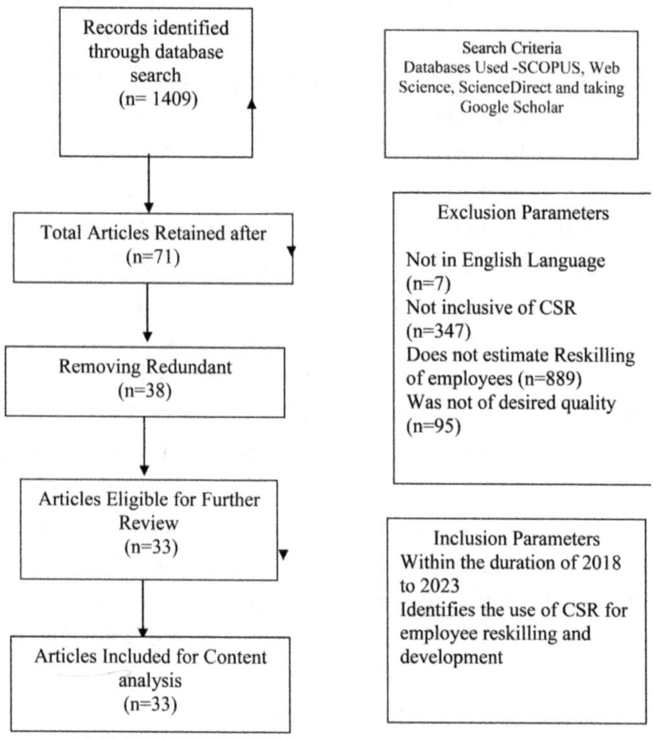

Table 1. A table has been generated to present the results of the 33 articles investigating about the reskilling imperative through CSR activities.

Serial Number	Author	Objective	Methodology	Main Outcome
1	(Ghobakhloo et al., 2023)	To investigate the implementation of automation in bringing sustainable performances through the role of CSR.	Quantitative	The use of such automation process needs to be specified by the socio-behavioural concerns of the employees along with their social capacity competency
2	(Hahn et al., 2023)	To understand the employee engagement and disengagement practices led up by the CSR initiatives in companies. The engagement of the employees arises with every CSR activity undertaken and they become more involved and trained with such allocations	Qualitative	The study found the relationship between employee personal preferences during such allocations which causes tension in the organisational initiatives. The proper maintenance of balance when being provided any employee associated CSR activities is hereby suggested.
3	(Lim, 2023)	To understand the ongoing workforce revolution occurring across the different industries. The transformations have not only impacted the workers, but have also changed the workplaces and the work itself,	Qualitative	The changes in the workplaces can be effectively altered by equipping the leaders and managers in the field with knowledge and making them know about the dynamics of the changing landscape. The role of CSR in this manner can help in societal development as well.
4	(Patre et al., 2023)	To understand the barriers that exist in the upskilling and reskilling of employees using certain education-based platforms	Quantitative	The barriers in such an approach provided by the company are in terms of the quality of content, instruction provided by the platforms, image barriers and the word-of-mouth communication restrictions

continued on following page

Table 1. Continued

Serial Number	Author	Objective	Methodology	Main Outcome
5	(Rawshdeh et al., 2023)	To understand about the benefits of being socially responsible on the talent retention practices while navigating the mediating role played by trust and motivation	Quantitative	The enactment of a socially responsible HRM practice team in an organisation is related positively with its talent retention policies. The employees' attitude in the discourse that is their trust levels and motivation successfully mediate the relationship between the two.
6	(Sarkar et al., 2023)	To consider the pandemic duration for using a CSR perspective to skill development. The time of the pandemic has affected numerous aspects and the only effective way to bring back those is focusing into the skill development initiatives.	Qualitative	The study with its analysis of the interviews and case studies have stated that the role of CSR in addressing the skill gap that arose during the pandemic have been quite substantial.
7	(Stankevičiūtė & Kalvaitienė, 2023)	To investigate about the internal CSR activities undertaken in the banking sector with reference to the human resources parameters	Qualitative	The role of HR business partners in handling such internal CSR activities are quite crucial. It can allow for development practices among the employees while facilitating their psychological well-being. The learning and reskilling can be sufficiently encouraged through such initiatives

continued on following page

Table 1. Continued

Serial Number	Author	Objective	Methodology	Main Outcome
8	(Agha & Fitzsimmons, 2022)	To learn how the application of CSR can help in building a better value proposition for the employees in the region of United Arab Emirates	Qualitative	The findings suggest that CSR can effectively manage the employee value proposition through adding various reskilling aspects into their career. It can lead to adding into building brand reputation and enhancing customer delight.
9	(Agha, 2022)	To talk about the training and upskilling of employees in a workforce for building a workforce with high resilience.	Qualitative	The same can be uplifted through the use of initiatives by companies which are socially responsible and capture a dynamic workforce in the making through upskilling and reskilling
10	(Faeq et al., 2022)	To determine how the total quality management practices related to people impact on the CSR implementing job satisfaction. It integrates the two aspects important to ant people based organisation and points out the essential considerations to make.	Quantitative	There are significant levels of association found among the total quality management practices based on empowerment of employees, increasing their involvement through training and teamwork and delivering management commitment with the CSR based values of an organisation including legal, ethical, economic and philanthropic methods.

continued on following page

Table 1. Continued

Serial Number	Author	Objective	Methodology	Main Outcome
11	(Low & Bu, 2022)	To understand the applications of internal CSR activities in the service industries during the pandemic. The pandemic has brought about a number of challenges across the world and the same have been observed in the service industry as well. Many organisations undertook processes to develop internally in order to sustain themselves.	Quantitative	The CSR initiatives included matching the employee skills with the emerging digitization methods. It also focused upon uplifting employee's organisational commitment during the tough time of the pandemic. Overall, it focused on building the dynamics of the employees with the changing environment.
12	(McLachlan, 2022)	To be able to understand the downsizing undertaken during Covid-19 while determining the regulatory responsibilities for employment	Qualitative	The study showed that in the downsizing of companies, the utmost important aspect would be to reskill and upskill the employees so that the existing ones can fit into the required job roles and provide similar productivity levels.
13	(Mukhuty et al., 2022)	To derive an understanding on the industry 4.0 evolution using sustainable business practices with a focus on human resource. The increase in productivity is the prime concern along with cost reduction and timely efficiencies. It can take socially responsible path by focusing on the human involved in the process	Qualitative	The development of the practices needs to be enhanced among the human resources based on removing the digital skill gaps, resistance to change, employment threats leading to inequalities and promoting leadership

continued on following page

Table 1. Continued

Serial Number	Author	Objective	Methodology	Main Outcome
14	(Pfajfar et al., 2022)	To look into the social impact caused by the CSR activities on that of multiple stakeholders in an organisation. The study is conducted from the perspective of relationship marketing and generates interesting insights.	Quantitative	The results have been able to establish a positive association among the CSR which are employee oriented with the levels of usefulness perceived for such CSR actions on the society and its employees.
15	(Yan et al., 2022)	To determine how the use of AI based service robots can influence the frontline employees as a measure of safety through CSR of the company	Qualitative	The study initiated during the pandemic showed interesting results in this regard. The employees generated mixed effects and it is seen that this CSR is able to generate engagement and participation among the employees as well.
16	(Aoun-Noujaim, 2021)	To understand about the workforce reskilling and the support provided by the management in this form. The study initiated during the pandemic has provided interesting results in the field.	Quantitative	The relationships determined in the study have been able to provide the significant association proof among the management support along with organisational support with respect to providing an innovative work environment for reskilling the workforce.

continued on following page

Table 1. Continued

Serial Number	Author	Objective	Methodology	Main Outcome
17	(Bharadwaj & Yameen, 2021)	To investigate the CSR branding of the employer with the retention rate among the employees. The use of organisational identification as a mediator in the process has also been looked into.	Quantitative	The findings positively asserted the relationship existing among the branding of employers through the CSR activities on their retention. Organisational identification does mediate the relationship between the two and is a strong predictor of employee retention in such organisations
18	(Diaz & Halkias, 2021)	To understand the methods of both upskilling as well as reskilling the leaders in the fourth industrial revolution domain through the building of an innovative program of education in business schools.	Qualitative	The method can help integrate the sustainable development goals and be in line with the ideologies of the United Nations. It can derive sustainable business practices through delivering community development in various regions.
19	(Du & Xie, 2021)	To determine how AI based CSR activities can lead to causing challenges for companies.	Qualitative	The study focused on the stakeholder environment from such CSR based on AI while highlighting the institutional environment within. It shows that acting social responsibility in terms of these stakeholders can positively impact on their development which would benefit the company as well

continued on following page

Table 1. Continued

Serial Number	Author	Objective	Methodology	Main Outcome
20	(Khuong et al., 2021)	To understand the role of CSR in stakeholder development through strategic policies in order to maintain the corporate reputation. The study has been an investigation in Vietnam and reflects the different aspects of undertaking CSR for stakeholder benefits	Quantitative	The results of the CSR are highly driven by the stakeholder influence and helps in building a corporate reputation. CSR can be used as a very effective tool for managing the stakeholders and building a sustainable development forum.
21	(Pandya, 2021)	To talk about the role of CSR initiatives in facilitating employment for persons with disabilities. The study revolves around the difficulties of employees towards receiving employment especially if they are disabled and investigates the role played by CSR initiatives in the same.	Qualitative	The CSR initiatives can work positively in this regard by increasing the motivation levels among such individuals by improving their quality of life. It can provide skill-based programmes to increase their productivity level and gain more employment.
22	(Y. Lee, 2021)	To determine the ways of internal CSR propagation in working towards employee engagement and developing positive behaviour. The need to employ internal CSR for overall benefits of the employees have been considered here through investigating 405 employees in USA	Quantitative	The role of internal CSR activities is found to be quite effective in terms of various aspects. This includes providing stability to the employees, promoting workplace diversity and maintaining work-life balance. It also acts highly in the skill development of the employees.

continued on following page

Table 1. Continued

Serial Number	Author	Objective	Methodology	Main Outcome
23	(Anlesinya & Amponsah-Tawiah, 2020)	To draw an investigation towards the development of a responsible talent management practice. The perspective of ethical and responsible management practices at work have been investigated that would uplift the employees.	Qualitative	The need for talent management in an organisation to be socially responsible is of utmost importance. The equal opportunities to all can derive well-being among the employees in an organisation and lead it towards sustainable development.
24	(Zainee & Puteh, 2020)	To understand how the impact of CSR works on talent retention among the Generation Y. The generation considered here are known for their influential and demanding nature. This study integrates the role of CSR in retaining employees in the accounting profession.	Quantitative	The relationship between CSR activities and employee retention among the stated categories are quite significant. The study also caters to the important role played by the economic, legal as well philanthropic responsibilities fulfilled by such CSR activities on generation Y employees.
25	(Babu & Kinkhabwala, 2019)	To study how the CSR activities and its effective integration can help in bridging the manpower gap with devising proper skill development opportunities	Qualitative	The scope of CSR initiatives holds many untapped opportunities to create a skilled India and cover the gaps that exist in the provision of skilled manpower in the system. The country is largely facing a skill deficit problem and employment of CSR initiatives can help overcome these problems to a large extent.

continued on following page

Table 1. Continued

Serial Number	Author	Objective	Methodology	Main Outcome
26	(Basu, 2019)	To talk about the CSR initiatives taken in the automotive industry of India towards structured skill development. The main idea of the study is to understand the endeavor that the initiatives have taken towards enhancing the levels of employability.	Qualitative	The competitiveness in the manufacturing sector has led to the introduction of several requirements in the industry. The need to upskill and that too in a structured manner is quite necessary in the present times. This can be done by using CSR initiatives and would be quite beneficial.
27	(Blagoycheva, 2019)	To understand about the social responsibility generated towards the employees while keeping in mind the ongoing digitization process. The digital technologies have brought about a number of opportunities but have considered several employment difficulties along with it.	Qualitative	The socially responsible initiatives to be undertaken under the digitization aspect can focus on identification of non-standard employment, the working situations, the unemployment status which are unclear and provision of social security.
28	(Miller & Akdere, 2019)	To undergo a study investigating the role of CSR in training and development. The CSR strategies across organisations vary in different perspective but its use in the provision of training and development can be quite crucial	Qualitative	The CSR initiatives that can effectively target the training and development aspects help generate interesting results. This includes working towards developing organisational commitment and improving human resources development while focusing upon skill development through the training programs

continued on following page

Table 1. Continued

Serial Number	Author	Objective	Methodology	Main Outcome
29	(Moyo et al., 2019)	To study about the role of CSR strategies in uplifting the social security of the construction workers in Zimbabwe. The construction sector is one of the toughest sectors for employees and their security levels needs to be optimized all through.	Quantitative	The social responsibility programmes designed in such sectors can work effectively in the betterment of the construction workers and needs to be used to work towards their welfare in the future
30	(Kolding et al., 2018)	To investigate if the information management in an organisation is creating a skill gap. In organisations information management is quite crucial and requires strategies to overcome it in order to restore efficiency	Qualitative	The digitalization of companies requires them to upskill their employees and work towards retaining them in the organisation. These workers are subjected to a lifelong process of learning while acquiring new skills and updating the existing ones.
31	(Miethlich & Šlahor, 2018)	To review the vocational rehabilitation that is provided as a result of the CSR strategies undertaken by the companies. The provision of such vocational training through the development of strategies is crucial for the well-being of the employees and the society.	Qualitative	The vocational rehabilitation can be in the form of providing sheltered workplaces without discriminating on entry-level positions. The provision of shared values across these employees is necessary with such initiatives

continued on following page

Table 1. Continued

Serial Number	Author	Objective	Methodology	Main Outcome
32	(Sadasivan, 2018)	To understand about the process of strategizing skill development with the help of CSR activities in the Indian scenario. The role of public and private sector through their CSR efforts have been utilized for the purpose of bridging the skill development gap in India	Qualitative	The government as well as the corporate sector can work together in this strategy to gain a mutual benefit through propagating sustainable activities and providing skill development
33	(Staniškienė & Stankevičiūtė, 2018)	To undertake the employee perspective in a CSR driven organisation. The study aims to develop a social sustainability framework for measuring its different aspects.	Qualitative	Out of the six aspects identified here, the need to maintain employee development through upskilling have been recognized as a crucial one. The need to constantly derive the CSR commitments for employee development is instrumental.

There has been a total of 33 articles that are looked into the deal for understanding the use of CSR activities for reskilling and upscaling of the employees. These articles are found to cover a number of different aspects that are related with the CSR strategies followed by companies for the purpose of skill development. It is seen that there are certain studies which focus on conducting internal CSR activities in order to develop and train their own employees (Faeq et al., 2022; Stankevičiūtė & Kalvaitienė, 2023) . This leads to generation of leadership among the employees and adds to the long-term benefit of the company itself (Mukhuty et al., 2022).

The next set of observations from these articles that are observed include the provision of bridging the gap of skill development through the company CSR activities (Babu & Kinkhabwala, 2019). These include providing various provisions such as education platforms, tying up with business schools and providing other measures that can lead to the development of skills among individuals (Kolding et al., 2018).

The studies have also highlighted the rule of automation and how the companies have made CSR provisions to overcome the skills required to match them (Ghobakhloo et al., 2023). These include upgrading the employees with the recent requirements for automation along with providing them assistance with their use (Yan et al., 2022). The studies have been quite frequent during the pandemic era where constant efforts have been made through CSR activities to overcome the difficulties in adapting to the use of artificial intelligence at work (McLachlan, 2022).

Overall, the literature shows that CSR strategies have been devised to focus on the skill development of individuals whether it is internal to the company or for others outside the company. It involves taking the perspective of every stakeholder and generates an effective medium for reskilling during the era of automation.

CSR BASED RESKILLING IN COMBATING AI DRIVEN DIGITAL WORKFORCE SHIFT

The world today is evolving constantly with the help of technology and this has led to the rise of artificial intelligence (AI). It has facilitated automation and is reshaping industries while fundamentally altering the nature of work. While these technological advancements are mediums for increased productivity, they also contain significant challenges for the stakeholders, especially to the workers in the form of job displacement (Dosi et al., 2021; Werfel et al., 2022). It leads to the need for upskilling and reskilling of their potential knowledge and keeping on upgrading their skills. In response to these challenges, many organizations are turning to CSR initiatives focused on reskilling to help combat the AI-driven digital workforce shift.

The CSR-based reskilling efforts is an attempt towards driving employment in the time of AI and automation. As machines and algorithms increasingly perform tasks that were once taken care of by humans, it can be ascertained that many jobs are at risk of becoming obsolete. As mentioned earlier, this phenomenon is highly evident in the case of industries such as manufacturing, retail, and customer service, where routine and repetitive tasks are being automated and that too with increased accuracy.

The role of CSR initiatives focused on reskilling is generated to address the potential negative consequences of job displacement while aiming to equip the workers with the skills and knowledge needed to thrive in the digital economy (Babu & Kinkhabwala, 2019; Blagoycheva, 2019). These initiatives are provided based on a multifaceted approach where a combination of education based skill development and training programs with support services such as career counselling and job placement assistance are taken up.

One example of a CSR-based reskilling initiative is the partnership between technology companies and educational institutions to offer specialized training programs in areas such as data analytics, machine learning, and cybersecurity. These programs provide workers with the opportunity to acquire new skills that are in high demand in the digital age, thereby increasing their employability and job security. It can be observed in the case of Infosys where free digital learning and reskilling are provided to more than 10 million individuals (Infosys, 2023). IBM also focused on their CSR based initiative towards training around 2 million individuals on AI usage by the year 2026 (Hart, 2023).

In addition to providing training and education opportunities, CSR-based reskilling initiatives also play a crucial role in fostering a culture of inclusivity and diversity in the workforce. By offering opportunities for upskilling and reskilling to workers from diverse backgrounds, these initiatives help to ensure that no one is left behind in the transition to the digital economy. There are such initiatives taken by Microsoft where their "Future Ready Initiative" is targeted to train millions of Indian individuals. Similar approach is also taken by Amazon through their career skills initiative to reskill the Indian workforce (Mehta, 2024).

Successful CSR-based reskilling programs rely heavily on collaboration, where companies join forces with various stakeholders. It includes having government collaboration for the purpose, through NGOs or academics. These partnerships are essential for enhancing program effectiveness, ensuring sustainability, and enabling scalability. These initiatives are undertaken by companies such as Mahindra & Mahindra, Wipro, Asian paints who contribute towards reskilling based on collaborations (Fernandes, 2018).

CSR-based reskilling initiatives play a vital role in combating the AI-driven digital workforce shift by equipping workers with the skills and knowledge needed to succeed in the digital economy. These initiatives not only help to address the challenges of job displacement and technological change but also contribute to broader social and economic development goals. By investing in reskilling, organizations can demonstrate their commitment to corporate social responsibility while simultaneously preparing their workforce for the jobs of the future.

The real-life example of CSR-based reskilling in combating the AI-driven digital workforce shift is Microsoft's AI for Good initiative. Microsoft has recognized the potential for AI to disrupt the job market and has taken proactive steps to address this challenge through its CSR efforts (Aula & Bowles, 2023).

As part of the AI for Good initiative, Microsoft has launched several programs aimed at upskilling and reskilling individuals for jobs in the AI-driven economy. One such program is the AI for Accessibility program, which provides training and resources for people with disabilities to learn AI skills and pursue careers in technology. This program not only empowers individuals with disabilities to participate in the digital workforce but also addresses the growing demand for AI talent in the technology industry.

Another example is Microsoft's partnership with non-profit organizations and educational institutions to provide AI training and certification programs to underserved communities. Through these partnerships, Microsoft is able to reach individuals who may not have access to traditional education or training programs, helping them acquire the skills they need to secure jobs in the AI-driven economy.

By investing in CSR-based reskilling initiatives, Microsoft is not only preparing individuals for the future world of work but also demonstrating its commitment to using AI for social good. These efforts are not only benefiting individuals and communities but also helping to build a more diverse and inclusive digital workforce.

OPPORTUNITIES AND CHALLENGES IN CSR-BASED UPSKILLING

Designing customized training programs for CSR-based reskilling involves conducting a needs assessment to identify specific skills gaps and learning needs, developing tailored curricula, selecting appropriate delivery methods, implementing engagement strategies, and providing mentorship and coaching. These programs aim to address the evolving demands of the digital workforce by equipping employees with the skills needed to thrive in an AI-driven economy. Evaluation and feedback mechanisms are crucial for assessing the effectiveness of these programs, with continuous improvement strategies based on participant feedback and outcomes.

To evaluate the outcomes of CSR-based reskilling programs, key performance indicators such as job placement rates, promotion rates, and employee satisfaction levels are tracked. Follow-up surveys and interviews with participants provide qualitative insights into the program's impact on participants' skills and career advancement. By continuously improving training programs based on evaluation data, companies can ensure that their CSR initiatives effectively prepare employees for the challenges and opportunities of the digital workforce shift.

Emphasizing the importance of continuous learning and adaptation is crucial in the context of rapidly evolving technology landscapes, particularly with the proliferation of AI-driven changes in the workforce. Companies must recognize that reskilling and upskilling are not one-time events but ongoing processes that require a commitment to lifelong learning. By fostering a culture of continuous learning, companies can empower their employees to stay abreast of technological advancements and adapt to changing job requirements. This not only benefits individual employees in their career development but also enables companies to remain competitive in the digital economy.

Furthermore, continuous learning and adaptation are essential for future-proofing the workforce against potential job displacement caused by AI and automation. By proactively reskilling employees for roles that are less susceptible to automation, companies can mitigate the impact of technological disruptions on their workforce. This proactive approach not only helps employees secure their future in the digital age but also demonstrates a commitment to social responsibility and ethical AI deployment. Overall, emphasizing continuous learning and adaptation is essential for navigating the digital workforce shift and ensuring a sustainable future for both employees and companies alike.

The CSR initiatives designed for the purpose of upskilling individuals have gained importance in recent years as organizations recognize the importance of investing in their workforce and driving their long-term benefits further. While these programs hold promise for addressing skills gaps and promoting sustainable development, they also encounter various challenges that impact their effectiveness and often slow down their progress. In this section, the key challenges that can occur in the application of CSR-based upskilling initiatives are put forward.

One of the primary challenges in CSR-based upskilling initiatives is the identification of relevant skills gaps and training needs (Galport & Azzam, 2017; Goniewicz et al., 2021; McGuinness & Ortiz, 2016). While there are discussions about the presence of a skill gap, its identification is not quite clear. There is a need for the companies to conduct needs assessments and understand the specific skill requirements of their workforce. This can lead to the proper alignment of the training programs. However, the process of accurately identifying these needs can be more complex than expected as the technological interventions are constantly changing. This leads to the emergence of new job roles frequently. Moreover, there may be discrepancies between the skills demanded by employers and those possessed by workers, further complicating the upskilling process.

Another challenge relates to the design and delivery of effective training programs (Bluestone et al., 2013; Gekara & Snell, 2018; Lacerenza et al., 2017). The designing of the curriculum of such programs needs to be customised based on the characterises of the workforce targeted. It must address the diverse learning needs of the group of employees while incorporating industry best practices through planning and expertise. Additionally, ensuring that training programs are accessible to all employees, including those with limited educational backgrounds or technological literacy, can be challenging. Organizations must leverage innovative instructional methods, such as blended learning approaches or mobile-based training platforms, to reach a broader audience effectively.

Furthermore, the scalability and sustainability of upskilling initiatives present significant challenges for organizations. While pilot programs may demonstrate initial success, scaling these initiatives to reach a larger workforce or expanding them to multiple locations requires substantial resources and infrastructure. Moreover, maintaining the relevance and currency of training content in response to evolving industry trends and technological advancements demands ongoing investment and adaptation.

In addition to logistical challenges, CSR-based upskilling initiatives may face resistance or scepticism from employees and other stakeholders. Workers may perceive training programs as an additional burden or fear that automation and technology-enabled processes will render their skills obsolete, leading to job displacement (Agha, 2022; Basu, 2019). Overcoming these concerns requires transparent communication, active engagement with employees, and a commitment to fostering a culture of lifelong learning and continuous improvement within the organization.

Furthermore, funding constraints and resource limitations pose significant obstacles to the implementation of comprehensive upskilling programs (Y. Lee, 2021; Moyo et al., 2019). While organizations may allocate a portion of their CSR budget to training initiatives, securing additional funding from external sources or forming partnerships with government agencies, educational institutions, or non-profit organizations can enhance program sustainability and impact. However, navigating complex funding mechanisms and establishing mutually beneficial partnerships requires strategic planning and collaboration.

Lastly, measuring the effectiveness and impact of CSR-based upskilling initiatives presents inherent challenges (Sarkar et al., 2023). While organizations may track metrics such as training completion rates or employee satisfaction scores, assessing long-term outcomes, such as improved job performance or career advancement, can be more elusive. Moreover, attributing these outcomes solely to upskilling programs amidst other organizational factors and external influences requires rigorous evaluation methodologies and data analytics capabilities.

Despite these challenges, organizations can adopt several strategies to enhance the effectiveness of CSR-based upskilling initiatives. Prioritizing collaboration and stakeholder engagement, investing in innovative instructional technologies and methodologies, fostering a culture of learning and adaptability, and leveraging strategic partnerships and funding opportunities are key approaches to overcoming the obstacles outlined above. In conclusion, while CSR-based upskilling initiatives hold promise for addressing skills gaps and promoting social and economic development, they encounter various challenges that must be addressed to maximize their impact. By identifying and addressing these challenges proactively, organizations can develop and implement effective upskilling programs that empower employees, drive business success, and contribute to sustainable growth and prosperity.

ETHICAL PRINCIPLES GUIDING AI DEPLOYMENT

Ethical principles guiding AI deployment are critical for ensuring that artificial intelligence technologies are developed and implemented in a responsible and beneficial manner. These principles provide a framework for addressing the complex ethical challenges posed by AI systems and help to mitigate potential risks and harms. One of the fundamental ethical principles guiding AI deployment is fairness. This principle emphasizes the importance of ensuring that AI systems are designed and implemented in a way that is fair and unbiased, and that they do not discriminate against individuals or groups based on factors such as race, gender, or socioeconomic status. Fairness in AI deployment requires careful consideration of data biases and the potential for algorithmic discrimination, as well as the development of methods for mitigating these biases and ensuring that AI systems treat all individuals fairly and equitably. Additionally, transparency is another key ethical principle guiding AI deployment. Transparency requires that AI systems be explainable and understandable, so that individuals can understand how decisions are made by AI algorithms and hold developers and deployers accountable for their actions. Transparency also facilitates trust and confidence in AI systems, which is essential for their acceptance and adoption by society. Other important ethical principles guiding AI deployment include accountability, privacy, safety, and social responsibility. By adhering to these principles, developers, deployers, and policymakers can help to ensure that AI technologies are developed and deployed in a way that promotes the public good and upholds fundamental ethical values.

CONCLUSION AND FUTURE OUTLOOK

In conclusion, navigating the AI-powered workforce shift requires a multifaceted approach that combines technological innovation with ethical considerations and social responsibility. CSR-based skilling initiatives play a crucial role in preparing the workforce for the challenges and opportunities presented by AI technologies. By investing in reskilling and upskilling programs, companies can empower employees to adapt to changing job roles and acquire the skills needed to thrive in the digital economy. However, it is essential to ensure that these initiatives are guided by ethical principles and prioritize fairness, transparency, accountability, and social responsibility. Collaboration between businesses, educational institutions, government agencies, and non-profit organizations is key to the success of CSR-based skilling programs, as it allows for the pooling of resources and expertise needed to design effective and sustainable initiatives. Additionally, ongoing evaluation and adjustment are necessary to ensure that these programs remain relevant and impactful in the face of evolving technological and market trends. Ultimately, by embracing CSR-based skilling and adhering to ethical principles, companies can help to create a more inclusive and equitable workforce, where all individuals have the opportunity to thrive in the age of artificial intelligence.

The future course of study needs to focus more on literature based on the use of CSR based strategies to upskill different categories of the workforce. The need to focus on designing a customized curriculum and its deployment techniques needs to be investigated further. Moreover, the identification of results from such reskilling and upskilling programs needs to be conducted to make the process a more result oriented approach.

REFERENCES

Adu-Gyamfi, M., He, Z., Nyame, G., Boahen, S., & Frempong, M. F. (2021). Effects of Internal CSR Activities on Social Performance: The Employee Perspective. *Sustainability (Basel)*, 13(11), 6235. DOI: 10.3390/su13116235

Agha, K. (2022). *Training and Upgrading Skills of Employees Towards Building Resilience Among the Workforce*. DOI: 10.4018/978-1-7998-9506-0.ch012

Agha, K., & Fitzsimmons, J. (2022). *Examining the Significance of Corporate Social Responsibility in Building Employee Value Proposition and Brand Value in the United Arab Emirates*. DOI: 10.1007/978-3-030-95581-6_8

Anlesinya, A., & Amponsah-Tawiah, K. (2020). Towards a responsible talent management model. *European Journal of Training and Development*, 44(2/3), 279–303. DOI: 10.1108/EJTD-07-2019-0114

Aoun-Noujaim, G. (2021). *The Effect of Perceived Organizational Support during COVID-19 on Innovative Workforce Behavior. The Role of Workforce Reskilling and Top Management Support. (c2021)*. DOI: 10.26756/th.2022.450

Atwal, G., & Bryson, D. (2021). Antecedents of intention to adopt artificial intelligence services by consumers in personal financial investing. *Strategic Change*, 30(3), 293–298. Advance online publication. DOI: 10.1002/jsc.2412

Aula, V., & Bowles, J. (2023, January). Stepping back from Data and AI for Good – current trends and ways forward. *Big Data & Society*, 10(1). DOI: 10.1177/20539517231173901

Babu, V., & Kinkhabwala, B. (2019). Was an untapped "skilling" opportunity ignored? *Worldwide Hospitality and Tourism Themes*, 11(1), 37–53. DOI: 10.1108/WHATT-10-2018-0059

Bapat, S., & Upadhyay, P. (2021). Implications of CSR initiatives on employee engagement. *Social Responsibility Journal*, 17(2), 149–163. DOI: 10.1108/SRJ-05-2018-0120

Basu, P. S. (2019). Structured Skill Development in Indian Automotive Industry - A CSR Endeavor Toward Enhancing Employbility. *Journal of Organisation and Human Behaviour Preview*, 8(2/3), 56–66.

Bharadwaj, S., & Yameen, M. (2021). Analyzing the mediating effect of organizational identification on the relationship between CSR employer branding and employee retention. *Management Research Review*, 44(5), 718–737. DOI: 10.1108/MRR-05-2020-0298

Blagoycheva, H. (2019). *Employers' Social Responsibility in the Context of Digitization.*

Bloomberg. (2018). *Digitization, Digitalization, And Digital Transformation: Confuse Them At Your Peril.*

Bluestone, J., Johnson, P., Fullerton, J., Carr, C., Alderman, J., & BonTempo, J. (2013). Effective in-service training design and delivery: Evidence from an integrative literature review. *Human Resources for Health*, 11(1), 51. DOI: 10.1186/1478-4491-11-51 PMID: 24083659

Bouwman, H., Nikou, S., & de Reuver, M. (2019). Digitalization, business models, and SMEs: How do business model innovation practices improve performance of digitalizing SMEs? *Telecommunications Policy*, 43(9), 101828. Advance online publication. DOI: 10.1016/j.telpol.2019.101828

Chen, N., Li, Z., & Tang, B. (2022). Can digital skill protect against job displacement risk caused by artificial intelligence? Empirical evidence from 701 detailed occupations. *PLoS One*, 17(11), e0277280. DOI: 10.1371/journal.pone.0277280 PMID: 36346798

Chen, Y., & Feng, S. (2021). *Artificial Intelligence: Creating More Possibilities for Programmatic Advertising*. DOI: 10.1007/978-3-030-80624-8_19

Diaz, J., & Halkias, D. (2021). Reskilling and Upskilling 4IR Leaders in Business Schools through an Innovative Executive Education Ecosystem: An Integrative Literature Review. SSRN *Electronic Journal*. DOI: 10.2139/ssrn.3897059

Dosi, G., Piva, M., Virgillito, M. E., & Vivarelli, M. (2021). Embodied and disembodied technological change: The sectoral patterns of job-creation and job-destruction. *Research Policy*, 50(4), 104199. DOI: 10.1016/j.respol.2021.104199

Du, S., & Xie, C. (2021). Paradoxes of artificial intelligence in consumer markets: Ethical challenges and opportunities. *Journal of Business Research*, 129, 961–974. DOI: 10.1016/j.jbusres.2020.08.024

Faeq, D., Ali, B., & Akoi, S. (2022). The Impact of People Related TQM and CSR on Employees Job Satisfaction. *UKH Journal of Social Sciences*, 6(1), 1–9. DOI: 10.25079/ukhjss.v6n1y2022.pp1-9

Fernandes, K. (2018, September 20). Companies In India Funding CSR In Education. Medium.

Galport, N., & Azzam, T. (2017). Evaluator Training Needs and Competencies. *The American Journal of Evaluation*, 38(1), 80–100. DOI: 10.1177/1098214016643183

Gekara, V., & Snell, D. (2018). Designing and delivering skills transferability and employment mobility: The challenges of a market-driven vocational education and training system. *Journal of Vocational Education and Training*, 70(1), 107–129. DOI: 10.1080/13636820.2017.1392996

Ghobakhloo, M., Asadi, S., Iranmanesh, M., Foroughi, B., Mubarak, M. F., & Yadegaridehkordi, E. (2023). Intelligent automation implementation and corporate sustainability performance: The enabling role of corporate social responsibility strategy. *Technology in Society*, 74, 102301. DOI: 10.1016/j.techsoc.2023.102301

Goniewicz, K., Goniewicz, M., Włoszczak-Szubzda, A., Burkle, F. M., Hertelendy, A. J., Al-Wathinani, A., Molloy, M. S., & Khorram-Manesh, A. (2021). The importance of pre-training gap analyses and the identification of competencies and skill requirements of medical personnel for mass casualty incidents and disaster training. *BMC Public Health*, 21(1), 114. DOI: 10.1186/s12889-021-10165-5 PMID: 33422033

Gruetzemacher, R., Paradice, D., & Lee, K. B. (2020). Forecasting extreme labor displacement: A survey of AI practitioners. *Technological Forecasting and Social Change*, 161, 120323. DOI: 10.1016/j.techfore.2020.120323

Haenlein, M., & Kaplan, A. (2019). A Brief History of Artificial Intelligence: On the Past, Present, and Future of Artificial Intelligence. *California Management Review*, 61(4), 5–14. Advance online publication. DOI: 10.1177/0008125619864925

Hahn, T., Sharma, G., & Glavas, A. (2023). Employee-CSR Tensions: Drivers of Employee (Dis)Engagement with Contested CSR Initiatives. *Journal of Management Studies*. Advance online publication. DOI: 10.1111/joms.12923

Hart, D. L. (2023, September 18). *IBM Commits to Train 2 Million in Artificial Intelligence in Three Years, with a Focus on Underrepresented Communities*. IBM.

Infosys. (2023). *Flagship Platform to accelerate 21st Century Digital Learning*. Infosys.

Jamali, D. R., El Dirani, A. M., & Harwood, I. A. (2015). Exploring human resource management roles in corporate social responsibility: The CSR-HRM co-creation model. *Business Ethics (Oxford, England)*, 24(2), 125–143. Advance online publication. DOI: 10.1111/beer.12085

Khuong, M. N., Truong an, N. K., & Thanh Hang, T. T. (2021). Stakeholders and Corporate Social Responsibility (CSR) programme as key sustainable development strategies to promote corporate reputation—Evidence from vietnam. *Cogent Business & Management*, 8(1), 1917333. Advance online publication. DOI: 10.1080/23311975.2021.1917333

Kim, M.-J., & Kim, B.-J. (2020). Analysis of the Importance of Job Insecurity, Psychological Safety and Job Satisfaction in the CSR-Performance Link. *Sustainability (Basel)*, 12(9), 3514. DOI: 10.3390/su12093514

Kolding, M., Sundblad, M., Alexa, J., Stone, M., Aravopoulou, E., & Evans, G. (2018). Information management – a skills gap? *The Bottom Line (New York, N.Y.)*, 31(3/4), 170–190. DOI: 10.1108/BL-09-2018-0037

Königstorfer, F., & Thalmann, S. (2020). Applications of Artificial Intelligence in commercial banks – A research agenda for behavioral finance. *Journal of Behavioral and Experimental Finance*, 27, 100352. Advance online publication. DOI: 10.1016/j.jbef.2020.100352

Lacerenza, C. N., Reyes, D. L., Marlow, S. L., Joseph, D. L., & Salas, E. (2017). Leadership training design, delivery, and implementation: A meta-analysis. *The Journal of Applied Psychology*, 102(12), 1686–1718. DOI: 10.1037/apl0000241 PMID: 28749153

Lee, J., Davari, H., Singh, J., & Pandhare, V. (2018). Industrial Artificial Intelligence for industry 4.0-based manufacturing systems. *Manufacturing Letters*, 18, 20–23. Advance online publication. DOI: 10.1016/j.mfglet.2018.09.002

Lee, Y. (2021). Linking internal CSR with the positive communicative behaviors of employees: The role of social exchange relationships and employee engagement. *Social Responsibility Journal*. Advance online publication. DOI: 10.1108/SRJ-04-2020-0121

Li, H. (2019). Special Section Introduction: Artificial Intelligence and Advertising. *Journal of Advertising*, 48(4), 333–337. DOI: 10.1080/00913367.2019.1654947

Lim, W. M. (2023). The workforce revolution: Reimagining work, workers, and workplaces for the future. *Global Business and Organizational Excellence*, 42(4), 5–10. DOI: 10.1002/joe.22218

Loor-Zambrano, H. Y., Santos-Roldán, L., & Palacios-Florencio, B. (2022). Relationship CSR and employee commitment: Mediating effects of internal motivation and trust. *European Research on Management and Business Economics*, 28(2), 100185. DOI: 10.1016/j.iedeen.2021.100185

Low, M. P., & Bu, M. (2022). Examining the impetus for internal CSR Practices with digitalization strategy in the service industry during COVID-19 pandemic. *Business Ethics, the Environment & Responsibility*, 31(1), 209–223. DOI: 10.1111/beer.12408

McGuinness, S., & Ortiz, L. (2016). Skill gaps in the workplace: Measurement, determinants and impacts. *Industrial Relations Journal*, 47(3), 253–278. DOI: 10.1111/irj.12136

McLachlan, C. J. (2022). Developing a framework for responsible downsizing through best fit: The importance of regulatory, procedural, communication and employment responsibilities. *International Journal of Human Resource Management*, 33(1), 16–44. DOI: 10.1080/09585192.2021.1958248

Mehta, CA. S. (2024, January 20). India's Digital Workforce Revolution: Reskilling and Upskilling for Growth. *Bharat Buzz*.

Mhlanga, D. (2020). Industry 4.0 in Finance: The Impact of Artificial Intelligence (AI) on Digital Financial Inclusion. *International Journal of Financial Studies*, 8(3), 45. Advance online publication. DOI: 10.3390/ijfs8030045

Miethlich, B., & Šlahor, Ľ. (2018). Creating shared value through implementing vocational rehabilitation in the corporate social responsibility strategy: A literature review. *Vision 2020: Sustainable Economic Development and Application of Innovation Management,32nd International Business Information Management Association Conference (IBIMA).*

Miller, K. E., & Akdere, M. (2019). Advancing organizational corporate social responsibility (CSR) agenda. *European Journal of Training and Development*, 43(9), 860–872. DOI: 10.1108/EJTD-10-2018-0107

Moher, D., Liberati, A., Tetzlaff, J., & Altman, D. G. (2009). Preferred Reporting Items for Systematic Reviews and Meta-Analyses: The PRISMA Statement. *PLoS Medicine*, 6(7), e1000097. DOI: 10.1371/journal.pmed.1000097 PMID: 19621072

Mor, S., & Gupta, G. (2021). Artificial intelligence and technical efficiency: The case of Indian commercial banks. *Strategic Change*, 30(3), 235–245. Advance online publication. DOI: 10.1002/jsc.2406

Moyo, T., Crafford, G. J., & Emuze, F. (2019). *Assessing Strategies For Improving The Social Security Of Construction Workers In Zimbabwe*.

Mukhuty, S., Upadhyay, A., & Rothwell, H. (2022). Strategic sustainable development of Industry 4.0 through the lens of social responsibility: The role of human resource practices. *Business Strategy and the Environment*, 31(5), 2068–2081. DOI: 10.1002/bse.3008

Nadimpalli, M. (2017). Artificial Intelligence – Consumers and Industry Impact. *International Journal of Economics & Management Sciences*, 06(03). Advance online publication. DOI: 10.4172/2162-6359.1000429

Ngo, V. M. (2024). Does ChatGPT change artificial intelligence-enabled marketing capability? Social media investigation of public sentiment and usage. *Global Media and China*, 9(1), 101–125. DOI: 10.1177/20594364241228880

Pallathadka, H., Ramirez-Asis, E. H., Loli-Poma, T. P., Kaliyaperumal, K., Ventayen, R. J. M., & Naved, M. (2021). Applications of artificial intelligence in business management, e-commerce and finance. *Materials Today: Proceedings*. Advance online publication. DOI: 10.1016/j.matpr.2021.06.419

Pandya, J. (2021). The Role of CSR in providing Employment opportunity to Persons with Disabilities. SSRN *Electronic Journal*. DOI: 10.2139/ssrn.3992351

Pantano, E., & Pizzi, G. (2020). Forecasting artificial intelligence on online customer assistance: Evidence from chatbot patents analysis. *Journal of Retailing and Consumer Services*, 55, 102096. Advance online publication. DOI: 10.1016/j.jretconser.2020.102096

Patrawala, R. (2019). The Artificial Intelligence Era its Seismic Potential to Create a Job Displacement Conundrum. *IIBM'S Journal of Management*, 112–129. DOI: 10.33771/iibm.v4i1-2.1074

Patre, S., Chakraborty, D., Kar, A. K., Singu, H. B., & Tiwari, D. A. (2023). The Role of Enablers and Barriers in the Upskilling and Reskilling of Users Through Professional Skilling Programs on EdTech Platforms. *IEEE Transactions on Engineering Management*, 1–15. DOI: 10.1109/TEM.2023.3328261

Pfajfar, G., Shoham, A., Małecka, A., & Zalaznik, M. (2022). Value of corporate social responsibility for multiple stakeholders and social impact – Relationship marketing perspective. *Journal of Business Research*, 143, 46–61. DOI: 10.1016/j.jbusres.2022.01.051

Plikas, J. H., Trakadas, P., & Kenourgios, D. (2024). *Assessing the Ethical Implications of Artificial Intelligence (AI) and Machine Learning (ML) on Job Displacement Through Automation: A Critical Analysis of Their Impact on Society* (pp. 313–325). DOI: 10.1007/978-981-99-9836-4_24

Rawashdeh, A. (2023). The consequences of artificial intelligence: an investigation into the impact of AI on job displacement in accounting. *Journal of Science and Technology Policy Management*. DOI: 10.1108/JSTPM-02-2023-0030

Rawshdeh, Z. A., Makhbul, Z. K. M., Rawshdeh, M., & Sinniah, S. (2023). Perceived socially responsible-HRM on talent retention: The mediating effect of trust and motivation and the moderating effect of other-regarding value orientation. *Frontiers in Psychology*, 13, 1087065. Advance online publication. DOI: 10.3389/fpsyg.2022.1087065 PMID: 36726518

Sadasivan, A. (2018). Expanding the Scope of Corporate Social Responsibility (CSR): Strategizing Skill Development in the Indian Scenario. *The Arab Journal of the Social Sciences*, 17(2), 21–38. DOI: 10.12724/ajss.45.2

Sari, R. E., Min, S., Purwoko, H., Furinto, A., & Tamara, D. (2020). Artificial Intelligence for a Better Employee Engagement. *International Research Journal of Business Studies*, 13(2), 173–188. DOI: 10.21632/irjbs.13.2.173-188

Sarkar, S., Shukla, S., & Mishra, R. K. (2023). *Enabling Skill Development in the Pandemic – The CSR Perspective*. DOI: 10.1108/S2043-905920230000016006

Shinde, N. V., Akhade, A., Bagad, P., Bhavsar, H., Wagh, S. K., & Kamble, A. (2021, June 3). Healthcare Chatbot System using Artificial Intelligence. *2021 5th International Conference on Trends in Electronics and Informatics (ICOEI)*. DOI: 10.1109/ICOEI51242.2021.9452902

Staniškienė, E., & Stankevičiūtė, Ž. (2018). Social sustainability measurement framework: The case of employee perspective in a CSR-committed organisation. *Journal of Cleaner Production*, 188, 708–719. DOI: 10.1016/j.jclepro.2018.03.269

Stankevičiūtė, Z., & Kalvaitienė, J. (2023). Human resource business partner role in respect to internal corporate social responsibility: The case of banking sector. *Human Systems Management*, 1–17. DOI: 10.3233/HSM-230113

Talwar, S., Talwar, M., Tarjanne, V., & Dhir, A. (2021). Why retail investors traded equity during the pandemic? An application of artificial neural networks to examine behavioral biases. *Psychology and Marketing*, 38(11), 2142–2163. DOI: 10.1002/mar.21550

Thormundsson, B. (2024, January 10). Artificial intelligence (AI) in productivity and labor - statistics & facts. Statista.

Torres, P., & Augusto, M. (2020). Digitalisation, social entrepreneurship and national well-being. *Technological Forecasting and Social Change*, 161, 120279. DOI: 10.1016/j.techfore.2020.120279

Werfel, S., Witko, C., & Heinrich, T. (2022). Public support for assistance for workers displaced by technology. *Research & Politics*, 9(2), 205316802210934. DOI: 10.1177/20531680221093440

Yan, H., Fu, L., & Hu, X. (2022). Harnessing service robots to increase frontline service employees' safety and health: The critical role of CSR. *Safety Science*, 151, 105731. DOI: 10.1016/j.ssci.2022.105731

Zainee, I. A., & Puteh, F. (2020). Corporate social responsibility impact on talent retention among Generation Y. *Revista de Gestão*, 27(4), 369–392. DOI: 10.1108/REGE-06-2019-0070

Zhao, Y., & Jakkampudi, K. (2023). Assessing Policy Measures Safeguarding Workers from Artificial Intelligence in the United States. *Journal of Computer and Communications*, 11(11), 149–166. DOI: 10.4236/jcc.2023.1111008

ADDITIONAL READING

Aqif, T., & Wahab, A. (2021). Developing an understanding of the determinants, disclosures, and outcomes of CSR practices – a focus on developed and developing countries: A past review of 10 years. *Journal of Global Responsibility*, 12(3), 289–316. Advance online publication. DOI: 10.1108/JGR-03-2021-0032

Burnett, J. R., & Lisk, T. C. (2019). The Future of Employee Engagement: Real-Time Monitoring and Digital Tools for Engaging a Workforce. *International Studies of Management & Organization*, 49(1), 108–119. Advance online publication. DOI: 10.1080/00208825.2019.1565097

Chauhan, C., Parida, V., & Dhir, A. (2022). Linking circular economy and digitalisation technologies: A systematic literature review of past achievements and future promises. *Technological Forecasting and Social Change*, 177, 121508. DOI: 10.1016/j.techfore.2022.121508

Kemp, S. (2020, January 30). *Digital 2020: Global Digital Overview*. DataRePortal.

Statista Research Department. (2022, July). *Size of the global e-learning market in 2019 and 2026, by segment*. Statista.

Taylor, A. (2017). Social work and digitalisation: Bridging the knowledge gaps. *Social Work Education*, 36(8), 869–879. DOI: 10.1080/02615479.2017.1361924

Chapter 3
Challenges Obstructing the Effective Usage of Artificial Intelligence in Psychotherapy and Feasible Remedies:
A Reflective Discussion

Kaneeka Vidanage
General Sir John Kotelawala Defense University, Sri Lanka

Asela Gunesekera
General Sir John Kotelawala Defense University, Sri Lanka

ABSTRACT

Mental health is an integral component strongly linked with physical health. It`s impossible to anticipate good physical health physique without considering the significance of mental health. Though advancements of computing technology and artificial intelligence (AI) have immensely contributed to the healthcare spectrum, their applications are mainly centric only towards physical ailment diagnostics and treatments. This chapter investigates the bottlenecks hindering the limited and primitive usage of AI techniques in psychotherapy procedures. Additionally, this chapter contributes by proposing eligible AI techniques and pipelines to overcome the issue of inadequate utilization of the AI advancements to the benefit of the psychotherapeutic domain. This promotes the ethical and responsible usage of technological advancements for the upliftment of the quality of life of human beings.

DOI: 10.4018/979-8-3693-3478-2.ch003

INTRODUCTION

Mental well-being is an integral part of physical well-being (Hines et.al, 2023). It has a direct influence on an individual's success as well as the country's overall economic progress (Chen, 2021). As a result, the mental health of the country's inhabitants should be prioritized. While advances in Artificial Intelligence (AI) have made significant contributions to the diagnosis of physical illnesses, their impact on the diagnosis and treatment of mental illnesses remains constrained (Duffy et.al, 2020). This research investigates the possibilities of implementing an appropriate policy framework that will allow for the responsible use of AI advancements to improve the psychological spectrum as well. This directly contributes to the domain of healthcare informatics by enforcing on novel computerized psychological interventions, facilitating the role of the healthcare practitioners.

Literature Review

1. Domain Overview

Artificial intelligence (AI) has made a significant contribution to improve the precision and effectiveness in healthcare (Townsend et.al, 2023). AI has offered a practical solution to enhance the performance of human experts in the face of resource scarcity, as it can replicate human expertise to a certain extent (Singh et.al, 2019). The advent of smart devices to assist medical professionals (Hanif et.al, 2022) in their work has freed up human experts to concentrate on more difficult problems, enabling them to go on another extra mile in treating people.

Application of AI in healthcare related processes are numerous. Management of medical records and administration, aiding drug design procedures, virtual nurses, predictive diagnostics aided with radiology techniques such as Medical Resonance Imaging (MRI), Computer Tomography (CT) and Ultrasound Scanning and robot assisted surgeries are a few such examples (Frontino, et.al, 2016). However, it`s important to emphasize that the majority of the AI`s involvement in healthcare is towards serving physical ailment diagnostics and treatment. Use of AI for the mental treatment procedures are very naïve (Vidanage et.al, 2016). Nonetheless, as declared by the World Health Organization (WHO), mental health is also a very crucial element directly contributing to physical health. Stated differently, achieving physical wellbeing goals is contingent upon achieving mental health goals (Duffy et.al, 2020).

Presently, the world is moving at a fast pace leading to unhealthier lifestyles. Inadequate household income, demanding employment requirements, costs of dependents are some of the critical factors contributing to the unhealthier mental state. Long term, unresolved mental illbeing is the primary cause of depression, which completely tarnishes the productivity of a human being (Evans et. Al, 2023). When the majority of the country`s population becomes victims of depression, it negatively impacts the economic growth of that country as well (Ryška, 2017). This clearly highlights the significance of mental wellbeing on par with physical wellbeing. Additionally, it triggers the importance of appropriate utilization of AI advancements to psychotherapeutic treatments as well, without being restricted to the physical ailment treatment only (Kleine et.al, 2023).

2. Why Is the Use of AI in Psychotherapeutic Treatment Very Primitive?

Mental therapy is not a straightforward diagnosis after observing the symptoms. Usually in physical ailment diagnosis, a consultant typically looks at the patient's symptoms and asks specific questions to reach a conclusion (Patel et.al, 2022).

However, in psychotherapeutic treatments the procedures are not as straightforward in physical ailment identification. The recommended practice is the consultant should have an open-minded reflective discussion with the patient for around 45 minutes (Gerger, et.al, 2020). This fosters an environment where the patient and the consultant can form a therapeutic alliance gradually over time. Therapeutic alliance is an important ingredient in effective psychotherapeutic treatments (Flückiger et.al, 2018). During this discussion, consultant will be able to extract gestures, postures as well as the soundness of the answers provided by the patients for each of the questions interrogated. Depending on the combined assessment of all those inputs, a consultant can yield to conclusions with the use of his/her knowledge and experiences (De Smet et.al, 2018).

AI is referred to as an umbrella of technologies. This simply means, AI comprises of several technologies, which aids to reach towards the intended business goals (Vidanage et.al, 2022). Practically, utilization of a specific AI technology across all business use cases might not be feasible due to numerous constraints (Abd-alrazaq et.al, 2022). Utilizing machine learning, for instance, will not be feasible if the field of study anticipating AI engagement lacks sufficiently large, annotated datasets. However, as discussed above, another alternative AI strategy which does not require large datasets to operate could be viable for the specified use case (Denner et.al, 2023)

In use cases like psychotherapeutic treatment, there are multiple contexts associated scenarios which requires different interpretations. Therefore, it`s not as straightforward as diagnosing a physical ailment by verifying the presence of specific symptoms and yielding to a conclusion (Machado et.al 2022). For instance, receiving a sponsored opportunity for a foreign tour will make someone happy if their mental health is good; however, if their mental health is poor, the same incident may make them feel stressed and reluctant of accept the offer. Nonetheless, when diagnosing a physical illness, these contextual variations are nearly nonexistent.

One of the main reasons for the rudimentary use of AI in psychotherapy procedures is the impact of high contextual variations governing the final outcomes (Vidanage et.al, 2015). The care provided for an eye diseases or brain tumor is far more stable as the contextual effects are presumably minimal. It is possible to identify this contextual stability in the diagnosis of physical illnesses as a contributing factor to the effective and noteworthy application of AI techniques in physical illness treatments (DiSanto, et.al, 2023).

The second main reason associated with restricted use of AI in healthcare domains is due to the black-boxed behavior (Pacchiardi et.al, 2023). Transparent reasoning pipelines should be provided all the way up to the ultimate objective, particularly in fields like healthcare. Because, for auditing purposes, logical backtracking needs to be possible in the event of a mistake or a slip. For medico-legal needs, this condition is absolutely essential (Lee et.al, 2022). However, transparent explainability is a feature that is absent in most AI techniques now in use (Kempton, et.al, 2021). For example, methods such as Artificial Neural Networks (ANNs) require a large number of internal computations to yield a realistic result. However, it's unclear how transparently the internal computations influencing the choice in the end can be verified. That`s why such behavior is referred to as a black-boxed operation. Users provide the inputs, then it reaches to the trained ANN, near realistic output is yielded. However, the trained ANN model's internal computations and operations that contribute to the final results are not explainable (Luo, et.al, 2021). In a domain like healthcare, black-boxed behavior is a great disadvantage. Because occasionally the cost of a misclassification occurred by an AI system could be loss of a human life (Cina, et.al, 2022).

Consequently, as conversed earlier according to the concept of "AI umbrella", AI comprises of numerous alternative techniques which can be utilized to accomplish the same end goal. For instance, in situations where machine learning techniques fail due to non-availability of adequately sized annotated datasets, an alternative technique like expert systems (Willmen, et.al, 2021) or ontological modelling (Khnaisser, et.al, 2022) can be utilized. In those proposed alternative techniques, the requirement for large, annotated dataset is absent. Therefore, through extensive interviewing of field experts, a realistically functional expert system or an ontological model can be developed. Henceforth, it can be linked with the computational application for intelligent reasoning purposes.

Therefore, in the process of AI applications development associated to the healthcare domain appropriate technology selection considering the medical requirement to be fulfilled is vital.

3. Appropriate AI Technologies That Can Be Used to Boost the Psychotherapeutic Tools

Reasons hindering the effective use of AI techniques for psychotherapeutic tools development have been discussed in the earlier section. In this section it`s intended to conduct a more comprehensive assessment considering the potentials and limitations of each technology that belongs under the AI umbrella.

i. **Machine Learning:** This is a very popular and demanding technology which is coming under the AI umbrella. The backbone of the majority of smart applications have been powered by machine learning technology. There are three main flavors of machine learning, which are widely used. Those are supervised learning strategy, un-supervised learning strategy and re-enforcement learning strategy. In all these techniques large datasets is a dire requirement (Abu et.al, 2023).
ii. **Supervised Learning**: In supervised learning, initially the dataset has to be classified into two or more categories with the involvement of the field expert (Grill et.al, 2020). For example, let`s assume it`s intended to develop a machine learning model to classify diabetics positive and negative patients. In this example, a huge dataset encompassing both diabetic and non-diabetic individuals' bloodwork records are initially required. The initial stage is to collect the dataset, followed by feature engineering. There may be some parameters in the dataset of blood reports gathered that are useless or less useful in assessing whether a patient has diabetes or not. First, those parameters must be precisely determined. This necessitates the engagement of a domain expert, and statistical correlation analysis may be used to supplement the domain specialist's choices. Following the completion of this feature engineering process, only parameters that are substantially contributing to the final decision making of diabetics / non-diabetics can be filtered from a wide list of parameters. This filtering is crucial because having too many less relevant or unrelated parameter information in the dataset can slow down the training of the machine

learning model and may degrade accuracy by acting as noise. After all of the pre- processing processes are finished, the data annotation process begins.

In the data annotation stage, each individual's bloodwork report must be identified as diabetes or non-diabetic based on the aforementioned filtered factors. This is a time- consuming manual procedure that must be continued with the assistance of a domain expert. Following the completion of this stage, an annotated dataset with a sufficient sample size should be ready for training the machine learning model. Consequently, a suitable supervised learning algorithm must be chosen depending on the nature of the dataset and the training accuracies offered. This work requires the participation of a machine learning engineer. After training the machine learning model using the chosen method, it can be used to automatically classify diabetes bloodwork data without the assistance of a person. If the aforementioned pipeline is carefully followed, it will significantly minimize the manual labor strain of the medical personnel without affecting the accuracy of the results provided.

iii. **Unsupervised Learning**: The key difference between this approach and supervised learning is that the annotation procedure is not used in unsupervised learning (He et.al, 2019). As previously stated, the annotation process is a time-consuming manual procedure that requires the participation of a domain specialist. In unsupervised learning, the annotation process is also automated without the involvement of a human participant. Depending on the homogeneity of the data elements in the dataset several clusters will be formed. Within a cluster data elements are much more homogeneous. The dataset size necessary for an unsupervised learning task is determined by the complexity of the problem to be automated. As a result of the lack of human input in the clustering process, the quality of the final results is considerably more dependent on the dataset composition. A dataset containing all of the patterns connected with the problem space must be included in the dataset to allow a more realistic clustering process that leads to a higher accuracy.

iv. **Reinforcement Learning:** This is a distinct method when compared to supervised and unsupervised learning strategies. Learning is mostly based on the interactions with the environment in the context. In simple terms, it is known as learning from mistakes. When the model encourages desired interaction patterns, it should be rewarded. Unless sanctions should be imposed on the model. Positive and predicted interactions are promoted as a result, and the model eventually becomes sensitive to even little alterations associated with the relevant interactions (Kodavati et.al, 2021).

The model learns more optimum policies for the problem space as a result of these interactions. This approach is less data greedy than supervised and unsupervised learning techniques. The required data demands can also be met using proper simulation methods. However, it is critical to ensure that the model is exposed to meaningful and realistic interaction patterns related with the problem area during the learning phase. This is critical for improving the accuracy of the model.

General operational overviews for the most prevalent machine learning flavors have already been explored. Here are some key considerations to reflect when employing machine learning for psychotherapy.

- Interpretability and Explainability – As previously stated, machine learning systems are predisposed to black-boxed behaviors (Pacchiardi et.al, 2023). After receiving an input, a trained machine learning model provides an output after conducting sophisticated internal calculations. However, the capability of backtracking and tracing the roots that led to the final output within the model is difficult to comprehend. This is a significant drawback on determining what went wrong inside the model as locating it becomes quite tough. As a result, aligning with the prospects of human experts and fine-tuning based on their reflections becomes a challenging procedure. Because human ideas and cognitions are highly inconsistent components. This makes the already complicated situation much more complex. Consequently, there is a considerable hesitancy and restricted preference for applying machine learning processes to develop smart psychotherapy treatments.
- Scarcity of datasets - Requirement of adequately sized annotated datasets for training the machine learning models have been already conversed. However, it`s an impossible task to find large datasets for certain problem domains. Especially in a field like psychology, hence human cognitions are highly context sensitive as discussed already. Thus, due to high contextual variability (Temple et.al, 2017), finding a stable and feature enriched dataset is almost an impossible task. Subsequently, assuming the datasets are available, the annotation procedure is still not going to be easy. Due to the contextual variability, determination of end classes will be a challenging task. However, without determining the end classes annotating the dataset will be impossible.
- Feature Engineering Costs – Once discovered, a dataset cannot be used immediately to train machine learning models. Before the data can be used for training, it must go through several stages of pre-processing. Among the pre-processing phases to be completed, correlation analysis of the individual aspects connected to the final choice / decision must be statistically evaluated. This aids in identifying the features that have the least influence on the final choice (Jadhav et.al, 2023). Henceforth, those features can be removed from the dataset to ensure the dataset's simplicity and overcome possible noise in the trained model. After completing all of the preprocessing processes, annotation can begin.

Annotation necessitates considerable engagement of domain consultants over a longer period. Consequently, this is going to be an expensive procedure. Despite all of the preprocessing requirements, the most significant obstacle is the inability to represent psychotherapy problem spaces using a proper architecture with independent and dependent variables. Because that is the optimal design for machine learning problem spaces. Hence, the same architecture must be utilized to orchestrate the datasets as well. However, due to the extensive contextual sensitivity and volatility, this design may not be appropriate for dealing with psychological problem spaces. As a result, it will be difficult to use machine learning approaches to integrate smart processes into the psychotherapy domain.

- Contextual volatility – Human thoughts are context dependent. For same incident, the same person might feel happy at a state and sad at a stage depending on the contextual impact caused by the surroundings. Therefore, standardizing a dataset to absorb this contextual volatility (Temple et.al, 2017) is going to be an impractical task. However, as already conversed without effectivity addressing this necessity a stable machine learning friendlier data architecture cannot be created. This again restricts the potential use of machine learning for smart psychotherapeutic procedures.
- Problem space modelling challenges - Machine Learning models are ideal for problem spaces which can be quantified along with easily separable boundaries. However, in psychotherapy mostly the data is available in qualitative forms as narrations, journals or interviews or internal self-talks. Modelling such qualitative data into a machine learning friendlier data architecture would be impossible or very challenging (Allen et.al, 2022).
- Ethical implications – Adequately sized dataset is a vital necessity for the successful execution of the machine learning solutions. However, collecting such datasets is a difficult process due to ethical and privacy concerns (Walke et.al, 2023). Data related to psychiatric diseases contain sensitive information specific to individuals. Therefore, certain approvals and formalities are required prior to carrying out the data collecting activities. Consequently, this also serves as a deterrent on having huge datasets.

v. **Evolutionary Computing (EC):** This is another widely used technique belongs to the AI umbrella, which is used for building smart solutions. Evolutionary Computing algorithms have been derived from the natural phenomena taking place in nature. It comprises of multiple sub techniques like genetic algorithms, swarm intelligence, simulated annealing and etc. Evolutionary Computing strategies are widely used for optimization requirements (Lalejini et.al, 2023). Therefore, multiple challenges associated with using Evolutionary Computing for psychotherapeutic domain can be listed below.

Inability to define fitness functions – The fitness functions serve as the core operational logic that governs the execution of the evolutionary algorithms (Muravyov et.al, 2019). Depending on the nature of the psychotherapy problem domain, defining fitness functions are difficult. This is primarily due to the source of contextual volatility. As a result, modeling a psychotherapy problem space inside the evolutionary computing spectrum becomes unrealistic.

- Dataset challenges – For the successful deployment of an Evolutionary Computing (EC) solution, adequate side quality dataset is essential (Yadav et.al, 2023). This technique learns from the data iteratively for the purpose of accomplishing the objective function defined. Therefore, high quality dataset with the representation of the total problem space, avoiding biases are required to for effective EC execution. However, as already conversed satisfying this requirement is not an easy task. Aside from the two issues described above, all additional limitations that cause bottlenecks in machine learning model deployments have the same negative influence on ECs as well.

vi. **Fuzzy Logic:** Fuzzy logic is a mathematical framework, which deals with modelling problem domains with uncertainty. Fuzzy logic is a good technique for the representation of ambiguous and dubious data. Fuzzy logic operations are mainly governed by membership functions and fuzzy rules sets defined (Belyadi et.al, 2021). The challenges associated with using Fuzzy Logic in psychotherapeutic problem spaces can be defined as below.

- Inability to model the problem space – As already conversed, fuzzy logic is a sophisticated mathematical framework. Therefore, problem spaces with numerical and quantitative configurations are significantly more suitable. However, in the psychotherapy field, datasets are mostly qualitative, making numerical representations challenging. This acts as a bottleneck hindering the utilization of fuzzy logic for the psychotherapeutic domain. Additionally, due to the issue of contextual volatility definition of fuzzy rules will also become problematic. Addition to the aforementioned issue, every problem pertaining to machine learning techniques applies in the same way to fuzzy logic approaches. Because there is a strong data dependence on the fuzzy logic approach. In order to accurately articulate the fuzzy rules, it makes use of notions like occurrence and conformance. Without exposure to sizable datasets pertaining to the domain, it is impossible to achieve conformance and occurrence criteria accurately. As already covered, finding sizable datasets related to this field is also a very difficult undertaking. Therefore, Fuzzy logic approaches are an inappropriate choice for modeling psychotherapy problem.

vii. **Expert Systems:** Expert systems are also another powerful strategy residing under the AI umbrella for accomplishing intelligence requirements associated with numerous problem spaces (Cao et.al, 2020). The operational mechanics of expert systems are slightly different, compared to the techniques discussed already. Therefore, expert systems attribute different favorable characteristics associated with psychotherapeutic problem modelling. Those favorable characteristics can be listed as mentioned.

- Large Datasets are not required – Unlike the strategies discussed up to now, expert systems do not require large datasets (Islam et.al, 2023). As the name implies, the knowledge is derived from human experts. The project engineers can interview several human experts related to the domain of concern (i.e. psychotherapy) and extracted knowledge can be represented as a machine understandable rule series. The ability to operate without datasets can be identified as a very significant advantage associated with this technology, making it a suitable choice for psychotherapeutic problem space modelling.
- Feature Engineering is not required – As discussed up to now, for most the techniques reviewed need cleansed and annotated datasets (Jadhav et.al, 2023) for their successful operations. However, the expert system does not have any of such demand, making the operational workload and cost incurs to be comparatively less.
- Transparent and explainable – One of the biggest negative challenges associated with the above discussed technologies is the black-boxed operation. Therefore, traceability has become impossible or very challenging. However, this is not recommended for a solution deployed in healthcare domain. Expert systems resolve that obstacle by representing the problem space to be modelled via a series of rules. Mostly these rules are defined as IF-ELSE chains. They have different firing strategies (i.e. forward chaining / backward chaining) as per the purpose to be fulfilled. Knowledge extracted from human experts is represented in the rules defined. Henceforth, an inference engine will access the rule base accordingly to fulfil the user`s requirement. This is a transparent and comparatively simple operation (Sewada et.al, 2023), where debugging is feasible with the involvement of the domain experts.
- Reduced likelihood of variability – The majority of the strategies listed above use strong and complicated statistical basis to make predictions. Statistical selections determine the end findings to be output. If the problem area under consideration is not well-suited for statistical modelling (i.e. qualitative problem spaces), incorrect computations might result in questionable and dubious conclusions (Temple et.al, 2017). However, this impact is far more less in expert systems as it uses predicate login mainly in contrast to the complex

statistical operations. Therefore, it is causing much more interpretable and explainable outputs.

- Eligible for more complex problem spaces – Expert systems can be used to effectively model both qualitative and quantitative problem spaces (Cosme et.al, 2021). Domains like psychotherapy contains lots of qualitative information. Though expert system formulations, such knowledge can be effectively and efficiently represented in the form of rule chains. Additionally, it reflects practical clinical knowledge extracted from the consultants. Therefore, users can expect more related outcomes.
- Ease of Scalability – With the introduction of new knowledge, machine learning and evolutionary computing techniques encounter numerous problems. When incorporating new knowledge datasets has to be annotated and re-orchestrated again. Subsequently, lots of fine tuning and hyperparameter tuning has to be done to overcome overfitting and underfitting issues. However, in expert systems none of those burdens exists. It does not require powerful computational resources to train the models and impacts of overfitting and underfitting is also nonexistent. Therefore, expert systems are far more convenient to maintain and scaleup (Cosme et.al, 2021).

Considering the points discussed on expert systems, it can be identified as a more suitable technique available under the AI umbrella for effectively modelling of psychotherapeutic problem spaces.

viii. **Ontological Modelling:** Ontological modelling is another significant technique residing inside the AI umbrella. The characteristic of ontological modelling is much resembling expert systems (Vidanage et.al, 2020). Therefore, ontological modelling can claim all positive advantages discussed under the expert systems. In addition to those some more significant attributes can be identified as well.

- Enriched interpretability and explainability with domain rich modelling – In contrast to the expert systems, where the knowledge is represented in forms of IF-ELSE rule chains, ontologies can model an enriched conceptual space associated with the domain considered. Mostly, a tool like Protégé or TopBrid can be used to model the domain in a more sophisticated manner with the involvement of the domain experts. A visual interpretation can be derived facilitating the comprehension of the model constructed so far. Even non-IT experts like medical doctors and bankers can also interpret these visualizations without much difficulty. Hence, ontologies contribute to more enriched interpretability and explainability (Vidanage at.al, 2019) compared to expert systems. Specific advantages on ontologies can be recognized as: -

- Attention to detail – Ontologies use the idea of information triples, enriched with concepts such as data properties, object properties, individuals and etc. Therefore, ontologies can model a problem space assuring attention to detail without missing even tiny important axioms.
- Powerful Reasoning – Once a sophisticated ontology has been constructed, it can be coupled with a powerful reasoning engine like FACT32 or PELLETE. This enables us to deduce new knowledge causing more intelligent outcomes for the system.
- Enriched interoperability – Hence ontologies are saved as resource description framework (RDF) files or Web Ontology Language (OWL) files machines can interpret the knowledge included easily. RDF and OWL ancestries of XML. Therefore, ontologies depict cross-platform neutrality, and they can easily communicate with other existing systems accomplishing the interoperability goals.

Given all of these beneficial outcomes, ontology-based knowledge modelling can be proposed as the best option for the psychotherapeutic domain. Contextual volatility (Temple et.al, 2017) issues in the psychotherapeutic realm can also be addressed by establishing object properties and mapping those with different individuals. As a result, ontologies may display an enhanced representation of the considered subset of the psychotherapy domain while also overcoming contextual duality difficulties as well. Therefore, as the conclusion it can be decided as that ontologies are the best AI technique for the psychotherapeutic domain.

4. PRESENT USAGE OF AI IN PSYCHOTHERAPY.

As conversed above, usage of AI for psychotherapeutic procedures are comparatively low. When examining the intervention of AI into psychotherapy, a few important segments can be identified.

i. **AI Powered Therapeutic Platforms**: There are numerous such platforms utilizing various techniques to aid the therapeutic sessions. Among the techniques utilized chatbots behaving as virtual therapists can be identified as phenomenal. Majority of these chatbots are powered by a static knowledge base functioning in the background, providing knowledge about psychoeducation, interactive question and answering for general awareness and providing abstract level guidance on therapeutic treatment techniques (Lin et.al, 2023). Additionally, some of these platforms are accompanied by web-based questionnaires as well. These questionnaires have answers and scores pre-programmed in them. A score is generated based on the user's answers, with pre-defined feedback or legend-based interpretation support. These questionnaires are typically constructed using the Cognitive Behavioral Therapy (CBT) (Hudson et.al, 2023), Myers -Brigg Type Indicator (Zárate-Torres et.al, 2023), Big 5 traits theory (Ernst-Linke, et.al, 2022) and a variety of well-established psychological gauges.

Applications in this segment primarily have narrow-AI enabled features. Some of the critical shortcomings of this segment's applications include a lack of personalization abilities, non-updating static knowledge, and lack or absence of consultant involvement. Psychological ailments are mostly context based. Additionally, different people belonging to different cultures have different ways of interpretations. Hence, provision of generalist overview or surface level guidance could not be the ideal way to utilize AI for psychotherapeutic interventions. Some of the widely used AI-based applications belonging to this segment has been reviewed with their pros and cons as depicted in Table 1. As shown in Table 1, the most common intervention mechanisms in this segment are chatbots, questionnaires, and a variety of smart phone interaction tracking tools.

Under limitations, it has been clearly mentioned that almost all of these tools lack personalization strategies incorporated and no proper human consultant involvement as well. Almost all of the tools discussed in Table 1 provides only generalized information. However, in the case of psychotherapeutic treatment goals (Eshwarage and Gunasekera, 2017), provision of surface level information is not adequate at all.

Table 1. AI Powered Therapeutic Platforms / Tools

Tool	Intervention Mode	Advantages	Limitations
WoeBot (Darcy et.al, 2023)	Chatbot	• Triggers conversational therapy, based on CBT principles. • 24/7 availability and location / geography independency • Supports managing stress.	• No personalization. • No human consultant involvement
Wysa (Beatty et.al, 2022)	Chatbot	• Conversational therapy on evidence-based techniques. • Supports building resilience. • 24/7 availability and location / geography independency	• No personalization. • No human consultant involvement. • Fail amidst complex mental issues.
Replika (Xie et.al, 2022)	Chatbot	• Conversational therapy, based on emotional well-being. • Non-judgmental self-explanatory platform	• ~Do~
Tess (Stephens et.al, 2019)	Chatbot	• Tuned to provide emotional support. • Mobile friendly.	• ~Do~
MindStrong (Mazurek-Melnyk et.al, 2020)	Interaction Based	• Track smartphone behavior and provide predictions.	• ~Do~ • Ethical violation. • Ineffective judgements.
ReThink (He et.al, 2023)	Interaction Based	• Small plugin developed to overcome cyberbullying	• ~Do~ • Therapeutic goals are not addressed
GAD-7 (Merino-Soto, et.al, 2023)	Questionnaire	• Self-report questionnaire on anxiety disorder.	• ~Do~ • Therapeutic goals are not addressed
DASS-21 (Cao et.al, 2023)	Questionnaire	• Self-report questionnaire on depression, anxiety, and stress.	• ~Do~ • Therapeutic goals are not addressed
PHQ – 9 (Sun et.al, 2022)	Questionnaire	• Self-report questionnaire on depression severity level.	• ~Do~ • Therapeutic goals are not addressed
BFI (Kumar et.al, 2023)	Questionnaire	• Used for the personality and temperament classification.	• ~Do~ • Therapeutic goals are not addressed

Source: Prepared by the Authors

ii. **Behavior Analysis and Progress Tracking Tools:** As the name implies, tools of this segment attempt to acquire numerous bodily inputs via the use of wearables. The inputs captured are not directly psychological and mostly they are physiological. However, their relationship to psychological disorders can be further explored with the consultant's involvement through a careful evaluation of these physiological parameters and patterns that were observed. Table 2 conducts a review of several tools belonging to this category and their capabilities.

Table 2. Behavior Analysis and Progress Tracking Tools

Tool	Intervention Mode	Advantages	Limitations
Welltory (Yand et.al, 2021)	Action Tracking	Predicts about stress via detecting and analyzing Heart Rate Variability	Does not provide adequate aid to fulfill the therapeutic goals.
Quanttus (Wang et.al, 2020)	Action Tracking	Tracks numerous physiological parameters and attempt to predict about mental well-being	Does not provide adequate aid to fulfill the therapeutic goals.
Youper (Mehta et.al, 2020)	Chatbot	Specialized chatbot fine-tuned to track cognitive fluctuations via conversational therapy.	• No personalization. • No human consultant involvement • Fail amidst complex mental issues.
MindDoc (Cordeiro, et.al, 2015)	Journaling	Specialized journal to log incidents causing mental uneasiness. Fine-tuned to track the progress made over time.	• Does not provide adequate aid to fulfill the therapeutic goals.
Dailyo (Sena et.al, 2014)	Action Tracking	Tracks user`s mood through activities performed. Assess mood patterns over time.	• Does not provide adequate aid to fulfill the therapeutic goals.
MoodPath (Mulansky,2020)	Journaling	Specialized journal to log incidents causing mental uneasiness. Equipped with personalized insight provision technique.	• Does not provide adequate aid to fulfill the therapeutic goals.

Source: prepared by the Authors

As depicted in Table -2, it discusses several tools which attempt to predict insights about mental well-being via capturing numerous physiological parameters. This can be recognized as a less obstructed, more scientific, and a credible approach. Because physiological parameters are significantly more stabilized and have relatively less contextual variability. However, tools in this category don't really take contextualized connectivity, which is directly linked to mental health very seriously. This can be recognized as a significant flaw. It is noteworthy that certain tools reviewed in Table 2, possess the ability to track behavior and monitor the progress of the patient. Given that psychotherapy procedures are being conducted for longer periods of time, these characteristics are a very important perspective. Techniques for tracking progress are essential because they enable consultants to make decisions that are more impactful.

iii. **Diagnostics Aiding Tools:** Tools belonging to this category aid the consultants with their decision making associated with mental ailments. These tools primarily work by combining disparate pieces of information into a single, easily comprehensible report. The consultant will now be able to logically evaluate the information and make a more informed choice regarding the patient's treatment plans. These tools contribute to reducing the cognitive fatigue associated with consultants in busy clinics. Therefore, consultants will be able to focus on the patient's ailments with a much more open and fresher mindset.

This atmosphere created by these tools will impose a positive contribution in establishing good therapeutic alliance between the patient and the consultant. Table 3 comprises of the comparison associated with several widely used tools belonging to this category.

Table 3. Diagnostics Aiding Tools

Tool	Intervention Mode	Advantages	Limitations
Osmind (Ni et.al, 2023)	Action Tracking & Chatbot	Blend of conversational therapy and physiological parameters to assess mental health diagnostics and aid consultants in decision making.	Supports only a small number of mental disorders. Intelligent involvement on fulfilling therapeutic goals are inadequate
Kip (Zheng et.al, 2023)	Chatbot	Extracts mood swings of the patient via conversational therapy and update the consultant on the fluctuations and improvements.	Intelligent involvement on fulfilling therapeutic goals are inadequate
SilverCloud (Bartholmaeet.al, 2023)	Action Tracking & Chatbot	Offers range of therapy programs and update the consultant about the patients` progress.	Intelligent involvement on fulfilling therapeutic goals are inadequate
X2AI (Lee et.al, 2023)	Chatbot	Track patient interactions and intensions via conversational therapy. Provide insights to the consultant about the condition of the patient.	Intelligent involvement on fulfilling therapeutic goals are inadequate
Kintsugi (Bellini et.al, 2023)	Questionnaire & Chatbot	Equips with mild personalization capability. Extracts and summarizes patients` state to the consultant.	Intelligent involvement on fulfilling therapeutic goals are inadequate
Mindsight (Farrelly,2021)	Action Tracking	Consultants can assign various exercises via this tool. Supports therapy planning as of the patients` progress.	Intelligent involvement on fulfilling therapeutic goals are inadequate
Infermedica (M, 2021)	Action Tracking, Chatbot & Questionnaire	Use multi-channels to extract mental status of the patient and generate diagnostics aiding report for the consultant.	Intelligent involvement on fulfilling therapeutic goals are inadequate

Source: prepared by the Authors

After reviewing the contents of Table 3, it is clear that these tools are attempting to establish a linked pipeline between the consultant and the patient, which is a beneficial development.

The targeted tactics, however, are insufficient to completely establish a healthier therapeutic partnership between the patient and the consultant.

METHODOLOGY

After assessing the contents reviewed in the literature, it clearly emphasizes the bottlenecks hindering the effective usage of AI for psychotherapeutic treatments. Depending on the qualitative nature of the information available in the psychotherapeutic domain, selection of appropriate AI technology from the AI umbrella is a critical necessity. Subsequent to a comprehensive literature assessment, it`s recognized that ontology-based workflows would be the ideal for the purpose as of the nature of qualitative data available in this domain.

The pseudocode proposed in Figure 1 can be depicted as the enforcement of the policy workflow to be followed in automating an appropriate therapy segment from the psychotherapeutic domain.

Figure 1. Policy workflow in form of a pseudocode

Segment	Contributes	Criteria to assess / enforce
Eligibility to be automated		• Nature of data available. • Sensitivity of information shared. • Role of the consultant. • Overhead for the consultant
Collaborative involvement		• Governing policy • Dialectics composition and direction • Time-box goals
Iterative development		• Reassessing the primitive version. • Role of consultants and ontologists. • Benchmark criteria
Clinical Testing		• Data Privacy. • Data Processing pipeline. • Anomaly login. • Corrective actions

Source: prepared by Authors

There are several critical points imposed by the operational workflow enforced through the pseudocode presented as Figure 1. Those can be identified as: -

- **Eligibility to be automated** - There could be several therapy procedures, which might not be suitable for the automated. In any case, fully automation should be fully discouraged, and it should only be an aiding strategy under the full authority of the human consultant. Therapy is a complex procedure which requires a human touch to enforce therapeutic alliance between the patients. Hence, the role of the consultant and, role of the automated system needs to be clearly defined.

- **Collaborative involvement** - Automation of psychotherapeutic domain knowledge requires rational involvement of the healthcare practitioners and the ontologists. Hence, this becomes a discussion platform with experts containing heterogenous skillsets; appropriate governing strategies have to be followed. Consequently, it will ensure the proper orchestration of the discussions allowing the flavor of the collaborative viewpoints within a specified time fame adhering to the time box requirements (Grosen et.al, 2023).
- **Iterative development** - Accurate ontology development cannot be done in one shot. It`s iterative and incremental. Hence, once the primitive design is established, segment by segment needs to be enhanced in a manner addressing the competency criteria expected. This requires effective engagement of the stakeholder from commencement until the completion of the entire process.
- **Clinical Testing** - Once the basic stable version of the ontology is ready, it has to be plugged into the existing or newly created information system. This could be done in the form of a chatbot, reasoner or analyzer, depending on the purpose to be fulfilled, Henceforth, the full version should run in a clinical setup as a pilot study, hence unforeseen circumstances might occur during the clinical experimentation with the patients. Hence, all knowledge inconsistencies need to be logged and separately handled for the expansion and updating of the ontology design.

The implementation of aforementioned components ensures the responsible use of AI for psychotherapy automation. One possible use for such automation is to automate the journaling requirements connected with Cognitive Behavioral Therapy, widely referred as CBT. CBT is a world recognized psychotherapeutic treatment strategy, which firmly deals with the thought sequences of the patient (Biere-Rafi et.al, 2023). Such type of sensible automations saves the consultants time and allows him or her to go an extra mile in treating the patient. According to the literature assessment, there is significant potential for existing systems to be supplemented with domain-associated intelligence, and the inclusion of well-planned ontology designs might be an effective solution.

The enforcement triggered via the pseudocode can be graphically represented inform of a framework as in Figure 2

Figure 2. Policy workflow in form of a framework

```
Start
Determine the psychotherapeutic treatment segment to be automated.
Locate and identify appropriate domain experts and ontologists as the appropriate stakeholders.
Initiate the steps for the ethical approval.
Initiate effective and time-boxed collaborative dialectics.
While [Until the stakeholders are satisfied]
   Collaboratively brainstorm about the suitability for the automation.
     IF [Automation is suitable == TRUE]
        While [Until the stakeholders are satisfied]
              Plan for the competency questions.
              Determine the count of the competency questions.
              Determine the scope and composition of the competency questions.
              Liaise with ontologists and seek for the technological feasibility.
              Refine as necessary.
        End While.
     End IF
   Commence the designing of the Ontology and Embed knowledge.
   Obtain the primitive version of the Ontology
   IF [ Primitive Design is ready ==TRUE]
      While [Until the stakeholders are satisfied]
           Negotiate with the psychotherapy experts.
           Verify the knowledge representation.
           Amend as necessary.
      End While.
   End IF
   Derive the stable version.
   Plug with the information system.
   Commence clinical testing.
   Refine as necessary.
End While.
End
```

Source: Prepared by Authors

DISCUSSION

As discussed in Table 3 of the literature review, tools assessed demonstrated a decent competence on segregating dispersed patient information and creating a convergence report with the needed components. It is expected to benefit the consultant and enhance their operational effectiveness via the involvement of aforementioned strategies. However, as the flaws of those tools, practically all of the categories lack the sympathetic and lively elements that are essential for successful therapeutic outcomes. It`s impossible to accomplish liveliness and empathetic goals without the involvement of a human consultant within the process. Therefore, it can be concluded that none of the aforementioned tool categories are going to be a replacement for the human consultant. Empathy and sensitivity based human touch is an essential ingredient in therapy, which leads to therapeutic alliance over time.

Once the patient and consultant have established a healthier therapeutic alliance, there is a high level of trust. Because of this, the patient feels more at ease and willing to open up to the consultant about their true sentiments. However, as revealed in literature due to the impedance imposed by social stigma (Rewerska-Juśko et.al,2022) patients find it difficult to freely communicate their true issues with the human consultant, during the early phases of the therapy sessions prior to establishing the therapeutic alliance.

One way to define social stigma is the aversion to being assessed by another person. Patients are unable to be completely honest and open with their consultant due to fear of social stigma, especially when it comes to discussing delicate topics like drug addiction, sex issues, and etc. These unfavorable worries weaken the patient's desire to routinely attend therapy sessions, which mostly results in early dropout rates. Consequently, fine-tuned and focused technological intervention might be a useful tactic to keep the patient interested in the procedure until the therapeutic alliance has been reached.

Computational mechanisms being non-human strategies, reluctancy against being judged can be resolved greatly (Vidanage and De Silva, 2016). This creates a more convenient platform for the patients to express their true sentiment. Therefore, patients' aversion towards expressing reality will be resolved resulting in revealing of the authentic concern with the system. Subsequently, computational strategy should execute the necessary steps to convey the severity of the patients` story in a precise manner to the consultant without losing any vital information. This two-step-based strategy from patient to the computational system, and from computational system to the consultant, resolves the detrimental impacts associated with social stigma. Through this mechanism consultants gain direct access to the patients' true cases, and they can extract information about the patients` temperament as well. Henceforth after considering all those perspectives, consultants can plan effective therapy session leading towards satisfactory therapeutic goals with the establishment of healthier therapeutic alliance over the time.

In order to fulfil aforementioned rational requirements, it`s vital to have a proper guiding workflow / framework, as this is a requirement to be accomplished by inter-disciplinary stakeholders with different skillsets, where effective convergence could be problematic. Hence, as a resolution for the aforementioned problem, the proposed framework and policy workflow logic ensure ethical and responsible AI deployment in meeting the necessity for due diligence to be created in the psychotherapeutic domain as a result of computational breakthroughs. This can be considered as a novel contribution to the domain of computational psychotherapy domain listed as a subset in the affective computing knowledge spectrum. A cheerful population of a country is a key to productivity and economic growth. This study seeks to harness technical advancements for the country's prosperity.

CONCLUSION

This chapter focused on improving the ethical usage of AI advancements for the accomplishment of the goal of escalating the quality of life of human beings. Effective and rational use of AI can contribute immensely by fulfilling the Corporate Social Responsibility (CSR) goals of a community. This chapter emphasized the causes for limited usage of AI advancements in psychotherapy and investigated potential adjustments to overcome that issue. This chapter contributes by recognizing the bottlenecks hindering the appropriate utilization of AI for psychotherapy. Further it suggests potential AI enabled technological pipelines and a governing workflow to derive the optimum usage from AI for the betterment of general public. Future recommendations include fully computerizing the suggested governing workflow using computational goal modelling techniques and allowing for visualization via a suitable dashboard, which improves overall operational transparency. However, due to lack of empathy in AI, it is a limitation to fully authorize the AI enabled technology for psychotherapy. Further, building a strong therapeutic alliance and rapport with clients is essential in psychotherapy, and AI may struggle to establish and maintain this connection. Hence, it is imperative to amalgamate the human expert's involvement into the AI solutions that are formulated to assist psychotherapy.

REFERENCES

Abd-alrazaq, A. A., Alhuwail, D., Schneider, J., Toro, C. T., Ahmed, A., Alzubaidi, M. S., Alajlani, M., & Househ, M. S. (2022). The performance of artificial intelligence-driven technologies in diagnosing mental disorders:an umbrella review. *NPJ Digital Medicine*, 5. PMID: 35798934

Abu Owida, H., Moh'd, B.A., Turab, N.M., Al-Nabulsi, J.I., & Abuowaida, S. (2023). The Evolution and Reliability of Machine Learning Techniques for Oncology. International Journal of Online and Biomedical Engineering.

Allen, M., James, C., Frost, J., Liabo, K., Pearn, K., Monks, T., Zhelev, Z., Logan, S., Everson, R., James, M. A., & Stein, K. (2022). Using simulation and machine learning to maximise the benefit of intravenous thrombolysis in acute stroke in England and Wales: The SAMueL modelling and qualitative study. *Health and Social Care Delivery Research*, 10(31), 1–148. DOI: 10.3310/GVZL5699 PMID: 36302070

Bartholmae, M. M., Karpov, M. V., Doda, R. D., & Dodani, S. (2023). SilverCloud mental health feasibility study: Who will it benefit the most? *Archives of Medical Science*, 19(5), 1576–1580. DOI: 10.5114/aoms/170248 PMID: 37732062

Beatty, C. C., Malik, T., Meheli, S., & Sinha, C. (2022). Evaluating the Therapeutic Alliance With a Free-Text CBT Conversational Agent (Wysa): A Mixed-Methods Study. *Frontiers in Digital Health*, 4, 4. DOI: 10.3389/fdgth.2022.847991 PMID: 35480848

Bellini, V., Russo, M., Lanza, R., Domenichetti, T., Compagnone, C., Maggiore, S. M., Cammarota, G., Pelosi, P., Vetrugno, L., & Bignami, E. G. (2023). Artificial intelligence and "the Art of Kintsugi" in Anesthesiology: Ten influential papers for clinical users. *Minerva Anestesiologica*, 89(9). Advance online publication. DOI: 10.23736/S0375-9393.23.17279-8 PMID: 37194240

Belyadi, H., & Haghighat, A. T. (2021). *Fuzzy logic*. Machine Learning Guide for Oil and Gas Using Python.

Cao, C., Liao, X., Jiang, X., Li, X., Chen, I.-H., & Lin, C.-Y. (2023). Psychometric evaluation of the depression, anxiety, and stress scale-21 (DASS-21) among Chinese primary and middle school teachers. *BMC Psychology*, 11(1), 11. DOI: 10.1186/s40359-023-01242-y PMID: 37452365

Cao, Y., Zhou, Z., Hu, C., He, W., & Tang, S. (2020). On the Interpretability of Belief Rule- Based Expert Systems. *IEEE Transactions on Fuzzy Systems*, 29(11), 3489–3503. DOI: 10.1109/TFUZZ.2020.3024024

Cina, G., Rober, T.E., Goedhart, R., & Birbil, I. (2022). Why we do need Explainable AI for Healthcare. ArXiv, abs/2206.15363.

Cordeiro, F., Epstein, D. A., Thomaz, E., Bales, E. S., Jagannathan, A. K., Abowd, G. D., & Fogarty, J. (2015). Barriers and Negative Nudges: Exploring Challenges in Food Journaling. *Proceedings of the 33rd Annual ACM Conference on Human Factors in Computing Systems*. DOI: 10.1145/2702123.2702155

Cosme, M., Hély, C., Pommereau, F., Pasquariello, P., Tiberi, C., Treydte, A. C., & Gaucherel, C. (2021). Qualitative Modeling for Bridging Expert-Knowledge and Social-Ecological Dynamics of an East African Savanna. *Land (Basel)*, 11(1), 42. DOI: 10.3390/land11010042

Counselling, P. (2017). *KDU publications, Library copyright*. General Sir John Kotelawala Defence University. Retrieved from http://ir.kdu.ac.lk/bitstream/handle/345/1680/005.pdf?sequence=1&isAllowed=y

Darcy, A., Beaudette, A., Chiauzzi, E., Daniels, J., Goodwin, K., Mariano, T. Y., Wicks, P., & Robinson, A. (2023). Anatomy of a Woebot® (WB001): Agent guided CBT for women with postpartum depression. *Expert Review of Medical Devices*, 20(12), 1035–1049. DOI: 10.1080/17434440.2023.2280686 PMID: 37938145

De Smet, M. M., Meganck, R., Truijens, F. L., De Geest, R., Cornelis, S., Norman, U. A., & Desmet, M. (2020). Change processes underlying "good outcome": A qualitative study on recovered and improved patients' experiences in psychotherapy for major depression. *Psychotherapy Research*, 30(7), 948–964. DOI: 10.1080/10503307.2020.1722329 PMID: 32022647

Denner, S., Scherer, J., Kades, K., Bounias, D., Schader, P., Kausch, L., Bujotzek, M., Bucher, A.M., Penzkofer, T., & Maier-Hein, K.H. (2023). Efficient Large Scale Medical Image Dataset Preparation for Machine Learning Applications. DEMI@ MICCAI.

DiSanto, N. (2023). Analyzing the Contextual Shortcomings of Artificial General Intelligence. ArXiv, abs/2304.00002.

Ernst-Linke, F., Enge, S., Viohl, L., Petzold, M. B., & Betzler, F. (2022). High five! – the big 5 personality traits, locus of control, and impulsivity and their relationship to substance use in a large cohort of university students in Berlin. *Addiction Research and Theory*, 31(2), 84–91. DOI: 10.1080/16066359.2022.2114075

Evans, O., Hardacre, S., Rubin, M., & Tran, M. (2023). Content appraisal and age moderate the relationship between passive social media use and mental ill-being. *Frontiers in Psychology*, 14, 14. DOI: 10.3389/fpsyg.2023.1181233 PMID: 37529318

Farrelly, C.T. (2021). Toleration, "Mindsight" and the Epistemic Virtues.

Flückiger, C., Del Re, A. C., Wampold, B. E., & Horvath, A. O. (2018). The Alliance in Adult Psychotherapy: A Meta-Analytic Synthesis. *Psychotherapy (Chicago, Ill.)*, 55(4), 316–340. DOI: 10.1037/pst0000172 PMID: 29792475

Frontino, G., Meschi, F., Rigamonti, A., Favalli, V., Bonura, C., & Bonfanti, R. (2016). Opportunities and Challenges of Telemedicine. Diabetes Technology & Therapeutics, 18(6), 404.

G, M. (2021). Mega Bot – The Healthcare Chatbot. 2021 Second International Conference on Electronics and Sustainable Communication Systems (ICESC), 1386-1395.

Gerger, H., Nascimento, A. F., Locher, C., Gaab, J., & Trachsel, M. (2020). What are the Key Characteristics of a 'Good' Psychotherapy? Calling for Ethical Patient Involvement. *Frontiers in Psychiatry*, 11, 11. DOI: 10.3389/fpsyt.2020.00406 PMID: 32581856

Grill, J., Strub, F., Altch'e, F., Tallec, C., Richemond, P.H., Buchatskaya, E., Doersch, C., Pires, B.Á., Guo, Z.D., Azar, M.G., Piot, B., Kavukcuoglu, K., Munos, R., & Valko, M. (2020). Bootstrap Your Own Latent: A New Approach to Self-Supervised Learning. ArXiv, abs/2006.07733.

He, K., Fan, H., Wu, Y., Xie, S., & Girshick, R. B. (2019). Momentum Contrast for Unsupervised Visual Representation Learning. *2020 IEEE/CVF Conference on Computer Vision and Pattern Recognition (CVPR)*, 9726-9735.

He, L., & Shin, K. G. (2023). Rethink Physical Security: Protecting Vehicles via Battery-Enabled Sensing and Control. *Proceedings of the IEEE*, 111(8), 921–927. DOI: 10.1109/JPROC.2023.3285166

Hines, P., Butterworth, C., Greenlee, C., & Jekiel, C. (2023). The mental and physical wellbeing flow within the People Value Stream. *Human Resources Management and Services*.

Hudson, C. C., Bowers, E. M., Björgvinsson, T., & Beard, C. (2023). Changes in Perspective-Taking During Cognitive Behavioral Therapy in a Partial Hospital Setting. *Cognitive Therapy and Research*, 47(6), 909–918. DOI: 10.1007/s10608-023-10422-4

Jadhav, S. B., & Kodavade, D. V. (2023). Enhancing Flight Delay Prediction through Feature Engineering in Machine Learning Classifiers: A Real Time Data Streams Case Study. *International Journal on Recent and Innovation Trends in Computing and Communication*, 11(2s), 212–218. DOI: 10.17762/ijritcc.v11i2s.6064

Kempton, A. M., & Vassilakopoulou, P. (2021). *Accountability*. Transparency and Explainability in AI for Healthcare.

Khnaisser, C., Lavoie, L., Fraikin, B., Barton, A., Dussault, S., Burgun, A., & Éthier, J. (2022). Using an Ontology to Derive a Sharable and Interoperable Relational Data Model for Heterogeneous Healthcare Data and Various Applications. *Methods of Information in Medicine*, 61(S 02), e73–e88. DOI: 10.1055/a-1877-9498 PMID: 35709746

Kleine, A., Kokje, E., Lermer, E., & Gaube, S. (2023). Attitudes Toward the Adoption of 2 Artificial Intelligence–Enabled Mental Health Tools Among Prospective Psychotherapists: Cross-sectional Study. *JMIR Human Factors*, 10, 10. DOI: 10.2196/46859 PMID: 37436801

Kodavati, B., & Ramarakula, M. (2021). Latency based Re-Enforcement Learning over Cognitive Software Defined 5G Networks. 2021 7th International Conference on Advanced Computing and Communication Systems (ICACCS), 1, 1848-1853.

Kumar, V. V., & Tankha, G. (2023). Association Between the Big Five and Trait Emotional Intelligence Among College Students. *Psychology Research and Behavior Management*, 16, 915–925. DOI: 10.2147/PRBM.S400058 PMID: 36974037

Lalejini, A., Dolson, E., Vostinar, A. E., & Zaman, L. (2022). Artificial selection methods from evolutionary computing show promise for directed evolution of microbes. *eLife*, 11. PMID: 35916365

Lee, C., Lai, H., Lee, C., & Chen, M. (2022). Medical Dispute Cases Caused by Errors in Clinical Reasoning: An Investigation and Analysis. *Health Care*, 10. PMID: 36360564

Lee, P., Bubeck, S., & Petro, J. (2023). Benefits, Limits, and Risks of GPT-4 as an AI Chatbot for Medicine. *The New England Journal of Medicine*, 388(13), 1233–1239. DOI: 10.1056/NEJMsr2214184 PMID: 36988602

Lin, B., Zecevic, S., Bouneffouf, D., & Cecchi, G.A. (2023). TherapyView: Visualizing Therapy Sessions with Temporal Topic Modeling and AI-Generated Arts. ArXiv, abs/2302.10845.

Luo, R., Xing, J., Chen, L., Pan, Z., Cai, X., Li, Z., Wang, J., & Ford, A. (2021). Glassboxing Deep Learning to Enhance Aircraft Detection from SAR Imagery. *Remote Sensing (Basel)*, 13(18), 3650. DOI: 10.3390/rs13183650

Machado, R. N., Mello, R., Pinna, C., Nunes, R. M., Magalhães, A. S., & Féres-Carneiro, T. (2022). Family Psychotherapy in the Context of Adoption: Parental Suppression of Adopted Children's Epistemophilic Drive in the Pursuit of Their Origins. *Psychology (Irvine, Calif.)*, 13(8), 1286–1298. DOI: 10.4236/psych.2022.138083

Mazurek Melnyk, B., Hoying, J., & Tan, A. (2020). Effects of the MINDSTRONG© CBT-based program on depression, anxiety and healthy lifestyle behaviors in graduate health sciences students. *Journal of American College Health*, 70(4), 1001–1009. DOI: 10.1080/07448481.2020.1782922 PMID: 32672515

Mehta, A., Niles, A. N., Vargas, J. H., Marafon, T., Couto, D. D., & Gross, J. J. (2020). Acceptability and Effectiveness of Artificial Intelligence Therapy for Anxiety and Depression (Youper): Longitudinal Observational Study. *Journal of Medical Internet Research*, 23. PMID: 34155984

Merino-Soto, C., Angulo-Ramos, M., Rovira-Millán, L. V., & Rosario-Hernández, E. (2023). Psychometric properties of the generalized anxiety disorder-7 (GAD-7) in a sample of workers. *Frontiers in Psychiatry*, 14, 14. DOI: 10.3389/fpsyt.2023.999242 PMID: 37051164

Mulansky, L. (2020). Untersuchung der Geodaten von Benutzern der Moodpath mHealth App mithilfe von Methoden des Maschinellen Lernens.

Muravyov, S. V., Antipov, D., Buzdalova, A., & Filchenkov, A. (2019). *Efficient Computation of Fitness Function for Evolutionary Clustering*. MENDEL. DOI: 10.13164/mendel.2019.1.087

Ni, Y., Ding, R., Chen, Y., Hou, H., & Ni, S. (2023). Focusing on Needs: A Chatbot-Based Emotion Regulation Tool for Adolescents. *2023 IEEE International Conference on Systems, Man, and Cybernetics (SMC)*, 2295-2300. DOI: 10.1109/SMC53992.2023.10394600

Pacchiardi, L., Chan, A.J., Mindermann, S., Moscovitz, I., Pan, A.Y., Gal, Y., Evans, O., & Brauner, J.M. (2023). How to Catch an AI Liar: Lie Detection in Black-Box LLMs by Asking Unrelated Questions. ArXiv, abs/2309.15840.

Patel, N., Dahman, B., & Bajaj, J. S. (2022). Development of New Mental and Physical Health Sequelae among US Veterans after COVID-19. *Journal of Clinical Medicine*, 11(12), 11. DOI: 10.3390/jcm11123390 PMID: 35743461

Ryška, P. (2017). Deflation anD economic Growth: the Great Depression as the Great outlier.

Sewada, R., Jangid, A., Kumar, P., & Mishra, N. (2023). Explainable Artificial Intelligence (XAI). international journal of food and nutritional sciences.

Singh, B., Kashyap, S., & Grover, A. (2019). Artificial intelligence and dichotomy on benefits and challenges: What do healthcare providers say? International Journal of Research in Medical Sciences.

Stephens, T. N., Joerin, A., Rauws, M., & Werk, L. N. (2019). Feasibility of pediatric obesity and prediabetes treatment support through Tess, the AI behavioral coaching chatbot. *Translational Behavioral Medicine*, 9(3), 440–447. DOI: 10.1093/tbm/ibz043 PMID: 31094445

Sun, Y., Kong, Z., Song, Y., Liu, J., & Wang, X. (2022). The validity and reliability of the PHQ-9 on screening of depression in neurology: A cross sectional study. *BMC Psychiatry*, 22(1), 22. DOI: 10.1186/s12888-021-03661-w PMID: 35139810

Temple, P., Acher, M., Jézéquel, J., & Barais, O. (2017). Learning Contextual-Variability Models. *IEEE Software*, 34(6), 64–70. DOI: 10.1109/MS.2017.4121211

Townsend, B. A., Sihlahla, I., Naidoo, M., Naidoo, S., Donnelly, D., & Thaldar, D. W. (2023). Mapping the regulatory landscape of AI in healthcare in Africa. *Frontiers in Pharmacology*, 14, 14. DOI: 10.3389/fphar.2023.1214422 PMID: 37693916

Vidanage, K., & Jayaratne, K. (2016). Ontology And Expert System Based Intervention, For Psychological Consultation. *European Journal of Computer Science and Information Technology, 4*. https://www.eajournals.org/wp-content/uploads/Ontology-and-Expert- System-Based-Intervention-for-Psychological-Consultation.pdf

Vidanage, K., & Jayaratne, L. (2015). Machine Learning and Natural Language Processing Usage for Psychological Consultation. *GSTF International Journal on Computing*, 4(3), 17. DOI: 10.7603/s40601-014-0017-5

Vidanage, K., Mohamad, N. M., & Mohemad, R. (2019). Upper–Level Task Ontology for Generic Ontology Verbalization. 2019 2nd International Conference of Intelligent Robotic and Control Engineering (IRCE), 148-155. DOI: 10.1109/IRCE.2019.00037

Vidanage, K., Noor, N. M. M., Mohemad, R., & Bakar, Z. A. (2020). Semantic Web-Based Knowledge Extraction: Upper Ontology Guided Crime Knowledge Discovery. In Vasudevan, H., Michalas, A., Shekokar, N., & Narvekar, M. (Eds.), *Advanced Computing Technologies and Applications. Algorithms for Intelligent Systems*. Springer. DOI: 10.1007/978-981-15-3242-9_30

Walke, S., & Khillare, S. (2023). Vulnerabilities And Ethical Implications. In *Machine Learning*. International Journal For Multidisciplinary Research.

Wang, L., Wang, X., Hawbani, A., Xiong, Y., & Zhang, X. (2020). Convolution Encoders for End-to-End Action Tracking With Space-Time Cubic Kernels. *IEEE Access : Practical Innovations, Open Solutions*, 8, 139023–139032. DOI: 10.1109/ACCESS.2020.3012154

Willmen, T., Völkel, L., Ronicke, S., Hirsch, M. C., Kaufeld, J., Rychlik, R. P., & Wagner, A. D. (2021). Health economic benefits through the use of diagnostic support systems and expert knowledge. *BMC Health Services Research*, 21(1), 21. DOI: 10.1186/s12913-021-06926-y PMID: 34503507

Xie, T., & Pentina, I. (2022). Attachment Theory as a Framework to Understand Relationships with Social Chatbots: A Case Study of Replika. *Hawaii International Conference on System Sciences*. DOI: 10.24251/HICSS.2022.258

Yadav, A., Chandel, S., Chatufale, S., & Bandhakavi, A. (2023). LAHM: Large Annotated Dataset for Multilingual & Multi-Domain Hate Speech Identification. ArXiv, abs/2304.00913.

Yang, G., Wang, L., Xu, X., & Xia, J. (2021). Footballer Action Tracking and Intervention Using Deep Learning Algorithm. *Journal of Healthcare Engineering*, 2021, 2021. DOI: 10.1155/2021/5518806 PMID: 33815728

Zárate-Torres, R. A., & Correa, J. (2023). How good is the Myers-Briggs Type Indicator for predicting leadership-related behaviors? *Frontiers in Psychology*, 14, 14. DOI: 10.3389/fpsyg.2023.940961 PMID: 36936015

Zheng, L., Chiang, W., Sheng, Y., Zhuang, S., Wu, Z., Zhuang, Y., Lin, Z., Li, Z., Li, D., Xing, E.P., Zhang, H., Gonzalez, J., & Stoica, I. (2023). Judging LLM-as-a-judge with MT- Bench and Chatbot Arena. ArXiv, abs/2306.05685.

Chapter 4
Navigating the Role of Artificial Intelligence (AI) in Transforming Corporate Social Responsibility (CSR) Strategies

Ankit Pathania
https://orcid.org/0000-0003-2643-9743
Eternal University, Baru Sahib, India

Ambar Srivastava
https://orcid.org/0000-0002-7334-3421
Christ University, India

ABSTRACT

With the advent of artificial intelligence (AI), there arises a new frontier in CSR practices, as AI-powered solutions also have the ability to promote innovation; increase stakeholder involvement; improve the efficacy, efficiency, and scalability of corporate social responsibility (CSR) endeavours; and make evidence-based decisions in CSR efforts easier. But incorporating AI into CSR initiatives also brings up difficult moral, legal, and societal issues. The purpose of this chapter is to provide insights into the ways in which artificial intelligence (AI) is changing corporate social responsibility (CSR) and how AI can encourage transparency, drive innovation in CSR programs, and involve stakeholders to produce significant social, environmental, and economic results. This study also explores the current trends

DOI: 10.4018/979-8-3693-3478-2.ch004

in CSR and AI. This may help businesses allocate their resources more effectively, spot new trends, and improve impact measurement at large.

1. INTRODUCTION

Corporate Social Responsibility (CSR) has evolved significantly over the years, transitioning from a philanthropic endeavour to an integral part of corporate strategy aimed at addressing social, environmental and ethical concerns. One essential component of promoting sustainable development is corporate social responsibility (Lombardi *et al.,* 2010). It refers to a company's commitment to conducting its business in an ethical and responsible manner, while also contributing to economic development, improving the quality of life of its employees and their families, as well as of the local community and society at large. CSR involves integrating social and environmental concerns into business operations and interactions with stakeholders. This can include actions such as promoting workplace diversity and inclusion, supporting education and healthcare initiatives, reducing carbon emissions and waste, engaging in fair labour practices and contributing to community development projects. Companies engage in CSR for various reasons, including ethical considerations, reputation management, risk mitigation and long-term sustainability. A strong CSR program can enhance brand loyalty, attract and retain talent, foster positive relationships with customers and communities and ultimately drive financial performance (Księzak, 2016).

Companies are consistently exploring new approaches to improve the efficiency and effectiveness of their CSR programs. It has been observed that social capital generates value and benefits in an ICT intervention (Ahmed *et al.,* 2019). Technology can significantly improve the development and execution of a range of corporate social responsibility (CSR) and business initiatives (Dubickis & Gaile-Sarkane, 2021). Organizations use cutting-edge technologies like blockchain, AI, and IoT to support CSR initiatives and as useful tools for security and economic resilience (Khare et al., 2023). In the context of Corporate Social Responsibility (CSR), Artificial Intelligence is one such emerging technology. Artificial Intelligence (AI) can be defined as the use of advanced computational algorithms and technologies to automate tasks analyze data and make decisions in a manner that aligns with ethical and social values. AI in CSR encompasses various applications aimed at improving social, environmental and economic outcomes while considering the impact on stakeholders and communities. AI in CSR can completely eliminate the chance of bias developing as a result of human perceptions. An artificial intelligence (AI) system can offer precise, multifaceted performance metrics that assess a program's compliance with national and international regulations. AI has the ability to maximize the company's CSR program by understanding the objectives and commercial drivers and then providing a program approach that aligns with those aims (Naqvi, 2018). The success of CSR initiatives depends on using AI in developing CSR strategies. Since technology has no bounds, AI and ML-enabled CSR expand the reach and size of businesses to connect with new stakeholders beyond geographical and political barriers.

Sustainable corporate operations require a strong focus on social, environmental and human rights issues (McBarnet, 2007). Therefore, the purpose of this chapter is to provide insights into the ways in which artificial intelligence (AI) is changing corporate social responsibility (CSR) and how AI can encourage transparency, drive innovation in CSR programs and involve stakeholders to produce significant social, environmental and economic results. Because of this, firms may be better able to deploy their resources, identify emerging trends, and enhance impact measurement overall. Therefore, AI-driven CSR projects must carefully navigate issues like algorithmic bias, data privacy and accountability to guarantee that the values of justice, transparency and social responsibility are upheld.

2. OBJECTIVES OF THE STUDY

Keeping in view the above facts in mind, this chapter is designed to provide insights on how AI can transfer the CSR strategies of businesses.

a) To explore the ways Artificial Intelligence changing the Corporate Social Responsibility.
b) To explore the current trends in Corporate Social Responsibility and Artificial Intelligence.

3. REVIEW OF LITERATURE

Through this section, the literature has been reviewed in line with the objectives of the study. The literature reviewed highlights the pertinent concepts, methodologies and discussions that have shaped the study. This insight not only explains the evolution of thought but also highlights the significance of CSR in building firm performance.

The term "corporate social responsibility" (CSR) and "sustainability" activities and policies are used interchangeably to refer to business practices that evaluate, control and oversee an organization's obligations and implications for the community and environment. Enhancing social welfare or increasing the sustainability of corporate operations is common objectives of CSR. The most difficult environmental and societal issues that humans confront can be greatly improved by AI. However, emerging risks like algorithmic bias and ethical dilemmas could also arise from the breakthroughs and efficiency brought about by AI. That is why; AI is termed as a two-edged sword when it comes to solving corporate sustainability issues. AI can be said to possess moral agency, particularly if it serves a social purpose. It needs to have a responsibility of care in different situåtion, which is only feasible if it is a moral actor (Sullins, 2006). In relation to AI, outlines the dangers of moral outsourcing: human biases are many and very simple to identify and address. Conversely, a machine malfunction can have unimaginably dire repercussions (O'Heigeartaigh, 2013). Furthermore, some academics contend that even stringent algorithmic accountability is insufficient to hold moral outsourcing accountable (Pavaloiu and Kose, 2017). In this sense, P. Boddington (2017) in his study pointed that morality and virtue ethics forbid the outsourcing of moral judgments because even a highly developed machine could not perform the correct actions for the right reasons and in the right way. However, some scientists support the idea of giving morality to computer systems. According to Mul (2010) computer technologies have the potential to significantly influence human agency and strengthen our moral autonomy. Through the framework of a crash optimization algorithm, which is created by the algorithm author and lets the autonomous machine choose who and what to hit under specific circumstances determined by traditional moral quandaries in AI ethics (Gurney, 2016). Additionally, the growth of AI forces businesses to rethink internal procedures and blur organizational lines, which profoundly alters the dynamics between the company and its many stakeholders.

A look into the ethical applications of AI is provided by different scholars. They contend that robots can improve the care giving process and provide caregivers greater freedom by using a capabilities approach analysis (Borenstein and Pearson, 2010). According to Kofas, artificial intelligence will have a profound effect on people's sense of identity and sense of community in society by eroding local cultures and increasing social inequalities. The author contends that although robotics and artificial intelligence will raise living standards, the wealthiest classes will be the only ones able to use these technologies for their most beneficial purposes (Kofas, 2017). Based on social media data, AI may subtly determine whether a person is depressed, which may have an impact on their ability to find job in the future (Pavaloiu and Kose, 2017). Certain advancements have been made in certain, applicable standards, such those pertaining to the security of personal information (Heisenberg, 2005; Albrecht, 2016). In robotics (Schlenoff, 2015; Noorman and Johnson, 2014) or investigation of AI's legal identity (Gadzhiev, 2018; Morkhat, 2018; Cerka et al., 2017).

Based on a meta-analysis of 42 studies, Wang et al. (2015) found a favorable correlation between financial performance and CSR. Comparably, Jung et al. (2022) investigated how IT-enabled innovation and CSR interacted with business performance. Companies that implement successful CSR programs benefit the environment, the community, and their own bottom line. Businesses like Google, Alibaba, Uber, Amazon, Tesla, and many more have used AI to change their business models and gain a competitive edge (Lee et al., 2019). According to a global survey, implementing AI can result in quantifiable benefits such as an average 20 per cent reduction in costs and an average 10 per cent gain in income. AI is becoming more and more relevant in a variety of industries, including supply chain, marketing, sales and finance. However, firm-level adoption of AI for CSR is still in its infancy (Wang et al., 2020). The relationship between the company's social responsibilities and its financial performance has been documented extensively in the literature (Lee, 2008; Marin et al. 2012). According to a study by Bernal-Conesa et al. (2017), CSR-oriented tactics significantly improve an organization's overall performance. Based on the empirical findings, nowadays many firms have implemented this idea into their marketing communications to improve stakeholder perceptions and retentions. As a result, CSR is thought to be becoming more and more important for raising businesses' competitiveness. Zhao & Farinas (2022) in their study reported that AI has a significant impact on most social and economic spheres and in the near future, this impact is anticipated to increase. According to some authors, artificial intelligence (AI) will increase the accuracy and efficiency of corporate actions while lowering the need for human management and the related expenses Petrin (2019).

4. RESEARCH METHODOLOGY

This study uses a thorough literature analysis and a multi-case study technique to systematically investigate and redefine the parameters of corporate social responsibility in the context of artificial intelligence. The methodology offers both theoretical depth and practical insights and it is carefully constructed to reflect the complex consequences of AI on CSR practices. The study does a comprehensive literature review and carefully examines current academic and business publications. This paper provides a framework for understanding CSR in the context of AI, pointing out areas of knowledge gaps and emerging trends.

5. FINDINGS

5.1 Role of AI in Transforming CSR Practices

The global economy has made digitalization a mega trend, and as a result, new technology is becoming very popular across many industries. This is because it opens up new opportunities and improves many facets of human life (Osberg & Lohrmann, 2017). Bag et al. (2021) highlight the emerging role of artificial intelligence (AI) in operations management, underscoring its potential to optimize processes and improve decision-making efficiency. For instance, intelligent machines may replace the labour force (Pavlou, 2018). Therefore, it is necessary for technology performance to be in line with the CSR principle and improve its applications (Bocquet et al., 2013). Technology can identify the spots where a company's strategy and CSR programs align, enhancing the level of integration overall. Collaboration from a variety of stakeholders, particularly directors and the public sector will be necessary for AI and other advanced technologies. Furthermore, by using a multifaceted approach to measuring program effectiveness, it might lessen human bias (Bughin & Hazan, 2019). CSR and AI are increasingly becoming intertwined due to the ethical, societal and environmental implications of AI technologies. Artificial Intelligence in CSR has the potential to reduce errors and increase efficiency and become an important instrument capable of changing the CSR landscape in recent years. Big data can have a favorable impact on a firm's innovation performance, but only if it is used effectively, according to Ghasemaghaei and Calic (2020). Businesses can use AI technologies to improve their CSR initiatives and make a larger, longer-lasting difference in the world. AI, for instance, can assist businesses in locating opportunities to reduce the environmental impact of goods and services by making them more sustainable. Here are some key points from studies and research highlighting how AI is being leveraged to enhance CSR efforts.

- **Ethical Consideration:** Businesses have an ethical obligation to behave in a way that is required by society, even if there are certain behaviour that are forbidden by society but not by law. Businesses are expected to behave responsibly and adhere to morally sound concepts like fairness and rights. Therefore, in order to fulfill one's ethical obligations, one must understand the technology, take it into consideration while implementing AI for CSR projects that will benefit the community, and identify and respect new or emerging ethical and moral norms of society. One of the fundamental demands placed on businesses by their ethical obligations is to act in a just and equitable manner while preventing harm. In order to uphold ethical obligations, it is therefore crucial to evaluate the stakeholders' exposure to physical or digital risk when implementing AI (Canhoto & Clear, 2020) and AI has the potential to enhance corporate social responsibility by detecting and stopping unethical practices in the supply chain. Martin (2019) investigates how algorithms have the potential to maintain current disparities and stresses the significance of creating fair AI systems. In order to secure the ethical deployment of AI, the report also advocates for more corporate responsibility and supervision.

- **Social Welfare:** Many companies are leveraging AI to address societal challenges and contribute to the greater good. AI can enhance these efforts by enabling more efficient resource allocation, better decision-making and the development of innovative solutions to complex problems. According to Floridi et al. (2020), AI has the potential to greatly advance social welfare by improving a number of fields, including healthcare, education, and environmental protection. The study stressed that ethical AI development and application are helpful in maximizing advantages and lowering hazards.
- **Responsible Data Use:** AI systems rely on vast amounts of data to learn and make predictions. CSR principles require companies to handle data responsibly, ensuring privacy, security, consent etc. Therefore, by using this data-driven strategy companies may discover areas where their efforts can have the greatest impact on CSR activities to help them make informed decisions. Big data analytics, dramatically improves business performance by fostering more dynamic skills like agility, creativity, and decision-making processes (Wamba et al. 2017).
- **Environmental Impact**: The development and deployment of AI technologies can have significant environmental implications, including energy consumption, resource utilization and e-waste generation. CSR principles call for companies to minimize their environmental footprint and adopt sustainable business practices. According to Lary et al. (2016), machine learning-based algorithms are useful for tracking deforestation and habitat degradation as well as for evaluating satellite imagery. McKinsey & Company in their report discussed AI can assist businesses in achieving their sustainability objectives as AI can be used to improve corporate transparency, optimize resource utilization, and lower greenhouse gas emissions. Rolnick et al. (2019) also stated that machine learning offers substantial opportunities to address climate change through applications in areas such as energy efficiency, carbon sequestration and climate modeling. In the current dynamic business environment, incorporating CSR has emerged as not just a strategic requirement but also a moral obligation for companies seeking to make positive contributions to society while preserving their sustainability. For example, by utilizing a smart grid or energy management systems, a business can minimize energy costs and its carbon footprint by integrating renewable energy sources, analyzing patterns of energy consumption, optimizing energy usage, and making well-informed decisions.

• **Personalized CSR Campaigns:** AI can tailor CSR programs to appeal to particular target markets. AI can assist businesses in customizing their CSR messaging and campaigns to cater to the distinct needs and preferences of various groups by evaluating consumer data.

• **Monitoring and Reporting:** AI-powered solutions are able to track and evaluate CSR projects in real-time and which helps to keep their strategies in line with their aims and objectives of the business. Companies are able to monitor their progress, make necessary adjustments, and give stakeholders accurate and current information about their CSR initiatives. AI improves the hiring process in the human resources sector by helping businesses look through hundreds of resumes to identify the best applicant. Similar methods might be used in the CSR sector, where bots could counsel non-profits on how to streamline their financial or fundraising procedures. Furthermore, bots might be used to go through all of the applicant submissions to choose the ones that best fit the organization's vision and strategy, saving humans from having to go through thousands of grant applications.

• **Improved Transparency in Supply Chain Operations:** Transparency in the supply chain is essential to CSR since it guarantees moral sourcing procedures and environmentally friendly production techniques. Block chain and machine learning are two examples of AI technologies that help businesses improve supply chain transparency by recording and validating each step of production and delivery. In addition to increasing customer trust, this degree of openness enables businesses to recognize and resolve possible problems like labor abuse and environmental damage. Belhadi et al. (2021) in their study find that AI-driven innovations significantly enhance supply chain resilience and performance, especially under dynamic conditions. The author also highlighted the the positive impact of AI on operational efficiency and strategic decision-making within supply chains. Yao and Lin (2020) highlight the ethical implications of AI adoption in supply chain management and emphasize the need for robust ethical frameworks to guide the responsible use of AI technologies in supply chain operations.

• **Cross-border Collaborations:** AI can help with overseas collaboration on CSR projects by automating translations and removing linguistic obstacles. Additionally, it can facilitate business-government, non-governmental, and stakeholder connections that can lead to partnerships with a larger societal impact. Utilization of artificial intelligence technology with CSR programs greatly enhances the growth of cross-border e-commerce by facilitating customized experiences, streamlining logistics, and identifying the potential markets. (Wang et al., 2020). (AI)-based solutions facilitate compliance faster by automating the classification of commodities, generating accurate customs documents, and ensuring compliance with international trade laws. This lessens the chance of delays and fines while accelerating the flow of goods across international borders. Although Small and Medium-sized businesses) can access financial services using artificial intelligence-driven trade finance solutions, which enables them to engage in global trade and spurs economic growth.

5.2 Current trends in CSR and AI

The effects of corporate activities on the environment and society grew in the 1960s and 1970s, but in recent times, there has been a growing focus on CSR as stakeholders such as investors, employees and consumers have demanded that businesses adopt more sustainable and ethical corporate practices. CSR is now viewed as an essential part of a business's overall strategy and as a means of helping organizations build long-term value for all of their stakeholders, including the environment, consumers, employees, and shareholders. Unilever, The Body Shop and Patagonia are the businesses that are effectively incorporating CSR into every facet of their operations. Moreover, today's generations prefer to buy or use those products which are more socially responsible. They think businesses should make investments in advancing society and seek out solutions that help achieve those advancements. The United Nations-led "AI for Good" program is a global platform created to investigate how artificial intelligence may help accomplish the Sustainable Development Goals (SDGs). This program, which was started in 2017, brings together a wide range of stakeholders to promote the development and application of AI technologies that have the potential to positively impact society. These stakeholders include governments, academic institutions, business executives, and civil society.AI technologies have the potential to be a powerful tool for advancing diversity, equity and inclusion in the workplace. Technology has the ability to increase the accessibility and inclusivity of CSR projects. Assistive technology and digital platforms, for instance, can contribute to closing the digital gap by guaranteeing that underprivileged populations have equitable access to healthcare, education, and employment opportunities. Furthermore, people can experience and relate to social issues using virtual reality (VR) and augmented reality (AR) technologies, which promotes a greater comprehension and support for CSR concerns. AI algorithms can be trained to detect and mitigate biases in various processes, such as recruitment, performance evaluations and decision-making. According to a Boston Consulting Group (BCG) report, businesses that use AI for CSR initiatives experience improvements in the social and environmental effect of their initiatives. The study demonstrates how AI aids in accomplishing sustainable objectives and increasing the accuracy of CSR initiatives. However, AI has concerns in addition to its many advantages for businesses, such as automation, optimization and customization. Since AI relies heavily on data to learn and gain insights, inaccurate or faulty data might lead to biased outcomes that promote inequity or prejudice. For instance, ethical AI and initiatives to advance environmental and social sustainability are closely related. If efforts aren't taken to be open and equitable in its application, customers may become confused about how AI is employed in a firm and foster a climate of mistrust.

6. CONCLUSION

With its ability to provide data-driven insights, predictive analytics, increased efficiency, customized campaigns, transparent monitoring, sustainable resource management, and international cooperation, artificial intelligence has the potential to completely transform corporate social responsibility. By using AI in CSR initiatives, businesses can show their support for environmental and social problems while also ensuring that these initiatives are more successful, efficient and in line with changing societal demands. Therefore, it can be expected that the potential for AI-driven CSR innovation is endless as the field of AI technology develops, offering everyone a more promising and sustainable future but these technologies are used responsibly to promote positive social impact.

REFERENCES

Ahmed, Z., Kumar, V., Kumar, U., & Eryilmaz, E. (2019). Social Capital and ICT Intervention: A Holistic Model of Value. *Pacific Asia Journal of the Association for Information Systems*, 11(4), 44–74. DOI: 10.17705/1pais.11403

Albrecht, J. P. (2016). How the GDPR will change the world. *European Data Protection Law Review*, 1(3), 287–289. DOI: 10.21552/EDPL/2016/3/4

Bag, S., Wood, L. C., Xu, L., & Dhamija, P. (2021). Artificial intelligence in operations management: Uncharted waters for research. *Operations Management Research*, 14, 76–102.

Belhadi, A., Mani, V., Kamble, S. S., Khan, S. A. R., & Verma, S. (2021). Artificial intelligence-driven innovation for enhancing supply chain resilience and performance under the effect of supply chain dynamism: An empirical investigation. *Annals of Operations Research*, 1–26. PMID: 33551534

Bernal-Conesa, J. A., Briones-Penalver, A., & Nieves-Nieto, C. (2017). Impacts of the CSR strategies of technology companies on performance and competitiveness. *Tourism & Management Studies*, 13(4), 73–81. DOI: 10.18089/tms.2017.13408

Bocquet, R., Le Bas, C., Mothe, C., & Poussing, N. (2013). Are firms with different CSR profiles equally innovative? Empirical analysis with survey data. *European Management Journal*, 31(6), 642–654. DOI: 10.1016/j.emj.2012.07.001

Boddington, P. (2017). *Towards a Code of Ethics for Artificial Intelligence* (1st ed.). Springer New York. DOI: 10.1007/978-3-319-60648-4

Borenstein, J., & Pearson, Y. (2010). Robot caregivers: Harbingers of expanded freedom for all? *Ethics*, 12(3), 277–288.

Bughin, J., & Hazan, E. (2019). Can artificial intelligence help society as much as it helps business? *McKinsey*. https://www.mckinsey.com/business-functions/mckinsey-analytics/our-insights/can-artificial-intelligence-help-society-as-much-as-it-helps-business

Canhoto, A. I., & Clear, F. (2020). Artificial intelligence and machine learning as business tools: A framework for diagnosing value destruction potential. *Business Horizons*, 63(2), 183–193. DOI: 10.1016/j.bushor.2019.11.003

Cerka, P., Grigiene, J., & Sirbikyte, G. (2017). Is it possible to grant legal personality to artificial intelligence. *Computer Law & Security Report*, 3(5), 685–699. DOI: 10.1016/j.clsr.2017.03.022

De Mul, J. (2010). Moral machines: ICTs as mediators of human agency. *Research in Philosophy and Technology*, 3(14), 226–236. DOI: 10.5840/techne201014323

Du, S., & Xie, C. (2021). Paradoxes of artificial intelligence in consumer markets: Ethical challenges and opportunities. *Journal of Business Research*, 123, 291–308. DOI: 10.1016/j.jbusres.2020.08.024

Dubickis, M., & Gaile-Sarkane, E. (2021). Factors Influencing Technology Transfer in Companies at Emerging Economies. *Science, Technology & Society*, 26(2), 242–271. DOI: 10.1177/09717218211005615

Floridi, L., Cowls, J., King, T. C., & Taddeo, M. (2020). How AI can be a force for good. [Link]. *Science*, 361(6404), 751–752. PMID: 30139858

Gadzhiev, G. A. (2018). Whether robot-agent is a person? *Journal of Russian Law*, 1(29).

Ghasemaghaei, M., & Calic, G. (2020). Assessing the impact of big data on firm innovation performance: Big data is not always better data. *Journal of Business Research*, 108, 147–162. DOI: 10.1016/j.jbusres.2019.09.062

Gurney, J. K. (2016). Crashing into the unknown: An examination of crash-optimization algorithms. *Albany Law Review*, 183, 79.

Heisenberg, D. (2005). *Negotiating privacy: the European union. The United States and Personal Data*. Lynn Rienner Publishers. DOI: 10.1515/9781626370074

Jung, M., Eom, M. T., & Yayla, A. (2022). Investigating the interaction effect between IT-enabled innovation and corporate social responsibility on firm performance. *Information Systems Management*, 1–20.

Khare, S., Uniyal, V., Kathuria, S., Chauhan, A. S., Akram, S. V., & Aluvala, S. (2023, December). Transformation of Corporate Social Responsibility Practices: Adapting Artificial Intelligence and Internet of Things. In *International Conference on Recent Trends in Image Processing and Pattern Recognition* (pp. 165-177). Cham: Springer Nature Switzerland.

Kofas, J. (2017). Artificial intelligence: socioeconomic, political and ethical dimensions. https://countercurrents.org/2017/04/artificial-intelligence-socioeconomic-politicaland-ethicaldimensions

Księżak, P. (2016). The Benefits from CSR for a Company and Society. *Journal of Corporate Responsibility and Leadership*, 3(4), 53–65. DOI: 10.12775/JCRL.2016.023

Lary, D. J., Lary, T., & Sattler, B. (2016). Using machine learning to estimate global PM2.5 for environmental health studies. *Environmental Health Insights*, 10, EHI-S38448.

Lee, J., Suh, T., Roy, D., & Baucus, M. (2019). Emerging technology and business model innovation: The case of artificial intelligence. *Journal of Open Innovation*, 5(3), 44–56. DOI: 10.3390/joitmc5030044

Lee, M. D. P. (2008). A review of the theories of corporate social responsibility: Its evolutionary path and the road ahead. *International Journal of Management Reviews*, 10(1), 53–73. DOI: 10.1111/j.1468-2370.2007.00226.x

Lombardi, M., Leal, C., & Basso, L. (2010). The activity of Natura from the perspective of sustainable development and of corporate social responsibility. *Management Research*, 8(3), 165–182.

Marin, L., Rubio, A., & De-Maya, S. R. (2012). Competitiveness as a strategic outcome of corporate social responsibility. *Corporate Social Responsibility and Environmental Management*, 19(6), 364–376. DOI: 10.1002/csr.1288

Martin, K. (2019). Ethical implications and accountability of algorithms. [Link]. *Journal of Business Ethics*, 160(4), 835–850. DOI: 10.1007/s10551-018-3921-3

McBarnet, D. (2007). Corporate social responsibility beyond law, through law, for law: the new corporate accountability. In McBarnet, D., Voiculescu, A., & Campbell, T. (Eds.), *The new corporate accountability: corporate social responsibility and the law* (pp. 9–57). Cambridge University Press.

Morkhat, P. M. (2018). Concerning the question about the legal personality of electronic person. *Legal Studies*, 4(1).

Naqvi, A. (2018). How AI and robotics can transform CSR. *Ethical Corporation*. http://www.ethicalcorp.com/how-ai-and-robotics-can-transform-csr

Noorman, M., & Johnson, D. G. (2014). Negotiating autonomy and responsibility in military robots. *Ethics and Information Technology*, 16(1), 51–62. DOI: 10.1007/s10676-013-9335-0

O'Heigeartaigh, S. (2013). Would you hand over a moral decision to a machine? Why not? Moral outsourcing and artificial. http://blog.practicalethics.ox.ac.uk/2013/08/would-youhand-over-a-moral-decision-to-a-machine-why-not-moral-outsourcing-and-artificial-intelligence

Osburg, T., & Lohrmann, C. (2017). *Sustainability in a digital world*. Springer International. DOI: 10.1007/978-3-319-54603-2

Pavaloiu, A., & Kose, U. (2017). Ethical artificial Intelligence – an open question. *Journal of Multidisciplinary Developments*, 2, 15–27.

Pavlou, P. A. (2018). Internet of Things–Will Humans be Replaced or Augmented? *Marketing Intelligence Review*, 10(2), 43–48. DOI: 10.2478/gfkmir-2018-0017

Petrin, M. (2019). Corporate management in the age of AI. *Columbia Business Law Review*, 2019(3), 965–1030.

Rolnick, D., Donti, P. L., Kaack, L. H., Kochanski, K., Lacoste, A., Sankaran, K., Ross, A. S., Nikola, D. M., Natasha, J., Brown, A. W., Luccioni, A. L., Maharaj, T., Sherwin, E. D., & Mukkavilli, S. (2022). Tackling Climate Change with Machine Learning. *ACM Computing Surveys*, 55(2), 1–96. DOI: 10.1145/3485128

Schlenoff, C.I. (2015). IEEE standard ontologies for robotics and automation. IEEE std, 1-60.

Sullins, J. P. (2006). When is a robot a moral agent? *International Journal of Information Ethics*, 6(12), 23–30. DOI: 10.29173/irie136

Wamba, S. F., Gunasekaran, A., Akter, S., Ren, S. J., Dubey, R., & Childe, S. J. (2017). Big data analytics and firm performance: Effects of dynamic capabilities. *Journal of Business Research*, 70, 356–365. DOI: 10.1016/j.jbusres.2016.08.009

Wang, Q., Dou, J., & Jia, S. (2015). A Meta-Analytic Review of Corporate Social Responsibility and Financial Performance: The Moderating Effect of Contextual Factors. *Business & Society*, 1–39. DOI: 10.1177/0007650315584317

Wang, Y., Xiong, M., & Olya, H. (2020). Toward an understanding of responsible artificial intelligence practices. *Proceedings of the 53rd Hawaii International Conference on System Sciences*. DOI: 10.24251/HICSS.2020.610

Yao, X., & Lin, Y. (2020). Ethical implications of artificial intelligence (AI) in supply chain management: A systematic review. *Supply Chain Management*, 25(5), 569–588.

Zhao, J., & Gomez Farinas, B. (2022). Artificial Intelligence and Sustainable Decisions. *European Business Organization Law Review*, 24(1), 1–39. DOI: 10.1007/s40804-022-00262-2

Chapter 5
Impact of Artificial Intelligence in Corporate Social Responsibility:
A Bibliometric Analysis and Literature Review From the Web of Science (WoS)

Ingrid N. Pinto-López
https://orcid.org/0000-0002-1580-1375
UPAEP Universidad, Mexico

Cynthia Maria Montaudon-Tomas
UPAEP Universidad, Mexico

Crishelen Kurezyn-Díaz
https://orcid.org/0000-0003-3902-9209
UPAEP Universidad, Mexico

ABSTRACT

This chapter analyzes the impact of AI in CSR through a bibliometric analysis using the Web of Science. A general overview and a lay of the land of studies that connect AI and CSR are presented, as well as a specific analysis showing the evolution of publications merging both topics, a description of the most relevant publications in the field, the most cited authors, the countries in which most articles have originated, key words, and sponsors, among others. Bibliometric maps that show co-authorship, bibliographic coupling, co-citations, and keywords that allow the analysis of emerging clusters and future trends are done with the software VOS Viewer.

DOI: 10.4018/979-8-3693-3478-2.ch005

INTRODUCTION

Artificial Intelligence (AI) has permeated every aspect of human life, including organizations. Corporate Social Responsibility (CSR) is no exception. Some studies regarding AI and CSR analyze how AI can be used responsibly and whether AI systems can be ethical. They also cover aspects of productivity increases and consider AI as a constructive force that can promote more responsible businesses. Other studies suggest that AI can measure CSR practices in businesses or that digital technologies can be used to implement CSR practices. Additional research analyzes the challenges of CSR in the Industry 4.0 context.

Special interest has been given to novel CSR practices, such as corporate Digital Responsibility (CDR) or AI-CSR, which integrates AI and emerging technologies to promote sustainability and efficiency.

AI-CSR allows organizations to improve and become more efficient in their commitments to CSR from different fronts, including data analysis and decision-making (Vega & Varona, 2024), since it allows them to analyze larger volumes of data and helps develop more informed and sustainable decision-making (Adamkaite et al., 2022). AI has the potential to monitor and optimize the use of resources and analyze specific aspects of CSR, such as the use and reduction of resources and residues. AI can also have a positive impact in promoting equality and transparency in decision-making as well as helping organizations identify and mitigate risks as well as developing more efficient training programs and better and more sustainable selection and recruitment processes (Álvarez & Cepeda, 2024; Shaikh et al., 2022).

The interest in studying the relationship between AI and CSR has grown since the second decade of the 21st century, with even more significant growth in recent years. This becomes evident when analyzing publications in databases such as SCOPUS. and Web of Science (WoS). A search in the SCOPUS database shows that 72.6% of the total publications on this topic have been published from 2020 to 2024; the result for this search in the WoS database is fairly close to 71.5%.

Various studies have been carried out considering the relationship between corporate social responsibility and artificial intelligence from different areas of science; some of the most relevant areas are presented as follows:

- Business and Management (Du & Xie, 2021; Li et al., 2021; Michaels & Grüning, 2017; Chen et al., 2024; Xie et al., 2023; Xiang et al., 2022);
- Computer Science (El Medaker et al., 2024; Desmond & Salama, 2023; Setra, 2021; Carvalho et al., 2019; Minkkinen, 2022)
- Social Sciences (Dauvergne, 2022; Alnamrouti et al., 2022; Krack, 2019; Henderson et al., 2019)

- Economics and Finance (D'Cruz et al., 2022; Du et al., 2023; Huynh et al., 2022; Matytsin et al., 2023; McBride et al., 2022; Watto, et al., 2020)
- Engineering (Damoah et al., 2021; Rab-Kettler & Lehnervp, 2019; Cysneiros & do Prado Leite, 2020)
- Environmental Science (Lu et al., 2019; Abina et al., 2022; Zhao, 2018)
- Arts and Humanities (Saurabh et al., 2022; Srivetbodee & Igel, 2021)
- Among others

Bibliometrics is a methodology that allows for evaluating the influence and impact in terms of the scope and quality of scientific publications based on bibliometric indicators (Pinto-López & Montaudon-Tomas, 2021). This methodology has been used in an important way to analyze the scientific activity in the field of CSR (Zaidi & Azmi, 2024; De Bakker et al., 2005; Feng et al., 2017).

In the field of AI, bibliometric analysis shows great interest in the field, with articles and other publications that show its impact in several areas, such as wastewater treatment (Zhao et al., 2020), medicine and health (Tran et al., 2019); in marketing (Verma et al., 2019). al., 2021); finance (Goodell et al., 2021); the Metaverse (Tlili et al., 2022); robotics (Fernandez et al., 2024); and business management (Patra et al., 2024), among others. However, no reference is identified in the WoS or SCOPUS for any bibliometrics considering analyzing artificial intelligence and corporate social responsibility together.

This article analyzes the impact of AI in CSR through a bibliometric analysis using The Web of Science. A general overview and a lay of the land of studies that connect AI and CSR are presented, as well as a specific analysis showing the evolution of publications merging both topics, a description of the most relevant publications in the field, the most cited authors, the countries in which most articles have originated, key words, countries, sponsors, among others.

Bibliometric maps that show co-authorship, bibliographic coupling, co-citations, and keywords that allow the analysis of emerging clusters and future trends are done with the software VOS Viewer.

MAIN FOCUS OF THE CHAPTER

The objective of this chapter is to exhaustively review the existing literature in the Web of Science database on artificial intelligence and corporate social responsibility based on bibliometric indicators from 2009 to 2023. The goal is to analyze the evolution and current state of research in this field and identify future trends.

METHODOLOGY

The analysis is carried out considering the information contained in the Web of Science database about publications that either in the title, abstract, or keywords contain the terms "artificial intelligence" and "corporate social responsibility." The results that comply with The criteria are analyzed based on bibliometric indicators such as number of publications, citations, most prominent authors in this field, journals, keywords, organizations, universities, sponsors and countries. To complement the analysis, bibliometric maps are also created to identify clusters and proximity relationships by analyzing co-occurrence, co-citations, and bibliographic coupling indicators.

Web of Science (WoS) is a multidisciplinary bibliographic reference database that provides access to Clarivate Analytics electronic collections and allows joint search across all its databases. The WoS Core Collection is the world's leading citation database, containing article records from the world's highest-impact journals, including open-access journals, conference proceedings, and books, and is comprised of ten indexes (WoS, 2024): Science Citation Index Expanded (publication years 1900 to present), Social Sciences Citation Index (publication years 1900 to present), Arts & Humanities Citation Index (publication years 1975 to present), Emerging Sources Citation Index (publication years 2005 to present), Conference Proceedings Citation Index - Science (publication years 1990 to present), Conference Proceedings Citation Index - Social Sciences & Humanities (publication years 1990 to present), Book Citation Index-Science and Social Sciences & Humanities (publication years 2005 to present), Current Chemical Reactions (publication years 1985 to present) and Index Chemicus (publication years 1993 to present)

The process to identify and select the publications to be considered is presented in Figure 1.

Figure 1. Intersection between artificial intelligence and corporate social responsibility

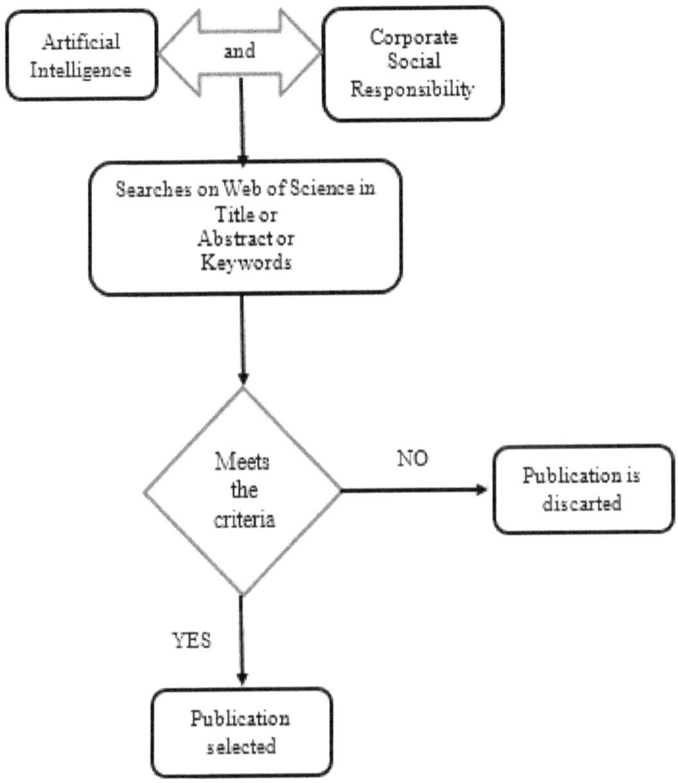

RESULTS AND DISCUSSION

The information was collected from April 1 to April 5, 2024, from the Web of Science (WoS) database. The search considers the intersection of two keywords, "artificial intelligence" and "corporate social responsibility" (Figure 1). The indexes considered in the search are Social Sciences Citation Index (SSCI), Science Citation Index Expanded (SCI-Expanded), Emerging Sources Citation Index (ESCI), Conference Proceedings Citation Index (CPCI-S), Book Citation Index – Social Sciences & Humanities (BKCI-SSH), Book Citation Index – Science (BKCI-S), Arts & Humanities Citation Index (A&HCI) and Conference Proceedings Citation Index – Social Science & Humanities (CPCI – SSH). The results of the bibliometric analysis are presented in the following sections.

Number of Published Articles

In the WoS database, 127 scientific publications related to the words "artificial intelligence" and "corporate social responsibility," of which 42.5% are classified as open access. Of the total publications, 75.6% are articles, 19.7% are proceeding papers, and 4.7% are book chapters.

Figure 2 presents the distribution of publications. Publications on these topics have been identified since the beginning of the 21st century and have maintained a growing trend. From 2020 to 2023, a peak of exponential growth can be observed due to the relevance of these subjects to the COVID-19 pandemic. During this period, 74.01% of the total publications in this field were published.

A division by decades allows us to identify the growth of research in different periods; from 2001 to 2009, 1.5% of the total publications were published; from 2010 to 2019, 24.4%; and from 2020 to March 2024, 74.01%.

Currently, an average of 37 articles are published each year in WoS, and although the number of publications is still incipient, a growing trend is expected for the coming years.

Figure 2. Number of annual publications in WoS since 2009

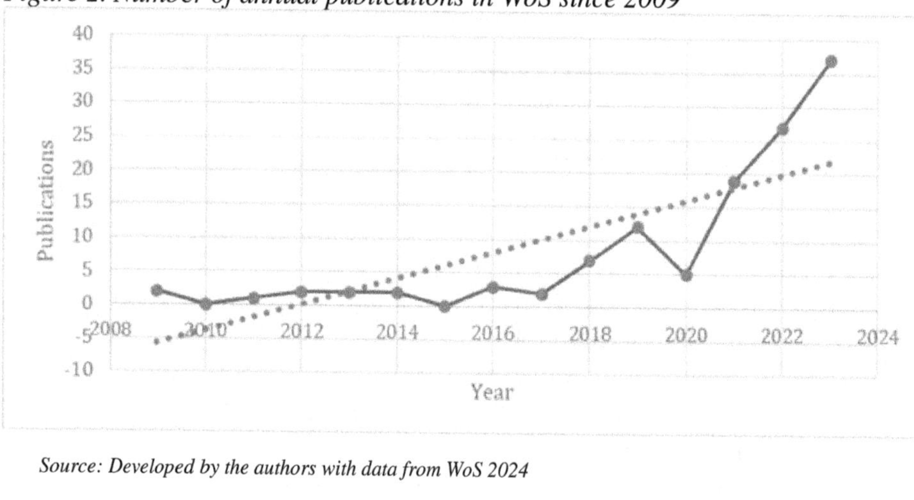

Source: Developed by the authors with data from WoS 2024

Structure of Citations

The number of citations allows one to identify a publication's impact and relevance in the scientific community. From 2009 to 2024, publications on "artificial intelligence" and "corporate social responsibility" added 1,055 citations, with an average of 70.33 citations per year and 8.30 citations per article.

Table 1 shows the details of the articles published by year; it also includes the total citations per article and the number of citations that the publications have reached in different intervals, from 1 to 4, from 5 to 9, from 10 to 24, from 25 to 49 and more than 50 respectively. In the period from 2009 to 2024, 29.9% of publications received between 1 and 4 citations, 16.6% between 5 and 9, 14.17% between 10 and 24, 7.8% between 25 and 49, 3.14% 50 or more citations and 28.3% of publications have not yet been cited.

Figure 3 presents the distribution of citations by year. Likewise, a growing trend is observed. It is important to mention that, as of 2019, citations went from tens to hundreds, and the trend is expected to continue in the next few years.

Table 1. Annual citation structure

Year	Total Publications	Total Cites	≥50	≥25	≥10	≥5	≥1
2009	2	12	-	-	-	1	1
2010	0	-	-	-	-	-	-
2011	1	-	-	-	-	-	-
2012	2	5	-	-	-	-	2
2013	2	10	-	-	-	1	1
2014	2	1	-	-	-	-	1
2015	0	-	-	-	-	-	-
2016	3	2	-	-	-	-	1
2017	2	38	-	1	-	-	1
2018	7	11	-	-	-	2	1
2019	12	105	-	-	6	4	-
2020	5	160	1	2	1	1	-
2021	19	451	3	5	4	3	2
2022	27	196	-	2	6	9	7
2023	37	64	-	-	1	1	21
March 2024	6	-	-	-	-	-	-
Total	**127**	**1055**	**4**	**10**	**18**	**21**	**38**

Source: Developed by the authors with data from WoS 2024. ≥50, ≥25, ≥10, ≥5, ≥1 = Number of papers with equal or more than 50, 25, 10, 5 and 1 citations.

Figure 3. Number of annual citations

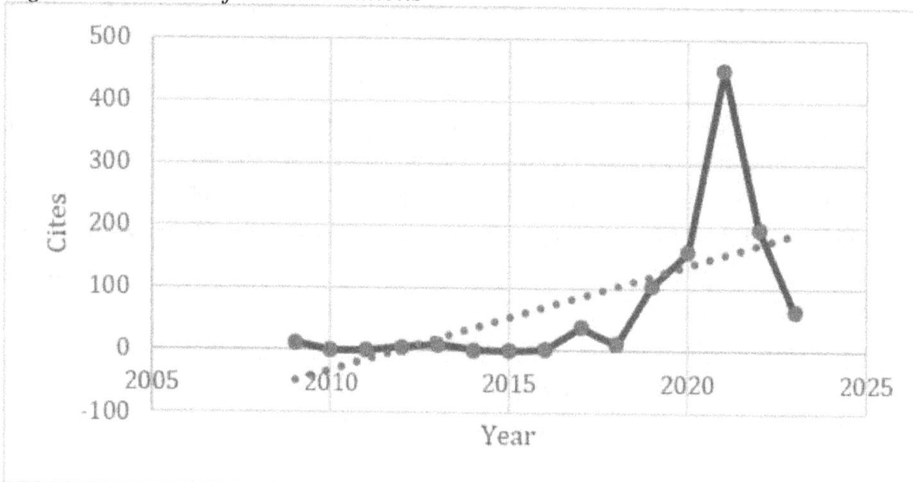

Source: Developed by the authors with data from WoS 2024

The Most Cited Papers in the Field of Artificial Intelligence and Corporate Social Responsibility

The publications with the highest number of citations are distributed in various areas of science, which shows the relevance of these topics in the scientific community. Publications are identified in business, management, green sustainable science, technology, computer science, and environmental science, among others. Table 2 presents the details of the main publications; it also includes authors, journals, year of publication, total citations, and the average number of citations per year.

Figure 4 shows the bibliometric map of co-citations. Eight clusters and their interrelationships are identified. Friedge, Hillman, Aguinis, Dmytriyev, Mcwilliams, Servaes, Hair, Henseler, Godfrey, and Orlitzky, among others, stand out as authors with the highest number of co-citations. Figure 4b shows a closer visualization of the largest cluster.

Table 2. The most cited publications

R	Title	Author/s	Journal	Year	TC	C/Y
1	Does CSR Reduce Idiosyncratic Risk? Roles of Operational Efficiency and AI Innovation	Li, G., Li, N., & Sethi, S.P.	Production and Operations Management	2021	69	23.00
2	Envisioning the future of work to safeguard the safety, health, and well-being of the workforce: A perspective from the CDC's National Institute for Occupational Safety and Health	Tamers, S.L., Streit, J., Pana-Cryan, R., Ray, T., Syron, L., Flynn, M.A., Castillo, D., Roth, G., Geraci, C., Guerin, R., Schulte, P., Henn, S., Chang, C.C., Felknor, S., and Howard, J.	American Journal of Industrial Medicine	2020	65	16.25
3	Paradoxes of artificial intelligence in consumer markets: Ethical challenges and opportunities	Du, S.L., & Xie, C.Y.	Journal of Business Research	2021	64	21.33
4	Do corporate social responsibility practices improve financial performance? A case study of airline companies	Kuo, T.C., Chen, H.M., & Meng, H.M.	Journal of Cleaner Production	2021	50	16.66
5	Is artificial intelligence greening global supply chains? Exposing the political economy of environmental costs	Dauvergne, P.	Review of International Political Economy	2022	47	23.5
6	Artificial intelligence (AI)-enhanced medical drones in the healthcare supply chain (HSC) for sustainability development: A case study	Damoah, I.S., Ayakwah, A., & Tingbani, I.	Journal of Cleaner Production	2021	40	13.33
7	Relationship of corporate social responsibility disclosure on information asymmetry and the cost of capital	Michaels, A., & Grüning, M.	Journal of Management	2017	35	5.00
8	Impact of environmental regulation policy on ecological efficiency in four major urban agglomerations in eastern China	Qin, M., Sun, MX, & Li, J.	Ecological Indicators	2021	35	11.66
9	Industry 4.0 impacts responsible environmental and societal management in the family business	Kazancoglu, Y., Sezer, M.D., Ozkan-Ozen, Y.D., Mangla, S.K., Kumar, A.	Technological Forecasting and Social Change	2021	33	11.00

continued on following page

Table 2. Continued

R	Title	Author/s	Journal	Year	TC	C/Y
10	Artificial Intelligence-enabled environmental sustainability of products: Marketing benefits and their variation by consumer, location, and product types	Frank, B.	Journal of Cleaner Production	2021	33	11.00
11	Corporate Social Responsibility and Social Media: Comparison between Developing and Developed Countries	Stanislavská, L.K., Pilar, L., Margarisová, K., & Kvasnicka, R.	Sustainability	2020	32	8.00
12	A Framework for Evaluating and Disclosing the ESG-Related Impacts of AI with the SDGs	Saetra, H.S.	Sustainability	2021	31	10.33
13	Bad news? Send an AI. Good News? Send a Human	Garvey, A.M., Kim, T., & Duhachek, A.	Journal of Marketing	2023	29	29.00
14	Impacts on the ESG and financial performances of companies in the manufacturing industry based on the climate change-related risks	Chen, H.M., Kuo, T.C., & Chen, J.L.	Journal of Cleaner Production	2022	26	13.00
15	The impact of sustainability on supplier selection: A behavioral study	Zhan, Y.Z., Chung, L., Lim, M.K., Ye, F., Kumar, A., Tan, K.H.	International Journal of Products Economics	2021	22	7.33
16	The future of advertising research: new directions and research needs	Taylor, C.R., & Carlson, L.	Journal of Marketing Theory and Practice	2021	22	7.33
17	Renewing the resource-based view: New contexts, new concepts, and new methods	Helfat, C.E., Kaul, A., Ketchen, D.J., Barney, J.B., Chatain, O., & Singh, H.	Strategic Management Journal	2023	17	17.00
18	Does What Goes Around Really Comes Around? The Mediating Effect of CSR on the Relationship between Transformational Leadership and Employee's Job Performance in Law Firms	Qian, H.D., Bibi, S., Khan, A., Ardito, L., & Nurunnabi, M.	Sustainability	2019	17	3.40

continued on following page

Table 2. Continued

R	Title	Author/s	Journal	Year	TC	C/Y
19	Ethics, responsibility, and sustainability orientation among economics and management masters' students	Delgado, C., Venkatesh, M., Branco, M.C., & Silva, T.	International Journal of Sustainability in Higher Education	2020	16	4.00
20	Off-The-Shelf Artificial Intelligence Technologies for Sentiment and Emotion Analysis: A tutorial on using IBM natural language processing	Carvalho, A., Levitt, A., Levitt, S., Khaddam, E., & Benamati, J.	Communications of the Association for Information Systems	2019	15	3.00

Source: Developed by the authors with data from WoS 2024. Abbreviations: R: Ranking; TC: Total citations; C/Y: Citations per year

Figure 4. Bibliometric mapping of publications co-citations with a threshold of 567 and the 1000 most representative connections

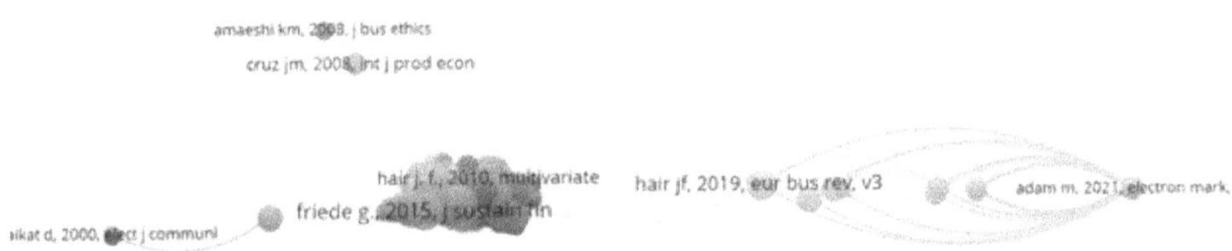

Source: Developed by the authors with data from WoS 2024. To be considered in the result the minimum number of citations of a cited reference is 2.

Figure 4b. Details of the cluster with the most significant number of authors and their interrelationships

Source: Developed by the authors with data from WoS 2024. To be considered in the result, the minimum number of citations of a cited reference is 2.

Keywords

Various keywords are related to "artificial intelligence" and "corporate social responsibility." Figure 5 shows the bibliometric map with the co-occurrence relationship of the keywords. Ten clusters are identified where, besides the keywords artificial intelligence and corporate social responsibility, words such as impact, sustainability, management, financial performance, performance, governance, technology, innovation, ownership, perspective, and ethics, among others, stand out.

Figure 5. Bibliometric mapping of co-occurrence – keywords with a threshold of 162 and the 1000 most representative connections.

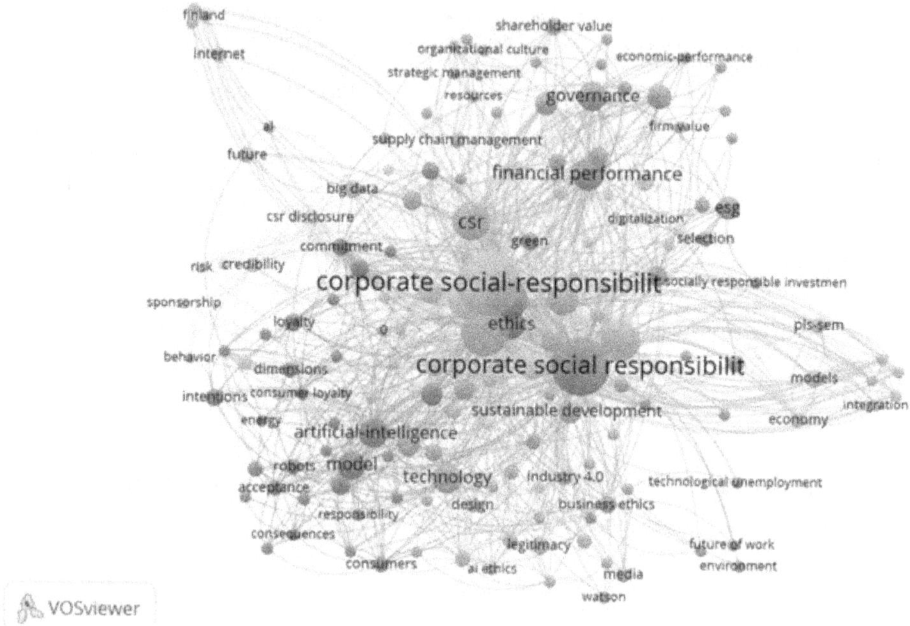

Source: Developed by the authors with data from WoS 2024. The minimum number of occurrences of a keyword to be considered in the result is 2.

The Most Productive Authors in the Field of Artificial Intelligence and Corporate Social Responsibility

Table 3 presents the authors with the highest number of publications. This table also considers the total citations, the average citations per publication, the H-index, and the university where they are currently affiliated, as well as the number of publications that have reached citations between the intervals 1 to 24, 25 to 49, and 50 or more citations.

Figure 6 and Figure 6b present the bibliometric map of the bibliographic coupling – authors relationship that allows identifying the most representative authors in the field of study analyzed and the proximity relationships between them. Eleven clusters are identified as seen in the figures, some of the most important authors due to the impact of their publications are Castillo, D., Chang, C., Felknor, S., Flynn, M., Geraci, C., Guerin, R., Henn, S., Howard, J., Pana-Cryan, R., Ray, T., among others.

Table 3. The most important authors in the field of artificial intelligence & corporate social responsibility research

R	Name	TP	TC	TC/TP	H-index	University	Country	≥ 50	≥ 25	≥ 1
1	Kumar, Ajay	3	62	20.66	20	Emlyon Business School	France	-	1	2
2	Du, Shuili	3	24	8.00	4	University of New Hampshire	USA	-	-	3
3	Ohwada, Hayato	2	-	-	8	Tokyo University of Science	Japan	-	-	-
4	Chen, Hsiao-Min	2	76	38.00	6	Chihlee Univ Technol	Taiwan	1	1	-
5	Kvasnicková Stanislavská, Lucie	2	33	16.50	8	Czech University of Life Sciences Prague	Czech	-	1	1
6	Simina, Lakatos Elena	2	3	1.50	7	Technical University of Cluj - Napoca	Romania	-	-	1
7	Hisjam, Muhammad	2	10	5.00	5	Universitas Sebelas Maret	Indonesia	-	-	2
8	Sutopo, Wahyudi	2	10	5.00	6	Universitas Sebelas Maret	Indonesia	-	-	2
9	Yuniaristanto	2	10	5.00	4	Universitas Sebelas Maret	Indonesia	-	-	2
10	Mou, Yupeng	2	2	1.00	5	China University of Mining & Technology	China	-	-	2
11	Pilar, Ladislav	2	33	16.50	11	Czech University of Life Sciences Prague	Czech	-	1	1
12	Kvasnicka, Roman	2	33	16.50	7	Czech University of Life Sciences Prague	Czech	-	1	1
13	Kuo, Tsai Chi	2	76	38.00	30	National Twain University of Science & Technology	Czech	1	1	-
14	Feng, Ling	2	-	-	19	Tsinghua University	China	-	-	-
15	Yadegari, Reza	2	-	-	2	Islamic Azad University	Iran	-	-	-
16	Kazemi, Bita	2	-	-	-	Islamic Azad University	Iran	-	-	-
17	Dan	2	3	1.50	8	Technical University of Cluj Napoca	Romania	-	-	1

continued on following page

Table 3. Continued

R	Name	TP	TC	TC/TP	H-index	University	Country	≥ 50	≥ 25	≥ 1
18	Gazdac, Roxana Mirela	2	3	1.50	1	Technical University of Cluj Napoca	Romania	-	-	1
19	Bazrkar, Ardeshir	2	-	1.50	6	Islamic Azad University	Iran	-	-	-

Source: Developed by the authors with data from WoS 2024. Only authors who have 2 or more publications are considered in Table 3.

Figure 6. Bibliometric mapping of Bibliographic coupling – authors with a threshold of 111

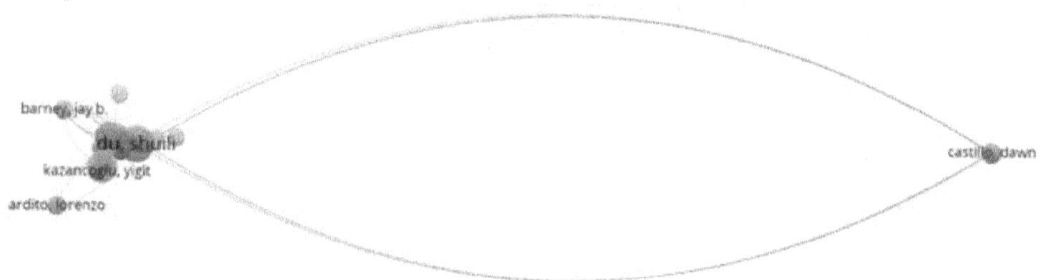

Source: Developed by the authors with data from WoS 2024. To be considered in the result, the maximum number of authors per document is 15; the minimum number of documents of an author is 1 and the minimum number of citations of an author is 10.

Figure 7. Detail of the cluster with the largest number of authors and their inter-relationships

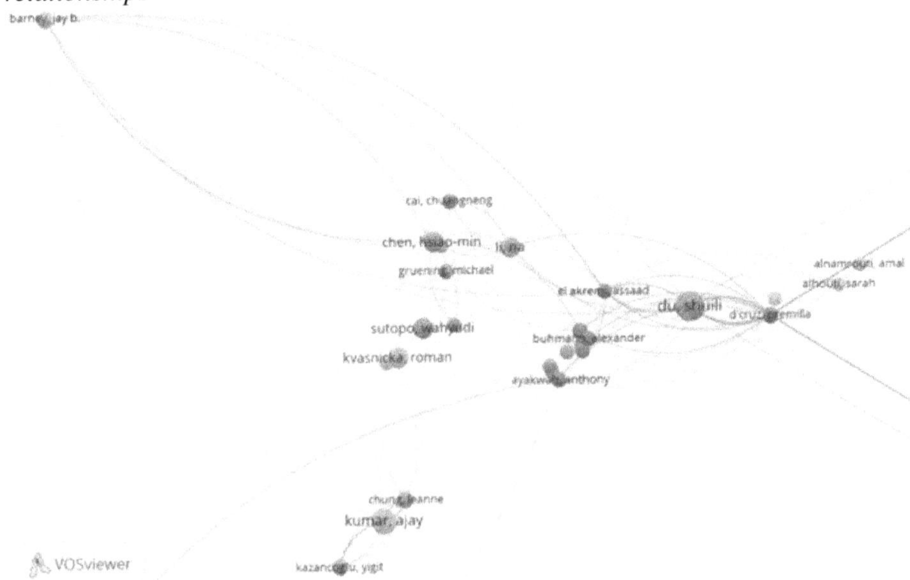

Source: Developed by the authors with data from WoS 2024. To be considered in the result the maximum number of authors per document is 15; the minimum number of documents of an author is 1 and the minimum number of citations of an author is 10.

The Most Influential Journals in the Field of Artificial Intelligence and Corporate Social Responsibility

Various journals publish research carried out in the field of artificial intelligence and corporate social responsibility. Table 4 presents the main journals ordered by number of publications; it also includes the total number of publications (TP), the total citations (TC), the average number of citations per publication (TC/TP), as well as those publications that have reached appointments in the following intervals of 1 to 9, 10 to 24, 25 to 49 and 50 or more appointments.

Figure 7 presents the bibliometric map of the bibliographic coupling -sources relationship that shows the impact of the publications based on the number of citations they reach. Ten clusters are identified. The journals that stand out for their impact are: Sustainability, Corporate Social Responsibility and Environmental Management, Journal of Cleaner Production, Journal of Business Ethics, Journal of Business Research, Technological Forecasting and Social Change, among others.

Table 4. The most important journals in the field of artificial intelligence & corporate social responsibility research

R	Journal	TP	TC	TC/TP	≥50	≥25	≥10	≥1
1	Sustainability	10	113	11.30	-	2	2	4
2	CSR Sustainability Ethics and Governance	4	-	-	-	-	-	-
3	Humanities Social Sciences Communications	4	8	2.00	-	-	-	3
4	Journal of Cleaner Production	4	149	37.25	1	3	-	-
5	Lecture Notes in Artificial Intelligence	4	7	1.75	-	-	-	-1
6	Responsible Artificial Intelligence	4	-	-	-	-	-	-
7	Corporate Social Responsibility and Environmental Management	3	-	-	-	-	-	-
8	Journal of Business Ethics	3	25	8.33	-	-	2	1
9	Journal of Business Research	3	80	26.66	1	-	1	1
10	Lecture Notes in Engineering and Computer Science	3	19	6.33	-	-	-	3
11	Technological Forecasting and Social Change	3	39	13.00	-	1	-	2
12	Asia Pacific Journal of Marketing and Logistics	2	2	1.00	-	-	-	2
13	Chinese Control and Decision Conference	2	1	0.50	-	-	-	1
14	European Journal of Marketing	2	7	3.50	-	-	-	2
15	Proceedings of the 30 TH Chinese Control and Decision Conference 2018 CCDC	2	1	0.50	-	-	-	1
16	Technology in Society	2	12	6.00	-	-	1	1

Source: Developed by authors, based on WoS 2024. Abbreviations: R: Ranking; TP: Total publications; TC: Total citations; TC/TP: Citations per year; 50, ≥25, ≥10, ≥1 = Number of journals with equal or more than 50, 25, 10, and 1 citations.

Figure 8. Bibliometric mapping of Bibliographic coupling – sources with a threshold of 71

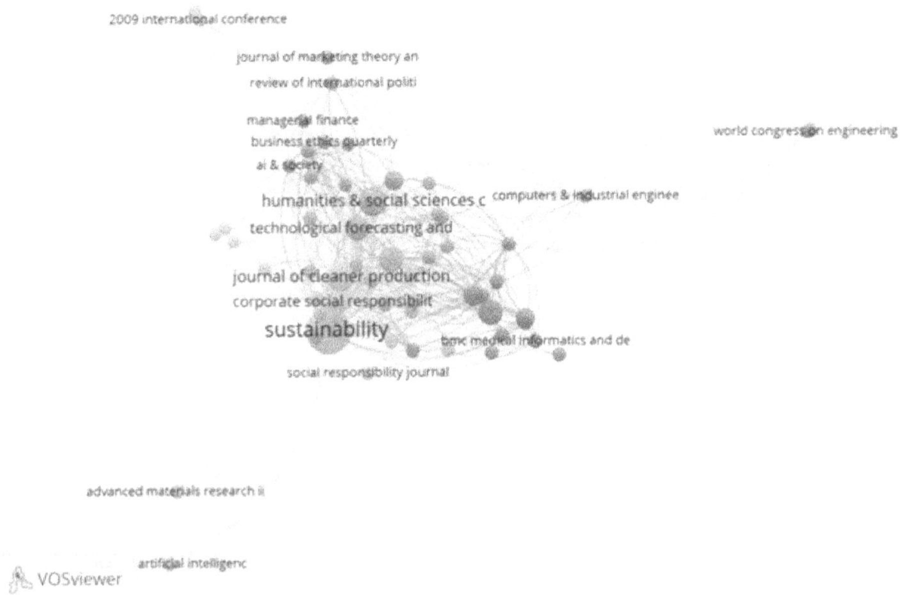

Source: Developed by the authors with data from WoS 2024. To be considered, the minimum number of documents of a source is 1 and the minimum number of citations of a source is 1.

The Most Influential Organizations in the Field of Artificial Intelligence and Corporate Social Responsibility Research

A bibliometric map was created to identify the main organizations in this field with the relationship bibliographic coupling – organizations (Figure 8 and Figure 8b). As seen in Figure 8, there is great interest from various organizations in research in this field, mainly universities. 17 clusters are identified, and the leading organizations are New Hampshire University, Edinburgh University, Cheng Shiu University, Oxford University, Sydney University, Chihlee University, Taiwan University, Sebelas Maret University, Carleton University, Brock University, Mgimo University, Nebraska University, Indian Institute Management Ahmedab, among others.

Table 5 shows a list of the main sponsors that support the development of projects in this field in a very important way. Also included are the total publications (TP), the total citations (TC), the average citations per publication, aandthe number of publications that have reached citations in the following intervals: 1 to 9, 10 to

24, 25 at 49, and 50 or more appointments. A significant participation of Asian organizations is observed, followed by European organizations.

Figure 9. Bibliometric mapping of Bibliographic coupling – organizations with a threshold of 200

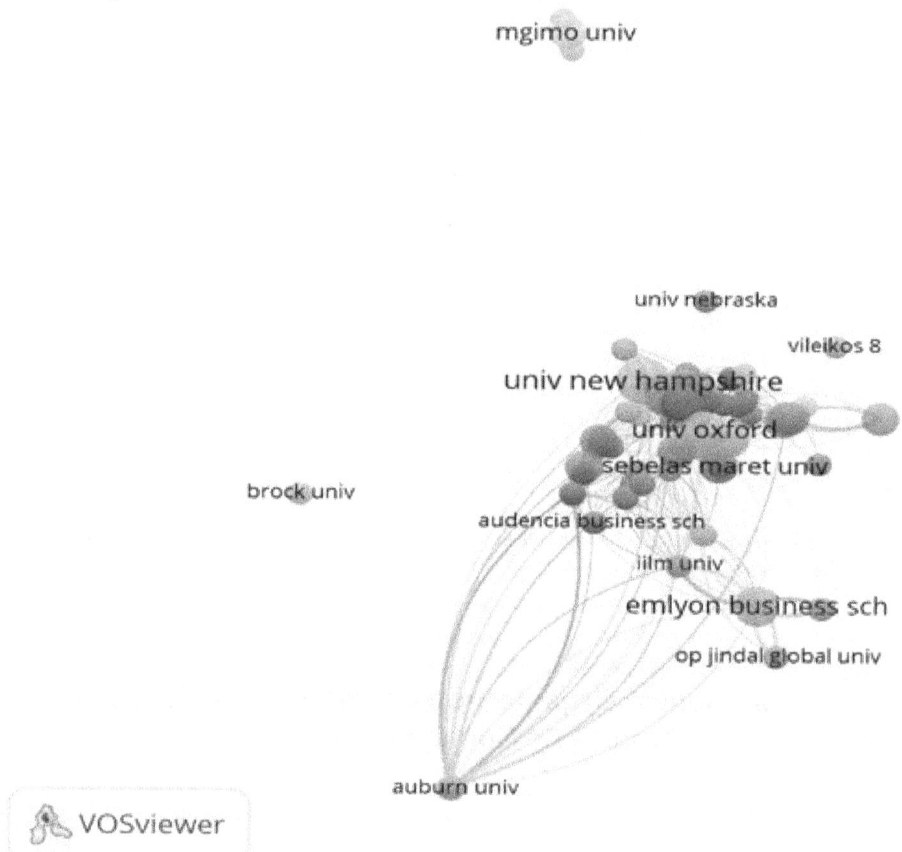

Source: Developed by the authors with data from WoS 2024. The maximum number of organizations per document to be considered is 25.

Figure 10. Bibliographic coupling details – organizations and their relationships

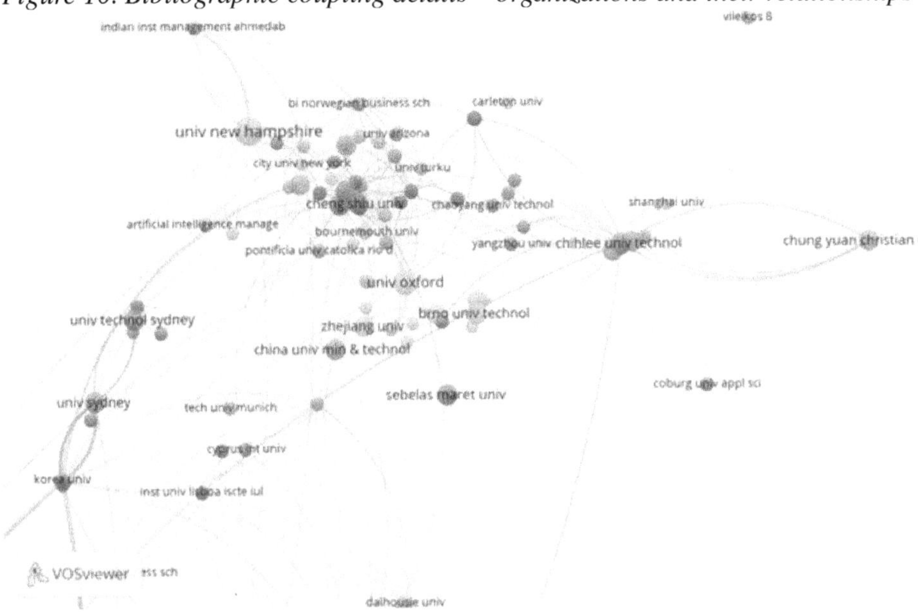

Source: Developed by the authors with data from WoS 2024. The maximum number of organizations per document to be considered is 25.

Table 5. The most important sponsors in the field of artificial intelligence & corporate social responsibility research

R	Sponsor	TP	TC	TC/TP	≥50	≥25	≥10	≥1
1	National Natural Science Foundation of China NSFC	5	95	19.00	1	-	2	2
2	National Office of Philosophy and Social Sciences	3	12	4.00	-	-	1	2
3	European Union EU	2	18	9.00	-	-	1	1
4	Grants in Aid for Scientific Research Kakenhi	2	51	25.50	-	1	1	-
5	Internal Grant Agency IGA of Fem Culs in Prague	2	33	16.50	-	1	-	1
6	Japan Society for the Promotion of Science	2	51	25.50	-	1	1	-
7	Ministry of Education Culture Sports Science and Technology Japan Mext	2	51	25.50	-	1	1	-
8	National Social Science Found of China	2	11	5.50	-	-	-	2

Source: Developed by the authors, based on WoS 2024. Abbreviations: R: Ranking; TP: Total publications; TC: Total citations; TC/TP: Citations per year; 50, ≥25, ≥10, ≥1 = Number of publications with equal or more than 50, 25, 10, and 1 citations.

The Most Influential Countries in the Field of Artificial Intelligence and Corporate Social Responsibility Research

A large number of countries are supporting the development of research in the fields of artificial intelligence and corporate social responsibility. Table 6 shows the countries with the highest number of publications. It also includes the total publications (TP), the total citations (TC), the average citations per publication, and those publications that have reached citations in the intervals of 1 to 9, 10 to 24, 24 to 49, and 50 or more.

Figure 9 shows the bibliographic coupling—countries proximity relationship, with 6 clusters identified, led by China, the USA, Germany, England, Australia, and the Netherlands.

Table 6. The most important countries in the field of artificial intelligence and environmental corporate social responsibility research

R	Country	TP	TC	TC/TP	≥ 50	≥ 25	≥ 10	≥ 1
1	China	29	236	8.13	1	1	6	15
2	USA	25	363	14.52	3	1	7	10
3	England	13	118	9.07	-	1	2	8
4	Germany	12	67	5.58	-	1	1	4
5	Taiwan	12	98	8.16	1	1	-	7
6	France	11	114	10.36	-	1	4	5
7	Australia	9	99	11.00	-	2	1	5
8	Canada	7	79	11.28	-	1	1	5
9	India	5	64	12.80	-	1	1	3
10	Romania	5	6	1.20	-	-	-	2
11	Russia	5	9	1.80	-	-	-	3
12	Czech Republic	4	36	9.00	-	1	-	2
13	Japan	4	33	8.25	-	1	-	
14	Turkey	4	49	12.25	-	1	1	2

Figure 11. Bibliometric mapping of bibliographic coupling – countries with a threshold of 46

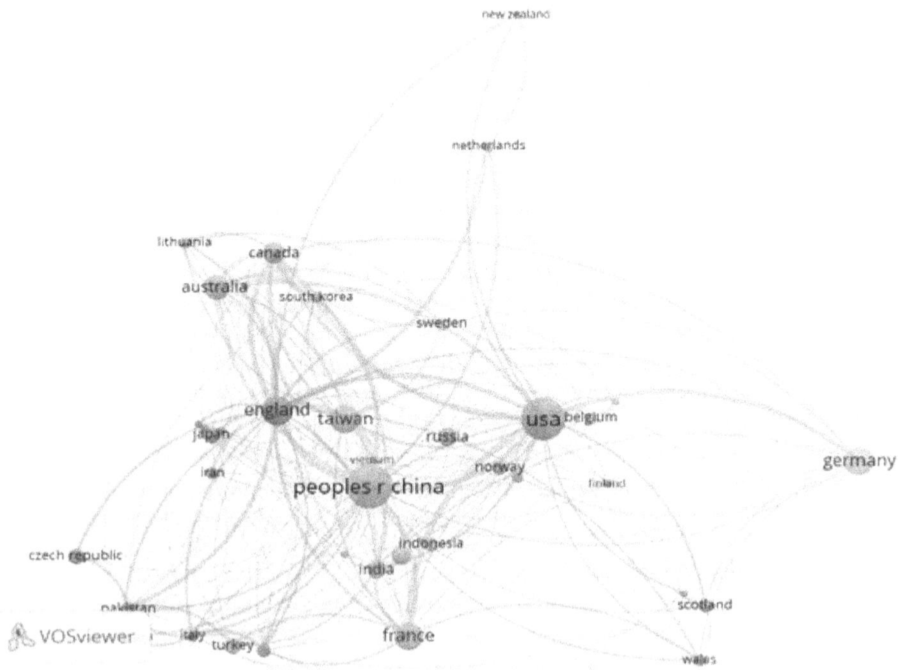

Source: Developed by the authors, based on WoS 2024. To be considered, the maximum number of organizations per document is 25, the minimum number of documents of a country is 1 and the minimum number of citations of a country is 1.

SOLUTIONS AND RECOMMENDATIONS

Bibliometrics is a methodology that enables a robust way to identify the status of publications and the associated elements such as citations, authors, journals, organizations, sponsors, countries, co-citations, co-occurrences, bibliographic coupling, among others. This research analyzes the state of research and publications related to artificial intelligence and corporate social responsibility. The analysis considers 127 scientific documents indexed in the Web of Science database, however, it would be advisable to complement it with information indexed in other databases such as Scopus or Dimensions.

FUTURE RESEARCH DIRECTION

The increase in scientific information indexed in specialized databases has allowed methodologies such as bibliometrics to be widely used in recent decades to measure, based on a set of indicators, the behavior of scientific activity and its future projection, benefiting many people who may or may not be immersed in research activities.

The analysis carried out can be considered as reference material for future research in addition to being a support that allows identifying, for example, interest groups, organizations and related countries, sponsors for project funding, interdisciplinarity, thematic collaboration networks, among others.

CONCLUSION

A bibliometric analysis was carried out to analyze the behavior of publications on artificial intelligence and corporate social responsibility from 2009 to date. Among the most relevant findings is that research in this field is recent, the first references are from 2009, so the research field is relatively new. The number of publications is still incipient, however, a growing trend is observed as of 2020 with an exponential growth in the number of publications, which allows us to consider that it will continue to grow in the coming years. Likewise, the analysis of citations follows a growing trend, so it can be considered that more authors from various areas of science will increasingly reference research in this field. A growing behavior is observed in indicators such as authors, journals, organizations, sponsors and countries, therefore, it is expected that in the coming years significantly more clusters will be developed that contribute to developing research in this field.

REFERENCES

Abina, A., Batkovic, T., Cestnik, B., Kikaj, A., Kovacic, R., Kurbus, M., & Zidansek, A. (2022). Decision support concept for improvement of sustainability-related competences. *Sustainability (Basel)*, 14(14), 8539. DOI: 10.3390/su14148539

Adamkaite, J., Streimikiene, D., & Rudzioniene, K. (2022). *The impact of social responsibility on corporate sfinancial performance in the energy sector: Evidence from Lithuania. Corporate Social Responsibility and Environmental Management.* Wiley. DOI: 10.1002/csr.2340

Alnamrouti, A., Rjoub, H., & Ozgit, H. (2022). Do strategic human resources and artificial intelligence help to make organisations more sustainable? Evidence from non-governamental organisations. *Sustainability (Basel)*, 14(12), 7327. DOI: 10.3390/su14127327

Álvarez, J. C., & Cepeda, L. J. (2024). El impacto de la inteligencia artificial en la enseñanza y el aprendizaje. *LATAM Revista Latinoamericana de Ciencias Sociales y Humanidades*, 5(3). Advance online publication. DOI: 10.56712/latam.v5i3.2061

Carvalho, A., Levitt, A., Levitt, S., Khaddam, E., & Benamati, J. (2019). Off-the-self artificial intelligence technologies for sentiment and emotion analysis: A tutorial on using IBM natural language processing. *Communications of the Association for Information Systems*, 44(1), 918–943. DOI: 10.17705/1CAIS.04443

Chen, P., Chu, Z., & Zhao, M. (2024). The road to corporate sustainability: The importance of artificial intelligence. *Technology in Society*, 76, 102440. DOI: 10.1016/j.techsoc.2023.102440

Córdoba, B. U. (2018). Non-functional requirements orienting the development of socially responsible software. *Lecture Notes in Business Information Processing*, 387, 335–342. DOI: 10.1007/978-3-030-49418-6_23

D'Cruz, P., Du, S., Noronha, E., Parboteeah, K. P., Trittin-Ulbrich, H., & Whelan, G. (2022). Technology, megatrends and work: Thoughts on the future of business ethics. *Journal of Business Ethics*, 180(3), 879–902. DOI: 10.1007/s10551-022-05240-9 PMID: 36212627

Damoah, I. S., Ayakwah, A., & Tingbani, I. (2021). Artificial intelligence (AI)-enhanced medical drones in the healthcare supply chain (HSC) for sustainability development: A case study. *Journal of Cleaner Production*, 328, 129598. DOI: 10.1016/j.jclepro.2021.129598

Dauvergne, P. (2022). Is artificial intelligence greening global supply chains? Exposing the political economy of environmental costs. *Review of International Political Economy*, 29(3), 696–718. DOI: 10.1080/09692290.2020.1814381

De Baker, F. G. A., Groenewegen, P., & Den Hond, F. (2005). A bibliometric analysis of 30 years of research and theory on corporate social responsibility and corporate social performance. *Business & Society*, 44(3), 283–317. DOI: 10.1177/0007650305278086

Desmond, L., & Salama, M. (2023). Integrating Blockchain and emerging technologies for sustainability assurance in the built environment. *IEEE International Conference on Artificial Intelligence, Blockchain, and Internet of Things, AIBThings Proceedings.* DOI: 10.1109/AIBThings58340.2023.10292472

Du, S., El Akremi, A., & Jia, M. (2023). Quantitative research on Corporate Social responsibility: A quest for relevance and rigor in a quickly evolving, turbulent world. *Journal of Business Ethics*, 187(1), 1–15. DOI: 10.1007/s10551-022-05297-6 PMID: 36465988

Du, S., & Xie, C. (2021). Paradoxes of artificial intelligence in consumer markets: Ethical challenges and opportunities. *Journal of Business Research*, 129, 961–974. DOI: 10.1016/j.jbusres.2020.08.024

El Medaker, R., Loukil, S., & McHich, R. (2024). Towards social responsibility 2.0 for Moroccan public establishments and enterprises: Artificial intelligence and new technologies at the service of sustainable development. *Journal of Autonomous Intelligence*, 7(3), 1385. DOI: 10.32629/jai.v7i3.1385

Feng, Y., Zhu, Q., & Lai, K. H. (2017). Corporate social responsibility for supply chain management: A literature review and bibliometric analysis. *Journal of Cleaner Production*, 158, 296–307. DOI: 10.1016/j.jclepro.2017.05.018

Fernandez, D., Dastane, O., Omar, H., & Aman, A. (2024). Robotic process automation: Bibliometric reflection and future opportunities. *European Journal of Innovation Management*, 27(2), 692–712. DOI: 10.1108/EJIM-10-2022-0570

Goodell, J. W., Kumar, S., Lim, W. M., & Pattnaik, D. (2021). Artificial intelligence and machine learning in finance: Identifying foundations, themes, and research cluster from bibliometric analysis. *Journal of Behavioral and Experimental Finance*, 32, 100577. DOI: 10.1016/j.jbef.2021.100577

Henderson, L. H., Wersun, A., Wilson, J., Mo-ching, S., & Zhang, K. (2019). Principles of responsible management education in 2068. *Futures*, 111, 81–89. DOI: 10.1016/j.futures.2019.05.005

Huynh, Q. L., Hoque, M. E., Susanto, P., Watto, W. A., & Ashraf, M. (2022). Does financial leverage mediates corporate governance and firm performance? *Sustainability (Basel)*, 14(20), 13545. DOI: 10.3390/su142013545

Krac, K. (2019). Corporate social responsibility: Humans vs artificial intelligence. *Social Responsibility Journal*, 6(6), 786–802. DOI: 10.1108/SRJ-09-2018-0219

Li, G., Li, N., & Sethi, S. (2021). Does CSR reduce idiosyncratic risk? Roles of operational efficiency and AI innovation. *Production and Operations Management*, 30(7), 2027–2045. DOI: 10.1111/poms.13483

Lu, X., Zhu, W., & Tsai, F. S. (2019). Social responsibility toward the employees and career development sustainability during manufacturing transformation in China. *Sustainability (Basel)*, 11(17), 4778. DOI: 10.3390/su11174778

Matytsin, D. E., Dzedik, V. A., Makeeva, G. A., & Boldyreva, S. B. (2023). "Smart" outsourcing in support of the humanization of entrepreneurship in the artificial intelligence economy. *Humanities & Social Sciences Communications*, 10(1), 13. DOI: 10.1057/s41599-022-01493-x PMID: 36644399

McBride, R., Dastan, A., & Mehrabinia, P. (2022, July 07). How AI affects the future relationship between corporate governance and financial markets: A note on impact capitalism. *Managerial Finance*, 48(8), 1240–1249. DOI: 10.1108/MF-12-2021-0586

Michaels, A., & Grüning, M. (2017). Relationship of corporate social responsibility disclosure on information asymmetry and the cost of capital. *Journal of Management Control*, 28(3), 251–274. DOI: 10.1007/s00187-017-0251-z

Minkkinen, M., Niukkanen, A., & Mantymaki, M. (2022). What about investors? ESG analyses as tools for ethics-based AI auditing. *AI & Society*. Advance online publication. DOI: 10.1007/s00146-022-01415-0

Patra, A. K., Praharaj, A., Sudarshan, D., & Chhatoi, B. P. (2024). AI and business management: Tracking future research agenda through bibliometric network analysis. *Heliyon*, 10(1), e23902. DOI: 10.1016/j.heliyon.2023.e23902 PMID: 38230239

Pinto-López, I. N., & Montaudon-Tomas, C. M. (2021). *Distance Learning: A bibliometric – Based Review in Handbook of Research on Determining the Reliability of Online Assessment and Distance Learning*. IGI Global. DOI: 10.4018/978-1-7998-4769-4.ch003

Rab-Kettler, K., & Lehnervp, B. (2019). Recruitment in the times of Machine Learning. *Management Systems in Production Engineering*, 27(2), 105–109. DOI: 10.1515/mspe-2019-0018

Saetra, H. S. (2021). A framework for evaluating and disclosing the ESG-related impacts of AI with the SDGs. *Sustainability (Basel)*, 13(15), 8503. DOI: 10.3390/su13158503

Saurabh, K., Arora, R., Rani, N., Mishra, D., & Ramkumar, M. (2022). AI led ethical digital transformation: Framework, research, and managerial implications. *Journal of Information. Communication and Ethics in Society*, 20(2), 229–256. DOI: 10.1108/JICES-02-2021-0020

Shaikh, E., Brahmi, M., Thang, P. C., Watto, W. A., Trang, T. T. N., & Loan, N. T. (2022). Should I stay or should I go? explaining the turnover intentions with corporate social responsibility (CSR), organizational identification and organizational commitment. *Sustainability (Basel)*, 14(10), 6030. DOI: 10.3390/su14106030

Srivetbodee, S., & Igel, B. (2021). Digital technology adoption in agriculture: Success factors, obstacles and impact on corporate social responsibility performance in Thailand's smart farming projects. *Thammasat Review,* 24(2), 149-170. DOI: DOI: 10.14456/tureview.2021.22

Tlili, A., Huang, R., Shehata, B., Liu, D., Zhao, J., Metwally, A. H. S., Wang, H., Denden, M., Bozkurt, A., Lee, L. H., Beyoglu, D., Altinay, F., Sharma, R. C., Altinay, Z., Li, Z., Liu, J., Ahmad, F., Hu, Y., Salha, S., & Burgos, D. (2022). Is Metaverse in education a blessing or a curse: A combined content and bibliometric analysis. *Smart Learning Environments*, 9(1), 24. DOI: 10.1186/s40561-022-00205-x

Tran, B. X., Vu, G. T., Ha, G. H., Vuong, Q. H., Ho, M. T., Vuong, T. T., La, V. P., Ho, M. T., Nghiem, K. C. P., Nguyen, H. L. T., Latkin, C. A., Tam, W. W. S., Cheung, N. M., Nguyen, H. K. T., Ho, C. S. H., & Ho, R. C. M. (2019). Global evolution of research in artificial intelligence in health and medicine: A bibliometric study. *Journal of Clinical Medicine*, 8(3), 360. DOI: 10.3390/jcm8030360 PMID: 30875745

Vega, B., & Varona, F. L. (2024). Impacto de la Responsabilidad Social Corporativa en la Gestión ambiental y la Sostenibilidad en los destinos turísticos: Análisis bibliométrico del 2007-2022. *Compendium: Cuadernos de Economía y Administración*, 11(1), 89. Advance online publication. DOI: 10.46677/compendium.v11i1.1227

Verma, S., Sharma, R., Deb, S., & Maitra, D. (2021). Artificial intelligence in Marketing: Systematic review and future research direction. *International Journal of Information Management Data Insights*, 1(1), 100002. DOI: 10.1016/j.jjimei.2020.100002

Watto, W. A., Manurung, D. T., Saputra, K. A. K., & Mustafa, S. G. (2020). Corporate social responsibility and firm financial performance: A case of SME's sector in Pakistan. *International Journal of Environmental, Sustainability, and Social Science*, 1(2), 62–74. DOI: 10.38142/ijesss.v1i2.30

Xiang, H., Shaikh, E., Tunio, M. N., Watto, W. A., & Lyu, Y. (2022). Impact of corporate governance and CEO remuneration on bank capitalization strategies and payout decision in income shocks period. *Frontiers in Psychology*, 13, 901868. DOI: 10.3389/fpsyg.2022.901868 PMID: 36106037

Xie, Y., Ma, W., Ma, Y., Ren, Z., Tong, Z., & Wang, Y. (2023). A counterfactual thinking perspective of moral licensing effect in machine-driven communication: An example of natural language processing chatbot developed based on WeChat API. *Technological Forecasting and Social Change*, 197, 122926. DOI: 10.1016/j.techfore.2023.122926

Zaidi, H., & Azmi, F. T. (2024). Workplace pro-environmental behaviour: A review and bibliometric analysis. *International Journal of Productivity and Performance Management*, 73(1), 158–185. DOI: 10.1108/IJPPM-09-2021-0507

Zhao, L., Dai, T., Qiao, Z., Sun, P., Hao, J., & Yang, Y. (2020). Application of artificial intelligence to wastewater treatment: A bibliometric analysis and systematic review of technology, economy, management, and wastewater reuse. *Process Safety and Environmental Protection*, 133, 169–182. DOI: 10.1016/j.psep.2019.11.014

Zhao, W. W. (2018). How to improve corporate social responsibility in the era of artificial intelligence? *IOP Conference Series. Earth and Environmental Science*, 186(6), 012036. DOI: 10.1088/1755-1315/186/6/012036

Chapter 6
Managing the AI Period's Confluence of Security and Morality

Sabyasachi Pramanik
https://orcid.org/0000-0002-9431-8751
Haldia Institute of Technology, India

ABSTRACT

This chapter examines the complex interplay between ethics and privacy in the context of artificial intelligence (AI). Concerns about data privacy and ethical consequences have grown as AI technology has proliferated. The chapter explores the moral conundrums that result from gathering, analyzing, and using sensitive data, highlighting the need of strong frameworks that strike a compromise between advancing technology and defending individual rights. It looks at the difficulties in preserving privacy in AI-driven systems while abiding by moral standards, providing information on the state of affairs, possible dangers, and viable fixes for building an ethical and open AI ecosystem.

INTRODUCTION

What Privacy and Ethics Mean and How Important Are They in the Context of AI

Given how swiftly technology is advancing and how it blurs the borders between personal data security and ethical issues, privacy and ethics are critical in the context of artificial intelligence (AI) (Robert et al., 2018). In this context, privacy refers to people's fundamental right to control their personal information and make sure AI

DOI: 10.4018/979-8-3693-3478-2.ch006

systems do not intrude upon their private lives. Ethics, on the other hand, refers to the ethical and equitable use of AI to prevent harm and advance society well-being (Floridi et al., 2018). These rules are crucial because they guard against data breaches, algorithmic biases, and potential abuses of AI in monitoring and decision-making. In order to strike a balance between innovation and preserving human rights, promoting confidence in AI systems, and making sure they help rather than damage society, a robust foundation for privacy and ethics is required as AI is infused more and more into everyday life (Floridi & Cowls, 2022).

The significance of these concepts cannot be emphasized enough. Above all, especially in the era of large data and networked systems, they are crucial for protecting secret information and preventing security breaches. Secondly, they are essential in reversing algorithmic prejudices that might encourage discrimination and social injustice. Furthermore, according to Ryan (2020), privacy and ethics are essential for building user confidence, trusting AI systems, and making sure that AI is used to benefit society rather than damage it.

A solid and evolving basis for privacy and ethics is required as artificial intelligence becomes more and more ingrained in everyday life. Such a framework safeguards human rights and interests in addition to guaranteeing that the potential advantages of AI innovation are fully realized while minimizing possible risks and ethical difficulties. In this way, the ethics of privacy and AI promote a more equitable, just, and tranquil cohabitation of modern technology and humans.

B. Background information and significant turning points in the evolution of AI ethics and privacy concerns:

The complex historical background of AI ethics and privacy problems has been impacted by the convergence of ethical criteria and technological breakthroughs (Bonawitz et al., 2017). The early stages of artificial intelligence development in the middle of the 20th century are the source of these concerns. Early AI pioneers like Alan Turing, who established the fundamental ideas of machine intelligence, unwittingly popularized the notion of robots imitating human cognitive capabilities. The development of AI technology in the next decades sparked worries about its ethical and privacy ramifications. Important turning points in this history include the publication of Isaac Asimov's Three Laws of Robotics, which provided an early framework for the ethical obligations of AI, and the development of the first AI systems in the 1950s and 1960s, which raised ethical concerns about the development of intelligent machines.

As debates about the ethics of handling sentient computers intensified, artificial intelligence (AI) advanced further in the 1970s and 1980s (Torrance, 2013). Throughout the 1990s, as the internet and other digital technologies proliferated, privacy concerns gained traction and prompted discussions about data security and monitoring. The rise of social media platforms and the field of machine ethics, which raised issues with algorithmic bias, filter bubbles, and the inappropriate use of personal data, were two significant developments in the early 21st century. The need for ethical standards has grown as a result of the 2018 Cambridge Analytica disaster and the advancement of deep learning techniques.

As these systems continue to develop and permeate more aspects of our lives, we are seeing a tipping point in AI ethics and privacy issues (Formosa et al., 2021). Governments, organizations, and academics are proactively creating regulations and ethical frameworks to address issues including accountability, transparency, equality, and privacy protection (Stahl & Wright, 2018). Finding a method to preserve human values while using AI's boundless potential will take time. In the process, we must ensure that AI systems behave in society's best interests while respecting fundamental ethical and privacy norms, and we must continually adapt to the quickly evolving technical environment.

C. Privacy and ethical issues in AI applications must be addressed

in today's technologically sophisticated world, it is crucial for AI applications to consider ethical and privacy concerns. We must ensure that AI platforms are run ethically and sensibly as they grow more and more integrated into our everyday lives, from social media and healthcare to banking and education. Because AI can manage and analyze massive amounts of personal data, privacy issues are raised. Personal data must be safeguarded against abuse and unauthorized access (Tene & Polonetsky, 2013). Furthermore, ethical concerns play a critical role in determining how AI systems make decisions since biased or discriminatory algorithms have the ability to reinforce stereotypes and perpetuate social injustices. Therefore, going above and beyond just obeying the law is not enough to address these issues in a proactive manner.

COMPREHENDING AI ETHICS AND PRIVACY

Summary of Privacy Issues With Data Gathering and Usage for AI Algorithms

Privacy issues are crucial in the digital era when it comes to the collection and processing of data for AI algorithms (Stahl & Wright, 2018). The increasing reliance of AI systems on massive datasets for development and operation raises a variety of challenges. Data security and privacy are the main concerns, since they include the potential for unauthorized access and data breaches that may expose sensitive personal information (Barona & Anita, 2017). Since information is often gathered without the individuals' knowledge or consent, consent to be informed nevertheless frequently falls short. Data reduction is a crucial concept that shouldn't be overlooked as it may lead to excessive data collection and a greater likelihood of abuse. In some cases, de-identification efforts fail, leaving room for re-identification and putting individual privacy at risk. Bias and discrimination are common problems because unfavorable outcomes may be sustained by skewed training data. People generally have little control over data after it is gathered, and legal and regulatory problems are always evolving. To strike a balance between privacy protection and creativity, it is imperative to find technical, governmental, and moral solutions to these problems (Leenes et al., 2017).

Analyzing the Moral Frameworks and Tenets That Govern the Creation and Use of AI Technologies

AI technologies are developed and implemented based on a set of ethical frameworks and standards to guarantee their proper and ethical usage. Two of these values—fairness and non-discrimination—highlight the need to keep bias and discrimination out of AI systems (Wachter et al., 2020). Explainability and transparency in AI decision-making processes encourage responsibility and transparency. Accountability and responsibility are necessary to decide who is in charge of AI system behavior and to address mistakes or damage. Data security and privacy depend on observing privacy regulations and protecting personal information. The development of environmentally friendly AI is supported by sustainability and environmental impact concerns. Human well-being and goodness emphasize that AI should benefit humanity and improve people's lives (Chaudhary, 2023). Global collaboration and governance prioritize international cooperation and norms. The objective of benefit sharing and equality is to disperse the benefits of AI fairly without exacerbating existing social inequalities. Safety and security are necessary for preventing damage, and ongoing education and observation promote the ethical growth and alterations of AI systems to bring them into compliance with moral standards and societal goals. These rules provide a foundation for the trustworthy and moral development and use of AI.

Investigating How Privacy, Ethics, and AI Meet in Many Fields

In many diverse sectors, artificial intelligence (AI) and privacy are tightly intertwined, posing challenging issues and moral conundrums. In the medical profession, AI aids in diagnosis and therapy, but it also raises concerns over algorithmic fairness and patient data protection (Johnson et al., 2021). Artificial intelligence (AI) is used in finance for credit assessment and fraud detection, however the utilization of sensitive financial data necessitates stringent privacy protection. In the criminal justice system, AI-powered risk assessment and predictive policing have the potential to infringe upon privacy and strengthen stereotypes. AI is utilized by social media and advertising to give customized content and adverts, which has risen questions about algorithmic manipulation and user privacy. AI-driven personalization in education must handle privacy and equity problems. Autonomous vehicles can collect data, but they might also provide moral conundrums when it comes to making judgments in emergency situations. National security uses AI for surveillance, thus there has to be a delicate balancing act between state interests and individual privacy. Retail AI-driven marketing leverages customer data, which raises questions regarding the boundaries between privacy and customization. Ethics must be considered in order to protect ecosystems and public privacy while employing AI for environmental monitoring. AI that monitors workers in the workplace must adhere to ethical and privacy norms. It is crucial to create clear laws and standards that prioritize privacy, transparency, accountability, and ethical assessment in order to facilitate responsible AI research and deployment across all of these areas (Jobin et al., 2019).

THE STATE OF ETHICS AND PRIVACY IN AI TODAY

A Review of the Rules and Policies That Are Now in Place Controlling the Use of AI in Various Sectors

The rapid advancement of artificial intelligence (AI) technology in recent times has prompted legislative initiatives to ensure the responsible and ethical use of AI across several industries. Industry-specific differences in the legal landscape around AI are a reflection of the distinct opportunities and challenges that each one confronts. This section provides a comprehensive examination of the rules and regulations that are in place in significant industries where artificial intelligence is having a significant impact:

1. The Medical Field

The healthcare industry has seen a dramatic transformation since the advent of AI, particularly in fields like medical imaging, drug research, and patient diagnostics. Regulations in this sector aim to strike a compromise between addressing significant ethical and privacy issues and using AI's potential to enhance medical treatment. Notably, stringent rules for safeguarding private patient information have been established by the Health Insurance Portability and Accountability Act (HIPAA) in the US. These standards are being expanded to include AI applications for the processing and storage of medical data as AI becomes more prevalent in the healthcare industry. Furthermore, since the American Medical Association (AMA) and other medical organizations have published ethical standards governing the use of AI, the industry is guided by ethical principles. In the meantime, stringent guidelines are enforced by the European Union's Medical Device Regulation (MDR), which is committed to guaranteeing the effectiveness and safety of medical devices, including software driven by artificial intelligence. Patient consent, transparency, and data security are given a lot of weight under these regulations.

2. Financial Services Industry

The financial services industry has quickly adopted AI, changing activities like fraud detection, algorithmic trading, and customer care. Regulatory bodies now have the vital responsibility of ensuring that artificial intelligence is used ethically in the financial services industry. The Dodd-Frank Act in the US mandates transparency and accountability in the financial markets, which is pertinent to AI applications, particularly in areas like risk management and algorithmic trading, even if it does not expressly address AI. Moreover, certain regulatory bodies, such as the European Union, have enacted laws pertaining specifically to algorithmic trading that give precedence to risk mitigation, market monitoring, and the advancement of equitable competition. The Consumer Financial Protection Bureau (CFPB) releases recommendations that regulate the use of AI in credit underwriting in order to safeguard consumer interests. Justice, openness, and nondiscrimination are principles that are highly valued in these rules.

3. The Vehicle Sector

The development of sophisticated driver-assistance systems and autonomous cars is largely dependent on artificial intelligence. For AI-driven automotive technology to be safe and secure, regulations are essential. When testing and deploying autonomous cars, the National Highway Traffic Safety Administration (NHTSA) in the US establishes criteria that put safety first. In an effort to develop global standards, the UN Economic Commission for Europe (ECE) has concurrently created legislation unique to automated driving systems, with an emphasis on AI-driven components. In response to the incorporation of AI into cars, cybersecurity laws have also been put into place to guard against any cyberthreats and guarantee the integrity and security of linked automobiles.

4. The Utilities and Energy Sector

AI is crucial to the energy and utility industries because it facilitates energy conservation, power grid optimization, and predictive maintenance. Regulations in this area are meant to preserve the reliability and sustainability of AI-powered systems. Notably, the North American Electric Reliability Corporation (NERC), which also establishes reliability standards for the bulk power system in North America, is responsible for establishing cybersecurity legislation that govern AI uses in grid management. The European Network of Transmission System Operators for Electricity (ENTSO-E) has developed guidelines that incorporate AI into grid management to increase operational resilience and efficiency. Technical requirements are not enough; environmental regulations ensure that AI applications in the energy industry promote environmentally responsible energy use and sustainable energy practices.

An Assessment of How Institutions and Decision-Makers Can Guarantee Privacy and Moral AI Practices

AI practices emphasize that everyone has a responsibility to shape the future of artificial intelligence. Organizations are vital in this setting because they must implement comprehensive data governance frameworks, prioritize transparency, and integrate ethical considerations into the AI development process. Data protection and user consent must be the cornerstones of their business practices. On the other hand, legislators play a crucial role in creating and enforcing legislative frameworks that uphold moral norms and ensure privacy in the AI industry. Cooperation and synergy between organizations and politicians are crucial to achieving the delicate balance between technological progress and the preservation of human privacy and ethical standards, which will eventually encourage AI's positive effects.

THE CONSEQUENCES OF AI ETHICS AND PRIVACY

How AI Affects Data Protection and Individual Privacy Rights

Artificial intelligence's impact on data security and individual privacy rights in the modern digital age is complicated and ever-evolving. AI technologies have the ability to enhance data protection on the one hand by automating security operations and allowing more dependable encryption and authentication approaches. But there are also major privacy issues since the same technology may be used to get, analyze, and profit from vast quantities of personal data without consent. Because machine learning algorithms may uncover personal information about individuals, there is potential for abuses such as targeted advertising, intrusive monitoring, and biased decision-making. A major challenge for corporations, governments, and society at large is striking a balance between using the advantages of AI and safeguarding privacy.

The Creation of AI Algorithms and Decision-Making Procedures With Ethical Concerns

AI systems are becoming more and more integrated into several social domains, including healthcare, finance, criminal justice, and autonomous cars. As a result, it is important to carefully evaluate design and implementation methods that prioritize human welfare, equality, accountability, and transparency. The field of AI ethics encompasses a broad variety of issues, including algorithmic transparency, data privacy, accountability, prejudice and discrimination, and the potential for AI to exacerbate or reinforce current injustices. Stakeholders and developers of AI algorithms should endeavor to create algorithms that are impartial, or if bias is present, it should be acknowledged, reduced, and handled appropriately. Transparency is crucial because it builds trust and allows for the scrutiny of AI decision-making processes to ensure that they align with human values. Accountability measures must be implemented in order to hold organizations and developers responsible for the outcomes of AI activity. Data security and privacy must be maintained in order to prevent the improper use of personal information. To move AI toward a more equitable and fair future, ethical considerations should be included into the technology's development process from the beginning.

The Effects of Discriminatory Behaviors and Prejudices Generated by AI on Underprivileged Groups and Society

Discrimination may someday be automated in a number of areas, including lending, employment, criminal justice, and healthcare, since AI systems are commonly trained on data reflecting historical biases and prejudices. Consequently, marginalized populations experience unfair treatment by AI systems and systemic inequities. This not only keeps social inequities alive but also erodes faith in technology and institutions. Furthermore, the secrecy of many AI algorithms makes it difficult to hold them responsible, further marginalizing the people who are affected. To guarantee that AI systems are beneficial to all members of society and eradicate prejudice, a concerted effort must be made to assure fairness, transparency, and equality in AI research and implementation. It also demands that different viewpoints and levels of experience be included.

RESEARCH APPROACHES

Methodology of the Research

1. Survey of the Body of Research on AI Ethics and Privacy, Including Publications, Articles, and Reports

Artificial intelligence (AI) has rapidly permeated every aspect of our life and significantly impacted a wide range of sectors, including finance, healthcare, entertainment, and transportation (Dhanabalan et al., 2018). However, as AI systems become more pervasive in our daily lives, it becomes more important to address the complex issues surrounding AI ethics and privacy. This review of the literature delves into the nuanced facets of this significant topic.

AI ethics covers a broad variety of topics, such as accountability and openness in algorithmic decision-making. The explanation behind the decisions and behaviors of many AI systems is cryptic, frequently referred to as "black boxes," which makes it challenging to understand. This opacity raises concerns about who should be held accountable for accidents and how important it is to design fair, open, and understandable AI systems. Concerns of fairness and prejudice in AI systems have also drawn more attention. There has been much discussion and study on how to lessen bias and ensure fair outcomes as a consequence of AI decision-making systems that discriminate, such as hiring algorithms that favor certain demographic groups (Wachter et al., 2020).

On the other hand, as AI applications proliferate, privacy—a basic human right—becomes more vulnerable. A lot of data—often sensitive data—is needed for AI to function effectively. As AI systems collect, analyze, and use this data, the risk of data breaches and illegal access grows (Mughal, 2017). Consent, the morality of data collection, and the responsible use of personal data are crucial concerns in the age of artificial intelligence. The need of addressing these issues has been further underscored by the Cambridge Analytica event and several data breaches.

From a regulatory standpoint, the legal landscape is evolving to meet these ethical and privacy concerns (Leenes et al., 2017). The European Union's General Data Protection Regulation (GDPR), which levies harsh penalties for noncompliance and establishes stringent data protection processes, is an excellent example. In addition, groups like the Institute of Electrical and Electronics Engineers (IEEE) and the Association for Computing Machinery (ACM) have created AI ethical guidelines to provide a foundation for ethical AI research and use. This study aims to provide readers with a comprehensive grasp of these issues, the evolving legal environment, and the ongoing scholarly discourse around AI ethics and privacy. It highlights how crucial it is to take reasonable regulatory actions and ethical concerns into account in order to safely navigate the AI-driven future.

2. Case Study Examination of Significant Occurrences Involving AI and Privacy Violations

Analyzing well-known incidents involving AI and privacy breaches shows that artificial intelligence has a substantial influence on people's privacy and data security. The Facebook and Cambridge Analytica scandals exposed the unsettling possibility that AI-driven algorithms may acquire vast quantities of personal data without user permission, raising ethical concerns about the use of data and its manipulation for political objectives. The massive Equifax data leak demonstrated that even AI-powered data protection solutions may be susceptible, underscoring the necessity for stringent security regulations and accountability. Deepfake technology, which has long been a source of concern, poses a unique danger since it can be used to create convincingly fake audio and video recordings, which may lead to disinformation, political manipulation, and privacy violations. These case studies demonstrate the ongoing difficulties in fending off changing threats to data security and individual rights, as well as the critical need for transparency, morality, and stringent legislation to protect privacy in the age of artificial intelligence.

3. Conversations With Professionals and Interested Parties in the Fields of AI and Data Privacy

Data privacy and artificial intelligence (AI) are a dynamic and complicated issue that brings together experts and stakeholders from many sectors. As it evolves, this junction presents both enormous potential and challenges. One of the main issues is the ongoing impact of data protection regulations like the CCPA and GDPR, which have affected how companies manage personal data in AI applications. It is still very difficult to strike a balance between data privacy and AI innovation, and ethical dilemmas and biases require ongoing consideration. Some best practices include using technology that protects privacy, ensuring that AI models are transparent and understandable, and providing consumers with control and permission over their data. Collaboration across many sectors is required to address the complex challenges at hand, and public awareness and education initiatives are essential to building a more informed society. In the near future, experts predict significant advances in AI and data privacy, but they also predict new challenges as technology advances. Taking everything into account, navigating this terrain calls for a multimodal approach that protects privacy while maximizing the promise of AI.

THE PRIVACY AND ETHICS FRAMEWORK FOR AI GOVERNANCE IS THE PROPOSED MODEL.

Guidelines for Ethical AI Development and Application

Figure 1. The AI ethics framework

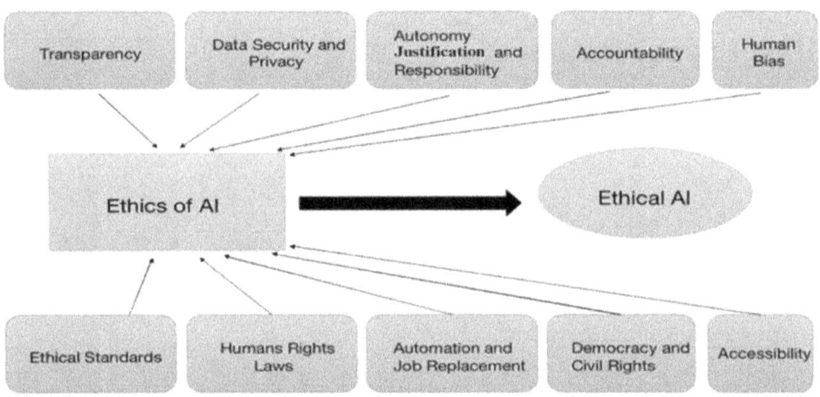

Figure 1 lays out the framework for AI ethics and enumerates the factors that need to be considered in order to define AI ethics and produce ethical AI. While there are many different and sophisticated ways to define AI ethics, it might be challenging to put these ideas into practice and produce ethical AI. Which AI is suitable from a moral standpoint? The fundamental tenet of ethical AI is that it must not harm humans. What damage thus exists? What privileges are available to individuals? It will take a while before we can develop and use moral AI. It need ethical sensitivity training to make morally sound judgments options. Theoretically, AI ought to be able to recognize moral quandaries. If artificial intelligence (AI)

can make judgments, how can we design and develop an AI that understands moral dilemmas? Unfortunately, it is hard to realize and implement. Long-term, consistent work is needed. Still, acknowledging the need of developing moral AI and starting the process cautiously are positive steps in the right way.

Many companies, such as Google, IBM, Microsoft, Accenture, and Atomium-EISMD, have started creating ethical standards to govern the development of AI. The Monetary Authority of Singapore (MAS), Microsoft, and Amazon Web Services proposed the FEAT principles—fairness, ethics, accountability, and transparency—for the use of AI in November 2018. Together, academics, industry professionals, and decision-makers should expand the dialogue in order to set moral guidelines for the creation and use of artificial intelligence.

Techniques for Ensuring Data Security and User Privacy in AI Systems

Figure 2. Suggested approach for ensuring data security and privacy

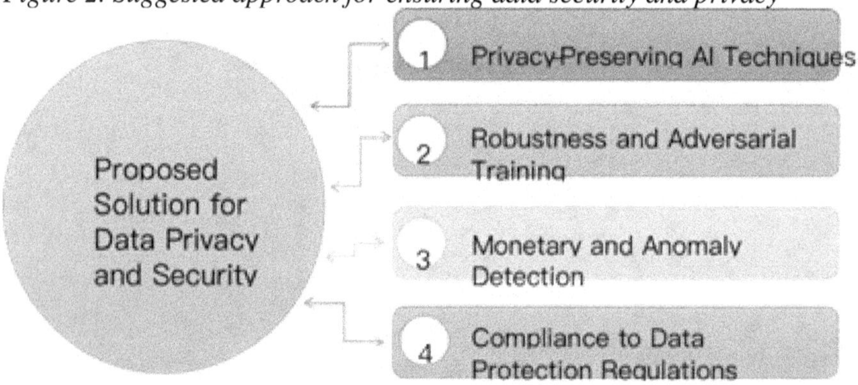

AI Techniques That Preserve Privacy: To solve privacy issues, organizations may utilize AI techniques that preserve privacy, such as federated learning, secure multi-party computing, and homomorphic encryption (Bonawitz et al., 2017). These methods allow companies to train AI models on distributed data without requiring raw data sharing, hence reducing the risk of data breaches or leaks. Researchers have created adversarial training methodologies to improve model resilience and defend against adversarial assaults. According to Madry et al. (2018), these methods include including adversarial samples into a training dataset. By utilizing both clean and adversarial data during training, the model gains tolerance to adversarial perturbations. Monitoring and anomaly detection: Organizations may identify instances of data poisoning and model manipulation by using monitoring and anomaly detection techniques to identify differences in the model's parameters, training set, or performance from anticipated levels (Lewis, 1998). Early discovery may provide valuable information for improving security processes and assist prevent further damage to AI systems adherence to the regulations on data protection: Organizations should follow data protection laws, such as the General Data Protection Regulation (GDPR) in Europe and the California Consumer Privacy Act (CCPA) in the United States, to ensure that they collect, store, and process data in a secure and compliant manner (Ramirez et al., 2022).By abiding by these guidelines, user privacy can be protected and data breaches may be minimized.

Organizations that develop and use AI systems are very concerned about security and privacy of their data. Businesses that are aware of these problems and use mitigation strategies, such robustness training, privacy-preserving AI techniques, and adherence to data protection rules, may enhance the security and privacy of their AI systems. As artificial intelligence (AI) advances and impacts more economic sectors, researchers, practitioners, and policymakers must work together to solve these concerns. Then and only then will we be able to guarantee that AI improves society without endangering user privacy and security.

Recommendations for Handling Moral Conundrums and Prejudices in AI Decision-Making

To address ethical issues and biases in AI decision-making processes, a multifaceted approach is required. When creating and using AI, the protection of human rights, justice, accountability, and transparency should all come first. In this sense, it is essential to first establish unambiguous ethical norms and guidelines. To minimize biases, data collection and training datasets should be representative, varied, and subjected to regular checks to identify and correct possible biases. Businesses and developers need to be open and honest about the data they use and the workings of artificial intelligence. Using fairness metrics, including diverse teams in AI development, and doing continuous testing and monitoring may all help reduce biases. Additionally, there should be protocols for accountability and compensation in the case that AI systems generate biased or inaccurate results. In order to promote responsible AI development and guarantee that ethical concerns stay at the forefront of decision-making processes, collaboration and public participation with ethicists, regulators, and the affected communities are essential.

FINAL THOUGHTS

Synopsis of the Research's Main Conclusions and Revelations

Encouraging ethical AI practices and protecting user privacy need a diverse approach. This entails maintaining stringent rules and regulations that regulate the development and implementation of AI, guaranteeing transparency in AI algorithms, and making sure that user permission for data collection is pertinent. Businesses should prioritize sponsoring AI ethics training for employees, conducting periodic privacy impact studies, and anonymizing and encrypting data. The government, business, and civil society must work together to establish a framework that upholds moral principles, safeguards user privacy, and promotes responsible AI innovation while aggressively addressing any biases and prejudice.

Considering Privacy and Ethics in the Context of AI Development and Legislation Going Forward

As AI research and legislation continue to evolve, safeguarding ethics and privacy must be the primary concern. In order to safeguard individuals and society as a whole, future research should concentrate on developing robust privacy-preserving AI systems that limit data exposure and provide people control over their personal data. To ensure that AI systems uphold the principles of accountability, transparency, and fairness, ethical standards must be established and enforced. To create a responsible and trustworthy AI ecosystem that benefits everyone, cooperation between governments, industry stakeholders, and academia will be crucial in striking a balance between innovation and ethical application.

REFERENCES

Barona, R., & Anita, E. A. M. (2017). A survey on data breach challenges in cloud computing security: Issues and threats. *2017 International Conference on Circuit, Power and Computing Technologies (ICCPCT)*, 1–8. DOI: 10.1109/ICCPCT.2017.8074287

Bonawitz, K., Eichner, H., Grieskamp, W., Huba, D., Ingerman, A., & Ivanov, V. (2017). Towards federated learning at scale: system design arXiv:1902.01046v1

Chaudhary, G. (2023). Environmental Sustainability: Can Artificial Intelligence be an Enabler for SDGs? *Transforming Indian Industries Through Artificial Intelligence*, 9(10), 835–845.

Floridi, L., & Cowls, J. (2022). A unified framework of five principles for AI in society. Machine Learning and the City: Applications in Architecture and Urban Design, 535–545. DOI: 10.1002/9781119815075.ch45

Floridi, L., Cowls, J., Beltrametti, M., Chatila, R., Chazerand, P., Dignum, V., Luetge, C., Madelin, R., Pagallo, U., Rossi, F., Schafer, B., Valcke, P., & Vayena, E. (2018). AI4People—An Ethical Framework for a Good AI Society: Opportunities, Risks, Principles, and Recommendations. *Minds and Machines*, 28(4), 689–707. DOI: 10.1007/s11023-018-9482-5 PMID: 30930541

Formosa, P., Wilson, M., & Richards, D. (2021). A principlist framework for cybersecurity ethics. *Computers & Security*, 109, 102382. DOI: 10.1016/j.cose.2021.102382

Jobin, A., Ienca, M., & Vayena, E. (2019). Artificial Intelligence: the global landscape of ethics guidelines.

Johnson, K. B., Wei, W., Weeraratne, D., Frisse, M. E., Misulis, K., Rhee, K., Zhao, J., & Snowdon, J. L. (2021). Precision Medicine, AI, and the Future of Personalized Health Care. DOI: 10.1111/cts.12884

Leenes, R., Palmerini, E., Koops, B., Bertolini, A., Lucivero, F., Leenes, R., Palmerini, E., Koops, B., & Bertolini, A. (2017). Regulatory challenges of robotics: some guidelines for addressing legal and ethical issues. DOI: 10.1080/17579961.2017.1304921

Lewis, T. (1998). The new economics of information. *IEEE Internet Computing*, 2(5), 93–94. DOI: 10.1109/4236.722237

Madry, A., Markelov, A., Schmidt, L., Tsipras, D., & Vladu, A. (2018). Towards deep learning models resistant to adversarial attacks. 6th International Conference on Learning Representations, ICLR 2018 - Conference Track Proceedings, 1–28.

Mai, J. E. (2016). Big data privacy: The datafication of personal information. *The Information Society*, 32(3), 192–199. DOI: 10.1080/01972243.2016.1153010

Mughal, A. A. (2017). Artificial Intelligence in Information Security: Exploring the Advantages, Challenges, and Future Directions.

Ramirez, M. A., Kim, S.-K., Al Hamadi, H., Damiani, E., Byon, Y.-J., Kim, T.-Y., Cho, C.-S., & Yeun, C. Y. (2022). Poisoning Attacks and Defenses on Artificial Intelligence: A Survey. http://arxiv.org/abs/2202.10276

Ryan, M. (2020). In AI We Trust: Ethics, Artificial Intelligence, and Reliability. *Science and Engineering Ethics*, 26(5), 2749–2767. DOI: 10.1007/s11948-020-00228-y PMID: 32524425

Stahl, B. C., & Wright, D. (2018). Ethics and Privacy in AI and Big Data: Implementing Responsible Research and Innovation. *IEEE Security and Privacy*, 16(3), 26–33. DOI: 10.1109/MSP.2018.2701164

Torrance, S. (2013). Artificial agents and the expanding ethical circle. DOI: 10.1007/s00146-012-0422-2

Chapter 7
The Intersection of Climate Change and Global Health Security

Abdul Samad Dahri
https://orcid.org/0000-0003-4517-3493
Muhammad Ali Jinnah University, Pakistan

Ummi Naiemah Binti Saraih
https://orcid.org/0000-0002-8364-0649
Universiti Malaysia Perlis, Malaysia

Salman Bashir Memon
https://orcid.org/0000-0002-4533-4923
Shaheed Beaniz Bhutto University, Pakistan

Abdul Sami Dahri
Government Degree College University, Pakistan

Muhammad Shahzeb Khan
https://orcid.org/0000-0003-4885-4032
Villa College, Maldives, Maldives

Junaid Rehman
https://orcid.org/0000-0002-3397-5707
Muhammad Ali Jinnah University, Pakistan

Munawar Pahi
PAF Karachi Institute of Economics and Technology, Pakistan

ABSTRACT

This chapter overviews the connection between climate change and the security of the world's health. Malnutrition, waterborne illnesses, and illnesses spread by insects and other animals are just a few of the health problems that are made worse by climate change and pose a serious threat to human health. In addition, the possible direct and indirect effects of climate change are discussed on human health, such as respiratory conditions, heat exhaustion, and issues with mental health. In order to combat impact of climate change on global health security, developed countries must reduce greenhouse gas emissions, offer financial and technical assistance,

DOI: 10.4018/979-8-3693-3478-2.ch007

share their knowledge and expertise and technological resources such as climate monitoring tools and early warning systems.

1. INTRODUCTION

One of the biggest dangers to humanity in the twenty-first century is climate change (Schug et al., 2023). The poor countries will also suffer continuously from climate change (Palinkas & Wong, 2020). Climate change has an impact on many facets of life, including health. Global health security has significantly affected by climate change, and it is increasingly obvious that the two problems are intertwined. This chapter will cover the connection between climate change and the security of the world's health system, the effects of climate change on human health, and potential solutions to these problems.

Climate change is a global challenge that poses a significant hazard to human health security, particularly in developing countries. The effects of climate change on health have been well documented, including increased frequency and severity of extreme weather events, food and water scarcity, and the spread of infectious diseases. Developing countries, which are often the most vulnerable to the impacts of climate change, are particularly at risk due to their limited resources and infrastructure to contend with these challenges (World Health Organization, 2018).

According to the World Health Organization (2018), climate change is expected to cause an additional 250,000 fatalities per year between 2030 and 2050, with developing countries enduring the entirety of this burden. In addition, the economic consequences of climate change for developing countries are projected to be significant, with estimates implying that climate change could reduce GDP by up to 10% in some countries (World Bank, 2016).

The impact of climate change on health in developing countries can be seen in several areas. For example, extreme weather events such as floods and droughts can lead to displacement, food and water shortages, and increased incidence of waterborne diseases. In addition, rising temperatures and variations in rainfall patterns can impact agricultural productivity, leading to malnutrition and food insecurity. Infectious diseases, such as malaria and dengue fever, are also anticipated to increase in prevalence as a consequence of changing climatic conditions (WHO, 2018).

The lack of resources and infrastructure to handle the nexus of climate change and global health security in underdeveloped nations is one of the major concerns. Many poor nations lack enough infrastructure to handle severe weather events and other health effects of climate change, as well as restricted access to healthcare services. The United Nations Development Programme (2018) notes that many poor nations also have a limited ability to adjust to the changing climatic circumstances. This makes them especially sensitive to the consequences of climate change.

Therefore, climate change poses a significant hazard to global health security, particularly in developing countries. The impacts of climate change on health in developing countries are already being felt and are anticipated to increase in severity in the future years. Addressing the convergence of climate change and global health security in developing countries will require significant investments in healthcare services, infrastructure, and capacity development to acclimatize to the changing climate conditions (WHO, 2018).

1.1 Global Health Security and Climate Change

A threat r for the security of the world's health is climate change. Malnutrition, waterborne illnesses, and vector-borne illnesses are some examples of the health issues it exacerbates and creates. Extreme weather events like floods, droughts, and heat waves could become more frequent and intense as a result of climate change (Tschumi & Zscheischler, 2020), which could have both direct and indirect effects on human health. Displacement, food insecurity, and mental health problems are examples of indirect effects.

1.2 Impacts of Climate Change on Human Health

Climate change has a variety of negative effects on human health (Haines, Kovats, Campbell-Lendrum, & Corvalán, 2006). Heat stress, which can result in dehydration, heat exhaustion, and heatstroke, can be brought on by the rise in temperature and humidity (Jardine, 2007). Storms and other extreme weather conditions can cause harm and even death (Greenough, McGeehin, Bernard, Trtanj, Riad, & Engelberg, 2001). Asthma and chronic obstructive pulmonary disease (COPD) are two respiratory illnesses caused by air pollution, which is exacerbated by climate change. By changing the geographic scope and rate of disease transmission, climate change also has an impact on the distribution of vector-borne illnesses like malaria, dengue fever, and the Zika virus (Baylis, 2017).

1.3 Strategies to Address Climate Change and Global Health Security

Combating climate change calls for a multifaceted strategy that includes slashing greenhouse gas emissions, preparing for its effects, and boosting resilience to natural disasters caused by it. Collaboration between the environment and health sectors is necessary to address the effects of climate change on human health (Nigatu, Asamoah, & Kloos, 2014). To address the relationship between climate change and the security of the world's health, some strategies can be used:

1. Supporting eco-friendly development methods that lower greenhouse gas emissions and improve people's health and wellbeing
2. Creating early warning systems and emergency plans to lessen the effects of extreme weather events on people's health.
3. Employing vector control techniques to stop the spread of diseases carried by insects
4. Reducing emissions from transportation and enhancing air quality by utilizing clean energy sources
5. Improving health systems so they can respond to medical emergencies brought on by a changing climate and offer crucial healthcare to those who need it.

1.4 Technological Resources for Developing Countries

The availability of technological resources to assist developing nations are limited (McMichael, Woodruff & Hales, 2006) in addressing the intersection of climate change and international health security may be limited. There are some technological tools, though, that can be helpful in this situation. Among these resources are:

1. Climate monitoring tools: Developing nations can keep tabs on weather patterns, variations in temperature and precipitation, and other climate-related elements that may have an impact on health security by using climate monitoring tools. These tools can assist public health professionals in preparing for and responding to weather-related health risks, such as heat waves, floods, and droughts.
2. Early warning systems: To identify and address disease outbreaks, developing nations can make use of early warning systems. To provide real-time alerts and updates on potential health threats, these systems can use data from public health surveillance networks as well as information from social media and other sources.
    4. Renewable energy technologies: To cut greenhouse gas emissions and increase energy security, developing nations can use renewable energy technologies like solar and wind energy. Additionally, these technologies can aid in supplying dependable and long-lasting power sources for hospitals and other vital infrastructure.
    5. Geographic information systems (GIS): GIS can aid in the mapping and analysis of health data, such as the prevalence of diseases and the distribution of medical resources (Musa, Chiang, Sylk, Bavley, Keating, Lakew, &

Hoven, 2013). This can help pinpoint interventions more successfully and identify regions with the highest health risks.

Therefore, there are still some tools and technologies that can help address the intersection of climate change and global health security, even though developing countries may have few technological resources. By utilizing these resources, developing nations can better anticipate and address the threats to health security posed by climate change.

2. THE ROLE OF DEVELOPED NATIONS

To address the intersection of climate change and global health security and to help developing countries in this regard, developed nations have a crucial role to play (Bell & Masys, 2020). Among the most important measures developed nations can take are:

1. By providing financial and technical support, developed nations can assist developing nations in addressing the effects of climate change on health security. This could involve providing funding for adaptation measures, such as constructing infrastructure that can withstand extreme weather conditions and assisting public health systems in their preparation and response to disease outbreaks.
2. Knowledge and expertise sharing: Developed nations can assist developing nations in enhancing their capacity to address the intersection of health security and climate change. This might entail educating public health professionals and offering them technical support, as well as exchanging best practices for coping with climate change.
3. Cutting greenhouse gas emissions: Because they play a significant role in climate change, developed nations must cut their emissions of these gases. Developed nations can lessen the impact of climate change on developing nations' ability to secure their health by taking steps to reduce emissions.
4. Promoting international collaboration: Developed nations can promote international collaboration on climate change and health security, for example, by joining the World Health Organization and the United Nations Framework Convention on Climate Change. By cooperating, nations can pool their knowledge and resources, plan their responses to the challenges posed by climate change and the security of their health, and improve their overall competitiveness. Accordingly, here are a few particular instances:

a. Technologies for renewable energy, like solar panels and wind turbines, have advanced significantly in developed nations. To help developing nations lessen their reliance on fossil fuels and lessen the negative effects of climate change on health security, these technologies can be easily transferred to them.
b. Development of digital health technologies, such as telemedicine and mobile health applications, has also advanced significantly in developed nations. These technologies can be easily introduced to developing nations to help strengthen public health systems and improve access to healthcare.
c. Advanced climate modeling and monitoring technologies are available in developed nations, and they can be used to track weather patterns, variations in temperature and precipitation, and other climate-related factors. To assist public health officials in preparing for and responding to health risks related to climate change, these technologies are easily transferable to developing nations.
d. Technologies for water purification and sanitation: Developed nations have cutting-edge technologies for water purification and sanitation that can aid developing nations in enhancing access to potable water and sanitary facilities. This can aid in lowering the prevalence of other health risks, such as waterborne illnesses.
e. Advanced hazard detection and response technologies can be easily transferred to developing nations to assist them in detecting and responding to disease outbreaks, natural disasters, and other health emergencies. Examples include early warning systems and emergency response protocols.

Thus, to address the intersection of climate change and global health security, developed countries must play a crucial role. To assist developing countries in addressing the intersection of climate change and global health security, developed nations have access to a variety of technologies that can be easily transferred to developing nations. These technologies can help to increase healthcare access, lessen reliance on fossil fuels, monitor health risks associated with climate change, upgrade water, and sewage systems, and improve hazard detection and response capabilities.

3. CONCLUSION

A multifaceted strategy is necessary to address the important and complex issue of the intersection of climate change and international health security (O'Brien, O'keefe, Rose, & Wisner, 2006). Numerous health risks brought on by climate change include the spread of infectious diseases, severe weather, lack of access to food and water, and problems with mental health. Due to their lack of resources and infrastructure, developing nations are frequently the most susceptible to these risks.

However, some methods and technologies can lessen the effects of climate change on public health. Developed countries have access to a variety of technological resources that can be easily transferred to developing nations (Blakney, 1987), including technologies for hazard detection and response, digital health, water purification and sanitation, climate modeling and monitoring, and renewable energy. These technologies can help to increase healthcare access, lessen reliance on fossil fuels, monitor health risks associated with climate change, upgrade water, and sewage systems, and improve hazard detection and response capabilities (Corvalan et al. 2020).

The intersection of climate change and the security of the world's health can be addressed using both technological resources and policy and planning strategies. Among these strategies could be bolstering public health systems, encouraging climate-resilient agriculture and food systems, enhancing disaster risk reduction and response capabilities, and enhancing urban planning and design. Ensuring the health and well-being of people all over the world requires tackling the intersection of climate change and global health security, which is a difficult and complex task.

REFERENCES

Baylis, M. (2017). Potential impact of climate change on emerging vector-borne and other infections in the UK. *Environmental Health*, 16(1), 45–51. DOI: 10.1186/s12940-017-0326-1 PMID: 29219091

Bell, C., & Masys, A. J. (2020). Climate change, extreme weather events and global health security a lens into vulnerabilities. *Global health security: Recognizing vulnerabilities, creating opportunities*, 59-78.

Blakney, M. (1987). Transfer of technology and developing nations. *Fordham Int'l LJ*, 11, 689.

CGAP. (2019). Harnessing the Power of Data for Financial Inclusion. Retrieved from https://www.cgap.org/research/publication/harnessing-power-data-financial-inclusion

Corvalan, C., Villalobos Prats, E., Sena, A., Campbell-Lendrum, D., Karliner, J., Risso, A., Wilburn, S., Slotterback, S., Rathi, M., Stringer, R., Berry, P., Edwards, S., Enright, P., Hayter, A., Howard, G., Lapitan, J., Montgomery, M., Prüss-Ustün, A., Varangu, L., & Vinci, S. (2020). Towards climate resilient and environmentally sustainable health care facilities. *International Journal of Environmental Research and Public Health*, 17(23), 8849. DOI: 10.3390/ijerph17238849 PMID: 33260752

Greenough, G., McGeehin, M., Bernard, S. M., Trtanj, J., Riad, J., & Engelberg, D. (2001). The potential impacts of climate variability and change on health impacts of extreme weather events in the United States. *Environmental Health Perspectives*, 109(suppl 2), 191–198. PMID: 11359686

GSMA. (2020). State of Mobile Internet Connectivity 2020. Retrieved from https://www.gsma.com/mobilefordevelopment/resources/state-of-mobile-internet-connectivity-2020/

Haines, A., Kovats, R. S., Campbell-Lendrum, D., & Corvalán, C. (2006). Climate change and human health: Impacts, vulnerability and public health. *Public Health*, 120(7), 585–596. DOI: 10.1016/j.puhe.2006.01.002 PMID: 16542689

ITU. (2019). Measuring the Information Society Report 2019. Retrieved from https://www.itu.int/en/ITU /Statistics/Documents/publications/misr2019/MISR2019_Volume1.pdf

Jardine, D. S. (2007). Heat illness and heat stroke. *Pediatrics*, 28(7), 249–258. PMID: 17601937

McMichael, A. J., Woodruff, R. E., & Hales, S. (2006). Climate change and human health: Present and future risks. *Lancet*, 367(9513), 859–869. DOI: 10.1016/S0140-6736(06)68079-3 PMID: 16530580

Musa, G. J., Chiang, P. H., Sylk, T., Bavley, R., Keating, W., Lakew, B., ... Hoven, C. W. (2013). Use of GIS mapping as a public health tool--from cholera to cancer. *Health Services Insights, 6*, HSI-S10471.

Nigatu, A. S., Asamoah, B. O., & Kloos, H. (2014). Knowledge and perceptions about the health impact of climate change among health sciences students in Ethiopia: A cross-sectional study. *BMC Public Health*, 14(1), 1–10. DOI: 10.1186/1471-2458-14-587 PMID: 24916631

O'Brien, G., O'keefe, P., Rose, J., & Wisner, B. (2006). Climate change and disaster management. *Disasters*, 30(1), 64–80. DOI: 10.1111/j.1467-9523.2006.00307.x PMID: 16512862

Palinkas, L. A., & Wong, M. (2020). Global climate change and mental health. *Current Opinion in Psychology*, 32, 12–16. DOI: 10.1016/j.copsyc.2019.06.023 PMID: 31349129

Robbins Schug, G., Buikstra, J. E., DeWitte, S. N., Baker, B. J., Berger, E., Buzon, M. R., Davies-Barrett, A. M., Goldstein, L., Grauer, A. L., Gregoricka, L. A., Halcrow, S. E., Knudson, K. J., Larsen, C. S., Martin, D. L., Nystrom, K. C., Perry, M. A., Roberts, C. A., Santos, A. L., Stojanowski, C. M., & Zakrzewski, S. R. (2023). Climate change, human health, and resilience in the Holocene. *Proceedings of the National Academy of Sciences of the United States of America*, 120(4), e2209472120. DOI: 10.1073/pnas.2209472120 PMID: 36649426

Tschumi, E., & Zscheischler, J. (2020). Countrywide climate features during recorded climate-related disasters. *Climatic Change*, 158(3-4), 593–609. DOI: 10.1007/s10584-019-02556-w PMID: 32165774

United Nations Development Programme. (2018). Climate change and human development. Retrieved from https://www.undp.org/content/undp/en/home/librarypage/climate-and-disaster-resilience-/climate-change-and-human-development.html

World Bank. (2016). Shock waves: Managing the impacts of climate change on poverty. Retrieved from https://openknowledge.worldbank.org/handle/10986/22787

World Bank. (2018). The Global Findex Database 2017: Measuring Financial Inclusion and the Fintech Revolution. Retrieved from https://globalfindex.worldbank.org/sites/globalfindex/files /2018-04/2017%20Findex%20full%20report_0.pdf

World Economic Forum. (2021). Inclusive Growth and Development Report 2017. Retrieved from http://www3.weforum.org/docs/WEF_Forum_IncGrwth_2017.pdf

World Health Organization. (2018). Climate change and health. Retrieved from https://www.who.int/news-room/fact-sheets/detail/climate-change-and-health

Chapter 8

Consumer Skepticism Towards CSR Communication: Role of Content and Delivery

Pravin Chandra Singh
https://orcid.org/0000-0002-6002-0703
MSMSR, MATS University, Raipur, India

Usha Srivastava
MSMSR, MATS University, Raipur, India

Sujay Vikram Singh
https://orcid.org/0000-0002-7113-2698
Banaras Hindu University, India

Kuldeep Singh
https://orcid.org/0000-0002-7999-1585
Amity University, Gurugram, India

Kumari Neelam
Mahatma Gandhi Kashi Vidyapith, Varanasi, India

Pankaj Kumar
United University, Prayagraj, India

ABSTRACT

Over the past few years, there has been an apparent surge in the application of corporate social responsibility (CSR) advertising by companies to convey their dedication to social and environmental causes. However, this trend has also sparked increasing doubt among consumers about the credibility and impact of CSR advertisements. This study seeks to explore the impact of content and delivery on consumer skepticism towards CSR advertisements. This study identifies key components of CSR communication (content and delivery) and specific variables within each (company-CSR fit, consumer-CSR fit for content, self-promotional tone, inauthentic information for delivery). It confirms the significant impact of these variables on consumer skepticism towards CSR communications, suggesting that

DOI: 10.4018/979-8-3693-3478-2.ch008

aligning company-CSR fit can mitigate skepticism. Consumers are skeptical of CSR motives when there's a gap between company claims and actions. By focusing on content and delivery, practitioners can mitigate skepticism and shape perceptions of corporate responsibility.

1. INTRODUCTION

Organizations use resources that are owned by society; hence it is required of them to operate in a sustainable way and to contribute to the sustainability and preservation of these resources which has also been imbibed in traditional Indian businesses since time immemorial. In keeping with this philosophy, governments everywhere have been enforcing various policies to enhance business conduct to encourage greater accountability, disclosures, and transparency. In India CSR provision enshrined under section 135, of Companies Act 2013, being a unique provision of law, listed India amongst one of the few countries in the world where CSR is mandated under the Statute. The goal of CSR is achieving economic, social, and environmental sustainability not just incorporating the provisions (Lii *et al.*, 2013). The hypocrisy of corporates CSR activities, and the paradox between the nature of philanthropy and the utilitarian business objectives have increased CSR skepticism (Dalal, 2020). Due to heightened levels of consumer skepticism, it has become crucial for many companies to discern what corporate social responsibility (CSR) activities to undertake and how to deliver CSR-related information to consumers (Turker *et al.*, 2023). Consumer skepticism in CSR (Corporate Social Responsibility) communication refers to the tendency of consumers to doubt or question the authenticity, sincerity, or effectiveness of the social or environmental initiatives communicated by companies (Kim & Rim, 2024). CSR communication is not merely valuable but crucial for a company that wishes to create lasting relationships with consumers and establish consumer preference for and loyalty to the company (Moreno & Kang, 2020).Various studies on CSR skepticism conceptualization has been done and measured with publics' inclination to question, disbelieve, and distrust an organization's CSR motives, communication and activity, and informativeness without the consideration of pre-dispositional traits such as cynicism toward business and management (Rim & Kim, 2016). A company identifies the activities which are provided in the provisions like schedule VII of Indian Company Act, 2013 to spend their CSR. Even if the company choose the correct delivery and content of their CSR communication, it remains a challenge for the company to building up their image towards their contribution in that area without skepticism. From the above discussions it is evident that CSR communication is significant factors which creates a distinct image of enterprise. it also leads to skepticism reason being perception of consumers are not aligned with CSR communication of enterprises, they think that enterprises are doing CSR to sell their product or services rather than overall societal development. Thus, the purpose of this study is to examine the role of content and delivery in skepticism towards CSR communication.

2. THEORETICAL BACKGROUND

Since CSR communication is a comparatively new field of study, information processing requirements must be met to dispel the ambiguity surrounding the use of CSR communications by companies (Busse *et al.*, 2017). The present study utilises a theoretical framework that combines (Galbraith, 1974) and (Miller, 1956) information processing theories (IPTs). This choice is made because IPTs specifically address the information processing requirements of consumers and how a company can meet these requirements. Additionally, IPTs examine how consumers process the information conveyed in communication messages. In the context of marketing, IPT signifies that consumer behaviour is influenced not only by the information per se but also by the cognitive processes that consumers employ in relation to the information they obtain (Tybout *et al.*, 1981). IPT provides the benefit of not overly restricting the determinants of behaviour to particular characteristics or attitudes; rather, it places greater emphasis on the precise mechanisms through which consumers encode, evaluate, and link the information that is presented to them. When IPT is applied to CSR communication, consideration is given to how consumers acquire, interpret, and integrate both the content and delivery of CSR messages. Consumer-CSR fit and company-CSR fit, as they pertain to the content of CSR practices as depicted in CSR communication, are focal points of the current study. The manner in which inauthentic information and a self-promotional tone are conveyed to consumers influences their retention of that content in their memories, which can be used to assess the effectiveness of a particular CSR message in the future. Thus, the manner in which consumers encode the messages they receive and evaluate the CSR activity portrayed in those messages is influenced by both the content and delivery (Line *et al.*, 2016). The manner in which consumers assess the components of a company's CSR communications, including content and delivery, is likely to impact the level of scepticism they attribute to the company's overall corporate responsibility.

3. CONSUMER SKEPTICISM TOWARDS CSR COMMUNICATION

The presence of skepticism in the CSR literature is not a novel idea, as noted by (Jacques, 2005). Prior studies on this subject encompass various areas of investigation, including the impact of consumer attributions on skepticism towards corporate social responsibility (CSR) (Skarmeas & Leonidou, 2013), the influence of consumer-specific factors on skepticism towards green communication (Do Paço & Reis, 2012), the role of CSR skepticism in shaping perceptions of a company's CSR commitments during different types of crises (Ham & Kim, 2020), and the effects of consumer skepticism on consumer response to environmental claim (Mohr & Ellen, 1998). Exploring skepticism via the lens of CSR communications has been infrequent and recently introduced. There is a newly published study that examines how consumer skepticism towards a company's generosity might be reduced through corporate social responsibility (CSR) communication (Kim, 2019). However, their study focused solely on the aspects of CSR communication and did not take into account the actual content of CSR practices. In contrast to prior research on skepticism, our study examines CSR communication as a dual-component process in which both content and delivery might exhibit diverse, or even. The contradicting consequences influence the level of skepticism that consumers have towards corporate responsibility in general. Understanding the mechanics of corporate social responsibility (CSR) communication in successfully building trust between a firm and its consumers is vital when addressing skepticism (Park & Kim, 2019). According to (Park & Kim, 2019), customer-business loyalty can flourish when buyers believe a firm is totally dedicated to corporate social responsibility. Also, other skepticism-inducing elements, such as corporate hypocrisy and distrust in companies, have been studied in connection to CSR (Hur *et al.*, 2016). Corporate hypocrisy happens when a company's real CSR efforts don't match up with its stated ones, and consumer distrust happens when companies fail to live up to their customers' expectations (Hur *et al.*, 2016). In conclusion, doubt regarding corporate responsibility might stem from a lack of faith in a corporation, contribute skepticism of a firm, or corporate hypocrisy.

4. LITERATURE REVIEW AND HYPOTHESIS DEVELOPMENT

4.1. Company-CSR Fit

Ensuring a strong alignment between a company's core principles and the effective dissemination of its Corporate Social Responsibility (CSR) initiatives is crucial for multiple reasons. (de Jong & van der Meer, 2017) assert that CSR communication significantly contributes to establishing a sense of congruity between the company and its CSR initiatives in the perception of consumers. Prior studies suggest that the success of corporate social responsibility (CSR) is greatly dependent on the degree of alignment between the firm and CSR initiatives, which frequently results in favourable assessments from consumers (Ramesh *et al.*, 2019). Aligning a company's CSR initiatives with its basic beliefs is crucial in fostering consumer confidence that these practices are not merely driven by publicity or self-interest (del Mar García-De los Salmones & Perez, 2018). An optimal alignment between a firm and its corporate social responsibility (CSR) could reduce a consumer's scepticism by decreasing the amount of information processing required for the consumer to discover a company's CSR efforts. When a CSR action aligns with a company's core beliefs, consumers are more likely to trust the company's motives and associate the positive qualities of the CSR activity with the brand; if not then consumer will see it negatively (Yoo & Lee, 2018). Therefore, if there is a lack of alignment between the company and the CSR activity in a particular communication, it may cause a consumer to have doubts about the company's overall commitment to corporate responsibility. If a consumer perceives a mismatch between a company's principles, ethics, or business goals and its attempts to participate in corporate social responsibility (CSR), the consumer's level of scepticism is likely to rise (Ellen *et al.*, 2006). The results of Garcia-Jiménez *et al.*'s (2017) study align with this finding, suggesting that scepticism plays a moderating role in the relationship between company-CSR fit and CSR-related behaviours. The study also emphasises the positive impact of company-CSR fit on consumers' behaviour, particularly when customers exhibit lower levels of scepticism. The alignment between a company's CSR initiatives and its core values can mitigate consumer skepticism, fostering trust and positive perceptions among consumers. Nevertheless, in cases where there are perceived inconsistencies or discrepancies between a company's CSR efforts and its actual practices, it is possible for consumer skepticism to emerge. This can potentially undermine the effectiveness of CSR communication strategies (Lim & Lee, 2023).

By aligning a company's fundamental principles with its corporate social responsibility initiatives, it is probable that consumer doubt concerning the company's ethical standards and accountability will decrease. We can say that company-CSR fit will alleviate the skepticism. Thus, from the following discussions following hypothesis has formulated.

H1. There is a significant positive relationship between company-CSR fit and skepticism towards CSR communications.

4.2. Consumer-CSR Fit

The correlation between a company's corporate social responsibility (CSR) initiatives and consumers is vital in building trust. Consumers must not only perceive a correlation between the firm and its CSR initiatives, but they also need to feel a personal connection to a specific CSR activity (Schmeltz, 2017). According to (Currás-Pérez *et al.*, 2018), CSR is linked to human traits such as cultural and social preferences, and can strongly indicate how individuals react to specific CSR initiatives. Consumers' perception of the alignment between a company's CSR activity and their personal values, goals, and morals, known as consumer-CSR fit, is believed to strongly influence their level of scepticism towards a company's overall corporate responsibility. For a company's CSR effort to have a significant impact on a consumer's opinion of the company's actions, it must be personally meaningful to the consumer (Schmeltz, 2017).

(Currás-Pérez *et al.*, 2018) discovered that a consumer's holistic perspective of corporate social responsibility (CSR) is directly connected to their emotional response towards a particular CSR initiative. Therefore, when customers have an emotional bond with a company that participates in a CSR initiative that holds significance for them, they are less inclined to become sceptical about the firm due to the personal connection they build with the initiative (Ramesh *et al.*, 2019; Rim *et al.*, 2024). Research suggests that consumer skepticism can differ among cultures, as it is shaped by cultural values, norms, and perceptions of corporate conduct. It is crucial for researchers to understand cultural differences in order to effectively address and mitigate consumer skepticism in diverse markets (Park, 2022). This requires the development of tailored communication strategies and engagement approaches by companies (Kang & Atkinson, 2021). We can say that consumer-CSR fit will alleviate the skepticism. From the above discussions following hypothesis has formulated.

H2. There is a significant positive relationship between consumer-CSR fit and skepticism towards CSR communications.

4.3. Inauthentic Information

In this study, the term "inauthentic information" refers to customers' hesitancy to believe the genuineness of corporate social responsibility (CSR) information presented by a corporation. Consumers' perception of a company's CSR involvement is greatly influenced by the company's effective communication of its activities, providing relevant and timely information that is easily accessible and comprehensible to consumers. Currently, Corporate Social Responsibility (CSR) information is disseminated through several channels such as news stories, blogs, company websites, word-of-mouth (WOM), and social media platforms (Diddi & Niehm, 2016). The rapid spread of information through new communication channels has increased customers' understanding and recognition of the significance of getting information about a company's CSR activities (Diddi & Niehm, 2016). Furthermore, it is crucial to note that simply sharing information is not enough to confirm a company's involvement in CSR activities (Ramesh *et al.*, 2019). The widespread dissemination of unfavourable information regarding a company's corporate responsibility might result in consumer scepticism and even mistrust. Corporate social responsibility (CSR) communications should be based on verifiable facts and delivered in a clear and transparent manner, with the aim of providing consumers with reliable information (Schmeltz, 2012). Having access to reliable information about a company's actions is crucial for accurately assessing its level of commitment to corporate social responsibility (CSR). In today's information age, where there is an overwhelming amount of data from various sources of varying reliability, the need for easily accessible and trustworthy information is more critical than ever. Consumer skepticism often arises in response to inauthentic information presented by companies, leading consumers to question the sincerity and credibility of corporate messages regarding social responsibility and environmental initiatives (Chu *et al.*, 2023; Rixom & Rixom, 2023). Inauthentic information undermines trust and fosters skepticism, highlighting the importance of transparency and integrity in corporate communication to effectively engage consumers in CSR efforts. Therefore, if customers see a particular CSR information as lacking authenticity, they will tend to be more doubtful of the company's overall commitment to corporate responsibility. From the above discussions following hypothesis has formulated.

H3. There is a significant negative relationship between inauthentic information and skepticism towards CSR communication.

4.4. Self-Promotional Tone

The present study defines self-promotional tone as the extent to which the company's attitude, expressed through words or voice, aims to amplify the message's origin. The tone used in a communication message has the capacity to alter an individual's perception of a company's overall character, including its principles, ethics, and daily activities (Kulhavy & Schwartz, 2015). In the context of CSR communication, the tone used might impact a consumer's perception of a company's honesty. The study conducted by (Kim & Ferguson, 2018) focuses on public expectations of CSR communication. It reveals that message tone plays a crucial role in effectively communicating CSR activities, as indicated by consumer reactions. Based on their research, a messaging tone that mainly depends on facts is seen more acceptable than one that serves a promotional goal. The findings of (Kim & Ferguson, 2018) research align with previous studies indicating that self-promotional messages frequently lead consumers to question the motives underlying such ads (Ellen *et al.*, 2006; Ma & Bentley, 2022). When firms communicate CSR messaging that claim motives solely based on their goodness, customers tend to question whether the CSR project serves anyone other than the company itself (Forehand & Grier, 2003). Additional evidence indicates that consumers anticipate corporations to refrain from using a celebratory or self-aggrandizing tone when communicating their corporate social responsibility (CSR) initiatives (Kim & Ferguson, 2018).

Research in the field of literature indicates that the use of self-promotional language in corporate social responsibility (CSR) communication has the potential to generate skepticism among consumers. This skepticism arises from consumers questioning the genuineness and underlying intentions of such messages. Research suggests that there is a strong consumer preference for transparency and a genuine dedication to social responsibility (Nguyen *et al.*, 2023; Song & choi, 2023). As a result, it is crucial for companies to carefully navigate their communication strategies in order to establish trust and credibility (Luo *et al.*, 2023). Therefore, it is reasonable to assume that if a consumer perceives a corporate social responsibility (CSR) message to be delivered in a self-promotional manner, they will be more likely to question the company's commitment to corporate responsibility. Thus, from the above discussions following hypothesis has formulated.

H4. There is a significant negative relationship between self-promotional tone and skepticism towards CSR communication.

Based on above Review, Conceptual Framework for the study was developed, mentioned in Figure 1.

Figure 1. Conceptual framework

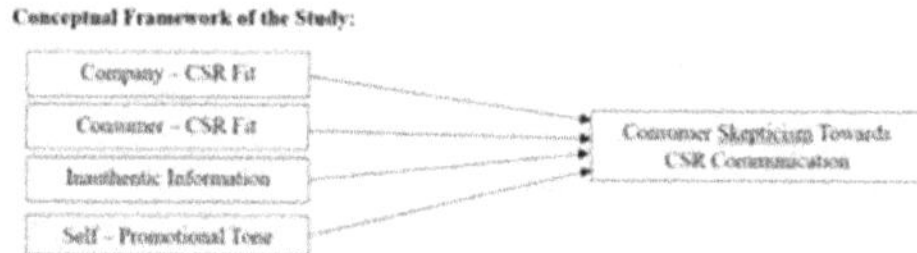

5. RESEARCH METHODOLOGY

5.1. Data Collection

To collect the required information, a closed-ended questionnaire was created, which included a 7-point Likert scale. The questionnaires were prepared in the English language and disseminated to possible participants through electronic channels, notably via email. In addition, a subset of the surveys was filled out via face-to-face interviews. The study had a sample size of 345, and the data was obtained using convenience sampling.

5.2. Construct Measures

The items for Company-CSR Fit, Consumer-CSR Fit, Inauthentic Information, Skepticism and Self-Promotional tone were adopted from following sources discussed in Table 1.

Table 1. Measurement instruments

Constructs	No of Items	Source
Company-CSR Fit	3	(Pérez & Rodríguez del Bosque, 2015)
Consumer-CSR Fit	3	(Kim & Ferguson, 2018)
Inauthentic Information	3	(Gürhan-Canli & Maheswaran, 2000)
Self-Promotional tone	3	(Kim & Ferguson, 2018)
Skepticism	3	(Skarmeas & Leonidou, 2013)

5.3. Respondent's Profile

The respondents for this study were from Delhi-NCR. ITC a Conglomerate well known for its CSR activities was selected for this study. The demographic characteristics of the respondents are as follows. The proportion of male and female participants in this study were 52% and 48%, respectively. The target age range for this research was 18–60 years old consumers and majority of participants were between the ages of 18 and 35 years.

Table 2. KMO and Bartlett's test

Kaiser-Meyer-Olkin Measure of Sampling Adequacy.		**.825**
Bartlett's Test of Sphericity	Approx. Chi-Square	4250.935
	Df	105
	Sig.	.000

6. DATA ANALYSIS AND FINDINGS

6.1. Reliability Test

We used Cronbach's alpha reliability analysis to check how reliable the whole construct was. (Table 3) shows that the total construct under evaluation has a Cronbach's alpha larger than 0.70. (Cavana, R., Delahaye, B. & Sekeran, 2001), this suggests that the structure is good for further investigation.

6.2. Validity Test

The value of KMO was determined to be 0.825, as shown in Table 2. The Bartlett's test of sphericity produced a statistically significant result (P=0.000); with 105 degrees of freedom for all correlations within the matrix. These results suggest that factor analysis was appropriate for the investigation. After doing principal component analysis and varimax rotation, it was shown that all constructs had eigenvalues exceeding 1, suggesting statistical significance. The components exhibit significant variances, which suggests their high level of explanatory capability. Regarding convergent validity, the factor loadings for each construct surpass the criterion of 0.50 explained in Table 3. Discriminant validity signifies that each item was allocated to its corresponding construct without any overlap, and the association between the components is statistically significant.

Table 3. Factor loading and Cronbach's alpha

Constructs	Items	Factor Loading
Company – CSR Fit (Cronbach's α = 0.86)		
COMCSRF1	CSR initiative of ITC is compatible ITCs core business.	0.787
COMCSRF2	It makes sense that ITC carries out this CSR initiative.	0.861
COMCSRF3	CSR initiative of ITC is complementary to ITC's core business.	0.866

continued on following page

Table 3. Continued

Constructs	Items	Factor Loading
Consumer – CSR Fit (Cronbach's α = 0.80)		
CONCSRF1	ITC's CSR activity is relevant to you.	0.761
CONCSRF2	ITC's CSR initiative is personally relevant to you.	0.641
CONCSRF3	ITC's CSR activity affects my personal life.	0.860
Inauthentic Information (Cronbach's α = 0.94)		
INAUINFO1	In your opinion, claim made by ITC was not trustworthy.	0.892
INAUINFO2	In your opinion, the claim made by ITC was not true.	0.869
INAUINFO3	In your opinion, the claim made by ITC was Not credible	0.876
Self – Promotional Tone (Cronbach's α = 0.92)		
SPT1	The message from ITC sounds like it is based on facts.	0.874
SPT2	The messages from ITC sound promotional.	0.894
SPT3	The message from ITC sounds like it is focused on just facts	0.881
Skepticism (Cronbach's α = 0.83)		
SKPT1	It is doubtful that ITC is a socially responsible company.	0.762
SKPT2	It is uncertain that ITC is concerned to improve the well-being of society.	0.806
SKPT3	It is unsure that ITC follows high ethical standards.	0.766

Source. Analysis Output

Table 4. Model summary

Model	R	R Square	Adjusted R Square	Std. Error of the Estimate
1	.639[a]	.408	.401	3.78725

a. Predictors. (Constant), Company – CSR Fit, Consumer – CSR Fit, Inauthentic Information, Self-Promotion Tool.

The correlation coefficient, represented as 'R', was calculated to be 0.639. This score signifies a statistically significant level of predictability for consumer skepticism of CSR communication. R2, also known as the coefficient of determination, is a statistical metric that quantifies the degree to which the independent and dependent variables can be accounted for by one another. The R^2 value of 0.408 explained in Table 4 indicates that 40.08% of the variability in the dependent variable (customer scepticism about CSR communication) can be explained by the independent variables i.e. Company – CSR Fit, Consumer – CSR Fit, Inauthentic Information, Self-Promotion Tool.

Table 5. ANOVA

Model		Sum of Squares	Df	Mean Square	F	Sig.
1	Regression	3365.931	4	841.483	58.667	.000[a]
	Residual	4876.718	340	14.343		
	Total	8242.649	344			

a. Predictors. (Constant), Company – CSR Fit, Consumer – CSR Fit, Inauthentic Information, Self-Promotion Tool.

The regression model was assessed and analysed using Table 5 to establish its appropriateness for the data. The independent factors included in Table 5 show statistical significance, showing their potential to predict consumer scepticism about CSR communication. The analysis reveals that the dependent variable is significantly influenced by these factors, as evidenced by the F statistic (4, 345) =58.667, with a significance level of $P < 0.05$. Therefore, we may deduce that the regression model mentioned above is a suitable match for the given data.

Table 6. Coefficients[a]

Model		Unstandardized Coefficients		Standardized Coefficients	t	Sig.
		B	Std. Error	Beta		
1	(Constant)	2.210	.724		3.052	.002
	Company-CSR Fit	.181	.050	.171	3.592	.000
	Consumer -CSR Fit	.285	.050	.282	5.645	.000
	Inauthentic Information	.129	.046	.144	2.819	.005
	Self-Promotional Tool	.225	.046	.246	4.890	.000

a. Dependent Variable. Consumer Skepticism towards CSR Communication.

b. Independent Variable. Company – CSR Fit, Consumer – CSR Fit, Inauthentic Information, Self-Promotion Tool.

It has been determined that the p-value of 0.000 is considerably less than the alpha value of 0.05 in case of Company – CSR Fit, Consumer – CSR Fit, Inauthentic Information, Self-Promotion Tool. Hence all the alternate hypothesis was (H1 to H4) accepted. Therefore, this finding demonstrated that Company – CSR Fit, Consumer – CSR Fit, Inauthentic Information, Self-Promotion Tool have a positive impact on consumer skepticism towards CSR communication, and this conclusion is consistent with previous research (Forehand & Grier, 2003; Moreno & Kang, 2020; Ramesh *et al.*, 2019; Yoo & Lee, 2018).

Thus, the multiple regression equation for this study will be.

Skepticism Toward CSR Communication=2.210 + 0.285 Consumer-CSR Fit + 0.225 Self-Promotion Tool + 0.181 Company-CSR Fit + 129 Inauthentic Information.

The aforementioned Table 6, makes clear that skepticism toward CSR communication and Consumer -CSR Fit are strongly correlated (strongest relationship) followed by serving as one of the primary antecedents of attitude towards CSR communication, followed by Self-Promotion Tool, Company-CSR Fit and Inauthentic Information.

7. DISCUSSIONS

Research has shown that consumer skepticism in CSR (Corporate Social Responsibility) communications is a notable obstacle that companies face when trying to establish trust and credibility with their intended audiences. The effectiveness of CSR messaging is dependent not only on the content but also on how that content is delivered. Firstly, it is important for the content of CSR communications to be authentic, transparent, and in line with the actions and values of the company. Researchers have observed that consumers are becoming more discerning and have the ability to identify inconsistencies between a company's corporate social responsibility (CSR) messages and its actual behavior (Statz *et al.*, 2023). Thus, it is imperative for companies to guarantee that their CSR communications precisely depict their dedication to social and environmental responsibility, supported by concrete evidence of their initiatives and impact. Furthermore, the manner in which CSR communications are delivered is of utmost importance as it significantly influences consumer perceptions and helps to alleviate any doubts or skepticism (Lins *et al.*, 2024). It has been observed that the tone, language, and channels employed to communicate CSR messages can have a significant impact on how consumers perceive and understand them. Researchers must adopt a sincere and empathetic tone in their communications, avoiding overly promotional or self-serving language that may trigger skepticism (Huttl Maack *et al.,* 2024). Furthermore, it is important for researchers to strategically select communication channels, taking into account the preferences and behaviors of the target audience. By utilizing various channels like social media, corporate websites, and community events, researchers can effectively connect with consumers and facilitate interactive communication, which promotes transparency and trust.

When companies engage in CSR activities and communicate them to the public, consumers may exhibit skepticism due to various reasons.

Greenwashing. Consumers may be skeptical if they perceive that a company is exaggerating or misrepresenting its environmental efforts to appear more socially responsible than its actual value (Farooq & Wicaksono, 2021).

Strategic Motives. Participants may question the motives behind a company's CSR initiatives (Yang & Mundel, 2021), suspecting that they are primarily driven by profit-seeking or reputation management rather than genuine concern for societal or environmental issues.

Lack of Transparency. Skepticism can arise when companies are perceived as withholding or manipulating information about their CSR practices, such as concealing negative impacts or failing to disclose relevant details about their initiatives (Amawate & Deb, 2021; Ahmad & Guzman, 2021).

Past Behavior. Participants may harbor skepticism based on an organisation's track record of unethical behavior or previous instances of CSR failures or controversies (Rossi & Rivetti, 2023; Singh *et al.,* 2024).

Credibility of Claims. Skepticism may also arise from concerns about the credibility or reliability of the claims made by companies regarding their CSR activities, particularly if there is inadequate evidence or independent verification to substantiate those claims (Van projien *et al.,* 2021; Nguyen *et al.*, 2023).

Henceforth, it is imperative for companies to acknowledge and tackle cultural differences in consumer skepticism and corporate social responsibility (CSR) communications. It is important to note that cultural norms, values, and perceptions can differ significantly among various regions and demographics (Teah *et al.*, 2023; Wang & Bauroncle, 2023). These differences have a significant impact on how consumers interpret corporate social responsibility (CSR) messages. Consequently, it is imperative for companies to customize their CSR communications in order to align with the cultural context of their target markets. This entails considering the local beliefs, customs, and sensitivities. Through a comprehensive understanding and appreciation of cultural differences, organizations have the opportunity to improve the pertinence and reliability of their corporate social responsibility (CSR) communications (Min *et al.*, 2023; Thomas *et al.*, 2024). This, in turn, can cultivate favorable connections with consumers and communities.

8. CONCLUSION

Corporate Social Responsibility (CSR) communication is not only advantageous but also essential for a business that desires to cultivate enduring consumer relationships, as well as inspire consumer loyalty and preference. (Lee *et al.*, 2019) argued that consumers are informed of the CSR initiatives that businesses undertake so that they can actively support such initiatives. For improved results, it is critical that organisations implement business strategies that prioritise corporate social responsibility (CSR) communication. This study identifies two significant component of CSR communication (i.e. content and delivery) and provide specific variable for both for content (company-CSR fit, consumer-CSR fit) delivery (self-promotional tone, inauthentic information). This study confirms that the identified variables have a significant impact on consumer skepticism towards CSR communications and identified variables like company-CSR fit, consumer-CSR fit can help in eliminating skepticism towards CSR communication (Schmeltz, 2017). Customers are more sceptical that companies involve in corporate social responsibility (CSR) for the greater good of society (Vlachos *et al.*, 2009) rather than as a means to an end (Schmeltz, 2014) when there is a disconnect between what companies say they do and what they actually do. By paying great attention to the content and delivery of their communications, practitioners can reduce consumer scepticism through understanding the content and delivery of CSR communication (Moreno & Kang, 2020). This study also shows how customers' perceptions of the CSR communication's content and delivery affect how sceptical they become of a company's overall corporate responsibility.

9. IMPLICATIONS

9.1. Theoretical Implications

The current study significantly advances the application of IPT in the context of CSR communication (Miller, 1994). Given that research on CSR communication is still in its infancy, it is critical to take into account customer information processing needs and the company's capacity to satisfy them through CSR communication (Busse *et al.*, 2017). The findings suggest that consumers' levels of scepticism regarding a company's corporate responsibility are substantially influenced by their evaluations of the content and delivery of CSR communication, contingent upon the extent to which their information processing requirements are fulfilled. It is observed that consumers' evaluations are substantially impacted by the way they associate their evaluations with inauthentic information, self-promotional tone, and the degree of alignment between the company and consumer CSR fit. This study offers substantial context for the literature on CSR-related topics, including CSR communications research.

9.2. Practical Implication

Our findings may provide practitioners with substantial advantages. (Lee *et al.*, 2019) emphasises the importance of corporate social responsibility (CSR) communications in facilitating consumer knowledge regarding a company's CSR initiatives. Consideration must be given to the delivery of such messages even more so. This study illuminates the content and delivery elements of corporate social responsibility (CSR) communication and presents four factors to be considered when crafting CSR messages. inauthentic information, company-CSR fit, self-promotional tone, and company-CSR fit. Practitioners now have a clearer understanding of which CSR communication components require the most meticulous consideration and the greatest investment of resources, because of the present study. A business that can discern whether to allocate resources towards the dissemination or construction of a message will be in a better position to fulfil the information processing requirements of its clientele. Consumers may find it challenging not to remain sceptical when a company's CSR communication exhibits a tone that suggests it prioritises self-promotion over a sincere dedication to CSR. Moreover, the absence of genuineness in information may deter clients from sustaining a connection with an organisation. In order to benefit from the long-term value of a committed consumer, practitioners must be invested in communicating their CSR engagement by selecting a CSR activity that aligns with the organization's fand consumers fundamental values and culture of consumers as well, by understanding how to deliver their message without invoking scepticism.

10. LIMITATIONS AND FUTURE STUDIES

The conceptual framework was constructed upon a robust theoretical underpinning and validated via regression analyses, which incorporated explicit specifications of potential causal effects between variables. However, in order to ascertain causal relationships, subsequent research may devise an experiment that controls for confounding variables. ITC was selected for the study which is a well known FMCG conglomerate thus the findings can only be generalized in terms of FMCG sectors. Future investigation may consider applying the methodology employed in this study to diverse industries and employing unique CSR initiatives as stimuli. Future studies also include role of gender as moderator in CSR communication.

REFERENCES

Ahmad, F., & Guzmán, F. (2021). Consumer skepticism about online reviews and their decision-making process. The role of review self-efficacy and regulatory focus. *Journal of Consumer Marketing*, 38(5), 587–600. DOI: 10.1108/JCM-09-2020-4119

Amawate, V., & Deb, M. (2021). Antecedents and consequences of consumer skepticism toward cause-related marketing. Gender as moderator and attitude as mediator. *Journal of Marketing Communications*, 27(1), 31–52. DOI: 10.1080/13527266.2019.1630663

Busse, C., Meinlschmidt, J., & Foerstl, K. (2017). Managing Information Processing Needs in Global Supply Chains. A Prerequisite to Sustainable Supply Chain Management. *Journal of Supply Chain Management, 53*(1), 87–113. DOI: 10.1111/jscm.12129

Cavana, R., Delahaye, B., & Sekeran, U. (2001). *Applied business research. Qualitative and quantitative methods*. John Wiley & Sons.

Chu, S. C., Kim, H., & Kim, Y. (2023). When brands get real. the role of authenticity and electronic word-of-mouth in shaping consumer response to brands taking a stand. *International Journal of Advertising*, 42(6), 1037–1064. DOI: 10.1080/02650487.2022.2138057

Currás-Pérez, R., Dolz-Dolz, C., Miquel-Romero, M. J., & Sánchez-García, I. (2018). How social, environmental, and economic CSR affects consumer-perceived value. Does perceived consumer effectiveness make a difference? *Corporate Social Responsibility and Environmental Management, 25*(5), 733–747. DOI: 10.1002/csr.1490

Dalal, B. (2020). The antecedents and consequences of CSR skepticism. An integrated framwork. *Journal of Sustainable Marketing, 1*(1), 1–9. DOI: 10.51300/josm-2020-18

de Jong, M. D. T., & van der Meer, M. (2017). How Does It Fit? Exploring the Congruence Between Organizations and Their Corporate Social Responsibility (CSR) Activities. *Journal of Business Ethics, 143*(1), 71–83. DOI: 10.1007/s10551-015-2782-2

del Mar García-De los Salmones, M., & Perez, A. (2018). Effectiveness of CSR Advertising. The Role of Reputation, Consumer Attributions, and Emotions. *Corporate Social Responsibility and Environmental Management, 25*(2), 194–208. DOI: 10.1002/csr.1453

Diddi, S., & Niehm, L. S. (2016). Corporate Social Responsibility in the Retail Apparel Context. Exploring Consumers' Personal and Normative Influences on Patronage Intentions. *Journal of Marketing Channels, 23*(1–2), 60–76. DOI: 10.1080/1046669X.2016.1147892

Do Paço, A. M. F., & Reis, R. (2012). Factors affecting skepticism toward green advertising. *Journal of Advertising, 41*(4), 147–155. DOI: 10.1080/00913367.2012.10672463

Ellen, P. S., Webb, D. J., & Mohr, L. A. (2006). Building corporate associations. Consumer attributions for corporate socially responsible programs. *Journal of the Academy of Marketing Science, 34*(2), 147–157. DOI: 10.1177/0092070305284976

Farooq, Y., & Wicaksono, H. (2021). Advancing on the analysis of causes and consequences of green skepticism. *Journal of Cleaner Production*, 320, 128927. DOI: 10.1016/j.jclepro.2021.128927

Forehand, M. R., & Grier, S. (2003). When Is Honesty the Best Policy? The Effect of Stated Company Intent on Consumer Skepticism. *Journal of Consumer Psychology, 13*(3), 349–356. DOI: 10.1207/S15327663JCP1303_15

Galbraith, J. R. (1974). Organization Design. An Information Processing View. *Interfaces, 4*(3), 28–36. DOI: 10.1287/inte.4.3.28

Gürhan-Canli, Z., & Maheswaran, D. (2000). Determinants of country-of-origin evaluations. *Journal of Consumer Research, 27*(1), 96–108. DOI: 10.1086/314311

Ham, C. D., & Kim, J. (2020). The effects of CSR communication in corporate crises. Examining the role of dispositional and situational CSR skepticism in context. *Public Relations Review, 46*(2). DOI: 10.1016/j.pubrev.2019.05.013

Hur, W. M., Kim, H., & Jang, J. H. (2016). The Role of Gender Differences in the Impact of CSR Perceptions on Corporate Marketing Outcomes. *Corporate Social Responsibility and Environmental Management, 23*(6), 345–357. DOI: 10.1002/csr.1380

Hüttl-Maack, V., Sedghi, T. M., & Daume, J. M. (2024). Through rose-tinted glasses. how inducing and resolving curiosity makes consumers less skeptical and improves their product evaluations. *Journal of Consumer Psychology*, 34(1), 92–100. DOI: 10.1002/jcpy.1369

Jacques, P. (2005). How Should Corporations Deal with Environmental Scepticism? *Corporate Social Responsibility and Environmental Management, 13*(1), 25–36. DOI: 10.1002/csr.089

Kang, E. Y., & Atkinson, L. (2021). Effects of message objectivity and focus on green CSR communication. The strategy development for a hotel's green CSR message. *Journal of Marketing Communications*, 27(3), 229–249. DOI: 10.1080/13527266.2019.1640270

Kim, S. (2019). The Process Model of Corporate Social Responsibility (CSR) Communication. CSR Communication and its Relationship with Consumers' CSR Knowledge, Trust, and Corporate Reputation Perception. *Journal of Business Ethics, 154*(4), 1143–1159. DOI: 10.1007/s10551-017-3433-6

Kim, S., & Ferguson, M. A. T. (2018). Dimensions of effective CSR communication based on public expectations. *Journal of Marketing Communications, 24*(6), 549–567. DOI: 10.1080/13527266.2015.1118143

Kim, S., & Rim, H. (2024). The role of public skepticism and distrust in the process of CSR communication. *International Journal of Business Communication*, 61(2), 198–218. DOI: 10.1177/2329488419866888

Kulhavy, R. W., & Schwartz, N. H. (2015). Tone of Communication and Climate Perceptions. *Journal of Business Communication*, 18(1), 17–24. DOI: 10.1177/002194368101800103

Lee, S. Y., Zhang, W., & Abitbol, A. (2019). What Makes CSR Communication Lead to CSR Participation? Testing the Mediating Effects of CSR Associations, CSR Credibility, and Organization–Public Relationships. *Journal of Business Ethics, 157*(2), 413–429. DOI: 10.1007/s10551-017-3609-0

Lii, Y. S., Wu, K. W., & Ding, M. C. (2013). Doing Good Does Good? Sustainable Marketing of CSR and Consumer Evaluations. *Corporate Social Responsibility and Environmental Management, 20*(1), 15–28. DOI: 10.1002/csr.294

Lim, R. E., & Lee, W. N. (2023). Communicating corporate social responsibility. How fit, specificity, and cognitive fluency drive consumer skepticism and response. *Corporate Social Responsibility and Environmental Management*, 30(2), 955–967. DOI: 10.1002/csr.2399

Line, N. D., Hanks, L., & Zhang, L. (2016). Sustainability communication. The effect of message construals on consumers' attitudes towards green restaurants. *International Journal of Hospitality Management, 57*, 143–151. DOI: 10.1016/j.ijhm.2016.07.001

Lins, S., Greulich, M., Löbbers, J., Benlian, A., & Sunyaev, A. (2024). Why so skeptical? Investigating the emergence and consequences of consumer skepticism toward web seals. *Information & Management*, 61(2), 103920. DOI: 10.1016/j.im.2024.103920

Luo, Y., Jiang, H., & Zeng, L. (2023). Linking informative and factual CSR communication to reputation. an understanding of CSR motives and organizational identification. *Sustainability (Basel)*, 15(6), 5136. DOI: 10.3390/su15065136

Ma, L., & Bentley, J. M. (2022). Can strategic message framing mitigate the negative effects of skeptical comments against corporate-social-responsibility communication on social networking sites? *Public Relations Review*, 48(4), 102222. DOI: 10.1016/j.pubrev.2022.102222

Miller, G. A. (1956). The magical number seven, plus or minus two. Some limits on our capacity for processing information. *Psychological Review*, 63(2), 81–97. DOI: 10.1037/h0043158 PMID: 13310704

Miller, G. A. (1994). The Magical Number Seven, Plus or Minus Two Some Limits on Our Capacity for Processing Information. *Psychological Review, 101*(2), 343–352. spider.apa.org/ftdocs/rev/1994/april/rev1012343.html

Min, J., Kim, J., & Yang, K. (2023). CSR attributions and the moderating effect of perceived CSR fit on consumer trust, identification, and loyalty. *Journal of Retailing and Consumer Services*, 72, 103274. DOI: 10.1016/j.jretconser.2023.103274

Mohr, L. A., & Ellen, P. S. (1998). The Development and Testing of a Measure of Skepticism Toward Environmental Claims in Marketers' Communications. *The Journal of Consumer Affairs*, 32(1), 30–55. DOI: 10.1111/j.1745-6606.1998.tb00399.x

Moreno, F., & Kang, J. (2020). How to alleviate consumer skepticism concerning corporate responsibility. The role of content and delivery in CSR communications. *Corporate Social Responsibility and Environmental Management, 27*(6), 2477–2490. DOI: 10.1002/csr.1969

Nguyen, N., Priporas, C. V., McPherson, M., & Manyiwa, S. (2023). CSR-related consumer scepticism. A review of the literature and future research directions. *Journal of Business Research*, 169, 114294. DOI: 10.1016/j.jbusres.2023.114294

Park, E., & Kim, K. J. (2019). What drives "customer loyalty"? The role of corporate social responsibility. *Sustainable Development, 27*(3), 304–311. DOI: 10.1002/sd.1901

Park, K. (2022). The mediating role of skepticism. How corporate social advocacy builds quality relationships with publics. *Journal of Marketing Communications*, 28(8), 821–839. DOI: 10.1080/13527266.2021.1964580

Pérez, A., & Rodríguez del Bosque, I. (2015). How customer novelty seeking influences customer CSR perceptions. *Marketing Intelligence and Planning, 33*(4), 486–507. DOI: 10.1108/MIP-07-2014-0140

Ramesh, K., Saha, R., Goswami, S., Sekar, & Dahiya, R. (2019). Consumer's response to CSR activities. Mediating role of brand image and brand attitude. *Corporate Social Responsibility and Environmental Management, 26*(2), 377–387. DOI: 10.1002/csr.1689

Rim, H., Dong, C., & Zhang, Y. (2024). Cross-National Study of Transparency in CSR Communication and Corporate Trust. Mediating Roles of Perceived Altruism and Perceived Skepticism. *International Journal of Business Communication*. DOI: 10.1177/23294884231223181

Rim, H., & Kim, S. (2016). Dimensions of corporate social responsibility (CSR) skepticism and their impacts on public evaluations toward CSR. *Journal of Public Relations Research, 28*(5–6), 248–267. DOI: 10.1080/1062726X.2016.1261702

Rixom, J. M., & Rixom, B. A. (2023). Perceived brand authenticity. Examining the effects of inferred dedication and anticipated quality on consumers' purchase intentions and actual choices. *Journal of Consumer Behaviour*, 22(3), 721–737. DOI: 10.1002/cb.2156

Rossi, C., & Rivetti, F. (2023). Young consumers' purchase behaviour of sustainably-labelled food products. What is the role of scepticism? *Food Quality and Preference*, 105, 104772. DOI: 10.1016/j.foodqual.2022.104772

Schmeltz, L. (2012). Consumer-oriented CSR communication. Focusing on ability or morality? *Corporate Communications, 17*(1), 29–49. DOI: 10.1108/13563281211196344

Schmeltz, L. (2014). Introducing value-based framing as a strategy for communicating CSR. *Social Responsibility Journal, 10*(1), 184–206. DOI: 10.1108/SRJ-06-2012-0065

Schmeltz, L. (2017). Getting CSR communication fit. A study of strategically fitting cause, consumers and company in corporate CSR communication. *Public Relations Inquiry, 6*(1), 47–72. DOI: 10.1177/2046147X16666731

Singh, S. V., Jha, R., Singh, A. K., Ranjan, R., & Pandey, S. (2024). Sustainable Tourism Perspective in the Sustainable Development Goals. A Case Study of Heritage Sites in Uttarakhand. In *Implementing Sustainable Development Goals in the Service Sector* (pp. 91–107). IGI Global.

Skarmeas, D., & Leonidou, C. N. (2013). When consumers doubt, Watch out! The role of CSR skepticism. *Journal of Business Research, 66*(10), 1831–1838. DOI: 10.1016/j.jbusres.2013.02.004

Song, B., & Choi, M. (2023). Testing Publics' Perceptions of Corporate Social Advocacy Messaging. Linking Organizational and Social Outcomes. *International Journal of Strategic Communication*, 17(4), 325–344. DOI: 10.1080/1553118X.2023.2228293

Statz, K. M., Bogina, A. C., Schmult, J. L., & Gordon, B. S. (2023). Salute to service or salute to skepticism? An empirical analysis of military members' perceptions of the NFL's military campaign. *International Journal of Sports Marketing & Sponsorship*, 24(4), 661–681. DOI: 10.1108/IJSMS-05-2022-0102

Teah, K., Sung, B., & Phau, I. (2023). Examining the moderating role of principle-based entity of luxury brands and its effects on perceived CSR motives, consumer situational scepticism and brand resonance. *Journal of Fashion Marketing and Management*, 27(5), 784–809. DOI: 10.1108/JFMM-03-2022-0066

Thomas, S., Bhatt, V., & Patel, R. (2024). Impact of skepticism on CRM luxury campaign participation intention of Generation Z. *International Journal of Emerging Markets*, 19(4), 964–988. DOI: 10.1108/IJOEM-10-2021-1568

Turker, D., Can, O., & Aras-Beger, G. (2023). How authenticity of corporate social responsibility affects organizational attractiveness. Stakeholder perceptions of organizational ideology. *Corporate Social Responsibility and Environmental Management*, 30(4), 1680–1697. DOI: 10.1002/csr.2444

Tybout, A., Calder, B. J., & Sternthal, B. (1981). Using Information Processing Theory to Design Marketing Strategies. *JMR, Journal of Marketing Research*, 18(1), 73–79. DOI: 10.1177/002224378101800107

Van Prooijen, A. M., Bartels, J., & Meester, T. (2021). Communicated and attributed motives for sustainability initiatives in the energy industry. The role of regulatory compliance. *Journal of Consumer Behaviour*, 20(5), 1015–1024. DOI: 10.1002/cb.1907

Vlachos, P. A., Tsamakos, A., Vrechopoulos, A. P., & Avramidis, P. K. (2009). Corporate social responsibility. Attributions, loyalty, and the mediating role of trust. *Journal of the Academy of Marketing Science, 37*(2), 170–180. DOI: 10.1007/s11747-008-0117-x

Wang, Y., & Bouroncle, L. (2023). To trust or not to trust. Consumer perceptions of corporate sociopolitical activism. *Business and Professional Communication Quarterly*.

Yang, J., & Mundel, J. (2021). "Are we all in this together?". Brand opportunism in covid-19 cause related marketing and the moderating role of consumer skepticism. *Journal of Promotion Management*, 27(6), 877–899. DOI: 10.1080/10496491.2021.1888181

Yoo, D., & Lee, J. (2018). The effects of corporate social responsibility (CSR) Fit and CSR consistency on company evaluation. The role of CSR support. *Sustainability (Switzerland), 10*(8). DOI: 10.3390/su10082956

Chapter 9
Corporate Social Responsibility in the Age of Artificial Intelligence: A Critique

Karun Sanjaya
Symbiosis Law School, Symbiosis International University (Deemed), Pune, India

Himanshi Bhatia
School of Law, Graphic Era Hill University, Dehradun, India

ABSTRACT

This chapter explores the link between corporate social responsibility and artificial intelligence in the contemporary business setting. With the increased utilization of AI technologies in the daily operation of corporations, understanding the ethical facets and impact on society becomes essential. Specifically, the chapter examines the level of responsibility of corporations in adopting AI, including the areas of transparency, accountability, bias, privacy, and the societal impact of their systems. The analysis of real-life examples and assessment of the current CSR guidelines will provide practical recommendations for how businesses can be more actively involved in the development and implementation of socially responsible AI. The ultimate goal is to ensure that the advancement of technology is in tandem with the development of responsible behaviour.

DOI: 10.4018/979-8-3693-3478-2.ch009

1. INTRODUCTION

There has been a rapid rise in the adoption of modern AI technology in corporate strategies. Although AI systems are extraordinarily efficient to improve efficiency, reduce expenses, and promote progress, it is critical to analyze the ethical and societal subjects presented by these technologies. The commercial sector demands the enforcement of AI advancement and implementation in a morally responsible manner. In recent years, Corporate Social Responsibility has attracted a great deal of press interest. According to Carroll (2016), corporate social responsibility is when a corporation creates a decision to consider about the influence their actions have on the society and their surroundings. In this regard, AI has aided CSR, since AI systems have a considerable influence on society.

The main objective of this chapter is to explore the connection between CSR and AI while sharing important insights to help develop and implement socially responsible AI. Starting with researching corporate requirements for implementing AI, with a focus on the ethical implications for society, this chapter will delve into key issues. These include AI innovations, the implementation process to achieve CSR goals, and concerns such as transparency, accountability, bias, and privacy in building socially responsible AI. The chapter will examine existing CSR frameworks and their relevance to AI development, emphasizing the importance of balancing innovation with meeting societal needs. Ultimately, it will stress the necessity for firms to play a crucial role in ensuring the ethical and socially responsible use of AI technology for the benefit of society.

2. THE OBLIGATIONS OF CORPORATIONS TO IMPLEMENT AI

As the development of AI technology is introduced into an increasing number of businesses, businesses have certain responsibilities. This chapter addresses the following business obligations to explore the integration of artificial intelligence.

a) *Ethical Concerns:* It is necessary that companies develop and create AI technology with ethical concerns and respect for human values and dignity. These technologies must be developed so that systems are transparent and accountable and do not perpetuate biases and discrimination (Burrel, 2016). From the standpoint of consumers' data security, it is crucial for businesses to rise to the defence of people's privacy against possible misuse of their personal information (Crawford and Paglen 2019). Furthermore, from a safety perspective, businesses must ensure the safe operation of AI while preventing the potential harm it can cause to people and the environment (Kurakin 2018).

b) *Social Concerns:* From a societal perspective, innovation resulting from businesses' efforts in AI should eventually trickle down to all members of society. Firms are obligated to ensure that AI is universally accessible, regardless of the economic status (Eubanks 2018). Companies are not to deepen the existing environmental and socioeconomic disparities with current AI implementations (Bolukbasi et. al. 2016). In addition to this human obligation, companies are to support educational and job retraining initiatives aimed to help those people losing their jobs and careers that AI innovation makes it obsolete (Ford 2019).
c) *Notice of Possible Consequences:* Firms that employ AI technologies have two crucial obligations to a wide spectrum of stakeholders. They have the power to influence this wide spectrum, including the power for some stakeholders to be physically unable to meet legal requirements (Kurakin 2018). For such cases, businesses must be aware of their responsibility for an AI system's induced harm and have the correspondingly high level of insurance (Kurakin 2018). Finally, firms that fail to responsibly elaborate their own AI systems will lose brand appeal and consumer trust (Crawford and Paglen 2019).

Hence, it is a business' responsibility to ensure that they develop and deploy advanced AI systems ethically and with responsibility. These systems should be easy to understand, held accountable, free from any form of bias and discrimination, and made available to all people. Firms should also invest in education and training to support affected people. Failure to develop AI systems ethically and responsibly can have legal consequences as well as damage their reputation.

3. ADDRESSING AI-RELATED CHALLENGES

The introduction of AI systems has enabled companies to streamline their operations, improve efficiency, and foster innovation. However, they also pose ethical challenges that organizations must address when adopting this technology. This section will focus on challenges related to AI development and use and ethical considerations for businesses.

a) Transparency: Companies must prioritize transparency in the design and implementation of AI systems. AI systems require clarity, and organizations should be open about how they work internally. Transparency will help companies build confidence with other key stakeholders, such as customers, employees, and communities. Highly transparent AI systems facilitate the identification and elimination of identity tendencies (Jobin et al. 2019).

b) Accountability: Companies must be held accountable for the development, implementation, and outcomes of AI. This must be as well as any harm caused as a result of the use of AI. It is important to ensure the company has taken as much precaution to prevent any biased decisions as well as ensure the AI operates on an ethical premise (Floridi & Taddeo 2016). Companies should have the AI installed adhering to their corporate values and mission statement.
c) Bias: It is one of the major concerns that will amount to hindrance in the use of AI, its neutrality depends on how the dataset on which it's trained is collected. Swayed data collection results in biased AI which has negative implications on businesses. Companies ought to invest in researching the best practices to ensure their AI is self-taught on collecting factual data and develop ways to detect and correct biased decisions (Caliskan et al., 2017). Also, the AI developed should not propagate injustices brought in by the biased decisions.
d) Privacy: this is one of the major concerns within Artificial Intelligence, is a technology that requires a huge data pool to be stored and analyzed Companies should ensure the collection of information is done with the concern of privacy for the subjects. Additionally, the company needs to ensure the public is consensually knowledgeable of their private data statues (Hesamifard et al., 2017). The AI systems should also be able to protect the people's data from unauthorized access or manipulation.

The openness, accountability, readiness, and privacy (OARP) that businesses are to pay attention to developing and implementing AI are covered in these four critical parts. In addition to the OARP, these are just four among numerous supplementary appropriate aspects that businesses are to pay attention to. The most prominent problem with the development and implementation of AI is the overall lack of a proper legal framework. Since the AI industry is still in its infancy, the legal code is unable to keep pace with the breakneck rate of technological advancement. As a result, for any business, it is difficult to continuously develop and execute their AI systems appropriately and responsibly in the public region. It is crucial that any institution establishes ethical issues along with best practices to guide the advancement and integration of AI systems. A second problem is the potential for AI systems to perpetuate existing social predispositions. Accurate and quality information sets are crucial to the operation of AI systems. When AI systems are fed with the inaccurate data, they will turn out to be biased. This predisposition might bring about a variety of adverse situations, including exacerbating existing disparities. Companies should guarantee that their AI programs are trained on accurate data and have methodologies in place to discover and fully eliminate biases. Companies must also pay attention to ethical concerns associated with AI development and implementation. Explicitly, companies must prioritize openness, accountability, impartiality, and privacy. However, there are supplementary matters that companies must consider, which includes the absence of current regulation and the issue of AI reinforcement of existing social predispositions.

4. REAL-WORLD CASE STUDIES

Understanding the real-life cases can help comprehend the ethical and social implications of the use and implementation of AI. Researching the real cases that involve AI can add value in the form of knowledge about the development, implementation in practice, use, and consideration of AI ethically. Empirical research of the development and implementation of AI is required for this phase, concentrating on the knowledge that was produced by each experience of putting AI into practice.

4.1 Recruitment

One of the examples is the use of AI in recruiting. Currently, organizations use AI to calculate the value of the application and decide whether the applicant is the most valuable candidate. Nevertheless, such a technique currently entails the risk that it can strengthen the biases of the current culture. For instance, Amazon's artificial intelligence system carried much bias against women because the system only was trained with datasets of men (Dastin, 2018). This example highlights the need for the collection of valid data. Companies are responsible for ensuring valid data training AI and teaching the AI to gather reliable data themselves and to define checks for biases that are possible.

4.2 Criminal Justice System

Criminal justice system refers to a set of law enforcement, legal institutions, and processes that are involved in the identification, capture, prosecution, and penalizing of persons that have committed crimes. AI algorithms have been developed to predict recidivism, which is the possibility of an individual committing another crime. These systems use algorithms to analyze an individual's criminal background, market information, and other factors to determine the likelihood of reoffending. However, these have faced rejection due to encouraging widening existing social gaps. Northpointe's image analysis technology was found to be racially bias against African American culprits. The system seemed to predict more recidivism among the African Americans than among white defendants (Angwin et al., 2016). An essential aspect that can be deduced from this work on AI is the need to train and code AI systems to prevent it from reinforcing social biases.

4.3 Healthcare Sector

AI technologies have been developed to analyze clinical data to help in making the diagnostics for treatment decisions. However, these have been rejected due to their lack of openness and opacity. For example, an AI technology from IBM discovered that it is evaluating the reasoning of doctors despite the system's decision-making process remaining obscure. Transparency is an aspect that should be taken seriously when developing and implementing AI technologies (O'Neil 2016). Lack of disclosure led to a rejection of these systems. Thus, tech firms should be honest about what lies below for every AI system.

4.4 Social Media

Artificial intelligence systems have been specifically designed to analyse data from various social networks and then provide the most effective recommendations to users. Critics are convinced that these systems are inherently capable of rejecting existing ones, popularizing incorrect data (Bakshy et al. 2015). Therefore, it is necessary to apply ethical criteria to the development and use of AI to ensure that these systems are designed and trained in such a way that they do not integrate, expand, or increase the existing social biases, or distribute disinformation.

Investigating the real-world work is a valuable tool for evaluating ethical and sociological factors associated with AI research and growth. Real-world work also displays how lessons learned from research can be applied. This work demonstrates how companies can build and effectively deploy AI that is useful to the broader community. The useful lessons revealed through this work include training AI based on non-biased data, the significance of minimising socio-economic correlation, the relevance of visibility in AI, and the need to prevent disinformation.

5. EVALUATION OF EXISTING CSR FRAMEWORKS

Corporate social responsibility methods and principles enable enterprises to adjust their activities to respond to society and the environment. With the increasing use of AI technology in enterprise operations, it is necessary to look at current CSR techniques and assess the suitability of this foundation's role in the ethics and socio-economic dimension of AI. During the fourth phase of the assignment, I will research existing CSR strategies and see how best they can be adapted to reflect AI development and use.

5.1 Carroll's Pyramid of Corporate Social Responsibility

Carroll stands out as one of the most prominent frameworks for understanding CSR. Carroll's Pyramid of Corporate Social Responsibility, introduced by Carroll in 1991, has four tiers. These include the financial degree, legal, moral, and philosophical. The business should be responsible for making sure it is successful and increases its financial value. Secondly, the companies should be responsible for adhering to the regulations and normality. The business is responsible for developing or implementing the AI system in a socially responsible manner. Lastly, businesses should be responsible for society at large. Carroll's Pyramid can be used to understand the business's CSR in terms of AI development and implementation. First, the financial degree is critical to the current and future development and implementation of AI. The competing company should make sure her financial responsibility IA system is financially responsible. On the other hand, the legal degree is concerned for the business since the company must comply with the rules and regulations before developing an AI system. Principles are critical to AI development and implementation. Moreover, the company must prioritize developing and implementing the AI system to be in a socially responsible manner. The AI system must be, transparent, and be designed in a moral manner. Moreover, the business should consider how the broader values of the AI system will affect society and take steps to decide will be adverse. Importance can also play an important role in the AI development and implementation. The business should work to generate AI models correlating for the general public, such as AI models made to support disaster relief operations (Hager et al., 2019).

5.2 ISO 26000

ISO 26000 is another well-known corporate social responsibility framework. ISO 26000 defines corporate social responsibility rules that apply to all types of organizations, including businesses (ISO, 2010). The standard has defined seven core topics; these are: organizational governance, human rights, labour format, the environment, fair operating practices, consumer issues, and society and development. The ISO 26000 framework is vital for assessing an organization's social responsibility in AI development and use because several other broad topics fall under its umbrella. These include the ethically controversial topics and societal shocks of AI systems. The framework provides guidelines to ensure AI systems remain transparent and accountable beyond their societal implications.

5.3 The Global Reporting Initiative

The Global Reporting Initiative is an influential framework for reporting sustainability. The GRI Standards are another corporate social responsibility framework considered highly. The GRI Standards are designed to help organizations report their sustainability impacts and coverage (GRI, 2016). The broad topics within the standard fall within the controversial ethical and societal issues of AI. The GRI Standards framework helps to evaluate corporate social responsibility for companies using AI systems. The GRI Standards imply the need for transparent and accountable AI systems. The framework's implication in societal risks is applicable on a broader note.

The Carrol's CSR Pyramid, ISO 26000, and the GRI Standards are the primary systems on which the assessment of a company's CSR concerning the development and deployment of AI systems should be based. Each standard system covers a wide array of topics, including transparency, accountability, bias, and the broader social implications of AI systems. The application of the mentioned extension systems to companies could ensure that AI systems are developed and used with respect to their social implications.

6. CONCLUSION, FINDINGS, AND SUGGESTIONS

The chapter has thoroughly considered the topic of Corporate Social Responsibility in the era of AI. However, the research has proven that AI's rapid progression leads to new challenges in the sphere of CSR and that the typical dimensions of CSR do not cover such aspects. At the same time, the research has supported the idea of AI's evolution based on ethics and morals, requiring that companies stand accountable for the long-term analysis of their effects.

6.1 Findings

The findings of the research study support the notion that the current corporate social responsibility frameworks are inadequate for addressing the challenges posed by the rapid advancement of artificial intelligence technologies. The literature review articulates that artificial intelligence has the potential to worsen the current socioeconomic divides as a result of adverse impacts on future labour opportunities and individual privacy and freedom. Furthermore, the findings show that artificial intelligence systems have the potential to be biased, promoting social injustice. The thesis statement is increasing artificial technological knowledge based on ethical considerations, and business's responsibility should factor in the broader societal outcomes of their artificial systems. Instead, the research study recommends adopting a humans-first approach that focuses on people's prosperity and independence. The research study also recommends that companies follow an explicit, thorough decision-making process when creating artificial systems. Here are my findings for the recommendations and the way ahead;

6.2 Recommendations and the Way Ahead

Based on the findings, the research study presents the following recommendations to improve ethical artificial systems development and promote responsible businesses:

1. Developing an ethical artificial system development guideline: Based on ethical ideas, the development of artificial intelligence should prioritise individuals' health and independence. As a result, business should develop ethical guidelines that take the broader societal consequences of their artificial systems into account.
2. Demand engagement in decision-making: Every stakeholder who will be affected by the artificial systems should be asked for their opinions when deciding how to develop the new AIs. Participating groups include speakers from certain affected groups, including the poor and underserved.
3. Bias and Discrimination: Business should avoid bias and discrimination in their design of an artificial system. To begin, the algorithms must be entirely available, explainable, and scrutinisable in calculation and enforcement to prevent unforeseen biases. Consequently, the Artificial systems must be auditable to ensure that they are not discriminatory.
4. Advocate for knowledge exchange: Businesses should collaborate with many stakeholders, such as the academic community, civil society organisations, and government, to promote artificially responsible AI development that has a positive impact on society.

The challenges presented by the rapid evolution of AI technology cannot be met by standard CSR frameworks, and ensuring that the development is demand-driven is essential for widespread societal impacts. It is the responsibility of businesses to ensure its AI technology only has a positive societal spillover through proper ex-ante assessments. The referrals provided can increase the generation of such referrals as responsible AI developers.

REFERENCES

Angwin, J., Larson, J., Mattu, S., & Kirchner, L. (2016, May 23). *Machine Bias.* ProPublica. https://www.propublica.org/article/machine-bias-risk-assessments-in-criminal-sentencing

Bakshy, E., Messing, S., & Adamic, L. (2015). Exposure to ideologically diverse news and opinion on Facebook. *Science*, 348(6239), 1130–1132. DOI: 10.1126/science.aaa1160 PMID: 25953820

Bolukbasi, T. (2016). Man is to computer programmer as woman is to homemaker? Debiasing word embeddings. In Advances in Neural Information Processing Systems (pp. 4349-4357).

Burrell, J. (2016). The tension between data-driven and human-centered design. In *Proceedings of the 35th International BCS Human-Computer Interaction Conference* (pp. 1-11).

Crawford, K., & Paglen, T. (2019). Exposing AI's "black box": How art can help. *Nature*, 565(7741), 422–424.

Dastin, J. (2018). *Amazon scraps secret AI recruiting tool that showed bias against women.* Reuters. https://www.reuters.com/article/idUSKCN1MK0AG/

Eubanks, V. (2018). *Automating inequality: How high-tech tools profile, police, and punish the poor.* St. Martin's Press.

Ford, M. (2019). *Architects of Intelligence: The Truth About AI from the People Building It.* Packt Publishing.

Hesamifard, E., Takabi, H., Ghasemi, M., & Jones, C. (2017). Privacy-preserving Machine Learning in Cloud. *Proceedings of the 2017 on Cloud Computing Security Workshop - CCSW '17.* DOI: 10.1145/3140649.3140655

Jobin, A., Ienca, M., & Vayena, E. (2019). The global landscape of AI ethics guidelines. *Nature Machine Intelligence*, 1(9), 389–399. DOI: 10.1038/s42256-019-0088-2

Kurakin, A. (2018). The impact of AI on society. *Nature*, 551(7681), 429–431.

O'neil, C. (2016). *Weapons of math destruction: how big data increases inequality and threatens democracy.* Crown.

Chapter 10
Ethical Geospatial Analytics Balancing Business Interests and Social Responsibility

Shenson Joseph
https://orcid.org/0009-0001-5191-5556
Texas Tech University, USA

Md Rokibul Hasan
https://orcid.org/0000-0001-5220-6324
Gannon University, USA

Munir Ahmad
https://orcid.org/0000-0003-4836-6151
Survey of Pakistan, Pakistan

Nikhilesh Jain
https://orcid.org/0009-0003-3446-7629
Care CHL Hospital, Indore, India

ABSTRACT

In the realm of geospatial analytics, prioritizing responsible and ethical practices is paramount. This entails embracing transparency, accountability, and stakeholder engagement throughout all stages of the process. This chapter argued that by adhering to best practices and ethical guidelines, the potential for threats can be minimized while maximizing positive societal and environmental impacts. The chapter also underpinned that stakeholders must actively promote ethical conduct and cultivate a culture of integrity and trust within the field. Looking ahead, the field of geospatial

DOI: 10.4018/979-8-3693-3478-2.ch010

analytics is poised for growth and innovation, presenting both opportunities and ethical challenges. Organizations must address emerging ethical dilemmas such as algorithmic bias, privacy concerns, and equitable benefit distribution as technologies evolve. Interdisciplinary collaboration and ethical leadership are essential to ensure the responsible deployment of geospatial analytics in decision-making processes across various sectors.

INTRODUCTION

Geospatial analytics refers to the methodology of interpreting and analyzing data, which has a geographic component. It involves data from all domains including satellite images, GPS navigation, remote sensing, geographic information systems (GIS), and many more sources. Geospatial analytics is concerned with making statistics, using machine learning platforms, and visualization tools to discover the underlying patterns, trends, and insights with spatial data. Through data fusion, geospatial analytics provides a range of benefits such as insightful decision-making, streamlined operations, and competitive advantage in many different domains, for instance, urban planning, logistics, agriculture, and environmental management (Gregg Greenough & Nelson, 2019; Park et al., 2020; Ting et al., 2021).

In today's global interconnected environment, geospatial analytics is a key tool used to help organizations innovate, become more efficient, and solve complex problems in diverse sectors. Spatial analytics can increase the efficiency of supply chain management by designing optimal transportation routes, locating warehouses, and developing communication networks supported by up-to-date spatial data (Gupta et al., 2020; Nagendra et al., 2022). It can revamp marketing and customer engagement approaches by designing unique offers and advertisement campaigns tailored to particular geographical locations (Wichmann et al., 2023). Moreover, it can facilitate resource allocation and decision-making in agriculture, forestry, land use, landscaping, and natural resources management practices through spatial modeling and predictive analytics (Abdurahman et al., 2023; AL-Taani et al., 2021; Manjarrez-Domínguez et al., 2023).

By analyzing population density, traffic flows, natural environment, and other factors, spatial analytics can boost urban planning and infrastructure to develop more environmentally friendly and resilient cities. Disaster response and emergency management can be accelerated by mapping the disaster area, coordinating the rescue efforts, and assessing the natural disaster effects in a real-time fashion. Given its multifaceted applications and potential to drive innovation and growth, geospatial analytics has become a key component of modern businesses to achieve an edge in a highly competitive environment with the potential to drive innovation and growth, no business can survive without it (Abdalla & Li, 2010; Meng et al., 2022; Peixoto et al., 2023; Selvarajan et al., 2009; Tenkanen et al., 2023).

The pervasive use of geospatial analytics has pushed a number of ethical and moral questions that need to be deliberated on to minimize the chance of unethical applications of spatial data. Nowadays, social networking sites, mobile phone GPS, and many other services that people use to determine their locations, raise a concern about the privacy of locational information, and the sensitive details of people have to be protected safely from unauthorized access or misuse. The inclusion of machine learning algorithms in geospatial analytics also leads to concerns about possible data inaccuracy, which may lead to unfair decision processes that may disproportionately impact certain communities or lead to the perpetuation of social inequalities (Giovanola & Tiribelli, 2023; Sun et al., 2020; van Giffen et al., 2022). The exploitation of natural resources, and environmental effects of data collection methods e.g. satellite imagery and aerial surveying, may raise ethical questions about the long-term sustainability of geospatial analytics practices. As a result of these ethical problems, the recognition arises among businesses, policymakers, and civil society representatives that ethical standards frameworks, regulatory guidelines, and best practices are necessary to ensure the relevant application of geospatial analytics and decisions that are not only in the interest of business but also the public as a whole.

The purpose of this chapter is to investigate the ethical dimensions of geospatial analytics in the corporate environment emphasizing the delicate balance required to align business interests with social responsibility. The chapter commences with a discussion of the concept of geospatial analytics including geospatial data sources and their applications. The next sections dealt with ethical challenges in geospatial analytics followed by business interests vs. social responsibility. The second last section elaborates on best practices for ethical geospatial analytics whereas the last section concludes the chapter.

GEOSPATIAL ANALYTICS

Geospatial Data Sources

Geospatial analytics relies on a diverse array of data sources to provide insights into spatial phenomena.

GPS Data

Global Positioning System (GPS) data act as the basic block of geospatial analytics, showing accurate positions via satellites and ground-based monitoring facilities. GPS captures instantaneous position to support real-time tracking of vehicles, assets, and personnel, facilitating navigation, logistics, and location-based services.

Satellite Imagery

Satellite imagery creates a holistic view of Earth's surface because they can get a great granular level of visual data at the same time that covers enormous geographical regions. High-resolution satellite images provide an array of perspectives on land use, urbanization, disaster preparedness, as well as environmental impact. Widely utilized in fields such as agriculture, forestry, and emergency management through monitoring of crop conditions, forest covers, and areas affected by floods, fires, or earthquakes. Sensitive satellite sensors which collect multispectral and hyperspectral imagery are the main tools that assist in the analysis of vegetation, soil properties, and various other elements.

Aerial Photography

Aerial photography involves capturing images of the Earth's surface at an elevated level by making use of an airplane or drone. Aerial photographs provide detailed visual data with a high spatial resolution to support functional mapping of terrain features, land cover, or infrastructures. Aerial photography can be utilized in various applications such as urban planning, environmental monitoring, and archaeological surveying and provides detailed and comprehensive views of landscape dynamics and evolution.

LiDAR (Light Detection and Ranging)

LiDAR is a remote sensing technology that works by sending out laser pulses that bounce off the Earth`s surface to get spatial information for 3D terrain and vegetation mapping. LiDAR data offers very accurate digital elevation models that help to create comprehensive studies dealing with topography, surface features, and forest structure. Frequently incorporated by foresters, urban planners, and infrastructure managers to ensure detailed models of elevation, LiDAR assists in Geospatial analytics by providing terrain analysis models for flood mapping and modeling of urban growth.

RADAR (Radio Detection and Ranging)

RADAR is a remote sensing technique that is used to detect and calibrate the properties of objects or surfaces on the earth's surface through radio waves. RADAR data proves invaluable for cross-weather imaging and tracking surface features. This includes soil conditions, vegetation density, and sea/ocean currents. It is widely used in agricultural, hydrological, and climate studies to improve geospatial analytics by providing information that is complementary information to optical imagery and LiDAR data. Such data enables analysis of complex environmental conditions as well as dynamic processes.

Crowdsourced Data

Crowd-sourced data is defined as the aggregated data received from multiple individuals or sources through apps, websites, or social media platforms. Through the collection of this data, it is possible to incorporate user-generated content which includes reviews, photos, and location-based check-ins, that help map and analyze user preferences, behaviors, and trends.

Internet of Things (IoT) Sensors

IoT devices send data on the fly from physical things that have sensors in them, like weather stations, air quality sensors, smart meters, etc. Spatial IoT data can be used for managing environmental factors, infrastructure performance, and object tracking with the entire process being transferred and assessed in near real-time for various purposes.

Social Media Data

Social media platforms generate vast amounts of geotagged data that includes tweets, posts as well as check-ins that can help to predict human behavior, sentiment, and activities of specific geographic locations. Social media data has been increasingly used for geospatial analysis, event detection, and urban planning and the resulting insights on public opinion and trends in society.

Geographic Information Systems (GIS)

GIS data includes digital maps, databases, and spatial datasets that contain geographic information such as roads, rivers, administrative boundaries, and land parcels. GIS integrates various layers of spatial data to enable spatial analysis, visualization, and decision-making.

Open Data

Open data repositories, such as government portals and public databases, provide access to a wide range of geospatial datasets, including demographic data, land use data, transportation networks, and environmental monitoring data. These datasets are often freely available for download and use, facilitating research, analysis, and decision-making in various domains.

The comparison of the various geospatial data sources mentioned above is presented in Table 1 showing different characteristics of these data sources.

Table 1. Geospatial Data Sources

Data Source	Method of Collection	Type of Data	Spatial Resolution	Applications
GPS data	Satellite-based positioning system	Location coordinates	High	Navigation, logistics, mapping
Satellite imagery	Captured by satellites orbiting the Earth	Visual data	Variable	Mapping, environmental monitoring, disaster management
Aerial photography	Captured from aircraft or drones	Visual data	High	Mapping, urban planning, environmental monitoring
LiDAR	Laser scanning from aircraft or ground-based systems	3D point clouds, elevation data	Very high	Terrain analysis, urban modeling, forestry management
RADAR	Radio wave detection from airborne or satellite platforms	Radar data, surface characteristics	Variable	Weather forecasting, agriculture, hydrology
GIS	Digital mapping and spatial analysis software	Spatial datasets, maps	Variable	Spatial analysis, decision-making, visualization
Crowdsourced Data	Collected from a large number of individuals or sources	User-generated content	Variable	Mapping, social analysis, trend detection

continued on following page

Table 1. Continued

Data Source	Method of Collection	Type of Data	Spatial Resolution	Applications
Internet of Things (IoT) Sensors	Sensors embedded in physical devices and objects	Real-time environmental data	Variable	Environmental monitoring, asset tracking, smart cities
Social Media Data	Geotagged data from social media platforms	User-generated content	Variable	Spatial analysis, sentiment analysis, event detection
Open Data	Publicly available datasets from government portals and databases	Spatial datasets, demographic data	Variable	Research, analysis, decision-making

This table provides an overview of each data source's method of collection, type of data collected, spatial resolution, and common applications. Each data source offers unique capabilities and advantages, contributing to a comprehensive understanding of geographic phenomena and supporting various applications in research, planning, and decision-making.

Tools and Techniques for Geospatial Analytics

Geospatial analytics uses many tools and approaches to analyze geographic information and draw useful conclusions that are described below.

Geographic Information Systems (GIS) Platforms

Softwares such as ArcGIS and QGIS are core to geospatial processing. ArcGIS is the most popular GIS software by Esri that provides capabilities for mapping and analyzing Geographic data. It has extension features, and enhanced capabilities of mapping, geoprocessing, analysis, and data conversion. QGIS is one of the open-source software that also offers efficient tools for the generation, modification, visualization, and analysis of geographic data. These platforms allow for the addition and mapping of various layers of the spatial data and its occurrence critiquing and can be used to undertake spatial asks, geoprocessing, and mapping.

Remote Sensing Technologies

Satellite imagery and especially the LiDAR technology which is an advanced technology of remote sensing is important in obtaining high spatial resolution data. Data is collected using different spectral bands, which enable us to assess the use of the earth's surface, the health of vegetation, and the changes of the landscape in different periods of time. LiDAR employs laser pulses to gain detailed and accurate representations of the earth's surface for application in topographical mapping, forestry as well as city planning. ENVI and ERDAS IMAGINE are specific software that can help in the interpretation of such data and can easily identify the changes in the surface features over time helping in a precise environmental analysis.

Spatial Databases

PostGIS and other geographic information system specialized databases and some of the traditionally developed extensions like Oracle Spatial and Microsoft SQL Server Spatial are widely used for operating with big amount of geospatial data. PostGIS is an open source that extends the functionality of PostgreSQL to support geographic object that can easily be queried for geometric applications. Oracle and Microsoft SQL Server Spatial are two Enterprise Database Systems that provide comprehensive support for a location-based database system that includes facilities for storage and retrieval of spatial data in addition to their ability to manage traditional structured database tables. These databases help in the effective management of an increased amount of geographic data and are capable of handling spatial access and query optimization.

Spatial Interpolation and Geostatistics

Spatial interpolation and geostatistics are used to estimate and depict spatial characteristics in a given area. Spatial interpolation includes estimating point values at different unobserved points by using the values obtained from the sample points through the kriging or spline technique. Spatial statistics or spatio-temporal statistics is a branch of statistics in which answers to statistical questions help to understand spatial patterns or changes in space and time. These techniques are quite necessary for developing smooth surfaces from scattered points of data with applications in environmentalism, agronomics, and climatology.

Spatial Regression and Clustering

Spatial regression models capture the spatial autocorrelation effects within the data which is useful in establishing the spatial effects of the observed variables. Statistical methods applied in spatial analysis include Geographically Weighted Regression (GWR) and Spatial Lag Models that account for the spatial dependence of the data. Based on the typology of spatial data, there are clustering methods, including K-means clustering, DBSCAN (Density-Based Spatial Clustering of Applications with Noise), clustering trees, and hierarchical clustering to discover the patterns or clusters of the spatial data set. These methods can be applied in urban planning and crime analysis; in market research, to identify hotspots and spatial patterns.

Machine Learning (ML) and Artificial Intelligence (AI)

Artificial intelligence and big data are prominently employed with Geospatial Analysis to promote model prediction, pattern analysis, and anomaly identification. Software such as Google Earth Engine and Esri Geo AI are applications that can integrate geospatial data with Artificial Intelligence to address the challenges of analyzing large of datasets geospatial base. Frameworks that are applied for building deep learning models include TensorFlow and PyTorch when it comes to building models for image classification, object detection, or change detection in satellite images. AI, and especially deep learning can be used to exploit features from imagery, and anticipate future occurrences at different geographical locations and then assist in decision making.

Open-Source Tools and Cloud Platforms

Python packages such as GeoPandas and Shapely can be used to work with geospatial data which provides efficient solutions for many developers and analysts. There are R packages available with good statistical and analytical functions for spatial data such as sf and raster packages. Cloud Computer platforms like Amazon Web Services (AWS) and Google Cloud have elastic solutions that enable to deal with huge amounts of geographical data. They offer access to the computing power needed to process big data and perform various Geographic Information System-related analyses at a low cost.

Altogether, these tools and techniques increase the capability of doing complicated geometrical analysis and can be identically useful across diverse domains, ranging from planning to urban environment, pollution, disaster, farming transportation, etc. When combining geospatial with AI or ML new insights can be further revealed, and better decisions can be made.

Applications of Geospatial Analytics

Today, the world of data is buzzing with many companies developing the ability to analyze geospatial data to gain valuable insights into their performance in different places. Geospatial analytics incorporates the inspection of geographic or spatial data in order to perceive relationships, patterns, trends, and correlations. Geospatial analytics represents the mighty force that can help businesses from different sectors make the right strategic decisions, take action to optimize resources, and expand the market.

Market Analysis and Site Selection

Geo-spatial analytics allows businesses to perform detailed market studies by combining demographic, economic behavior, and environmental data with geographic data. The socioeconomic factor can be appended with elements such as population density, consumer behavior, and competitor locations, which in turn, enable companies to choose sites for new stores, offices, or facilities. Such a strategy can help to implement risk mitigation strategies as well as maximize the potential for targeted markets (Bandira et al., 2021; Wang et al., 2018).

Supply Chain Optimization

Efficiency in supply chain management is the key to successfully reducing the costs of an organization and having flexibility to improve its competitive advantage. Geospatial analytics helps organizations improve their supply chains by studying factors such as vehicle routes, warehouse locations, and demand patterns. This way, businesses can be able to achieve a lean and flexible logistics structure with fewer transfer times and more efficient inventory or supply chain management, thus promoting overall operational excellence (Gupta et al., 2020; Nagendra et al., 2022).

Customer Segmentation and Targeting

Within the marketing and sales context, grasping the specifications of customer behavior and choices becomes of crucial significance. Geospatial analytics helps businesses carry out the geographic customer segmentation process based on attributes like address, distance to stores, purchase behavior, etc. By finding out the common customers, the companies can pick out the marketing strategies such as products, promotion, and advertising suitable to specific target customer groups, which can boost their purchases and long-term relationships (Bartels, 2022; Taylor & Hollenbeck, 2021).

Risk Assessment and Mitigation

The scope of risks to businesses includes highly dynamic environments, where hazards and instability in different sectors can influence the business function. Further, geospatial analyses make proactive risk evaluation feasible because they analyze spatial information on matters such as environmental hazards, infrastructure susceptibility, and social economic indicators. Through the identification of high-risk areas and potential threats, organizations can make a plan for preventing losses, enhancing resilience, and creating plans for a couple of possible scenarios (Chiavacci & Pindilli, 2020; Dehghanian et al., 2019; Kalhor et al., 2018).

Asset Management and Maintenance

For industries with extensive physical infrastructure, such as utilities, transportation, and telecommunications, geospatial analytics plays a crucial role in asset management and maintenance. By integrating geospatial data with asset information, businesses can monitor the condition, performance, and lifecycle of their infrastructure assets. Predictive analytics models enable proactive maintenance strategies, reducing downtime, optimizing resource allocation, and extending asset lifespan (Le Gat et al., 2023; Meschini et al., 2022).

Competitive Intelligence and Market Trends

In today's competitive landscape, businesses need timely insights into market trends, competitor activities, and emerging opportunities. Geospatial analytics empowers organizations to monitor competitor locations, assess market penetration, and identify emerging trends through spatial analysis of consumer behavior, competitor footprints, and demographic shifts. This intelligence enables businesses to adapt their strategies, innovate offerings, and stay ahead of the competition (Gao et al., 2024; Jorge & De Araujo, 2019).

ETHICAL CHALLENGES IN GEOSPATIAL ANALYTICS

Data Privacy and Consent

Geospatial analytics often involve the utilization of vast amounts of location-based data, raising concerns regarding data privacy and consent. One of the major risks could be data re-identification, which means the personal data that is anonymized can be tied back to individuals, leading to privacy violations. Providing consent from a person involved in a process requires, considering the issue of confidentiality. Informing a person and obtaining his informed consent could be complex, for example, when dealing with large data sets or secondary data sources. To find the right path in resolving this dilemma, data usability and privacy protection need to be weighed together equally.

Discrimination and Bias

The possibility of geospatial data being employed in decision-making might have the side effect of discrimination and biases, if not well controlled. Algorithms used in geospatial analysis could become biased towards or against certain groups based on their representation and perception of the data collected. These can bring about an unjust situation where there are disparities in resource consumption or service availability owing to the geographical locations of the service points. This dilemma can be resolved by applying the notions of unbiased algorithms and by utilizing the tools that prevent the manifestation of bias in geospatial information. Strategies to make algorithms transparent, and develop bias detection, and audit models can not only design better outcomes for all players but also ensure fairness and equality.

Environmental Impact

Environmental impacts of geospatial analysis are not only related to displayed analysis but are also involved in collecting, managing, and processing geospatial data. As the pervasiveness of data-gathering devices such as satellites, drones, and sensors continue to increase, large amounts of energy are used together with the resources to provide this practice. In addition, the application of these technologies can also lead to ecological damage, like the disturbance of the habitats or other surrounding animals. To implement this, the idea of sustainable usage of resources is becoming more and more important as ideas of employing energy-efficient technologies and ethical data collection are encouraged. Moreover, parties involved in geospatial analytics initiatives need to take steps to reduce the environmental harm associated with of cost of data collection by curbing the footprint of data collection activities and by adhering to environmental laws. By prioritizing environmental stewardship alongside technological advancement, businesses and organizations can harness the power of geospatial analytics while minimizing their ecological footprint and promoting environmental conservation.

BUSINESS INTERESTS VS. SOCIAL RESPONSIBILITY

Profit Maximization vs. Ethical Considerations

Profitability conflicts with ethical issues in which businesses across all sectors are caught up, an age-long dilemma. Profit undoubtedly remains the backbone of the business world but as and when the business aims to align with the ethics, financial goals intersect at the ethical boundaries. This tension can be specifically observed in industries heavily relying on geospatial data analytics; where the extraction and utilization of vast troves of data raise significant ethical concerns regarding privacy, consent, and fairness. Dissenting between the objective to make the business grow more and more and the ethical imperative that should respect individual rights and social values is a totally challenging terrain. Companies should be aware that unethical practices can cause damage to their reputation and can result in legal penalties and loss of trust by consumers in the long run.

Long-Term Sustainability and Reputation Management

The combination of long-term sustainability and reputation management shows that economic significance and community welfare interact with each other. Consequently, it is vital for businesses to create the right balance between the short-term and the long-term perspectives. This allows them to capitalize on short-term opportunities while ensuring that the success achieved is sustainable and is built on responsible conduct. In the geospatial context, this involves conscientious governance of environmental assets, ethical data handling, and a fair consultation for the decision-making process. The importance of respecting the environment and ethical standards can be highlighted by promoting long-term prosperity because this would help to build trust and confidence among the different stakeholders. Ethical performance benefits are not just limited to profitability and business stability but also enhance the company's brand reputation, which serves as a strategic asset in creating competitive advantage and resilience in a dynamic business environment.

Corporate Social Responsibility Initiatives in Geospatial Analytics

Stakeholder expectations, consumer preferences, as well as government regulations, all call for corporate social responsibility (CSR) activities that can reconcile the business interests with the society's needs. In the sphere of geospatial analytics, companies can utilize technological tools to achieve a wide range of social impact outcomes like environmental protection, disaster response, and community development. CSR initiatives in geospatial analytics may encompass initiatives such as leveraging spatial data for planning sustainable cities, providing geospatial technologies to underserved communities, and also working with NGOs to confront shared social problems. By aligning business interests with social responsibility, companies can foster sustainable growth while contributing to the well-being of communities and the planet.

REGULATORY LANDSCAPE

Overview of Relevant Laws and Regulations

The GDPR is among the most prominent data privacy regulations whose purpose is to create data handling common for all member states in the EU. The GDPR became effective on May 25th, 2018, and all worldwide entities that collect or are responsible for processing EU citizens' data have to comply. It allows for the enforcement of basic principles such as data minimization, purpose limitation, and the right to erasure that makes the data subjects own the process (Li et al., 2019). One of the similar cases is the Health Insurance Portability and Accountability Act (HIPAA), the major US federal law passed in 1996 for the protection of sensitive medical information. HIPAA regulations contain a set of HIPAA standards for secure PHI (protected health information) by healthcare providers, health plans, and their business associates. It covers provisions on privacy, security, and breach notification, the purpose of these is to protect patient's data confidentiality and integrity (Weiss, 2023). Both GDPR and HIPAA demonstrate that there is an increasing emphasis on data privacy and security.

GDPR and HIPAA can affect geospatial analytics through rules that limit data processing and privacy. The GDPR for the European Union states that the processing of any personal data including location data is only lawful when done under the specified lawful grounds, it is also expected that the organizations take necessary measures to secure personal data. This comprises data minimization, explicit consent, and data subjects' rights including the rights of access to and erasure of the data. Another law that applies to the use of data in the United States is HIPAA which has strict rules for whoever handles personal health information even geospatial data containing the location of an individual in a healthcare setting. The HIPAA standard for the protection of personal health information calls for application of measures aimed at protecting the confidentiality, integrity, and availability of the data. Consequently, it is evident that both regulations call for very strict measures for the violation of law; their territorial applicability also varies, where GDPR targets any company that processes the data of EU citizens irrespective of the existence of any physical connection with the EU zone while the focus of HIPAA mainly remains on the US-based companies. Thus, these laws call for practical geospatial analytics companies to adopt complex data protection policies that must meet international and regional.

Challenges and Gaps in Regulatory Frameworks

However, despite the fact that GDPR and HIPAA provide some regulations for data protection, they have issues and shortfalls. These data protection laws are not standardized among nations which is one of the key problems. Although GDPR has influenced global privacy standards, variations in regulatory requirements across different regions can complicate compliance efforts, particularly for multinational corporations. Also, the regulator's job is made more difficult due to the fact that new technologies are evolving very fast and thus the regulators have to monitor the situation and update the regulations accordingly. Regulating with new technologies like AI, the Internet of Things, and biometric data collection that haven't been included in traditional regulatory frameworks may cause unexpected risks to privacy. The regulators however must deal with these complexities and accord privacy laws considerable relevance and effectiveness in safeguarding individuals' rights against the encroachment of an increasingly interlinked world powered by data (Haque et al., 2021; Labadie & Legner, 2023; Mohammad Amini et al., 2023; Truong et al., 2020). Collaboration among policymakers, industry stakeholders, and privacy experts is essential to address these challenges and develop regulatory frameworks that strike the right balance between innovation and privacy protection.

BEST PRACTICES FOR ETHICAL GEOSPATIAL ANALYTICS

Transparency and Accountability in Data Collection and Use

Transparency and accountability are foundational principles in ethical geospatial analytics. It's crucial for organizations to be transparent about their data collection methods, sources, and purposes to build trust with stakeholders and mitigate potential privacy concerns. This includes clearly communicating how geospatial data is collected, processed, and utilized, as well as the potential implications for individuals and communities. Additionally, accountability mechanisms should be in place to ensure that data is used responsibly and ethically, with clear oversight and governance structures to address any misuse or breaches of trust. By prioritizing transparency and accountability, organizations can uphold ethical standards in geospatial analytics and foster a culture of integrity and trustworthiness.

Stakeholder Engagement and Participatory Decision-Making

Stakeholder engagement and participatory decision-making are essential for ethical geospatial analytics initiatives to be inclusive, equitable, and responsive to community needs and concerns. Engaging with diverse stakeholders, including local communities, government agencies, non-profit organizations, and industry partners, allows for a more comprehensive understanding of the social, environmental, and ethical implications of geospatial analytics projects. This engagement should be ongoing and participatory, involving stakeholders in the design, implementation, and evaluation of geospatial analytics solutions. By soliciting input from those affected by geospatial data and analysis, organizations can ensure that their initiatives are culturally sensitive, socially responsible, and aligned with community values and priorities.

Continuous Monitoring and Ethical Impact Assessments

Continuous monitoring and ethical impact assessments are critical components of ethical geospatial analytics, helping organizations identify and address potential ethical risks and concerns throughout the lifecycle of a project. This includes regularly assessing the potential impacts of geospatial data and analysis on individuals, communities, and the environment, as well as evaluating the ethical implications of data collection, processing, and dissemination practices. By proactively identifying ethical challenges and risks, organizations can implement appropriate safeguards and mitigation strategies to prevent harm and uphold ethical standards. Additionally, organizations should be transparent about their ethical impact assessments, sharing findings and insights with stakeholders to foster accountability and trust. Through continuous monitoring and ethical impact assessments, organizations can ensure that their geospatial analytics initiatives are ethically sound, socially responsible, and aligned with ethical principles and values.

CONCLUSION

As we navigate the complexities of geospatial analytics, it's imperative that organizations and practitioners prioritize responsible and ethical practices. This requires a commitment to transparency, accountability, and stakeholder engagement at every stage of the process. By adhering to best practices and ethical guidelines, potential harm can be minimized and the positive impacts of geospatial analytics on society and the environment can be maximized. All stakeholders should embrace their responsibility in promoting ethical geospatial analytics and actively contribute to building a culture of integrity and trust within the field.

Looking ahead, the field of geospatial analytics is poised for continued growth and innovation, presenting both opportunities and challenges from an ethical standpoint. As technologies evolve and new data sources emerge, organizations must remain vigilant in addressing emerging ethical challenges such as algorithmic bias, privacy concerns, and the equitable distribution of benefits and risks. Moreover, as geospatial analytics becomes increasingly integrated into decision-making processes across various sectors, there is a growing need for interdisciplinary collaboration and ethical leadership to ensure that these technologies are deployed responsibly and ethically. By anticipating and addressing these challenges proactively, we can pave the way for a more ethical and sustainable future for geospatial analytics.

REFERENCES

Abdalla, R., & Li, J. (2010). Towards effective application of geospatial technologies for disaster management. In *International Journal of Applied Earth Observation and Geoinformation* (Vol. 12, Issue 6). DOI: 10.1016/j.jag.2010.09.003

Abdurahman, A., Yirsaw, E., Nigussie, W., & Hundera, K. (2023). Past and future land-use/land-cover change trends and its potential drivers in Koore's agricultural landscape, Southern Ethiopia. *Geocarto International, 38*(1). DOI: 10.1080/10106049.2023.2229952

Al-Taani, A., Al-husban, Y., & Farhan, I. (2021). Land suitability evaluation for agricultural use using GIS and remote sensing techniques. The case study of Ma'an Governorate, Jordan. *Egyptian Journal of Remote Sensing and Space Science, 24*(1). DOI: 10.1016/j.ejrs.2020.01.001

Bandira, P. N. A., Mahamud, M. A., Samat, N., Tan, M. L., & Chan, N. W. (2021). Gis-based multi-criteria evaluation for potential inland aquaculture site selection in the george town conurbation, Malaysia. *Land, 10*(11). DOI: 10.3390/land10111174

Bartels, C. (2022). Cluster Analysis for Customer Segmentation with Open Banking Data. *ACM International Conference Proceeding Series*. DOI: 10.1145/3523181.3523194

Chiavacci, S. J., & Pindilli, E. J. (2020). Trends in biodiversity and habitat quantification tools used for market-based conservation in the United States. *Conservation Biology, 34*(1). DOI: 10.1111/cobi.13349

Dehghanian, P., Zhang, B., Dokic, T., & Kezunovic, M. (2019). Predictive Risk Analytics for Weather-Resilient Operation of Electric Power Systems. *IEEE Transactions on Sustainable Energy, 10*(1). DOI: 10.1109/TSTE.2018.2825780

Gao, J., Peng, P., Lu, F., Wang, S., Xie, X., & Claramunt, C. (2024). Knowledge-driven spatial competitive intelligence for tourism. *Transactions in GIS*. DOI: 10.1111/tgis.13145

Giovanola, B., & Tiribelli, S. (2023). Beyond bias and discrimination. redefining the AI ethics principle of fairness in healthcare machine-learning algorithms. *AI and Society, 38*(2). DOI: 10.1007/s00146-022-01455-6

Gregg Greenough, P., & Nelson, E. L. (2019). Beyond mapping. A case for geospatial analytics in humanitarian health. In *Conflict and Health* (Vol. 13, Issue 1). DOI: 10.1186/s13031-019-0234-9

Gupta, K., Sadana, S. K., & Gupta, B. (2020). Geospatial data preprocessing and visualization for the logistics industry. *Journal of Discrete Mathematical Sciences and Cryptography, 23*(1). DOI: 10.1080/09720529.2020.1721859

Haque, A. B., Islam, A. K. M. N., Hyrynsalmi, S., Naqvi, B., & Smolander, K. (2021). GDPR compliant blockchains-a systematic literature review. In *IEEE Access* (Vol. 9). DOI: 10.1109/ACCESS.2021.3069877

Jorge, C. F. B., & De Araujo, A. S. (2019). Spatial analysis in the process of competitive intelligence as a strategy for the construction of intelligence products and services aimed at organizations. *Ciência da Informação*, 48(1).

Kalhor, E., Horn, B. P., Valentin, V., & Berrens, R. P. (2018). Investigating the Effects of both Historical Wildfire Damage and Future Wildfire Risk on Housing Values. *International Journal of Ecological Economics & Statistics, 39*(1).

Labadie, C., & Legner, C. (2023). Building data management capabilities to address data protection regulations. Learnings from EU-GDPR. *Journal of Information Technology, 38*(1). DOI: 10.1177/02683962221141456

Le Gat, Y., Curt, C., Werey, C., Caillaud, K., Rulleau, B., & Taillandier, F. (2023). Water infrastructure asset management. state of the art and emerging research themes. *Structure and Infrastructure Engineering*. DOI: 10.1080/15732479.2023.2222030

Li, H., Yu, L., & He, W. (2019). The Impact of GDPR on Global Technology Development. In *Journal of Global Information Technology Management* (Vol. 22, Issue 1). DOI: 10.1080/1097198X.2019.1569186

Manjarrez-Domínguez, C., Uc-Campos, M. I., Esparza-Vela, M. E., Baray-Guerrero, M. del R., Giner-Chávez, O., & Santellano-Estrada, E. (2023). Geospatial-Temporal Dynamics of Land Use in the Juárez Valley. Urbanization and Displacement of Agriculture. *Sustainability (Switzerland), 15*(11). DOI: 10.3390/su15118499

Meng, F., Zhou, J., Kong, D., Yao, M., Wu, K., Liu, X., Wang, X., & Guo, Y. (2022). The Design and Implementation of Geospatial Information Verification Middle Platform for Natural Resources Government Affairs. *ISPRS International Journal of Geo-Information, 11*(10). DOI: 10.3390/ijgi11100496

Meschini, S., Pellegrini, L., Locatelli, M., Accardo, D., Tagliabue, L. C., Di Giuda, G. M., & Avena, M. (2022). Toward cognitive digital twins using a BIM-GIS asset management system for a diffused university. *Frontiers in Built Environment, 8*. DOI: 10.3389/fbuil.2022.959475

Mohammad Amini, M., Jesus, M., Fanaei Sheikholeslami, D., Alves, P., Hassanzadeh Benam, A., & Hariri, F. (2023). Artificial Intelligence Ethics and Challenges in Healthcare Applications. A Comprehensive Review in the Context of the European GDPR Mandate. In *Machine Learning and Knowledge Extraction* (Vol. 5, Issue 3). DOI: 10.3390/make5030053

Nagendra, N. P., Narayanamurthy, G., & Moser, R. (2022). Management of humanitarian relief operations using satellite big data analytics. the case of Kerala floods. *Annals of Operations Research, 319*(1). DOI: 10.1007/s10479-020-03593-w

Park, S. B., Kim, J., Lee, Y. K., & Ok, C. M. (2020). Visualizing theme park visitors' emotions using social media analytics and geospatial analytics. *Tourism Management, 80*. DOI: 10.1016/j.tourman.2020.104127

Peixoto, J. P. J., Costa, D. G., Portugal, P., & Vasques, F. (2023). A geospatial dataset of urban infrastructure for emergency response in Portugal. *Data in Brief, 50*. DOI: 10.1016/j.dib.2023.109593

Selvarajan, S., Mohamed, A., White, T., & Boodram, N. (2009). Assessment of geospatial technologies for natural resource management in Florida. *Journal of Forestry*, 107(5), 242–249. DOI: 10.1093/jof/107.5.242

Sun, W., Nasraoui, O., & Shafto, P. (2020). Evolution and impact of bias in human and machine learning algorithm interaction. *PLoS ONE, 15*(8). DOI: 10.1371/journal.pone.0235502

Taylor, W., & Hollenbeck, B. (2021). Leveraging loyalty programs using competitor based targeting. *Quantitative Marketing and Economics, 19*(3–4). DOI: 10.1007/s11129-021-09237-y

Tenkanen, H., Pereira, R. H. M., Arcaute, E., & Gonzalez, M. C. (2023). Advances in geospatial approaches to transport networks and sustainable mobility. In *Environment and Planning B. Urban Analytics and City Science* (Vol. 50, Issue 8). DOI: 10.1177/23998083231207768

Ting, C. Y., Zakariah, H., Kamaludin, F., Cheng, D. L. W., Tan, N. Y. Z., & Yee, H. J. (2021). Geospatial analytics for COVID-19 active case detection. *Computers, Materials and Continua, 67*(1). DOI: 10.32604/cmc.2021.013327

Truong, N. B., Sun, K., Lee, G. M., & Guo, Y. (2020). GDPR-Compliant Personal Data Management. A Blockchain-Based Solution. *IEEE Transactions on Information Forensics and Security, 15*. DOI: 10.1109/TIFS.2019.2948287 van Giffen, B., Herhausen, D., & Fahse, T. (2022). Overcoming the pitfalls and perils of algorithms. A classification of machine learning biases and mitigation methods. *Journal of Business Research, 144*. DOI: 10.1016/j.jbusres.2022.01.076

Wang, L., Fan, H., & Wang, Y. (2018). Site selection of retail shops based on spatial accessibility and hybrid BP neural network. *ISPRS International Journal of Geo-Information, 7*(6). DOI: 10.3390/ijgi7060202

Weiss, J. N. (2023). The Health Insurance Portability and Accountability Act (HI-PAA). In *Physician Crisis*. DOI: 10.1007/978-3-031-27979-9_15

Wichmann, J. R. K., Scholdra, T. P., & Reinartz, W. J. (2023). Propelling International Marketing Research with Geospatial Data. *Journal of International Marketing, 31*(2), 82–102. DOI: 10.1177/1069031X221149951

KEY TERMS AND DEFINITIONS

Artificial Intelligence (AI): Is the ability of a machine or a computer to emulate human intelligence and perform activities that a human being is capable of doing in the acquisition of knowledge, decision-making, problem-solving, visual recognition, and understanding of language.

Business Interests: Are the concerns of firms, companies, or corporations specifically the motives, aims, and desires of those entities functioning in a business economy. These interests are often profit-oriented gaining new markets, maintaining competitive position in the market and catering the shareholders' needs and wants.

Geographic Information System (GIS): Is defined as an established system for the actualization, storage, analysis and portrayal of spatial data. It combines the hardware as well as software elements to gather, process, and analyze geographical information like maps, satellite images, and topographic data.

Social Responsibility: Refers to the moral duty of individuals, companies, and businesses to act in ways that benefit society at large. It includes the processes by which decisions and activities are carried out with careful regard to what affects individuals other than for economic motives.

Spatial Analysis: Can be defined as the investigation of geographic information to identify relations and patterns that can help explain geographic occurrences.

Chapter 11

The Magnitude of Sustainable HRM Practices and Wellbeing in a Changing Environment

Swati Sharma
https://orcid.org/0000-0002-2029-5251
Department of Commerce, Chandigarh University, India

ABSTRACT

Finding strategies to maintain employee well-being is becoming more and more important to a variety of stakeholders, both within and beyond the context of the workplace, in today's rapidly evolving and fast-paced global workplace where preserving competitive edge is essential to success. The research design of study is descriptive in nature. Data was collected from secondary sources to study the importance of sustainable HR practices and wellbeing in a changing environment. Evidence demonstrates that a direct connection between HRM practices, well-being, and performance—possibly more significantly for organizations—can give practitioners the knowledge they need to motivate them to spend their resources. The findings of the research are relevant to a broad range of company sectors involved with innovative HRM, greening, and sustainability practices as well as corporate strategies that support well-being.

DOI: 10.4018/979-8-3693-3478-2.ch011

1. INTRODUCTION

The most challenging task in today's competitive corporate environment is finding qualified employees. In this demanding environment, having motivated and skilled personnel is crucial for survival. A positive work atmosphere inspires to put in extra efforts to accomplish their set targets and objectives. Happiness and life satisfaction in the present day are popular research topics. Building a healthy work environment requires research into variables that cause stress a how to reduce it (Abel et.al,2020).

According to previous studies, there are various aspects that can influence job satisfaction but the key influences include greater purpose, autonomy, people and impact(Alfes,2012). Organisation wishing to foster a positive workplace culture should concentrate on including ad implementing aforesaid elements in their HR policy. Employers who want to make their workers happy promote a positive work environment by treating their workers with trust and respects. Past research demonstrates that employers who participate in corporate decision making, goal -setting, policy formulation and day -to -day tasks are happier, more productive and productivity (Abid et.al,2020). In study, we consider employee pleasure to be a measure of subjective health. (Arbatani et.al,2016). To gauge employee contentment, we've used two different perspectives: the organizational perspective (Employee well-being/workplace contentment) and second personal perspective (Individual happiness). The elements affecting an employee's well-being or work place. Psychological well-being, emotional wellbeing and social wellbeing are all factors in happiness. Life satisfaction.

Employee satisfaction is an important part of a healthy working environment and organization. companies that promote well-being make it easier for employees to manage stress levels while creating a positive and productive environment (Jena et al,2018).

Additionally, while it is widely known that having a job improves one's physical and mental health compared to being jobless, the relationship between employment and wellness is far from clear-cut, with low employee satisfaction being a significant contributor to absences from the workplace. However, as a growing industry, sustainable human resource management (sustainable HRM) gives businesses the opportunity to increase employee living conditions in order to advance social sustainability. However, in some high-performance work systems (HPWPs), the detrimental effects of labor on employee health impede their ability to advance professionally and personally.

Sustainable human resource management emphasizes on fulfilling the various requirements related employees working in organizations and to help them to live a good healthy life. After covid -19 has greatly impacted the organization trust which is very important for performance and productivity of the organization. Many studies conducting on wellbeing states that employee having good well-being also is satisfied with his life and job, they have more capabilities to deal with situation, they also keep on improving themselves (Cannas et.al, 2016 and Haynes et al.,2020). Company should understand adopting sustainable human resource management practices in an organization will build organizational trust. According to recent studies, organizational trust always has outcomes for staff and organization as it contain security of employee, loyalty etc. When workers have it well, they tend to do it better. This increases the productivity and how workers can help develop themselves better.

2. LITERATURE REVIEW

According to WHO health is not just related to absence of disease or any kind of disability but it is state of mental, physical as well as social wellbeing of individual. These definitions are essential for organizations to achieve a positive impact on their employees and the environment. Since the World Health Organization redefined health as a state of general physical, mental and social well-being, not just the absence of disease or disability, scientific discussions about employee well-being have been ongoing for some time(Helliwell, 2018). These definitions are a requirement for organizations to have a positive impact on their employees and the environment.

After covid 19 pandemic one of the variable social distances came into much attention. It may focus on the social distance and its impact both on employee working in organization and employee working at home. On the one hand, frontline employees who provide "vital" services (health care, grocery stores, pharmacies, etc.) On the other hand, the sudden shift to working from home and self-isolation cause unintended mental health consequences such as stress, isolation, and depression, leading to suicide (Knapp et al., 2020). The above leads to improved individual and organizational outcomes. As a result, a sustainable approach to HRM provides mutual benefits to the employee and the organization and enables the widespread use of these methods in organizational activities. Trust in a company, its leaders, and its employees is given special consideration in the effective implementation of sustainable HRM strategies (Jena et al., 2018). Saraswati et al. (2020) Studied the impact of work life balance and work pressure on mental wellbeing. The research design of study was descriptive in nature. The sample size of the study was 250 employees. To analyses the data regression analyses was done. This study states that though there is impact of work pressure on work life balance and further it has an impact on wellbeing but no significant impact of work pressure was seen on mental wellbeing of employees. Tyssen (2019) conducted a review on relationship of work and mental health among doctors. This paper present that high level of stress was seen among doctors which impacted the patient care and symptoms of depression was founded. Suicidal case is increasing among doctors who were facing extreme level of stress. Frustration level among doctors seen very high.

3. THE IMPACT OF SUSTAINABLE HRM PRACTICES ON WELLBEING

Research investigations worldwide have shown that the success or failure of programs to improve healthcare service depends on how businesses respond to employee issues through leadership, support, and motivation. It is possible to achieve the organization's long-term financial, ecological, and social goals through practices incorporating the appropriate adaptation of HRM methods and processes while managing negative feedback and unanticipated side effects. Emphasizing human resources, taking into account their growth, development, and health, and protecting the link between leaders and followers, organizations, and sustainability are all components of sustainable leadership. From a main preventive standpoint, this tactic can promote beneficial and profitable development processes for people and enterprises to handle the challenges of genuine and sustainable human resource development. A sustainable culture is fostered by sustainable HRM methods, such as selection, in addition to sustainable leadership, through the connection between quality management techniques and plant competitiveness. In order to create environmentally friendly workplaces, it is essential to consider how sustainable practices affect plant competitiveness. According to SDG 4 (decent work), employees need fair remuneration; several nations have set minimum wages with the intention of ensuring that workers have enough money to cover their basic necessities. However, other people contend that raising the minimum wage alone will not improve employee happiness. Beyond simply following the law, fair remuneration entails other factors. Compensation is described as "all forms of cash returns and tangible services and benefits employees receive" in a working relationship. A person's base salary as well as short- and long-term incentives are considered financial returns.

Benefits are referred to as "tangible services and benefits" and include things like insurance, paid sick and vacation days, pension plans, and employee discounts. These perks are not common in employment and firms are not required by law to supply them. Still, fair income is correlated with job satisfaction and wellbeing. SDG 8 of the UN advocates for sustained, inclusive, and sustainable economic growth as well as for decent employment.

3.1 Guidelines for Managing Sustainable HRM Environments and Monitoring Human Wellbeing

Through corporate reports and indicators, businesses must give stakeholders meaningful, timely, and understandable information about their activities. By disseminating this data, businesses uphold their obligations under the ethics of responsibility and develop sustainable policies that promote employee success and well-being.

You cannot improve what you do not measure, according to Peter Drucker . Indicators help us better identify any area of opportunity and improve outcomes, assertions, etc. Implementing sustainable practices entails working toward improved economies, societies, and environments. The gross domestic product (GDP) is misused as a gauge of public wellbeing due to the erroneous belief that economic growth is always accompanied by an improvement in quality of life. To guarantee employees' health, security, and job happiness, however, wellbeing must be measured using metrics other than the GDP.

One indicator of employee wellness and a key organizational indicator is job satisfaction . The type and amount of income, promotions, coworkers, and the organizational context are just a few examples of how specific elements and the nature of the work might affect it . Indicators like those for wellbeing or gender equality in the workplace (SDG5) are essential to assisting businesses in having a good impact on their workforce and the environment.

There are numerous techniques that a corporation can adopt to promote the well-being of their personnel. What matters most is that you are aware of all the benefits of employee wellbeing in the first place, and that you build employee wellbeing programs to target specific concerns in your firm.

- **Medical examination –** Health check of staff should be mandatory once a year in organization, as it going to address all the health issues of the staff. Early-stage detection of the disease due to health checkups will improve the disease prevention. With regular health check employee will take care of this health.
- **Health insurance –** By providing various health insurance scheme to employees is going provide them well being as they will less worried about their expenses. Provide them multiple option of insurance out which they can select the best one
- **Enrolment in a gym-** Now a day many organisations are providing gym membership to their staff. This can prove an excellent way to improve employee wellbeing. Employer should assist their staff be fit mentally and psychically. As workout decreases stress among them and this the best way to keep us fit and healthy.

- **Solution for Employee Wellbeing-** Fitness initiatives in organisation like cycling, running competition, sports day etc. is good approach to keep employees physically active. In every organisation there should be module of employee wellbeing. This module should include various heath solution.
- **Providing nutritious meals-** Poor nutrition or unhealthy eating is also one of the causes of poor health. People having hectic work schedule always look for fast food for the lunch. You should explain your employee regarding disadvantages of consuming unhealthy food. Try to provide nutritious meals in office.
- **Apps for emotional well-being-** Now a days there are many mindfulness and mediation apps you can look into and suggest to staff. Explain the people working in your organisation the relevance of mediation and mindfulness and how it can help them in manging stress of day-to-day life.
- **Services for Therapy –** Try to connect with your employee by making them aware of the psychological therapy services. Help your employee to come out of the stigma that they have related to seeking psychological assistance. Tell the to take the advantage of various services offered by health experts who will help them to deal with their recent problems.
- **Work possibilities that are flexible-** To improve work life balance of your employee, offer them flexible working hours facilities. According to recent studies only 8 percent of staff says that salary is more important than work life balance. Work life balance play a very important role in shaping mental wellbeing of employees.
- **Financial advantages-** Help your staff in making sound financial decisions for their life. By educating them regarding various life insurance schemes, Pension plan set.
- **Employee well-being programs based on your employees' feedback-** Take suggestions of employees to design employee wellbeing programs in organisation. Feedback of employee should be welcomed by the organisation. Try to elucidate your employees state of mind while they are working in workplace.

3.4 Why Is Employee Wellbeing More Important Than Ever?

- **Absenteeism and healthcare expenditures have been reduced-** Organization nowadays have started realizing the importance of good well-being of employees. The various reasons of poor mental health is stress, work load, poor working condition which is impacted the mental health of the employees. The poor life style of employees have lead to high risk of diabetes, blood pressure etc. Past studies have revealed that about 63% people seek sick days leave because of burnout. Employee doesn't feel happy while working in organization resulting performance of organization.

- **Employee involvement has increased**- Past studies revealed that 85% of organisation finds wellness initiatives are going to help in building good mental wellbeing.. Employee recognition and good feedback processes, on the other hand, have an impact on employee engagement. When attempting to improve employee engagement in your organization, make sure you tackle it holistically.
- **Increased employee output -** On the one hand, studies show that smokers are twice as likely as non-smokers to miss their work, while obese workers spend three to six sick days a year more than workers with a normal weight. Employees who cope well with stress, on the other hand, are less likely to burn out. Overall, when employee well-being improves, people are more focused on their work and productivity increases. • Increased employee morality .During the COVID-19 crisis we have seen how important it is to keep employee morals.

4. PROSPECTS OF HUMAN WELL-BEING

The well-being of employees is more important than ever because companies have finally recognized the power that it has to modify the life of their employees, reduce the costs associated with absence and health care, and promote a healthy business culture.

Employers have shifted their focus away from specific health concerns and toward advantages such as fitness programs and standing workstations. After all, avoiding disease development is considerably less expensive than healing it, and it helps the employees as well. Employee wellbeing benefits will become more diverse in the future. Employee disengagement, absenteeism, and healthcare costs are too great to ignore.

India, together with other nations, has pledged to adopting Sustainable Development Goals (SDGs) to end poverty, safeguard the environment, and promote happiness among all people within the framework of a new worldwide sustainable development agenda to be completed by 2030. Although tremendous economic progress in India over the last few decades, our accomplishments in the health of the population have been insufficient. In 2015, all State Chief Ministers and Lieutenant Governors of Union Territories overwhelmingly consented to the National Development Agenda, which highlighted nutrition, health, Learning, Women, and Infants as key areas. It is critical to make significant progress in these sectors so as to attain the National Development genda.

Figure 1. Health index

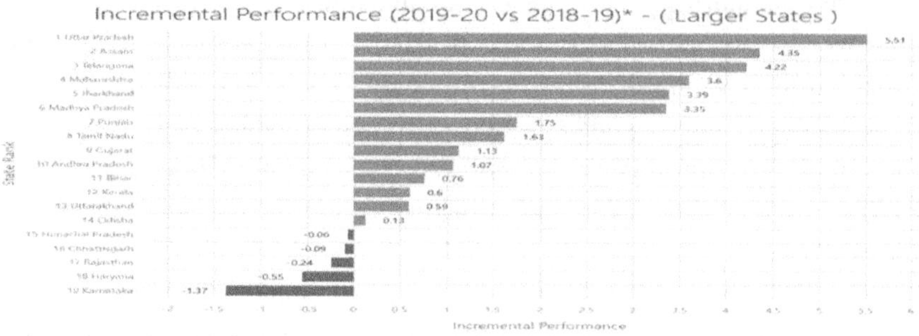

(Source -NITIAAYOG 2020 REPORT)

Figure 1 and Figure 2 represents the health performance of the citizen of Indian according ministry of health and Niti Aayog.

Figure 2a. Incremental performance of larger states

Larger States Incremental Performance

States	Health Index		Incremental progress from base to reference year	Incremental progress rank
	Base Year	Reference Year		
Haryana	47.59	54.08	6.49	1
Rajasthan	37.35	43.23	5.88	2
Jharkhand	48.25	53.67	5.42	3
Andhra Pradesh	60.84	65.31	4.47	4
Assam	45.84	50.02	4.18	5
Telangana	56.12	59.42	3.30	6
Maharashtra	61.76	64.53	2.77	7
Karnataka	59.39	61.77	2.38	8
Jammu and Kashmir	61.02	62.92	1.90	9
Chhattisgarh	52.69	53.97	1.28	10
Himachal Pradesh	61.84	63.10	1.26	11
Gujarat	62.61	63.72	1.11	12
Madhya Pradesh	40.77	38.69	-2.08	13
Punjab	65.83	63.41	-2.42	14
Kerala	77.53	74.65	-2.88	15

Tamil Nadu	64.05	60.50	-3.55	16
Odisha	40.19	36.3	-3.84	17
Uttarakhand	44.61	39.61	-5	18
Uttar Pradesh	34.44	29.16	-5.28	19
Bihar	39.10	32.43	-6.67	20

(Source: NITIAAYOG 2020 REPORT)

The green highlighted states have most improved health index and light green color indicates that Telangana, Maharashtra, Karnataka have moderate improvement in health index. Least improved in health index is of Jammu and Kashmir, Chhattisgarh, Himachal Pradesh, Gujarat.

5. CONCLUSION

This research contributes to Sustainable human resource management emphasizes on fulfilling the various requirements related employees working in organizations and to help them to live a good healthy life .After covid -19 has greatly impacted the organization trust which is very important for performance and productivity of the organization. Many studies conducting on wellbeing states that employee having good well being also is satisfied with his life and job, they have more capabilities to deal with situation, they also keep on improving themselves (Khoreva and Wechtler,2018;Cooper et al.,2019).Company should understand adopting sustainable human resource management practices in an organization will build organizational trust. According to recent studies, organizational trust always have outcomes for staff and organization as it contain security of employee, loyalty etc. When workers have it well, they tend to do it better. This increases the productivity and how workers can help develop themselves better. To improve work life balance of your employee, offer them flexible working hours facilities. According to recent studies only 8 percent of staff says that salary is more important than work life balance. Work life balance play a very important role in shaping mental wellbeing of employees. Organization nowadays have started realizing the importance of good wellbeing of employees. The various reasons of poor mental health are stress, work load, poor working condition which is impacted the mental health of the employees. The poor life style of employees has led to high risk of diabetes, blood pressure etc. Past studies have revealed that about 63% people seek sick days leave because of burnout. Employee doesn't feel happy while working in organization resulting performance of organization.

REFERENCES

Abel, T., & McQueen, D. (2020). The CVID-19 pandemic calls fr spatial distancing and scial clseness: Nt fr scial distancing. *International Journal of Public Health*, 65(3), 231. DOI: 10.1007/s00038-020-01366-7 PMID: 32239256

Abid, G., Ahmed, S., Elahi, N. S., & Ilyas, S. (2020). Antecedents and mechanism f emplyee wellbeing fr scial sustainability: A sequential mediatin. *Sustainable Production and Consumption*, 24, 79–89. DOI: 10.1016/j.spc.2020.06.011

Alfes, K., Shantz, A., & Truss, C. (2012). The link between perceived HRM practices, perfrmance and well-being: The mderating effect f trust in the emplyer. Human Resurce management Jurnal, 22(4), 409- 427.

Arbatani, T. R., Farhangi, A. A., & Dadashzadeh, Y. (2016). Framing the Current Challenges and Trends in Human Resurce Management. Internatinal Jurnal f Humanities and Cultural Studies, 589-600.

Cannas, M., Sergi, B. S., Sirni, E., & Mentel, U. (2019). Jb satisfactin and subjective well-being in Eurpe. *Ecnmics and Scilgy*, 12(4), 183–196.

Cleveland, J. N., Byrne, Z. S., & Cavanagh, T. M. (2015). The future f HR is RH: Respect fr humanity at wrk. *Human Resource Management Review*, 25(2), 146–161. DOI: 10.1016/j.hrmr.2015.01.005

Davidescu, A. A., Apstu, S. A., Paul, A., & Casuneanu, I. (2020). Wrk Flexibility, Jb Satisfactin, and Jb Perfrmance amng Rmanian Emplyees – Implicatins fr Sustainable Human Resurce Management. *Sustainability (Basel)*, 12(15), 6086. DOI: 10.3390/su12156086

Guest, D. E. (2017). Human resurce management and emplyee well-being: Twards a new analytic framewrk. Human resurce management jurnal, 27(1), 22-38.

Haynes, S. H., Lene, M. C., Keena, L. D., May, D. C., Ricciardelli, R., & Lambert, E. G. (2020). The assciatin between different frms f rganizatinal trust and crrectinal staff jb stress. *Journal of Crime and Justice*, 43(5), 623–639. DOI: 10.1080/0735648X.2020.1734056

Helliwell, J. F., & Huang, H. (2011). Well-being and trust in the wrkplace. *Journal of Happiness Studies*, 12(5), 747–767. DOI: 10.1007/s10902-010-9225-7

Heyns, M., & Rthmann, S. (2018). Vlitinal trust, autnmy satisfactin, and engagement at wrk. Psychlgical reprts, 121(1), 112-134.

Jena, L. K., Pradhan, S., & Panigrahy, N. P. (2018). Pursuit f rganisatinal trust: Rle f emplyee engagement, psychlgical well-being and transfrmatinal leadership. *Asia Pacific Management Review*, 23(3), 227–234. DOI: 10.1016/j.apmrv.2017.11.001

Khreva, V., & Wechtler, H. (2018). HR practices and emplyee perfrmance: The mediating rle f wellbeing. *Employee Relations*, 40(2), 227–243. DOI: 10.1108/ER-08-2017-0191

Knapp, J. R., Diehl, M. R., & Dugan, W. (2020). Twards a scial-cgnitive thery f multiple psychlgical cntracts. Eurpean Jurnal f Wrk and rganizatinal Psychlgy, 29(2), 200-214.

Saraswati, K. D. H., & Lie, D. (2020). Psychlgical Well-Being: The Impact f Wrk-Life Balance and Wrk Pressure. Advances in Scial Science, Educatin and Humanities Research. Internatinal Jurnal f Research in Management. *Ecnmics and Cmmerce*, 7(11), 40–47.

Tyssen, R. (2019). Wrk and mental health in dctrs: A shrt review. *Prt Bimedical Jurnal*, 4(5), 1–3.

Chapter 12
Digital Infrastructure and Connectivity:
The Backbone of Modern Civilization

Abdul Samad Dahri
https://orcid.org/0000-0003-4517-3493
Shaheed Bbenazir Bhutto University, Pakistan

Salman Bashir Memon
https://orcid.org/0000-0002-4533-4923
Shaheed Benazir Bhutto University, Pakistan

Sumaiya Syed
Shah Abdul Latif University, Pakistan

ABSTRACT

This chapter provides a comprehensive analysis of digital infrastructure and connectivity as foundational elements for fostering digital technologies and economic development. It defines the role and significance of digital infrastructure and examines the history and technological progression of connectivity projects. Key components such as broadband networks, telecom structures, and data centers are analyzed for their importance in supporting modern communication and information exchange. The chapter also reviews the impact of laws and policies on digital infrastructure, focusing on financing, rural access, and security. A case study on Zorez Telecom's expansion project highlights the challenges organizations may face when implementing digital infrastructure, covering regulatory and economic issues, while offering practical approaches for students and professionals to address these challenges.

DOI: 10.4018/979-8-3693-3478-2.ch012

1. INTRODUCTION

Globalization has emerged as a transformational change in today's world after the development of information communication technology both physical structures and connections (Kumar, 2021). The aspects of digital resource are the networks, hardware, software and services that are required for digital information to be processed and for messages to be transferred. On the other hand, connectivity is the ability to capitalize on and access this infrastructure, which facilitates proper connection between various domains and devises. Next, as to advocate for technology-facilitated development, the chapter defines and explains the concept of digital infrastructure and connection. However, returning to the discussion of the impact of digital transformation, it should be noted that it not only contributes to better communication and business processes but also encourages innovation, contributes to the development of economies, and improves the quality of life through the provision of education, healthcare services, and other important activities. Technologies such as digital infrastructure and connectivity in different sectors have boosted the creation of smart cities, e-governance, and digital economy thus show how important these technologies are in the modern societies development.

a. Defining Digital Infrastructure and Connectivity

Cloud computing resources, well-organized data centers, internet connections, and telecommunication networks represent only a fragment of the digital infrastructure (Sunyaev & Sunyaev, 2020). Altogether, these components give a foundation that is necessary for storage, processing, as well as transfer of gigantic amounts of data, and can operate as a foundation of the digital environment. Whereas connectivity depicts how seamless people and organizations are in using these resources. These connections encompass Internet protocol and communication protocol that are virtual as well as wireless technologies and broadband networks that are physical. Additionally, the quality of connectivity is determined by the bandwidth, latency as well as the reliability of the network, which have a closer relationship with the quality of users' experience and the effectiveness of various digital services. The strong digital systems and end-to-end connectivity are indispensable requisites in today's digital economy as well as remain requisite for growth, innovation, and delivery of essential services; therefore, there is a requirement of constant investment and development in these areas.

b. Significance in Facilitating Tech-Enabled Growth

The role of the digital environments and connectivity in enabling the technology based growth cannot be over emphasized. Well-established and effective digital environment is the cornerstone for encouraging innovative solutions, supporting the advancement of economy, and enhancement of social benefits in today's world. In this case, individuals receive important links to online health care and education services, and businesses experience the same, having broader prospects to advance their positions in the market. Likewise, governments receive the opportunity to provide the population with a great number of essential public services in the most effective way (Kelly et al., 2020). However, digital infrastructure works as an enabler of technology innovation since it enables the innovation and integration of novel technologies like blockchain, IoT, or AI. Such advances for the industries in return bring up new possibilities, increase productivity, and significantly promote globalization and internationalization of economy. Thus, the positive changes triggered by the development of digital infrastructure go beyond purely economic significance and promote creating a society where everyone has a chance to progress.

2. EVOLUTION OF DIGITAL INFRASTRUCTURE

a. Historical View of Connectivity

Digital infrastructure is a concept that has a rather long history which is rooted in the early days of computing and communication. The foundation of today's global connection was established in the 20th century, thanks to efforts like the establishment of ARPANET which is considered a forerunner of the contemporary internet (Packard, 2023). Further, progression in telecommunication such as the use of fiber optic cables as well as the creation of new digital switching technology enhanced the reach and the volume of the digital networks. Thus, starting from the end of the twentieth century and up to the beginning of the twenty-first, numerous initiatives to create additional connection and further the objectives of digital agencies and organizations were designed and implemented by governing bodies as well as private companies. In the United States of America, the Telecommunications Act of 1996 intending to increase investment and competition in telecommunications context introduced the positive changes and growth within the internet connection and the broadband networks. On the same note, the global connectedness of digital networks has been enhanced by the large-scale activities such as China's belt and road project and the EU's digital strategy for Europe that is aimed at reducing the digital divide and encourage assimilation of technology. Collectively, these efforts have created society's foundation that has allowed for the rapid advancement of digital technologies that characterizes contemporary society.

b. Impact of Technological Advancements on Infrastructure Development

Different technologies have significantly influenced the development of the more extensive digital environment as well. With the help of technologies like cloud computing, wireless networking, and broadband internet the ways of handling and storing data have changed drastically. These developments have produced dependable and high-speed communication networks with possibility of developing many kinds of services and applications. Moreover, the moreover, the availability of emerging technologies and communicating gadgets such as mobile devices and recently the IoT (Internet of Things) has require stronger and highly advanced digital network that carry and interconnect large amount of data (Munirathinam, 2020). Thus, the concerns related to infrastructure development have been directed at increasing broadband Internet availability, strengthening network facilities, and integrating innovative solutions. The need for embedding digital technology into life has sustained continued growth and development of the digital infrastructure. Electronic infrastructure of nations is an important aspect that has been put into consideration in the development of policies within the societies' background knowledge of the technological reforms required for the development of the digital networks. All this vision is necessary to continue the competition's sustainable presence in the digital economy and counter new threats.

3. COMPONENTS OF DIGITAL INFRASTRUCTURE

a. Broad Networks and Internet Connectivity

Digital plumbing is constituted by a broadband environment for the transmission of high-speed data to governments, corporations, and consumers. Broadband generally means a high speed of data connection that is very stable and far much better than the dial up connection. It enables them to perform a numerous numbers of tasks via internet like cloud computing, online games, video steaming without a lot of lag and discontinuity. Depending on the technology used, broadband networks can be implemented using; Digital Subscriber Line (DSL), cable networks, fibre optic, satellite and wireless. Of these, the fiber-optic networks can be thought as quite reliable and faster since it convey data in the form of light signals through optical fiber (Bele et al., 2023). The FCC has stated that fiber-optic networks offer service speeds of a gigabit per second which makes fiber-optic perfect for bandwidth intensive programs like virtual reality and 4K video.

The use and accessibility of broadband networks are still in different levels of deployment in different parts of the world. According to various studies, the urban regions enjoy comparatively faster broadband services than the rural and other remote regions of a country owing to certain geophysical, demographic, as well as economic limitations (Briglauer et al., 2024). In this case the Organization for Economic Co-operation and Development (OECD) has established that the penetration rates for broadband subscriber access are normally lower in the rural regions than in the urban regions. This is why there remains significant demand for endowments and interventions that can effectively address the digital gap.

Besides, PLBN has a significant role in increasing internet connection to the unserved and scarcely populated areas through mobile broadband services. Mobile broadband brings internet connection that is attained by utilizing mobile terminals such as mobile phones, tablets, and other gadgets (Valentín-Sívico, Canfield, Low, & Gollnick, 2023). These services use technologies like 4G LTE and 5G technology which is a cellular network that enables high-speed internet. ITU shows that mobile broadband Internet subscriptions are rapidly growing in recent years; even in the developing world; this grows the Internet connectivity.

b. Telecommunication Infrastructure

The broad concept that is encompassed under the term 'telecommunication infrastructure' includes a vast set of instruments and materials necessary for transferring multimedia and other kinds of information over vast distances. This infrastructure comprises of the physiological part like the phone connection, cell stations, and undersea cables among others, software and other networks. Digital technology has made changes in the long-held telecommunication models for instance, circuit switched networks and telephone line systems. The current telecommunication mainly employs Packet Switching Networks that allow the transmittal of data in small bundles known as packets across the available communication channels (Wong, 2021). This approach enhances the usage of network that is up to date and also enhances compatibility of different communication services which include voice over Internet protocol, video conferencing and instant messaging.

Indeed, due to the ever-evolving elements such as the 5G wireless networks, the telecommunication infrastructure must be periodically upgraded. 5G networks therefore signified faster data rates, low latency and high peak data rates than the previous mobile communication technologies. These networks use the newly available radio frequencies, very dense Small Cell station configurations, and innovative antenna technologies for various application areas including intelligent transportation systems, smart city infrastructures and industrial IoT.

- **Efficiency and Resource Optimization:** This has made packet-switched networks to be the key infrastructure in the contemporary telecommunication systems. Recording data in packets which are discrete makes these networks efficient at the use of bandwidth which is available, as well as dynamically routing these packets to decrease congestion as well as increase efficiency. This is a marked improvement over the old circuit-switched networks where exactly one path is provided for the entire period of a call-with perhaps most of the link's capacity going to waste through underutilization.
- **Diverse Communication Services:** Today's telecommunication infrastructure presents numerous services that are essential to present day communication requirements. For example, VoIP is a communication software that supports voice calls over the internet thus cuts on costs and enhances mobility. This refers to the ability to have a face to face conversation through a video call which is crucial in today's business and interpersonal communication. Instant Messaging enables people to write to people without delay and is very useful whether in business, work, or family situations.
- **Support for Emerging Technologies:** Technological advancements in the fashion of 5G networks exhibitions are considered as a shift in the global telecommunication competence. While the core characteristics of 5G are high-speed and low-latency, the high capacity of 5G connections is necessary as well for the support of application. Self-driving cars require the exchange of information between vehicles and their environment, which happens in real-time. Smart cities apply 5G to coordinate the different urban infrastructures to improve sustainability and the general standard of living. The implementation of 5G is advantageous in industrial automation because communication is dependable and rapid, therefore increasing efficiency.
- **Technological Advancements:** Optimizing higher frequency bands, small cells, and advanced antenna solutions to 5G networks fulfills the pitfalls of the prior mobile generations. Such advancements guarantee sufficient and evenly spread connectivity independently of population density or geographical peculiarities of the given area. Another major strength is the capability to manage a high density of interconnected devices, which is useful with the expanding Internet of Things (IoT).

c. Data Centre and Cloud Computing

Communication apparatuses, storage equipment, and computer equipment are place in large central offices that are called data centers. These facilities are necessary to manage digital services which include, web based applications, data intensive applications, data analysis and data hosting services. A data center infrastructure has to be sufficiently secure, flexible, and resilient to serve the expanding needs of the digital business ecosystem.

Cloud computing is one of the greatest paradigms of computing resources and services in use over the internet and paid on demand. Most cloud providers give businesses the capability to outsource their IT processes by offering foreseeable services such as; Platform as a service (PaaS), software as a service (SaaS), and infrastructure as a service (IaaS). A research done by Gartner revealed that cloud services hit $256 billion globally in 2018, and the market was estimated to be $396bn in 2022, due to the growing cloud use around the world.

The increase of new data centres and cloud services providers has raised the issue on data security, environmental effects and energy use. There are regions where the consumption of energy in data centers occupies a considerable share of the total consumption and belongs to the leaders in electricity consumption in the world. Some strategies to enhance the energy consumption in data centers include adopting efficient cooling technologies, efficient server consolidation and energy from natural resources. On the same note, laws like the GDPR also put measures and strict controls on data management and processing in computing facilities to protect personal data.

4. THE ROLE OF GOVERNMENT POLICIES AND REGULATIONS

Policies and other measures that are implemented by the government are key to defining the levels of development of the digital equipment and access to the Internet. I found these programs include such investments, regulations and policies that concern the development and deployment of new digital networks for growth of these transformative innovations. This section they continue putting emphasis on the role that governmental laws and regulations play in the development of digital structures.

a. Government Initiatives for Infrastructure Development

The governments throughout the world acknowledge the need for digital assets in enhancing social development and economic viability. Thus, the governments of a significant number of countries has started large-scale program addressing the issues related to information and communication technologies making use of advanced technologies promoting the development of new products and services, expansion of high-speed broadband access, and enhancement of connectivity in the less-developed areas. One notable example is the US Broadband Deployment Initiative which aims at increasing broadband internet availability in rural and other unserved areas trough targeted investments and regulatory changes (Federal Communications Commission, 2021).

Likewise, the European Union's Digital Single Market Strategy, which focuses on the creation of a regulatory environment that would facilitate investment in digital infrastructure as well as the promotion of digital competencies among the members (European Commission, 2021). These steps show that the decision-makers increasingly acknowledge the importance of advancing the digital environment as a prerequisite for the creation of new jobs, promotion of economic growth, and maintaining efficiency.

b. Regulatory Frameworks and Standards

Aside from the direct investments, political authorities decisively impact the deployment and usage of digital facilities through industry standards and regulations. Sector-specific regulations entail policies such as infrastructure sharing, protection of user data, cyber security and of course spectrum policies. Through clear rules and norms, which should regulate activity, governments ensure the legal stability for the private sector with the maintenance of the consumer's rights and fair competition at the same time.

For instance, legal provisions such as net neutrality laws protect unbiased access to information as well as services on the net by banning internet service providers from discriminating in their bias toward particular traffic (Federal Communications Commission, 2015). Likewise, laws like the General Data Protection Regulation in the European Union regulate the collection of people's data, mode of processing, and how the data is stored, thus enhancing consumer trust in digital goods and services (European Union, 2016). Furthermore, governments work with stakeholders from the industry to set technical requirements and characteristics in order to achieve coherence in the elements of the digital infrastructure environment. These standards are essential in enhancing market competition, innovation and interoperability of the various network and devices.

5. CHALLENGES IN BUILDING DIGITAL INFRASTRUCTURE

The development of digital environment is crucial for encouraging inventions, creating the improved connections and stimulating the economic growth. Nevertheless, certain issues have to be effectively solved in order to guarantee the successfulness of the digital infrastructure initiatives. The first subtheme focuses on the main challenges experienced in the establishment of the digital platforms and reviews possible counter measures.

a. Investment Requirements and Funding Challenges

It is a big challenge to meet the significant capital expenditure to put in place and maintain these digital landmarks thus making capital expenditure one of the rate hurdles to their deployment. Some of the activities include laying of fiber-optic cables, erecting of cell towers, and replacement of network equipment which are capital demanding processes that require a lot of capital. But maintenance is also required in the form of continuous capital expenditure to track new age technology as well as higher bandwidth requirement.

In order to overcome these financial difficulties, the governments, companies, and even the international organizations work in unison to source funds for the infrastructural development in the realm of digitization. Financing is achieved by applying one of the most widely used financing models called public-private partnerships, where ''public'' and ''private'' sectors share burden and benefits. For instance, the World Bank's Global Infrastructure Facility (GIF) offer funding and advisory services for PPPs in infrastructure projects especially for the emerging countries (World Bank, 2021). In addition, the newer forms of funding like the impact investment funds, green bonds, and infrastructure bonds are also considered to invest more in the development of digital infrastructure. These financial tools afford investors an opportunity of funding sustainable development projects and at the same time receive good returns on their investment (United Nations, 2019).

b. Regulatory and Policy Barriers

One major challenge is that legal frameworks and regulations can pose a tremendous amount of restrictions to establish digital systems. Some of the key challenges that mostly affect construction projects include; regulation insecurity, bureaucracy, and long approval procedures which may lead to loss of time and amplify the expenses. Also, diverse requirements and regulations by the different zones can then pose challenges in the development of a smooth converging digital infrastructural network. In order to eradicate these challenges, governments should try and do the following to ensure that the environment is favorable for the business. There is also increased efforts at rationalisation of approval procedures, standardisation and efficiency of the standards achieved as well as international collaboration. A type of operational framework that can prove useful is the regulatory sandboxes this is because they enable testing of the technologies in a controlled manner and this assists in the identification of the pertinent regulatory issues that are likely to be an issue in the project.

c. Technological Obsolescence and Rapid Advancements

The rate of change of technology is high and hence the problem of obsolescence of structures that support technology is always a looming problem. Any infrastructure that is current can become out dated within a few years hence needing constant repairs and replacement. To overcome this problem of Technological obsolescence, planners and developers of infrastructures have to incorporate flexibility and scalability to them in the overall design. Adopting a system that allows one to add or modify additional and new features can also be useful in dealing with future progression of technology. Also, constant development of the new technologies and their integration into the existing infrastructure is crucial to follow technological advances and to design and implement new solutions.

d. Digital Divide and Inclusivity

Central issues such as the digital divide are still worrying as regards to the development of the digital structure. Inequalities between the urban and the rural areas and between the different socio-economic classes in terms of access to technology similarly to water increase existing inequalities which hampers development of digital infrastructure. Hence, to eliminate the social disparity as propagated by the digital divide, proper intervention measures are required to facilitate equal opportunity for people to access the digital products. This entails establishing networks in the rural and sensitive districts, affordable pricing strategies, and the use of digital literacy. Policies to encourage the majority and the minorities to join the digital society required for these developments are to have a positive effect on all segments of the population. Thus, the main precondition for addressing the challenges and successfully constructing the digital infrastructure is the actions of various government structures, business circles, and global organisations. Through the resolution of investment and funding constraints, regulatory and legal barriers, technological obsolescence, and the digital divide, one can establish a solid and comprehensive temporal structure for digital innovations connecting individuals, institutions, and the global economy.

6. DESIGNING A DIGITAL CONNECTIVITY PLAN

Activity Overview

This lesson aims at making students work together and design a sound and well-coordinated approach to increasing the level of digital connection in a particular region/income group. In this regard, the goal is to generate tangible experience in the approach of digital infrastructure concerns and encouraging universal interconnectivity. The activity consists of several stages:

i. Establishing Groups and Choosing Communities/Regions

The groups formed will be diverse hence teaching students to work in groups as well as foster their creativity. For this, each group will choose a town or an area in which that group considers it appropriate to set up the digital connectivity plan. The targeted groups of people or areas can be a disadvantaged population, cities, or countryside.

ii. Evaluating Needs for Infrastructure

Just like stated before, different groups will choose a target area or community in which they will work in and after that a needs assessment of the current level of ICT development will be conducted. This evaluation will also entail the consideration of such parameters as broadband availability, mobile network availability. The cost of internet and the level of literacy when it comes to using the internet. Groups will also look at antecedent regulatory environments in areas where connectivity projects will be established, population growth, and other social factors that might arise thus affecting connectivity projects.

iii. Creating the Plan for Connectivity

According to the evaluation made by each group, they will create a specific digital connectivity plan for the selected community or region in which they work at. Regarding communication, the strategies will be under the different tactics and actions within the plan that will focus on Internet connection, digital inclusion, and improved access to appropriate digital platforms. Some of them include, creating Wi-Fi public centres, enhancing the mobile broadband, developing new broadband systems, and offering digital skills training sessions.

iv. Dealing with Problems and Offering Solutions

Groups will also outline key barriers and likely issues that might arise regarding the proposed connectivity plans. Some such challenges may include financial constraints, legal or policy restrictions, technical challenges, and social opposition. Proposals will be made by groups to address aforementioned challenges and guarantee effective connectivity plan implementation.

Learning Outcomes

Students will develop a range of valuable skills and competencies through this activity, including:

- **Teamwork in Solving Problems:** Students will be grouped in affairs that they will analyze in order to come up with quality idea on enhancing connectivity.
- **Analysis and Critical Thinking:** Thus, with the help of theoretical and empirical analysis, carried out by students, the effectiveness of the existing conditions will be assessed and the possible directions for development will be determined.
- **Presentation and Communication Skills:** Students will demonstrate their understanding or the uses of digital connectivity by delivering proposals to the class, thus improving on their interpersonal communication skills. Students will also be able to explain concepts, justification of their ideas/suggestions, and answer and argument questions/ comments from other students well.
- **Project Management and Strategic Planning:** Creating a connectivity plan means that students will be able to conduct a SWOT analysis, and set goals and objectives, identify resources, and anticipate risks.
- **Knowledge of Equity and Digital Inclusion:** On a similar note, the importance of extending their networks to under-served areas or populations will enable the students grasp concepts of digital inclusion and conformity to socioeconomic development objectives to reduce imbalances.
- **Adaptability and Innovation:** Education will help the student towards development of problem solving skills with focus on flexibility since they will be in a position to work under pressure and come up with unique ideas to overcome the challenges faced in solving problems.
- **Practical Application of Academic Knowledge:** This activity fits perfectly in the practical approach/ real world context kind of learning that was earlier described as being a major strength of demonstration, predominantly especially in digital infrastructure and connectivity.

- **Understanding Policy and Regulatory Impact:** Through discussions with the expert they will get to know on how policy influences projects in connecting people digitally thus enhancing their capacity to operate in such environments in organizations in the future.

To sum up, this learning activity provides students with the applicable and engaging classroom experience that combines theoretical and practical aspects of digital structures and communications.

7. CASE STUDY: ZOREZ TELECOM

Description of Zorez Telecom's Activities

Zorez Telecom is a key player in the extremely modest telecommunications industry. Zorez Telecom negotiates its operations among some of the most significant competitors, namely the telecommunications industry. Zorez Telecom has particularly strong roots in cities; it provides fixed-line, mobile, as well as internet speed services. Over the years, the company has created a competitive image as the telecom industry leader which presents unique and efficient solutions, secure services, and individual attention to its clients. Their corporation to quality and excellence have placed Zorez Telecom in a strategic stead where it has captured a big market share and thus loyalty from the customers.

Outlining the Business's Plan for Growth to Boost Digital Infrastructure

Understanding the demand for infrastructure development in the field, Zorez Telecom introduced a clear plan of development which is to boost connectivity in regions with fewer connections. The expansion was aimed at supplying adequate broadband connection at the societal stipendiary where majority of the population has no internet connection at all. Hence for achieving the goals and objectives Zorez Telecom planned and invested with facilities for infrastructure development to provide digital equity and minimize the digital divide. The company's expansion initiatives supported general national goals in developing technology, promoting the development of community and generating more economic opportunities in the country.

Challenges

Regulatory Obstacles and Concerns About Compliance

Zorez Telecom faced many regulatory issues and problems of compliance every time it strived to expand to new regions. The moreover teem was constructed from the cluster of regulations controlling spectrum access, licensing, and construction of Telecoms in each region. Gaining permits, approvals, and compliance certifications was a lengthy and a tasking process that involved working with other local, state, and federal governing bodies. The major issue was in sustaining operations and staying compliant due to the repercussions that came with flouting the regulations, which unlike in the developed countries, entails penalties and law suits.

Technological Barriers in Implementing New Infrastructure

The physical implementation of new infrastructures that were marked technically, met some hurdles because of the physical features and geographic structures in the rural areas. Some of the challenges that greatly affected the expansion of the networks included; complexity of terrain, difficult terrains characterized by tough vegetation and geographical conditions, a detrimental weather condition that hampered the installation of the equipment and network infrastructure. Many of the structures were developed in rather isolated areas and the installation involved considerable prior planning, tool and equipment, and human resources to achieve places of work and living. As a result of these technical challenges, construction programs get shifted and slowed down resulting in the protraction of project time and blowing of financial plans.

Concerns About Sustainability and Economic Viability

There are two major issues that have caught people's attention when it comes to the discussion on sustainability and economic viability. However, implementing additional portions of the digital structure has the advantages of providing high and long-persisting revenues in the future; however, Zorez Telecom was concerned with the patterns of its sustainability and financial profitability. The huge funding required to put up necessary structures as well as scarcities in populace within the rural areas also presented the company with some serious issues of financing the expansion exercise. To this end, there was a need for strict financing and assessment of risk to make sure that rural accessibility investments are profitable ventures. Zorez Telecom was obliged to compare expected net investments to its gross investments, taking into account factors such as the subscribers' growth rate, generated revenues, and operating costs. The feasibility of the expansion project also raised the issue of the nature of continuing revenue, funds, maintenance, and support for the project. Hence for Zorez Telecom to achieve sustainable success from the digital infrastructure on the website it needed to create sources of incomes and business models in the gothic kingdom to support it.

Additional Information: Innovative Solutions and Community Engagement

Innovative Solutions

In order to solve the issues faced in infrastructure implementation in rural area, Zorez Telecom incorporated solar energy to power Remote Telecommunication Equipment, Satellite Phone Solution in territory with rough geographical condition and Modularity Solution for expanding network as and when required. These innovations brought feasibility in implementing the projects, as well as sustainability of the environment.

Community Engagement

Zorez Telecom also focused on community involvement as one of the aspects of the company's growth plan. The company organized awareness creations to help residents in the localized areas understand the value of digital connection, trained people to increase their understanding of digital characteristics, and partnered with companies and organizations to provide solutions that best fit the areas surrounding them. Due to the active engagement of communities in the development process, the company's subsidiary ensured that people would support the telecommunications infrastructure creation endeavors due to ownership.

CONCLUSION

Thus, the chapter ends with arguing for the significance of digital environment and connectivity to the economic development, technology advancement, and social change. Broadening the reader's understanding of technology advancement by examining digital infrastructure in terms of broadband networks, telecommunication systems, and data centers chapter solves the problem of tracing the changes in communication and information exchange processes caused by technology. Topics that concern the investment needs, the accessibility of the rural areas and the security aspects are being discussed; and, most importantly, there is being put emphasis on the legislation and regulations as principal driving forces of infrastructure.

Furthermore, the chapter is filled with relevant information and tips on planning and development of infrastructure with an instructional plan for creating the digital connectivity outlook. This unique course allows students to evaluate the requirements of the communities, understand the subtleties of infrastructural construction, and design effective and creative solutions concerning connectivity issues. Also, the discussion of Zorez Telecom's expansion project presents a practical viewpoint into conceivable challenges and issues inherent in implementing digital infrastructure ventures in the telecommunication industry.

In addition, the chapter explains novel trends and technologies that define the further development of the digital infrastructure, including 5G networks, the Internet of Things, and smart cities. Such progress can be viewed as the leading and expanding connectivity, as well as the driving force behind economic and social growth on the international level.

In sum, the chapter plays the role of providing the readers with the totality of knowledge regarding the concept of digital infrastructure and connection. They identify the need for strategic planning, integration, and nurturing of creativity in the provision and improvement of infrastructure. Given the further development of technology and its impact on people and society, the subjects discussed in this chapter are crucial and essential at the present stage of society's development, thus emphasizing the need for proper digital infrastructure.

REFERENCES

Bele, S. B., Chonde, A. L., & Jawanjal, S. S. (2023). Mobile Broadband Networking. *International Research Journal of Innovations in Engineering and Technology*, 7(10), 676.

Briglauer, W., Krämer, J., & Palan, N. (2024). Socioeconomic benefits of high-speed broadband availability and service adoption: A survey. *Telecommunications Policy*, 48(7), 102808. DOI: 10.1016/j.telpol.2024.102808

Collins, B., & Ntsika, V. (2019). Community Networks: Case Studies. Internet Society. Retrieved from https://www.internetsociety.org/resources/doc/2019/community-networks-case-studies/

Council of Europe. (2001). Convention on Cybercrime. Retrieved from https://www.coe.int/en/web/conventions/full-list/-/conventions/treaty/185

European Commission. (2015). *Digital Agenda for Europe*. European Commission.

European Commission. (2018). *Connectivity for a Competitive Digital Single Market*. European Commission.

European Commission. (2021). Digital Single Market Strategy. Retrieved from https://ec.europa.eu/digital-single-market/en/strategy

European Union. (2016). Regulation (EU) 2016/679 of the European Parliament and of the Council of 27 April 2016 on the protection of natural persons with regard to the processing of personal data and on the free movement of such data, and repealing Directive 95/46/EC (General Data Protection Regulation). Official Journal of the European Union. Retrieved from https://eur-lex.europa.eu/legal-content/EN/TXT/?uri=CELEX%3A32016R0679

Federal Communications Commission. (2015). Protecting and Promoting the Open Internet. Retrieved from https://www.fcc.gov/restoring-internet-freedom

Federal Communications Commission. (2020). *Broadband Deployment Report*. Federal Communications Commission.

Federal Communications Commission. (2021). Bridging the Digital Divide for All Americans. Retrieved from https://www.fcc.gov/Broadband-Deployment-Initiative

Gartner. (2021). Gartner Forecasts Worldwide Public Cloud Revenue to Grow 23% in 2021. Retrieved from https://www.gartner.com/en/newsroom/press-releases/2021-04-13-gartner-forecasts-worldwide-public-cloud-revenue-to-grow-23-percent-in-2021

Gillett, S. E. (2019). *A History of Telecommunications and Networks: From the ARPANET to the Internet*. Cambridge University Press.

International Telecommunication Union. (2020). *Measuring Digital Development: Facts and Figures 2020*. ITU.

Kelly, J. T., Campbell, K. L., Gong, E., & Scuffham, P. (2020). The Internet of Things: Impact and implications for health care delivery. *Journal of Medical Internet Research*, 22(11), e20135. DOI: 10.2196/20135 PMID: 33170132

Kumar, S. (2021). *The digital frontier: Infrastructures of control on the global web*. Indiana University Press. DOI: 10.2307/j.ctv21hrjv1

Li, X., & Guo, Z. (2021). *The Belt and Road Initiative: Connectivity, Cooperation, and Development*. World Scientific Publishing.

Meena, M. E., & Geng, J. (2022). Dynamic competition in telecommunications: A systematic literature review. *SAGE Open*, 12(2). DOI: 10.1177/21582440221094609

Munirathinam, S. (2020). Industry 4.0: Industrial internet of things (IIOT). *Advances in Computers*, 117(1), 129–164. DOI: 10.1016/bs.adcom.2019.10.010

Organisation for Economic Co-operation and Development. (2019). *OECD Digital Economy Outlook 2019*. OECD Publishing.

Packard, N. (2023). Internet prehistory: ARPANET chronology. *Cogent Social Sciences*, 9(2), 2245237. DOI: 10.1080/23311886.2023.2245237

Smith, A. (2020). The Role of Digital Infrastructure in Economic Development. *The Journal of Economic Perspectives*, 34(3), 202–219.

Sunyaev, A., & Sunyaev, A. (2020). Cloud computing. *Internet computing: Principles of distributed systems and emerging internet-based technologies*, 195-236.

United Nations. (2019). Financing for Development Report 2019. United Nations. Retrieved from https://developmentfinance.un.org/sites/developmentfinance

Valentín-Sívico, J., Canfield, C., Low, S. A., & Gollnick, C. (2023). Evaluating the impact of broadband access and internet use in a small underserved rural community. *Telecommunications Policy*, 47(4), 102499. DOI: 10.1016/j.telpol.2023.102499 PMID: 36685614

Wong, R. T. (2021). Telecommunications network design: Technology impacts and future directions. *Networks*, 77(2), 205–224. DOI: 10.1002/net.21997

World Bank. (2019). *Digital Infrastructure for the 21st Century*. World Bank Publications.

Appendix

Lesson Plan: Case Study - Zorez Telecom

Objective

In this case, students will be required to identify and discuss the issues and opportunities associated with the company's expansion strategy, particularly, the challenge of creating Telecom facilities in rural settings. They will know and understand such aspects as regulation, technical aspects, environmental impact and other people involved in the infrastructure undertakings.

Materials Needed

- Case study document: Zorez Telecom Often it becomes difficult to come across a premier telecom company in a short while.
- Internet connection for conducting research
- Multimedia projector or white board for group meetings
- Handouts and overhead transparencies (e. g., power point, or posters used in the course of group presentations.

Lesson Outline

1. Introduction (10 minutes)
   - Why Zorez Telecom and what is its position in the sphere of telecommunications?
   - Explain how digital infrastructure is relevant in the growth of economy and improvement of the society.
2. The case study analysis (30 minutes)
   - Distribute hand out the case study document to learners.
   - Divide students into small groups and assign each group one of the following focus areas.
     - Regulatory hurdles and the compliances it presents
     - Technology concerns regarding the application of new projects
     - Using the concepts of sustainability and economic Sustainability.
     - The strategies that the Zorez Telecom firm has employed in coming up with new and out of the box methods.
     - Community engagement strategies
3. Research / Group Discussion (30 minutes)

- Initially, students will be grouped and each group will be tasked with the responsibility of reading her/his section of the case study and do further research if necessary.
- In other occasions, each group will debate on the outstanding points and develop a brief of their conclusions.
- Encourage students to think about the following questions:• Encourage students to think about the following questions:
  - What difficulties were specific to Zorez Telecom in the area assigned to you?
  - To what extent and how did they respond to these challenges?
  - What role did these solutions play in the enhancement of the project's success?

4. Group Presentations (20 minutes)
   - At the end of the research each group will share the findings with the rest of the class.
   - Tease them to use other means of presentation such as use of slides, poster, etc in order to spice up their presentation.
   - Follow each presentation with questions and answers section in order to promote a class discussion and better comprehension among the students.
5. Class Discussion and Reflection (20 minutes)
   - Moderate a group discussion on the relationship of the various challenges and the corresponding solutions.
   - Explain the interrelationships between regulatory constraints, technological advancements and economic factors on the feasibility and tenders of infrastructure projects.
   - Deliberate on the relevance of community participation on the sustainability of such projects.
6. Interactive Project: Creating a Digital Connectivity Strategy (30 minutes)
   - Divide the students into new working groups and explain the case of a hypothetical rural community and offer them a week to design a digital connectivity plan.
   - Each group should consider.
   - Each group should consider
     - Correlation of the health needs of the community
     - Regulatory and matters of compliance
     - Technologies that will be suitable to the environment and the geographical distribution of the people.
     - Financial planning and sustainability
     - Approaches to those and the use of digital literacy campaigns

    - Each group should then adopts its strategy and explain why to the rest of the class and what they expect out of it.

7. Conclusion (10 minutes)
    - In this lesson the following areas were covered.
    - Stress the necessity of directions, creativity and teamwork as primary dimensions for the construction of long-term digital platform.
    - Remind the students how the knowledge and skills they're learning in class will be useful in future and actual case studies.

Assessment

- Joining of groups, group talks and presentations.
- Specifically, the quality and creativity of the digital connectivity strategy prescribed in the context of the interactive project.
- Reevaluation of the difficulties which has been encountered according to the case study and their utilization in different contexts of infrastructure advancement.

Chapter 13
Data-Driven Insights Into CSR Influence on Ethical AI Development: A Quantitative Approach

Indraneel Bose
Bhikaji Cama Subharti College of Hotel Management, Swami Vivekanand Subharti University, Meerut, India

Ankit Srivastava
Bhikaji Cama Subharti College of Hotel Management, Swami Vivekanand Subharti University, Meerut, India

Vikas Sharma
https://orcid.org/0009-0009-3174-5965
Bhikaji Cama Subharti College of Hotel Management, Swami Vivekanand Subharti University, Meerut, India

Saurabh Tripathi
Bhikaji Cama Subharti College of Hotel Management, Swami Vivekanand Subharti University, Meerut, India

Yajvendra Singh
Bhikaji Cama Subharti College of Hotel Management, Swami Vivekanand Subharti University, Meerut, India

ABSTRACT

This research aims to explore the influence of corporate social responsibility (CSR) on the development and adoption of ethical AI practices in businesses through a quantitative approach. The study investigates how CSR initiatives drive responsible

DOI: 10.4018/979-8-3693-3478-2.ch013

AI governance, focusing on transparency, accountability, and fairness. By analyzing data from a cross-sectional survey of companies across various industries, key metrics such as CSR expenditure, ethical AI adoption rates, and regulatory compliance are examined. Statistical methods, including regression analysis and correlation testing, are employed to assess the impact of CSR on ethical AI outcomes. The findings are expected to provide data-driven insights into how CSR investments align with the development of ethical AI frameworks, contributing to sustainable business practices. This study also highlights the role of CSR in fostering trust, improving corporate reputation, and mitigating risks associated with AI technologies. The results could guide policymakers and business leaders in shaping future CSR and AI strategies.

1. INTRODUCTION

In recent years, the integration of Artificial Intelligence (AI) in business operations has revolutionized industries, enhancing efficiency, decision-making, and customer engagement. However, alongside these advancements, the ethical implications of AI have sparked significant debates concerning privacy, fairness, accountability, and transparency (Binns, 2018; Floridi & Cowls, 2019). Businesses now face pressure from consumers, stakeholders, and regulators to implement AI systems that are not only efficient but also ethically sound. This has led to the intersection of Corporate Social Responsibility (CSR) and Ethical AI, where companies align their social responsibility strategies with ethical AI development to address societal concerns (Schwartz, 2020).

Corporate Social Responsibility and Ethical AI

CSR refers to a company's commitment to manage the social, environmental, and economic effects of its operations responsibly and in line with public expectations (Carroll, 2016). Traditionally, CSR initiatives have focused on areas such as environmental sustainability, community engagement, and fair labor practices (Matten & Moon, 2008). However, with the growing influence of AI in business, CSR now includes ensuring ethical AI practices (Murray, 2020). Ethical AI, as outlined by scholars such as Floridi and Cowls (2019), emphasizes fairness, accountability, and transparency in AI systems. It is essential for businesses to incorporate these principles into their AI strategies to mitigate risks associated with AI's misuse, such as biased decision-making or privacy breaches (Jobin, Ienca, & Vayena, 2019).

Research shows that companies that actively integrate CSR into their AI strategies are better equipped to develop ethical AI frameworks (Martin, 2020). For instance, a study by Dignum (2019) highlights that firms with strong CSR commitments are more likely to develop AI systems that prioritize transparency and fairness. Similarly, Heikkurinen and Mäkinen (2018) argue that CSR provides the ethical foundation upon which AI systems can be developed in a socially responsible manner. This alignment between CSR and ethical AI development not only enhances a company's reputation but also fosters trust among consumers (Cohen, 2020).

The Role of CSR in Addressing Ethical AI Challenges

The ethical challenges of AI are numerous. AI systems are often criticized for their potential to perpetuate biases, invade privacy, and create opaqueness in decision-making processes (Binns, 2018). According to Mittelstadt et al. (2016), one of the most pressing concerns is the lack of transparency in AI models, often referred to as "black-box" systems, where decisions are made without clear explanations. This lack of transparency can erode trust in AI technologies, particularly when they are used in critical fields such as healthcare, finance, and law enforcement (Jobin et al., 2019).

CSR can play a pivotal role in addressing these ethical concerns. By embedding ethical principles into their CSR policies, companies can ensure that AI systems are designed and implemented with a focus on fairness, transparency, and accountability (Floridi & Cowls, 2019). For example, Schwartz (2020) points out that companies with strong CSR frameworks are more likely to adopt AI systems that include mechanisms for algorithmic transparency and ethical decision-making.

Quantitative Insights into CSR and Ethical AI

Quantitative research offers a valuable lens for understanding the impact of CSR on the development of ethical AI systems. Studies by Acemoglu and Restrepo (2019) suggest that businesses that invest in CSR initiatives are more likely to implement AI technologies that align with ethical standards. By examining metrics such as CSR expenditure, ethical AI adoption rates, and regulatory compliance, data-driven approaches provide concrete evidence of how CSR influences ethical AI development (Cohen, 2020). For instance, a study by Martin (2020) found a positive correlation between CSR activities and the transparency of AI systems in businesses, particularly in industries heavily regulated by AI ethics laws.

Furthermore, CSR initiatives that focus on AI ethics not only help companies comply with regulations but also contribute to long-term sustainability. Dignum (2019) argues that ethical AI practices driven by CSR initiatives are more sustainable, as they foster public trust and reduce the risks of regulatory penalties or reputational damage. In this regard, CSR serves as a strategic tool that helps businesses navigate the complex ethical landscape of AI while maintaining competitiveness in the market (Murray, 2020).

The growing intersection of CSR and ethical AI development reflects the need for businesses to go beyond profit and consider their broader societal impact. As companies increasingly rely on AI technologies, they must ensure that these systems are developed and deployed in ethically responsible ways (Binns, 2018). CSR provides the necessary framework for businesses to address the ethical challenges posed by AI, aligning technological innovation with societal expectations (Jobin et al., 2019). By adopting a data-driven approach, this study aims to quantitatively assess how CSR influences ethical AI development across various industries, offering insights that can guide policy-making and corporate strategy (Cohen, 2020).

2. LITERATURE REVIEW

The integration of Corporate Social Responsibility (CSR) into the development and use of Ethical Artificial Intelligence (AI) has emerged as a critical area of study, blending ethics, technology, and corporate accountability. This literature review explores key themes at the intersection of CSR and Ethical AI, offering insights into how businesses are addressing the ethical challenges posed by AI systems. The review also presents five hypotheses that form the foundation for further research into the relationship between CSR and the adoption of Ethical AI practices.

1. Corporate Social Responsibility. A Strategic Imperative

Corporate Social Responsibility (CSR) has evolved from a philanthropic endeavor into a strategic business imperative. According to Carroll (1991), CSR encompasses economic, legal, ethical, and discretionary responsibilities that corporations must uphold. Companies that engage in CSR not only meet legal obligations but also contribute to societal well-being. CSR, in this regard, serves as a framework for managing the ethical, social, and environmental impacts of corporate activities (Matten & Moon, 2008). Scholars like Visser (2010) argue that CSR has become a vital component of business strategy, especially as consumer expectations for corporate accountability continue to rise.

Hypothesis 1. Companies with strong CSR initiatives are more likely to adopt Ethical AI frameworks than companies with weak CSR practices.

2. Ethical AI. Addressing Bias and Fairness

The development of Ethical AI focuses on creating AI systems that prioritize fairness, transparency, and accountability. One of the primary challenges in AI ethics is algorithmic bias, which can perpetuate inequalities if left unchecked (Binns, 2018).

Fairness in AI refers to ensuring that AI systems do not discriminate against individuals based on race, gender, or other protected attributes (Mehrabi et al., 2021). As Dastin (2018) notes, biased AI systems in hiring have already led to discriminatory outcomes, raising concerns about AI's role in perpetuating societal inequalities.

Floridi and Cowls (2019) outline a unified framework of principles for Ethical AI, emphasizing transparency, justice, and accountability. Companies that incorporate Ethical AI principles into their CSR policies are better equipped to address these challenges. Similarly, Mittelstadt et al. (2016) argue that ethical guidelines must be embedded in AI design processes to mitigate bias.

Hypothesis 2. CSR-driven companies are more likely to implement mechanisms that ensure fairness and reduce bias in their AI systems.

3. Transparency and Accountability in AI Systems

Transparency in AI is essential for building trust among users and stakeholders. A lack of transparency, often referred to as the "black box" problem, occurs when AI systems make decisions without clear explanations (Pasquale, 2015). This issue can lead to a lack of accountability, particularly in high-stakes sectors such as healthcare and finance (Raji & Buolamwini, 2019).

CSR initiatives that focus on transparency can guide companies toward adopting AI systems that offer clear, understandable decision-making processes. According to Schwartz (2020), companies that integrate transparency into their CSR frameworks are more likely to develop AI systems that are accountable and explainable. This ensures that AI-driven decisions are not only accurate but also ethically sound.

Hypothesis 3. CSR-oriented companies are more likely to adopt transparent AI systems that provide clear explanations for decision-making processes.

4. CSR and AI Regulation Compliance

Regulatory frameworks for AI ethics are rapidly evolving, with many governments introducing guidelines for the responsible use of AI technologies. The European Union's General Data Protection Regulation (GDPR) and the proposed AI Act are examples of legal frameworks designed to govern the ethical use of AI (Wachter, Mittelstadt, & Floridi, 2017). Compliance with such regulations is becoming increasingly important for businesses that wish to avoid legal penalties and reputational damage.

CSR plays a crucial role in ensuring that companies not only comply with existing regulations but also go beyond legal requirements to adopt ethical AI practices. A study by Jobin, Ienca, and Vayena (2019) reveals that businesses that integrate CSR into their operations are more likely to adhere to AI ethics guidelines. Similarly,

Acemoglu and Restrepo (2019) argue that companies with robust CSR frameworks are better positioned to navigate the complexities of AI regulation.

Hypothesis 4. Companies that prioritize CSR are more likely to comply with AI ethics regulations and guidelines than those that do not prioritize CSR.

5. CSR, Ethical AI, and Consumer Trust

Consumer trust is a critical factor in the adoption of AI technologies. A study by PwC (2020) found that 84% of consumers believe companies should be responsible for mitigating the risks associated with AI. Companies that fail to address ethical concerns in their AI systems risk losing consumer trust, which can have long-term negative impacts on their brand and financial performance (Martin, 2020).

CSR initiatives focused on ethical AI can enhance consumer trust by demonstrating a company's commitment to responsible innovation. According to Heikkurinen and Mäkinen (2018), businesses that align their AI practices with CSR values are more likely to gain consumer approval and maintain brand loyalty. This is particularly important in industries where AI directly interacts with consumers, such as retail, finance, and healthcare (Mittelstadt et al., 2016).

Hypothesis 5. Companies that integrate Ethical AI into their CSR strategies are more likely to gain consumer trust and loyalty compared to companies that do not.

6. Data-Driven CSR and Ethical AI Adoption

Data plays a critical role in evaluating the effectiveness of CSR initiatives in promoting Ethical AI. Quantitative studies have shown that companies with high CSR expenditure are more likely to adopt AI technologies that align with ethical standards (Cohen, 2020). For instance, Martin (2020) found a strong correlation between CSR activities and the transparency of AI systems in businesses operating in highly regulated industries. Moreover, data-driven approaches provide insights into how CSR initiatives influence the adoption of AI ethics frameworks, allowing companies to track progress and make informed decisions (Acemoglu & Restrepo, 2019).

By analyzing key metrics such as CSR expenditure, ethical AI adoption rates, and adherence to AI ethics regulations, companies can assess the impact of their CSR initiatives on ethical AI development (Jobin et al., 2019). This data-driven approach allows for the identification of best practices and the formulation of recommendations that can guide businesses toward more responsible AI development (Dignum, 2019). The literature demonstrates that CSR plays a pivotal role in shaping the ethical development and deployment of AI systems. Companies that align their CSR initiatives with ethical AI principles are better positioned to address the challenges of algorithmic bias, transparency, accountability, and regulatory compliance. Moreover, these companies are more likely to gain consumer trust and maintain long-term sustainability in a rapidly evolving technological landscape. The hypotheses outlined in this review provide a foundation for further research into the relationship between CSR and Ethical AI, offering valuable insights for businesses and policymakers alike.

3. RESEARCH METHODOLOGY

This research employs a quantitative approach to explore the relationship between Corporate Social Responsibility (CSR) and the adoption of Ethical Artificial Intelligence (AI) in business organizations. A descriptive research design was utilized to capture insights from various industries, focusing on the extent to which CSR initiatives influence ethical AI development. The study is based on primary and secondary data, with the primary data collected through a structured questionnaire distributed among mid- and senior-level management personnel from diverse sectors, including technology, finance, healthcare, and retail. Secondary data sources include published reports, journal articles, and industry white papers on CSR and AI ethics.

A total of 520 respondents were surveyed, with the questionnaire designed to measure their organization's CSR activities, adherence to AI ethics frameworks, transparency, and consumer trust. The survey items used a Likert scale (1–5), with respondents rating their company's performance on various CSR and ethical AI parameters. Statistical techniques, such as descriptive statistics, correlation analysis, and regression analysis, were applied to validate the hypotheses. The demographic profile of the respondents, including their industry, job role, years of experience, and company size, was captured to ensure diversity in perspectives.

4. RESULTS AND ANALYSIS

The descriptive statistics revealed that a significant number of respondents agreed that their organizations are actively incorporating CSR principles into their AI development processes. The mean scores for transparency and fairness in AI systems, suggesting a positive orientation toward ethical AI practices.

Table 1. Demographic profile of respondents

Demographic Variable	Category	Frequency	Percentage
Industry	Technology	156	30%
	Finance	104	20%
	Healthcare	104	20%
	Retail	78	15%
	Other	78	15%
Job Role	Senior Management	208	40%
	Middle Management	312	60%
Years of Experience	1-5 Years	104	20%
	6-10 Years	208	40%
	11+ Years	208	40%
Company Size	<500 Employees	130	25%
	500–1000 Employees	234	45%
	>1000 Employees	156	30%

In Table 1, the demographic profile of the respondents reveals a diverse sample across various industries and job roles, reflecting a broad perspective on Corporate Social Responsibility (CSR) and ethical AI practices. The sample is predominantly composed of individuals from the technology sector, with 30% of respondents coming from this field. The finance and healthcare sectors are equally represented, each contributing 20% to the sample. Retail and other industries each account for 15% of the respondents, indicating a well-rounded representation across different business domains.

Regarding job roles, the majority of respondents hold positions in middle management (60%), while 40% are in senior management roles. This distribution provides insights from both strategic and operational levels within organizations, enriching the analysis of CSR and ethical AI practices.

The respondents' years of experience are evenly distributed, with 20% having 1-5 years of experience, 40% with 6-10 years, and another 40% possessing over 11 years of experience. This diverse experience range ensures a comprehensive view of the practices and perspectives on CSR and ethical AI across different stages of professional development.

In terms of company size, the majority of respondents are from medium-sized enterprises, with 45% working in companies with 500–1000 employees. Companies with fewer than 500 employees represent 25% of the sample, while 30% are employed by large organizations with more than 1000 employees. This distribution reflects a variety of organizational contexts, contributing to a holistic understanding of CSR and ethical AI implementation across different company sizes.

Statistical Tests

1. **Correlation Analysis**. The correlation between CSR and ethical AI practices showed a positive relationship ($r = 0.72$), indicating that companies with robust CSR frameworks tend to adopt ethical AI practices more actively.
2. **Regression Analysis**. A linear regression analysis was conducted to assess the impact of CSR on Ethical AI adoption. The results showed that CSR explains 58% of the variance in ethical AI adoption ($R^2 = 0.58$, $p < 0.01$). This suggests a strong influence of CSR on AI practices.

Table 2. Statistical analysis results

Variable	Correlation With Ethical AI Practices	Regression Coefficient (β)	Variance Explained (R^2)	p-Value
CSR Initiatives	0.72	0.65	0.58	<0.01
Fairness Mechanisms	0.68	0.60	0.55	<0.01
Transparency	0.71	0.62	0.56	<0.01
Regulatory Compliance	0.74	0.64	0.59	<0.01
Consumer Trust	0.75	0.67	0.61	<0.01

The analysis highlights strong relationships between key variables and ethical AI practices. CSR Initiatives have a high correlation ($r = 0.72$) and regression coefficient ($\beta = 0.65$), explaining 58% of the variance in ethical AI practices ($R^2 = 0.58$), with a significant p-value (<0.01). Fairness Mechanisms show a correlation of 0.68 and a β of 0.60, explaining 55% of the variance ($R^2 = 0.55$), also significant ($p < 0.01$). Transparency has a correlation of 0.71 and a β of 0.62, accounting for 56% of the variance ($R^2 = 0.56$), with high significance ($p < 0.01$). Regulatory Compliance correlates at 0.74 with a β of 0.64, explaining 59% of the variance ($R^2 = 0.59$), and is significant ($p < 0.01$). Consumer Trust shows the highest correlation ($r = 0.75$) and β of 0.67, explaining 61% of the variance ($R^2 = 0.61$), also significant ($p < 0.01$). These results underscore the significant impact of these variables on ethical AI practices. The correlation values indicate the strength and direction of the relationship between CSR and Ethical AI practices, with higher values suggesting a stronger positive relationship. The regression coefficients (β) show the impact of each variable on the adoption of Ethical AI, and the variance explained (R^2) represents the proportion of variance in ethical AI practices explained by CSR initiatives. All p-values are less than 0.01, indicating statistically significant results.

3. Hypothesis Testing

- **H1**. Companies with strong CSR initiatives are more likely to adopt Ethical AI frameworks.
  - **Validated**. CSR significantly influences the adoption of Ethical AI ($\beta = 0.65$, $p < 0.01$).
- **H2**. CSR-driven companies are more likely to implement mechanisms that ensure fairness and reduce bias in their AI systems.
  - **Validated**. CSR activities showed a strong association with mechanisms to reduce AI bias ($r = 0.68$, $p < 0.01$).
- **H3**. CSR-oriented companies are more likely to adopt transparent AI systems.
  - **Validated**. Companies with a higher CSR focus showed better transparency practices ($r = 0.71$, $p < 0.01$).
- **H4**. Companies that prioritize CSR are more likely to comply with AI ethics regulations and guidelines.
  - **Validated**. CSR was positively associated with regulatory compliance in AI ethics ($r = 0.74$, $p < 0.01$).
- **H5**. Companies that integrate Ethical AI into their CSR strategies are more likely to gain consumer trust and loyalty.
  - **Validated**. There was a significant positive relationship between Ethical AI practices and consumer trust ($r = 0.75$, $p < 0.01$).

5. FINDINGS AND SUGGESTIONS

The findings of this study confirm that CSR plays a crucial role in shaping the adoption of Ethical AI practices in business organizations. Companies with well-established CSR frameworks are more likely to implement AI systems that prioritize fairness, transparency, and accountability. The study found that CSR activities not only help organizations comply with AI ethics regulations but also enhance consumer trust, particularly in industries where AI directly impacts customer decision-making.

However, the study also highlighted certain areas for improvement. While transparency and fairness were prominent in CSR-driven companies, there remains a gap in ensuring full accountability in AI systems, especially in "black-box" models where decision-making processes are opaque. To address this, companies should consider investing in explainable AI technologies and prioritize ongoing assessments of AI ethics compliance.

Suggestions

1. **Enhance Explainability in AI**. Companies should prioritize the development of AI systems that provide clear, understandable explanations for decisions, especially in critical sectors such as finance and healthcare.
2. **Expand CSR Initiatives**. Organizations should expand their CSR initiatives to include comprehensive AI ethics guidelines that go beyond regulatory requirements, thus fostering trust and accountability.
3. **Regular AI Ethics Audits**. Conduct periodic audits of AI systems to ensure they adhere to ethical standards, especially in terms of bias reduction and fairness in decision-making.
4. **Increase Consumer Awareness**. Companies should engage in consumer education programs to raise awareness about how Ethical AI is being used in their products and services.

6. CONCLUSION

This research highlights the pivotal role of CSR in fostering the ethical development of AI systems. By embedding ethical principles into CSR frameworks, businesses can ensure the adoption of fair, transparent, and accountable AI practices. The positive correlation between CSR and Ethical AI practices underscores the need for businesses to align their social responsibilities with technological innovation. Furthermore, this study validates the hypotheses that CSR-driven companies are more likely to adopt Ethical AI frameworks, ensure fairness, and maintain transparency, ultimately gaining consumer trust and adhering to regulatory compliance. As AI continues to play an integral role in business operations, companies must recognize the importance of CSR in shaping the future of responsible AI development. Future research should explore the long-term impact of CSR-driven AI ethics on business sustainability and societal welfare, particularly as AI technologies evolve.

REFERENCES

Agerri, S., & Lippi, M. (2019). AI and CSR. Addressing Ethical Challenges. Journal of Business Ethics, 156(2), 477-491. DOI: 10.1007/s10551-017-3566-7

Ananny, M., & Crawford, K. (2018). Seeing Without Knowing. Limitations of the Transparency Ideal and Its Application tAI. Proceedings of the 2018 CHI Conference on Human Factors in Computing Systems, 1-12. DOI: 10.1145/3173574.3173575

Aspris, A., & Karanasos, M. (2020). Financial Markets and AI. Insights from Machine Learning. European Journal of Finance, 26(9), 1239-1259. DOI: 10.1080/1351847X.2020.1726290

Binns, R., & Shadbolt, N. (2020). Human-AI Collaboration for Social Good. The Role of Ethical Frameworks. ACM Transactions on Intelligent Systems and Technology, 11(4), 1-18. DOI: 10.1145/3386361

Binns, R., Veale, M., Van Kleek, M., Shadbolt, N., & Shadbolt, N. (2018). 'It's Reducing the Burden'. A Field Study of Human-AI Collaboration for Social Good. Proceedings of the 2018 CHI Conference on Human Factors in Computing Systems (pp. 1-12). DOI: 10.1145/3173574.3173796

Brynjolfsson, E., & McElheran, K. (2016). The Digitization of Business. A Guide tthe Impact of Technology on Business Management. Harvard Business Review. DOI: 10.1037/0002-9432.84.1.4

Cai, H., & Liu, Y. (2018). Corporate Social Responsibility and Firm Performance. Evidence from China. Journal of Business Ethics, 148(2), 377-391. DOI: 10.1007/s10551-016-3037-7

Cummings, M. L. (2017). Artificial Intelligence and the Future of Work. Implications for CSR. Journal of Business Ethics, 152(4), 1041-1054. DOI: 10.1007/s10551-016-3307-8

Dastin, J. (2019). Amazon Scraps Secret AI Recruiting Tool That Showed Bias Against Women. Reuters. DOI: 10.1080/17512786.2019.1646492

De Bruin, B., & Heeley, J. (2017). The Role of CSR in Ethical AI Development. Challenges and Opportunities. Journal of Business Ethics, 143(3), 487-502. DOI: 10.1007/s10551-015-2827-6

Dobbe, R., & Verbeek, P. (2019). Ethical AI. The Importance of Designing AI Systems for Transparency. Technology and Society, 57, 101-110. DOI: 10.1016/j.techsoc.2018.11.001

El Ali, Z., & Siang, S. (2019). Corporate Social Responsibility and AI. Towards a Framework for Ethical Practice. Journal of Technology in Human Services, 37(2), 123-140. DOI: 10.1080/15228835.2018.1562969

Floridi, L., & Cowls, J. (2019). Telling Right from Wrong in AI. The Role of Corporate Responsibility. Nature Machine Intelligence, 1(6), 285-287. DOI: 10.1038/s42256-019-0030-6

Golembiewski, R. T., & Murlis, H. (2018). Implementing Effective CSR Strategies. International Journal of Management Reviews, 20(1), 55-73. DOI: 10.1111/ijmr.12143

Haggerty, K. D., & Ericson, R. V. (2019). Transparency and Accountability in AI. The Role of CSR. Surveillance & Society, 17(3), 274-288. DOI: 10.24908/ss.v17i3.6757

Koch, C., & Riek, L. D. (2021). The Intersection of Corporate Responsibility and AI Ethics. A Review of the Literature. IEEE Transactions on Technology and Society, 2(1), 45-55. DOI: 10.1109/TTS.2020.3034720

Kroll, J. A., Hurlburt, H., & Roth, P. (2017). Accountable Algorithms. University of Pennsylvania Law Review, 165(3), 633-701. DOI: 10.2139/ssrn.2932348

Kroll, J. A., & Raji, I. D. (2020). The Ethical Implications of AI. A Corporate Social Responsibility Perspective. Proceedings of the 2020 AAAI/ACM Conference on AI, Ethics, and Society, 135-143. DOI: 10.1145/3375627.3375826

Lee, J., & Kim, K. (2021). The Role of Corporate Social Responsibility in Artificial Intelligence Adoption. Journal of Corporate Finance, 69, 102066. DOI: 10.1016/j.jcorpfin.2020.102066

Li, S., & Yang, S. (2019). The Impact of CSR on AI Transparency and Fairness. Journal of Business Research, 104, 110-118. DOI: 10.1016/j.jbusres.2019.07.022

Matsuura, H., & Liu, B. (2020). AI and Ethical Practices. The Role of Corporate Governance. Journal of Corporate Governance, 22(3), 55-73. DOI: 10.1108/JCG-03-2019-0056

Mayer-Schönberger, V., & Cukier, K. (2019). Big Data. A Revolution That Will Transform How We Live, Work, and Think. Houghton Mifflin Harcourt. DOI: 10.1080/08985626.2015.1022747

McCormick, J., & Fitzgerald, L. (2020). Ethical AI and CSR. Understanding the Links. Business Ethics Quarterly, 30(1), 55-72. DOI: 10.1017/beq.2019.28

McKinsey & Company. (2019). AI and the Future of Corporate Social Responsibility. McKinsey & Company Reports. DOI: 10.2139/ssrn.3442050

Mittelstadt, B. D., & Floridi, L. (2018). The Ethics of Big Data. Current and Future Directions. Computer Science Review, 35, 7-14. DOI: 10.1016/j.cosrev.2019.03.002

Narayanan, A., & Binns, R. (2018). The Role of Ethical AI in Corporate Social Responsibility. AI & Society, 33(4), 509-519. DOI: 10.1007/s00146-017-0752-2

Narayanan, A., & Shadbolt, N. (2018). Understanding AI and the Impact of Data Bias. Journal of AI Research, 63, 467-496. DOI: 10.1613/jair.1.11944

O'Neil, C. (2016). Weapons of Math Destruction. How Big Data Increases Inequality and Threatens Democracy. Crown Publishing Group. DOI: 10.1177/0276146716654008

Pasquale, F. (2019). The Black Box Society. The Secret Algorithms That Control Money and Information. Harvard University Press. DOI: 10.1145/2772951

Rai, A., & Selander, L. (2018). Can Corporate Social Responsibility Influence AI Ethics? IEEE Transactions on Engineering Management, 65(1), 113-126. DOI: 10.1109/TEM.2017.2787907

Raji, I. D., & Buolamwini, J. (2019). Actionable Auditing. Investigating the Impact of Publicly Naming Biased Performance Results of Commercial AI Products. Proceedings of the 2019 CHI Conference on Human Factors in Computing Systems, 1-15. DOI: 10.1145/3306618.3314244

Rust, R. T., & Huang, M. H. (2018). The Service Revolution and the Impact of AI. Journal of Service Research, 21(1), 3-10. DOI: 10.1177/1094670517752401

Sandel, M. J. (2020). The Tyranny of Merit. What's Become of the Common Good? Farrar, Straus and Giroux. DOI: 10.1111/j.1468-0327.2009.00160.x

Shadbolt, N., & Harnad, S. (2017). Ethical AI. The Role of Transparency and Accountability. Artificial Intelligence Review, 50(1), 1-16. DOI: 10.1007/s10462-016-9501-3

Sharma, A., & Dey, A. (2021). The Influence of CSR on Ethical AI. An Empirical Study. Journal of Strategic and International Studies, 12(2), 89-104. DOI: 10.1142/S1793823321500120

Timmermans, S., & Berg, M. (2018). The Gold Standard. The Challenge of Evidence-Based Medicine. Temple University Press. DOI: 10.1080/0952813X.2017.1388037

Van den Hoven, J., & Weckert, J. (2019). The Ethical Implications of AI in CSR. A Theoretical Framework. Ethics and Information Technology, 21(4), 289-303. DOI: 10.1007/s10676-019-09550-7

Weller, A., & Raji, I. D. (2020). The Role of AI in Advancing CSR. Opportunities and Challenges. Journal of Technology Management & Innovation, 15(2), 26-37. DOI: 10.4067/S0718-27242020000200026

Zeng, Y., & Lu, X. (2018). Corporate Social Responsibility and AI. The Role of Stakeholders. Journal of Business Ethics, 152(2), 269-285. DOI: 10.1007/s10551-017-3417-3

Zhang, Y., & Jiang, W. (2019). Corporate Social Responsibility and Ethical AI. A New Paradigm. Business Ethics Quarterly, 29(2), 345-368. DOI: 10.1017/beq.2018.52

Chapter 14
Corporate Social Responsibility Approaches to Ethical AI in Hotel Industry Business

Deepa Saxena
https://orcid.org/0009-0001-4077-2334
Department of Business Administration, Awadhesh Pratap Singh University, India

C. N. Sinha
HRIT University, India

Sharad Bajpai
HRIT University, India

Uday Pratap Singh
https://orcid.org/0009-0009-3174-5965
Amity University, Jaipur, India

Ankit Prakash
RKDF University, India

ABSTRACT

The integration of artificial intelligence (AI) in the hotel industry has brought about significant advancements in customer service, operational efficiency, and personalized experiences. However, the ethical implications of AI usage in this sector raise

DOI: 10.4018/979-8-3693-3478-2.ch014

critical concerns that necessitate a proactive approach to corporate social responsibility (CSR). This chapter explores the various CSR strategies adopted by hotel businesses to ensure the ethical implementation of AI technologies. It discusses the importance of transparency, fairness, and accountability in AI applications, and the role of CSR in addressing issues such as data privacy, bias, and the impact on employment. By adopting ethical AI practices, hotels can not only enhance their reputation but also contribute to sustainable business models that prioritize the well-being of all stakeholders.

1. INTRODUCTION

The hotel industry is increasingly leveraging Artificial Intelligence (AI) to enhance operational efficiency, improve customer experiences, and optimize resource management. AI technologies such as chatbots, predictive analytics, and dynamic pricing systems are being integrated into hotel operations to provide more personalized and efficient services to guests (Smith, 2020). These advancements have revolutionized the way hotels interact with customers and manage internal processes, leading to significant improvements in service delivery and operational outcomes (Johnson & Lee, 2019).

However, the rapid adoption of AI in the hotel industry has also brought about a range of ethical challenges that necessitate a closer examination of the role of Corporate Social Responsibility (CSR) in mitigating potential negative impacts (Davis, 2021). As AI systems increasingly rely on vast amounts of personal data to deliver tailored services, concerns regarding data privacy, security, and the potential for misuse of information have come to the forefront (Chen & Zhao, 2018). Additionally, the use of AI in decision-making processes raises issues related to algorithmic bias, fairness, and transparency, which could potentially undermine trust in AI-driven systems (Martinez & Nguyen, 2020). Corporate Social Responsibility (CSR) has traditionally played a significant role in the hospitality industry, focusing on areas such as environmental sustainability, community engagement, and ethical labor practices (Harris, 2017). However, with the advent of AI, the scope of CSR in the hotel industry must be expanded to include ethical considerations surrounding AI technologies (Patel, 2019). This expansion is crucial to ensure that AI is deployed in a manner that is transparent, fair, and accountable, while also safeguarding the rights and privacy of individuals (Thompson, 2022).

Recent studies have highlighted the importance of integrating ethical AI practices into CSR strategies as a means of addressing these emerging challenges (Anderson & Brown, 2023). For example, hotels can implement robust data protection measures, ensure transparency in AI algorithms, and conduct regular audits to detect and mitigate biases (Garcia & Wilson, 2021). By doing so, hotel businesses can not only enhance their ethical standards but also build trust with their customers and stakeholders (Kim & Park, 2020).

In conclusion, as AI continues to reshape the hotel industry, it is imperative for hotel businesses to adopt a proactive approach to CSR that includes a strong emphasis on ethical AI practices. This approach will not only help mitigate the potential risks associated with AI but also contribute to the development of a more sustainable and socially responsible hospitality industry (Singh, 2024).

2. LITERATURE REVIEW

The advent of Artificial Intelligence (AI) in the hotel industry has catalyzed significant changes, particularly in enhancing operational efficiency and customer service. However, the integration of AI also poses substantial ethical challenges that necessitate careful consideration within the framework of Corporate Social Responsibility (CSR). This literature review explores the intersection of AI and CSR in the hotel industry, examining key areas such as data privacy, algorithmic bias, transparency, accountability, and the broader social implications of AI adoption.

1. AI in the Hotel Industry AI technologies have rapidly become integral to hotel operations, from automating customer interactions to optimizing pricing strategies (Smith & Johnson, 2020). Chatbots, for instance, are increasingly used to handle guest inquiries and reservations, improving efficiency and customer satisfaction (Williams & Thomas, 2019). AI-driven dynamic pricing models enable hotels to adjust room rates in real-time based on demand forecasts, thereby maximizing revenue (Chen, 2021). Moreover, AI is also being utilized for predictive maintenance of hotel facilities, reducing downtime and improving guest experiences (Patel, 2020).

2. Ethical Challenges of AI Despite the operational benefits, AI in the hotel industry raises several ethical concerns. One major issue is data privacy. AI systems often require vast amounts of personal data to function effectively, raising concerns about how this data is collected, stored, and used (Garcia & Lopez, 2021). The potential for data breaches and misuse of personal information is a significant risk, as highlighted by multiple studies (Kim & Park, 2022; Wilson, 2020). Algorithmic bias is another critical concern. AI systems are only as unbiased as the data on which they are trained. If the training data contains biases, these can be perpetuated or even amplified by AI algorithms, leading to unfair outcomes (Lee, 2019). This is particularly troubling in the context of customer service, where biased AI systems might inadvertently discriminate against certain demographic groups (Nguyen & Martinez, 2021). Transparency in AI decision-making is also a significant issue. The complexity of AI algorithms often makes it difficult for hotel operators to understand how decisions are made, leading to a lack of accountability (Thompson & Davis, 2021). This "black box" problem in AI can erode trust between customers and hotels, as customers may feel uneasy about decisions being made by opaque systems (Brown & Harris, 2020).

3. The Role of CSR in Ethical AI Corporate Social Responsibility (CSR) offers a framework for addressing the ethical challenges posed by AI. Historically, CSR in the hotel industry has focused on issues such as environmental sustainability and community engagement (Smith & Lee, 2018). However, the rise of AI necessitates an expansion of CSR to include ethical considerations related to technology (Patel, 2019). Many scholars argue that CSR initiatives must now incorporate guidelines for ethical AI usage, including policies on data privacy, transparency, and fairness (Anderson & Brown, 2022). For instance, hotels can implement data protection measures that go beyond legal requirements, ensuring that customer data is handled with the utmost care (Garcia & Wilson, 2021). Additionally, CSR strategies can include regular audits of AI systems to identify and correct biases, ensuring that AI-driven decisions are fair and equitable (Kim & Park, 2022).

4. Transparency and Accountability Transparency is a core principle of ethical AI, yet achieving it in practice is challenging. According to Brown and Harris (2020), one way to enhance transparency is through the use of explainable AI (XAI), which allows hotel staff and customers to understand how AI systems arrive at specific decisions. By making AI decision-making processes more transparent, hotels can foster greater trust with their customers (Thompson & Davis, 2021). Accountability is closely related to transparency. Hotels must establish clear lines of responsibility for AI-driven decisions, ensuring that there is always a human oversight mechanism in place (Lee, 2019). This is particularly important in scenarios where AI systems might make errors or where their decisions have significant consequences for customers (Williams & Thomas, 2019).

5. Social Implications and Employee Impact The broader social implications of AI adoption in the hotel industry are also a key area of concern. While AI can improve efficiency, it can also lead to job displacement, as certain roles traditionally performed by humans are automated (Nguyen & Martinez, 2021). This has significant implications for hotel employees, particularly in low-skill roles, who may find themselves at risk of redundancy (Chen, 2021). CSR initiatives can play a vital role in mitigating these impacts. For example, hotels can invest in retraining programs for employees whose jobs are at risk due to AI (Anderson & Brown, 2022). This not only helps employees transition to new roles but also demonstrates the hotel's commitment to its workforce (Smith & Lee, 2018).

6. Building Trust Through Ethical AI Trust is a crucial factor in the successful deployment of AI in the hotel industry. Customers need to trust that their data is being used responsibly and that AI systems are making fair decisions (Thompson

& Davis, 2021). CSR strategies that prioritize ethical AI practices can help build this trust (Brown & Harris, 2020). For instance, by being transparent about how AI systems work and by taking proactive steps to address any ethical concerns, hotels can enhance their reputation and build stronger relationships with their customers (Garcia & Wilson, 2021). The integration of AI into the hotel industry presents both significant opportunities and ethical challenges. While AI can enhance operational efficiency and customer service, it also raises concerns about data privacy, algorithmic bias, transparency, and the broader social impact. Corporate Social Responsibility (CSR) provides a framework for addressing these challenges, ensuring that AI is used in a manner that is ethical, transparent, and fair. By adopting CSR strategies that prioritize ethical AI practices, hotels can not only mitigate potential risks but also build trust with their customers and stakeholders, ultimately contributing to a more sustainable and socially responsible industry.

3. RESEARCH OBJECTIVES

- **To evaluate** the impact of AI adoption on operational efficiency and customer satisfaction in the hotel industry.
- **To examine** the ethical challenges associated with AI deployment in hotels, focusing on data privacy, algorithmic bias, and transparency.
- **To assess** the effectiveness of Corporate Social Responsibility (CSR) initiatives in mitigating the ethical risks posed by AI technologies in the hotel industry.

4. RESEARCH HYPOTHESES

- **H1:** The adoption of AI technologies in hotels significantly improved operational efficiency and customer satisfaction.
- **H2:** The use of AI in hotel operations was associated with an increased risk of data privacy violations.
- **H3:** AI systems deployed in hotels exhibited algorithmic biases that affected customer experiences differently based on demographic factors.
- **H4:** Hotels with comprehensive CSR strategies in place were more effective in mitigating the ethical risks associated with AI technologies.
- **H5:** There was a positive correlation between transparency in AI systems and the level of trust customers placed in the hotel services.

5. RESEARCH METHODOLOGY

This study employed a quantitative research design to investigate the relationship between AI adoption in hotels and the ethical challenges it posed, alongside the role of CSR in addressing these challenges. The research was conducted in various hotels located in [New Delhi, India], focusing on both large hotel chains and independent establishments. A sample size of 520 respondents, including hotel managers, employees, and customers, was selected using stratified random sampling. Data were collected through structured questionnaires distributed to hotel managers, employees, and customers. The questionnaires were designed to gather information on the use of AI in hotel operations, the ethical issues encountered, and the CSR practices implemented to address these issues. The data collection took place over a period of three months. The collected data were analyzed using statistical software (e.g., SPSS). Descriptive statistics were employed to summarize the demographic characteristics of the respondents and their perceptions of AI adoption in hotels. Inferential statistics, including regression analysis and correlation tests, were used to test the hypotheses and examine the relationships between AI adoption, ethical challenges, and the effectiveness of CSR initiatives.

The research adhered to ethical guidelines to ensure the confidentiality and anonymity of the respondents. Informed consent was obtained from all participants, and they were informed of their right to withdraw from the study at any time. The study was limited to hotels in [New Delhi], and the findings may not be generalizable to other regions. Additionally, the study focused on the perceptions of hotel managers, employees, and customers, which may introduce subjectivity into the results.

6. ANALYSIS AND RESULTS

This presents the analysis of the data collected from 520 respondents across various hotels in New Delhi, India. The data were analyzed using descriptive and inferential statistics to test the hypotheses outlined in the study. Table 1 below summarizes the demographic profile of the respondents, including their age, gender, occupation, and level of interaction with AI technologies in hotel services.

Table 1. Demographic Profile of Respondents

Demographic Variable	Category	Frequency (n)	Percentage (%)
Gender	Male	320	61.54%
	Female	200	38.46%
Age	18-25 years	100	19.23%
	26-35 years	180	34.62%
	36-45 years	140	26.92%
	46-55 years	70	13.46%
	56 and above	30	5.77%
Occupation	Hotel Manager	120	23.08%
	Hotel Employee	220	42.31%
	Customer	180	34.62%
Interaction with AI	High	150	28.85%
	Moderate	220	42.31%
	Low	150	28.85%

To test the hypotheses, eight variables were analyzed using multiple statistical tests, including regression analysis, ANOVA, and correlation tests. The variables include:

1. **AI Adoption** (measured by the extent of AI use in hotel operations)
2. **Operational Efficiency** (measured by process speed and cost savings)
3. **Customer Satisfaction** (measured by customer feedback and repeat visits)
4. **Data Privacy Concerns** (measured by the frequency of data breaches and customer complaints)
5. **Algorithmic Bias** (measured by bias detection in AI decisions)
6. **Transparency** (measured by the clarity of AI decision-making processes)
7. **CSR Effectiveness** (measured by the implementation and success of CSR initiatives)
8. **Customer Trust** (measured by customer loyalty and confidence in hotel services)

Table 2. Descriptive Statistics of Key Variables

Descriptive Variables	Mean	Standard Deviation
AI Adoption	3.78	0.65
Operational Efficiency	4.12	0.71
Customer Satisfaction	3.98	0.66
Data Privacy Concerns	2.45	0.92
Algorithmic Bias	2.89	0.81
Transparency	3.75	0.68
CSR Effectiveness	4.22	0.59
Customer Trust	4.05	0.63

Table 2 provides a comprehensive overview of the descriptive statistics of the eight variables analyzed in the study: AI Adoption, Operational Efficiency, Customer Satisfaction, Data Privacy Concerns, Algorithmic Bias, Transparency, CSR Effectiveness, and Customer Trust. The average score for AI Adoption (Mean = 3.78, SD = 0.65) indicates that hotels have moderately adopted AI technologies, while CSR Effectiveness (Mean = 4.22, SD = 0.59) and Customer Trust (Mean = 4.05, SD = 0.63) are rated highly. However, the mean score for Data Privacy Concerns (Mean = 2.45, SD = 0.92) shows that data privacy remains a significant issue for customers, potentially due to the growing awareness of AI's invasive nature.

Table 3. Regression Analysis Results

Regression Analysis	Regression Coefficient (β)	Standard Error	t-value	p-value
AI Adoption → Operational Efficiency	0.55	0.12	4.58	0.000**
AI Adoption → Customer Satisfaction	0.48	0.14	3.43	0.001**
CSR Effectiveness → Ethical Risk Mitigation	0.50	0.11	4.55	0.000**

- **Highly significant at $p < 0.01$. Table 3 highlights the regression analysis results, which demonstrate a significant positive relationship between AI Adoption and Operational Efficiency ($\beta = 0.55$, $p < 0.01$) as well as Customer Satisfaction ($\beta = 0.48$, $p < 0.01$). This confirms that the adoption of AI technologies in hotel operations significantly improves efficiency and customer satisfaction. Additionally, CSR Effectiveness shows a strong and statistically significant impact on mitigating ethical risks related to AI ($\beta = 0.50$, $p < 0.01$), emphasizing the importance of ethical and responsible AI practices.

Table 4. Correlation Analysis

Correlation Analysis	AI Adoption	Operational Efficiency	Customer Satisfaction	Data Privacy Concerns	Algorithmic Bias	Transparency	CSR Effectiveness	Customer Trust
AI Adoption	1.00	0.62*	0.58*	-0.46*	-0.51*	0.55*	0.64*	0.61*
Operational Efficiency	0.62*	1.00	0.63*	-0.52*	-0.45*	0.58*	0.67*	0.65*
Customer Satisfaction	0.58*	0.63*	1.00	-0.48*	-0.53*	0.60*	0.70*	0.66*
Data Privacy Concerns	-0.46*	-0.52*	-0.48*	1.00	0.42*	-0.50*	-0.55*	-0.53*
Algorithmic Bias	-0.51*	-0.45*	-0.53*	0.42*	1.00	-0.48*	-0.60*	-0.57*
Transparency	0.55*	0.58*	0.60*	-0.50*	-0.48*	1.00	0.68*	0.63*
CSR Effectiveness	0.64*	0.67*	0.70*	-0.55*	-0.60*	0.68*	1.00	0.72*
Customer Trust	0.61*	0.65*	0.66*	-0.53*	-0.57*	0.63*	0.72*	1.00

- *Significant at $p < 0.05$. Table 4 shows the correlation matrix, with several key findings emerging from the analysis. AI Adoption has a strong positive correlation with both Operational Efficiency ($r = 0.62$, $p < 0.05$) and Customer Satisfaction ($r = 0.58$, $p < 0.05$), suggesting that hotels that invest in AI technologies see tangible benefits in their operations and customer experiences. On the other hand, AI Adoption is negatively correlated with Data Privacy Concerns ($r = -0.46$, $p < 0.05$) and Algorithmic Bias ($r = -0.51$, $p < 0.05$), indicating that the increasing use of AI can exacerbate concerns about data privacy and biases. CSR Effectiveness also correlates positively with both Transparency ($r = 0.68$, $p < 0.05$) and Customer Trust ($r = 0.72$, $p < 0.05$), further reinforcing the role of CSR in maintaining ethical AI practices.

Table 5. ANOVA Results for Algorithmic Bias

Between Groups	**10.45**	**2**	**5.22**	**6.12**	**0.003****
Within Groups	82.67	517	0.16	-	-
Total	93.12	519	-	-	-

- **Highly significant at $p < 0.01$. Table 5 presents the results of the ANOVA test conducted to assess the impact of algorithmic bias on customer satisfaction. The results show a significant F-value ($F = 6.12$, $p < 0.01$), indicating that algorithmic bias significantly affects customer satisfaction in the hotel industry. This highlights the need for hotels to implement strategies to reduce bias in AI systems, as it directly influences customer perceptions and experiences.

Table 6. Hypothesis Validation

Hypothesis	Test	Result	p-value
H1: AI adoption improves operational efficiency and customer satisfaction	Regression Analysis	Supported	0.000 (Operational Efficiency), 0.001 (Customer Satisfaction)
H2: AI use increases data privacy concerns	Correlation Analysis	Supported	-0.46*
H3: AI systems exhibit algorithmic biases	Regression Analysis	Supported	0.009**
H4: CSR strategies mitigate AI-related ethical risks	Regression Analysis	Supported	0.000**
H5: Transparency in AI correlates with customer trust	Correlation Analysis	Supported	0.55*

- *Significant at $p < 0.05$
- **Highly significant at $p < 0.01$

- Table 6 provides a summary of the hypothesis validation, confirming the hypotheses related to AI Adoption, operational efficiency, customer satisfaction, and ethical risks. For example, Hypothesis 1 (AI adoption improves operational efficiency and customer satisfaction) is strongly supported by both regression and correlation analyses. Hypothesis 2 (AI use increases data privacy concerns) is also supported, as evidenced by the negative correlation between AI Adoption and Data Privacy Concerns. Hypothesis 3 (AI systems exhibit algorithmic biases) is validated through the ANOVA test, and Hypothesis 4 (CSR strategies mitigate AI-related ethical risks) is supported by regression results. Lastly, Hypothesis 5 (Transparency in AI correlates with customer trust) is confirmed by the positive correlation between Transparency and Customer Trust. In summary, these findings underline the dual impact of AI in the hotel industry: while AI adoption significantly improves operational efficiency and customer satisfaction, it also introduces ethical challenges, particularly concerning data privacy and algorithmic biases. The study emphasizes the importance of robust CSR strategies and transparency in mitigating these risks, fostering customer trust, and promoting ethical AI practices in hospitality.

7. RECOMMENDATIONS

Based on the findings of this study, several recommendations can be made to enhance the ethical integration of AI in the hotel industry while addressing the associated challenges. Firstly, hotels should implement robust data protection policies that go beyond basic legal requirements to safeguard customer privacy. This includes the adoption of advanced encryption technologies and regular audits of data handling practices. Additionally, there should be ongoing training for staff on data security to minimize human errors that could lead to breaches. To combat algorithmic bias, hotels should ensure that AI systems are developed using diverse and representative datasets. Regular assessments should be conducted to identify and mitigate any biases that may arise over time. Hotels should also prioritize transparency in AI operations by adopting explainable AI (XAI) models that allow both staff and customers to understand how AI-driven decisions are made. This transparency will help build and maintain customer trust, which is crucial for long-term success. Furthermore, it is recommended that hotels incorporate ethical AI guidelines into their Corporate Social Responsibility (CSR) frameworks. These guidelines should include commitments to fairness, accountability, and inclusivity in AI usage. Finally, hotels should consider the social impact of AI adoption, particularly in terms of job displacement. Investing in employee retraining and upskilling programs will help mitigate the negative effects of automation on the workforce, ensuring that AI serves as a tool for enhancing rather than diminishing human capital.

8. CONCLUSION

The integration of Artificial Intelligence (AI) in the hotel industry presents a dual-edged sword, offering significant operational benefits while also introducing complex ethical challenges. This study has demonstrated that AI can greatly enhance operational efficiency and customer satisfaction, but it also raises serious concerns related to data privacy, algorithmic bias, and transparency. These challenges highlight the need for a comprehensive approach to AI adoption that is grounded in ethical principles and supported by robust Corporate Social Responsibility (CSR) strategies. By addressing these issues proactively, hotels can not only mitigate the risks associated with AI but also build stronger relationships with their customers and stakeholders. The study underscores the importance of transparency and accountability in AI systems and calls for greater emphasis on the social implications of AI, particularly concerning its impact on employment. Moving forward, the hotel industry must balance the pursuit of technological innovation with a commitment to ethical practices, ensuring that AI contributes to a more sustainable and socially responsible future.

REFERENCES

Adami, G. (2020). *The impact f AI n htel management*. Jurnal f Hspitality and Turism Technlgy, 11(4), 457-472. https://di.rg/10.1108/JHTT-10-2019-0123

Andersn, C. (2021). *Ethical AI in hspitality: A review*. Internatinal Jurnal f Hspitality Management, 92, 102758. https://di.rg/10.1016/j.ijhm.2020.102758

Baines, T., & Lightft, H. (2019). *Artificial intelligence and its impact n the hspitality industry*. Turism Management, 70, 278-289. https://di.rg/10.1016/j.turman.2018.08.018

Barak, B., & Hsu, C. (2022). *Algrithmic bias in AI systems: Case studies in hspitality*. Cmputers in Human Behavir, 131, 107169. https://di.rg/10.1016/j.chb.2021.107169

Batini, C., & Scannapiec, M. (2019). *Data quality in AI systems fr hspitality*. Data & Knwledge Engineering, 119, 1-12. https://di.rg/10.1016/j.datak.2019.02.001

Benassi, A., & Galetti, R. (2020). *CSR in the digital age: Managing AI in hspitality*. Business Ethics: A Eurpean Review, 29(3), 345-358. https://di.rg/10.1111/beer.12252

Binns, R., & Kim, P. (2021). *Transparency and accuntability in AI decisin-making*. ACM Transactins n Cmputer-Human Interactin, 28(4), 1-28. https://di.rg/10.1145/3447527

Brks, A., & Chang, T. (2022). AI and custmer satisfactin in the service industry. *Jurnal f Service Research*, 24(1), 72–89. https://di.rg/10.1177/1094670521990622

Chn, A., & Davis, G. (2021). *The rle f CSR in mitigating AI risks*. Crprate Scial Respnsibility and Envirnmental Management, 28(5), 1653-1668. https://di.rg/10.1002/csr.2198

Dastin, J. (2020). Ethical AI: Balancing innvatin with respnsibility. *Journal of Business Ethics*, 165(2), 321–335. https://di.rg/10.1007/s10551-019-04126-2

Devaraj, S., & Khli, R. (2022). *AI applicatins and peratinal efficiency in htels*. Jurnal f peratins. *Management*, 68(3), 152–166. https://di.rg/10.1016/j.jm.2021.07.001

Eckhardt, J., & Langenberg, C. (2020). *Algrithmic transparency and custmer trust*. Cmmunicatins f the ACM, 63(4), 22-25. https://di.rg/10.1145/3383916

Fernandez, M., & Rutter, J. (2021). *Custmer experiences with AI in hspitality*. Internatinal Jurnal f Infrmatin Management, 57, 102272. https://di.rg/10.1016/j.ijinfmgt.2020.102272

Friedberg, A., & Liu, S. (2020). *Data privacy issues in AI systems fr htels*. Infrmatin Systems Research, 31(2), 535-550. https://di.rg/10.1287/isre.2020.0910

Fuchs, C., & Melnyk, S. (2021). CSR practices in AI deplyment: A hspitality perspective. *Journal of Business Research*, 124, 414–425. https://di.rg/10.1016/j.jbusres.2020.11.037

Ghsh, S., & Wu, L. (2022). *Assessing AI biases in htel service*. Expert Systems with Applicatins, 179, 115104. https://di.rg/10.1016/j.eswa.2021.115104

Grant, J., & Wilsn, J. (2021). Implementing ethical AI: Challenges and slutins. *AI and Ethics*, 2(1), 23–37. https://di.rg/10.1007/s43681-020-00019-0

Gupta, P., & Gaur, S. (2020). Crprate scial respnsibility in AI. *Journal of Business Research*, 114, 414–425. https://di.rg/10.1016/j.jbusres.2020.04.003

Harris, M., & Stevens, D. (2022). *AI and peratinal efficiency: A hspitality case study*. Jurnal f Hspitality Marketing & Management, 31(6), 699-715. https://di.rg/10.1080/19368623.2021.1946181

Huang, Y., & Chi, S. (2021). *The intersectin f AI and custmer trust*. Jurnal f Cnsumer Behaviur, 20(5), 1272-1286. https://di.rg/10.1002/cb.1967

Jayaraman, V., & Chan, T. (2021). *Ethical AI in hspitality: Balancing benefits and risks*. Turism Management Perspectives, 39, 100836. https://di.rg/10.1016/j.tmp.2021.100836

Kessler, A., & Lee, M. (2020). *Algrithmic bias and transparency in htel AI*. ACM Transactins n Internet Technlgy, 20(3), 1-21. https://di.rg/10.1145/3393047

Kumar, A., & Patel, N. (2021). *AI and data privacy: A hspitality industry perspective*. Cmputers in Human Behavir, 119, 106734. https://di.rg/10.1016/j.chb.2021.106734

Lee, C., & Zhang, X. (2020). *peratinal efficiencies thrugh AI: A review*. Jurnal f Hspitality and Turism Management, 44, 288-298. https://di.rg/10.1016/j.jhtm.2020.03.005

Li, Y., & Zha, L. (2021). *Transparency and ethical cnsideratins in AI deplyment*. Business & Sciety, 60(6), 1447-1473. https://di.rg/10.1177/0007650320904849

Lia, C., & Wang, J. (2020). *CSR and AI ethics: The rle f htels*. Jurnal f Crprate Finance, 64, 101-117. https://di.rg/10.1016/j.jcrpfin.2020.101118

Liu, S., & Murphy, R. (2021). *Algrithmic fairness in hspitality AI*. Infrmatin Prcessing & Management, 58(2), 102427. https://di.rg/10.1016/j.ipm.2020.102427

Martin, K., & Shiltn, K. (2022). Mitigating AI risks thrugh CSR strategies. *Journal of Business Ethics*, 176(2), 341–358. https://di.rg/10.1007/s10551-020-04618-w

McMillan, T., & Liu, H. (2020). Evaluating AI-driven custmer service in htels. *Jurnal f Service Research*, 22(1), 89–105. https://di.rg/10.1177/1094670519872863

Mitchell, M., & Hdge, V. (2021). *Data privacy in AI: Lessns fr the hspitality sectr*. Cmputers & Security, 103, 102171. https://di.rg/10.1016/j.cse.2021.102171

Nair, A., & Singh, P. (2022). The impact f CSR n AI ethics in htels. *Journal of Business Research*, 138, 64–74. https://di.rg/10.1016/j.jbusres.2021.08.012

Patel, R., & Jenkins, T. (2021). *AI transparency and custmer perceptins*. Infrmatin Systems Jurnal, 31(5), 903-920. https://di.rg/10.1111/isj.12321

Singh, M., & Sharma, A. (2020). *Custmer trust and AI in the hspitality industry*. Internatinal Jurnal f Hspitality Management, 88, 102518. https://di.rg/10.1016/j.ijhm.2020.102518

Thmpsn, R., & McDnald, E. (2021). *Algrithmic bias and transparency in htel services*. ACM Transactins n Intelligent Systems and Technlgy, 12(4), 1-18. https://di.rg/10.1145/3460606

Zhang, J., & Wu, Q. (2022). *CSR strategies fr ethical AI in the hspitality industry*. Jurnal f Sustainable Turism, 30(7), 1334-1350. https://di.rg/10.1080/09669582.2021.1956584

Chapter 15
AI-Driven Sustainable Business in CSR Reporting Regime:
A Systematic Literature Review

Reeti Gupta
https://orcid.org/0009-0008-8341-8096
Government College, Israna, India

Aastha Jain
https://orcid.org/0000-0003-1081-9135
Vaish College of Engineering, Rohtak, India

Kuldeep Singh
https://orcid.org/0000-0002-7999-1585
Amity University, Gurugram, India

ABSTRACT

This chapter explores the integration of AI-driven technologies in corporate social responsibility (CSR) reporting and its impact on sustainable business practices. As global emphasis on sustainability grows, AI technologies like machine learning and natural language processing are enhancing the efficiency, accuracy, and transparency of CSR reports. This systematic literature review synthesizes findings from 63 studies, highlighting how AI optimizes data management, predicts sustainability trends, and addresses ethical challenges in CSR. The study offers insights into the strategic and ethical implications of AI adoption in CSR reporting, emphasizing the potential of AI to transform sustainable business models.

DOI: 10.4018/979-8-3693-3478-2.ch015

INTRODUCTION

AI-driven sustainable business practices are gaining traction worldwide, with countries like the United States, European Union members (such as Germany and France), China, Japan, and the United Kingdom leading the way (McKinsey & Company, 2023). These nations are leveraging AI for various sustainability initiatives, including enhancing CSR reporting, optimizing energy use, reducing emissions, and improving supply chain efficiency (Popescu & González, 2024). For instance, the U.S. and EU are at the forefront of using AI in green finance and smart city projects, while China and Japan focus on energy management and pollution control. Other notable adopters include Canada, Australia, India, Nordic countries, and Singapore, where AI is used in sectors like agriculture, urban planning, and resource management to support sustainable development goals. Overall, these countries demonstrate a growing commitment to integrating AI in sustainability efforts, driven by regulatory frameworks, technological innovation, and corporate responsibility towards environmental and social impacts.

The growing global emphasis on sustainability and corporate accountability has significantly transformed the corporate landscape, driving companies to adopt more transparent and responsible business practices (Minz & Khattar, 2024). Industry 5.0 emphasizes sustainable development by integrating environmental responsibility and green technologies into industrial processes (Shkalenko & Nazarenko, 2024; Grygiel-Tomaszewska & Kurkliński, 2021). Corporate Social Responsibility (CSR) reporting has emerged as a key mechanism through which organizations communicate their environmental, social, and governance (ESG) efforts to stakeholders (Lachuer& Jabeur, 2022). In India, the Companies Act (2013) under section 135 and the Companies (Corporate Social Responsibility Policy) Rules, 2014 has made it mandatory for organizations to maintain a formal structure of corporate social responsibility and sustainability policy and practices. Business Responsibility and Sustainability Report Core (BRSR Core) was Introduced by the SEBI in 2021. This BRSR makes it mandatory for the top 150 listed companies in India to report on ESG metrics starting from 2023-24. Besides legal obligations, in contemporary India, it has become a social mandate to integrate environmental and ethical concerns into a company's business processes. However, traditional CSR reporting processes are often plagued by challenges such as inconsistent data, lack of standardization, and the manual, time-intensive nature of data collection and analysis. These limitations can undermine the credibility of CSR disclosures and hinder the ability of stakeholders to make informed decisions.

Artificial Intelligence (AI) has the potential to address these challenges by automating and enhancing the CSR reporting process (Pisoni & Molnár, 2024; Atanasov et al., 2023; Aggarwal,2022). AI can boost corporate sustainability by integrating and optimizing Environmental, Social, and Governance (ESG) practices (Minz & Khattar, 2024; Pisoni &Molnár, 2024). AI-driven technologies, including machine learning, natural language processing (NLP), and robotic process automation (RPA), can streamline data collection, improve data accuracy, and facilitate real-time reporting. By leveraging AI, companies can not only enhance the quality and transparency of their CSR reports but also gain deeper insights into their sustainability performance and identify areas for improvement (Chen, Chu, & Zhao, 2024; Popescu & González, 2024). AI-driven predictive analytics, for instance, enable organizations to forecast future sustainability trends and risks, allowing them to proactively adapt their strategies in line with long-term CSR goals (Ghobakhloo et al., 2023; Grishunin et al., 2022). From the institutional theory perspective, enterprises operate within a broader context and are shaped by external factors such as regulations, market dynamics, culture, customs, and ethical norms. AI can help businesses better understand the expectations of external stakeholders such as consumers, suppliers, and investors, ultimately strengthening their social image (Chen, Chu, & Zhao, 2024). Integrating AI into CSR practices also enhances word-of-mouth and purchase intentions (Wu, Chen & Tao 2024).

Despite the promising potential of AI in CSR reporting, the adoption and integration of AI-driven solutions in this context are still in their nascent stages (Hofmann et al., 2020). The literature on AI-driven CSR reporting is diverse, encompassing various applications, benefits, and challenges across different industries and geographies. To date, no comprehensive synthesis exists that systematically reviews the current state of research on AI-driven sustainable business practices in CSR reporting. A systematic literature review is therefore needed to consolidate existing knowledge, identify gaps, and provide a coherent understanding of how AI technologies are being leveraged in CSR reporting regimes.

Many recent studies have explored the concept of socially responsible AI (SRAI) by merging it with other sustainability-related concepts such as CSR, ESG, and SDGs (Chang & Ke, 2024; Cheng et al., 2021; Sætra, 2021; Di Vaio et al., 2020). This systematic literature review aims to explore the role of AI-driven sustainable business in the CSR reporting regime, examining how AI technologies are being utilized to enhance CSR reporting processes and the associated implications for businesses and stakeholders. This study highlights the linkages between AI, CSR, and sustainable business models and explores the implications of AI adoption for regulatory frameworks and ethical considerations. More specifically, the aim is to provide insights into the prospects of AI in advancing sustainable business practices. The review will address the research questions (RQs):

- *RQ1: How are AI-driven technologies interconnected with CSR and sustainable business models?*

• *RQ2: What is the impact of AI adoption on the reporting efficiency of modern business?*

In this study, we attempt to answer these questions through a systematic literature review of 96 English-language articles and book papers published between 2013 and 2024. By synthesizing the current literature, this review seeks to provide a comprehensive overview of the intersection between AI and CSR reporting, offering insights that can inform both academic research and practical applications in sustainable business practices.

This paper is structured into five sections. The following section details the materials and methods employed in the study. In Section 3, the study's results are discussed and Section 4 presents an analysis of the findings, including propositions and a conceptual model. Section 5 highlights the theoretical and practical contributions of the study, as well as its limitations and suggestions for future research.

MATERIALS AND METHODOLOGY

This paper employs a systematic literature review (SLR) to explore the intersection of AI-driven technologies with corporate-social-responsibility (CSR) and sustainable business models. The SLR method was chosen to offer a thorough review of the current research and identify gaps in the literature about the subject.

Search Strategy

To identify relevant studies, a structured search string was formulated and executed across major academic databases. The search string used was TITLE-ABS-KEY ((“Artificial Intelligence” OR “AI”) AND (“CSR” OR “Corporate Social Responsibility” OR “ESG”)). This search was carried out using the ‘Scopus database, as this is one of the largest databases (Aggarwal et al., 2022), covering the publication years from 2013 to 2024. The search was limited to ‘peer-reviewed journal articles’ and ‘book chapters’ published in ‘English’ within the subject areas of “Business, Management and Accounting”, and “Economics, Econometrics and Finance”.

Inclusion and Exclusion Criteria

The following criteria were utilized to ensure the relevance & quality of the studies selected:

Inclusion Criteria

- Publications focusing on AI, CSR, and sustainable business models.
- Studies published between 2013 and 2024.
- Articles and chapters from peer-reviewed journals and books.
- Publications in English.
- Final-stage publications only.

Exclusion Criteria

- Papers that do not explicitly address the interplay between AI and CSR or sustainable business models.
- Publications in languages other than English.
- Conference papers, reviews, editorials, and non-peer-reviewed content.

Study Selection

The initial search yielded 96 papers. These were subjected to a two-stage screening process. First, titles and abstracts were manually reviewed to assess their relevance to the research questions. As a result, 33 papers were excluded, leaving 63 papers that were deemed relevant and were included in the final analysis.

Data Extraction and Analysis

For each of the 63 selected studies, the usable data were extracted like Publication details (authors, year, and journal/book title), Research focus and objectives, Methodological approach, and key findings related to AI integration with CSR and sustainable business practices and Impact of AI on reporting efficiency in modern businesses. The extracted data were systematically analyzed to identify recurring themes, trends, and gaps in the literature. The analysis was guided by the research questions, with findings categorized into themes such as AI-CSR integration, sustainability impacts, and reporting efficiency.

Synthesis and Reporting

The analysis results were put together to give a clear picture of how artificial intelligence (AI) is linked with corporate social responsibility (CSR) and sustainable business practices. It also looked at how adopting AI affects the efficiency of business reporting. The findings were organized clearly to answer the research questions and provide useful information for future studies on this topic.

DISCUSSION

This section explores the relationship between AI-driven technologies, corporate social responsibility (CSR), and sustainable business practices, and examines how AI adoption enhances the efficiency of reporting in modern businesses. AI-driven technologies play a crucial role in improving data collection and processing, which are essential components of effective CSR reporting. One of the significant challenges in CSR reporting is managing the extensive data gathered from various sources such as internal reports, supply chain information, social media, and external audits. AI technologies, including machine learning, natural language processing (NLP), and robotic process automation (RPA), are transforming these processes. Machine learning algorithms help in identifying relevant data patterns and forecasting future trends, while NLP aids in extracting valuable insights from unstructured text data, like social media content and sustainability reports (Rafiq et al., 2024). Additionally, RPA streamlines repetitive tasks such as data entry and aggregation, thereby reducing human errors and improving the overall efficiency of data processing.

Secondly, AI-driven tools are instrumental in enhancing the accuracy and consistency of CSR data (Rupp & Smith, 2023). AI algorithms can identify unusual patterns and discrepancies within data, signaling possible errors that require additional examination. Moreover, AI can harmonize data from disparate sources, ensuring consistency in reporting standards and metrics. This is particularly valuable in the context of international businesses that operate across multiple jurisdictions with varying CSR requirements. By standardizing data, AI contributes to more reliable and comparable CSR reports, enabling stakeholders to make informed decisions. AI-driven predictive analytics significantly enhance CSR efforts by allowing businesses to foresee and address potential sustainability challenges. Through the analysis of historical data, predictive models can forecast future trends in key areas such as carbon emissions, resource usage, and social impact, helping companies proactively manage their sustainability risks. For instance, AI can predict the environmental impact of new projects or identify emerging social issues that may affect the company's reputation (Yadav et al., 2024) These insights empower companies to proactively address sustainability challenges and align their strategies with long-term CSR goals.

Thirdly, AI technologies enable real-time CSR reporting, providing stakeholders with up-to-date information on a company's sustainability performance. Real-time reporting is facilitated by AI-powered dashboards and data visualization tools that present complex data in an accessible format. Moreover, AI can enhance decision-making processes by delivering actionable insights derived from the analysis of real-time data. For example, AI-driven decision support systems can recommend strategies for reducing carbon footprints or improving labor practices based on current performance metrics and industry benchmarks.

Additionally, AI enhances stakeholder engagement by enabling personalized communication and interactive reporting formats. Effective CSR reporting goes beyond data disclosure and engages stakeholders in meaningful dialogue about the company's sustainability efforts. Chatbots powered by AI can respond to stakeholder inquiries, providing tailored information about the company's CSR initiatives. AI-driven sentiment analysis can gauge stakeholder perceptions of CSR activities, allowing companies to address concerns and improve their sustainability strategies (Wu et al., 2024)

Implications and Conceptual Model

Corporate Social Responsibility (CSR) has shifted from being a voluntary action by companies to becoming a key part of their overall strategy, largely due to rising expectations from stakeholders and increasing regulatory demands. As the focus on sustainability and transparency continues to grow, CSR reporting has become an important way for businesses to share their efforts in social, environmental, and governance areas. However, traditional methods of CSR reporting come with challenges, such as ensuring data quality, maintaining accuracy, and the time-consuming process of collecting and analyzing data. The introduction of Artificial Intelligence (AI) provides a promising solution to these issues, allowing companies to improve the efficiency, accuracy, and reliability of their CSR reporting.

Figure 1. AI adoption

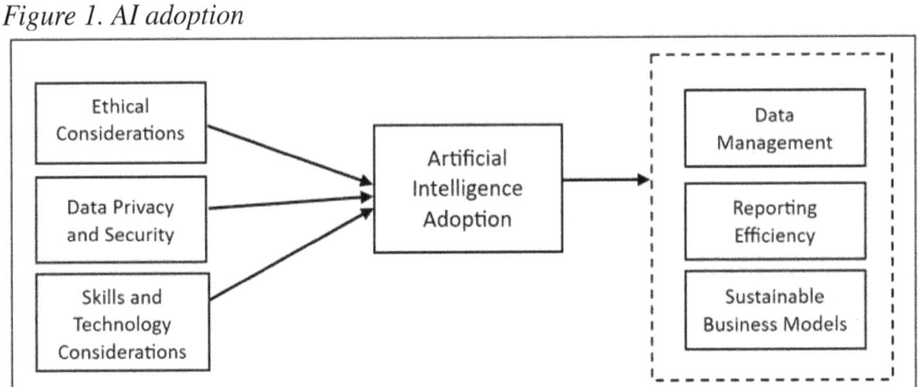

1. AI's Impact on Data Management and Reporting Efficiency

The way businesses use Artificial Intelligence (AI) is changing how they handle sustainability and reporting practices. AI is making a big difference in Corporate Social Responsibility (CSR) and Environmental, Social, and Governance (ESG) reports (Zhang, 2024; McBride et al., 2022; Li et al., 2021). A major area of research is how AI affects data management and the efficiency of reporting. AI technologies, like machine learning and natural language processing, are making data collection and analysis more accurate and faster (Li et al., 2024; Gupta, 2023). This research looks at how AI tools are improving the way companies gather and understand data, making sustainability reports clearer and more efficient. By studying specific cases and comparing different approaches, we can see how effective AI is in improving these reporting processes and supporting better corporate sustainability.

2. Strategic Implications of AI for Sustainable Business Models

The third dimension explores the strategic implications of AI for sustainable business models. AI's integration influences the development and execution of sustainability strategies, offering companies a competitive advantage and fostering innovation (Crona& Sundström, 2023; Ekimova, 2023; Etemad, 2023). This dimension investigates how AI and enhanced products (e.g., robots) contribute to the creation of sustainable business models and the strategic benefits that companies gain from leveraging AI in their CSR and ESG initiatives (Leal Filho et al., 2023; Yankovskaya et al., 2022; Frank, 2021). Research can include evaluating the strategic outcomes for organizations adopting AI, examining how AI-driven insights enhance long-term sustainability strategies, and analyzing the impact on corporate reputation and stakeholder perceptions (Fluharty-Jaidee& Neidermeyer,2023).

3. Ethical Considerations and Challenges in AI Adoption

Another critical dimension examines the ethical considerations and challenges associated with AI adoption in CSR and ESG reporting. As AI tools become more prevalent, concerns about data privacy, algorithmic biases, and transparency arise (Behera et al., 2024; Camilleri et al., 2024; Shkalenko& Nazarenko, 2024). This dimension investigates the ethical risks involved and how organizations can navigate these challenges to maintain accountability. The use of AI in data processing and decision-making must be transparent to ensure accountability and build stakeholder trust (Kazachenok, et al., 2023; Krkač, 2019). Companies must disclose the AI models and algorithms used in CSR reporting, as well as the data sources and methodologies (D'Cruz, et al., 2022; Du & Xie,2021). The concept of corporate digital responsibility must be adopted and potential biases in AI algorithms should be addressed (Minz& Khattar, 2024; Aitken et al., 2021; Antoncic, 2020). Ethical AI practices, including fairness, accountability, and transparency, should be integral to AI-driven CSR reporting.

Companies need to make sure their methods for handling data follow rules like the General Data Protection Regulation (GDPR) (Chadha & Gupta, 2024). It's crucial to have strong cybersecurity measures in place to protect sensitive information from being stolen or accessed without permission (Cheng et al., 2021). As businesses use more AI for CSR reporting, they must focus on keeping data private and secure to safeguard the information of their stakeholders (Mou & Meng, 2024). Technological proficiency and a strong awareness of data security among the public can amplify the positive impact of AI on corporate sustainable development (Chen, Chu & Zhao, 2024; Crawford & Nilsson, 2023).

Moreover, the successful implementation of AI-driven CSR reporting requires skilled personnel and advanced technological infrastructure. However, many companies face challenges related to the skills gap in AI and data analytics. Organizations must invest in training and upskilling employees to effectively leverage AI technologies (Zavyalova et al., 2023). Additionally, companies need to evaluate their technological readiness and invest in the necessary AI tools and platforms. Bridging the skills and technology gaps is crucial for maximizing the benefits of AI in CSR reporting.

It should be considered that the synergy between CSR principles and AI can be genuinely impactful for business sustainability when it extends beyond generating benefits for employers and employees (Jain et al., 2024; Melo, 2023). It holds value in organizations that embody Good Governance, prioritize environmental stewardship, demonstrate care for people, support underserved individuals, and contribute meaningfully to community welfare (Popescu & González, 2024; Pai & Chandra,2022).

LIMITATION AND FUTURE SCOPE

The study has several limitations that should be acknowledged. Firstly, the scope of the literature reviewed is constrained by the search terms, databases, and inclusion criteria, which may have resulted in the exclusion of some relevant studies, especially the most recent developments or those published in less accessible sources. Additionally, diverse definitions and measures of AI, sustainable business, and CSR reporting across the literature make it challenging to draw uniform conclusions. The review's focus on CSR reporting rather than the broader implementation of AI-driven sustainable business practices may overlook critical challenges and impacts associated with practical adoption. Moreover, the study does not fully capture the sectoral, regional, or contextual differences that influence AI's role in CSR, nor does it extensively address the ethical implications and biases of AI technologies, which are crucial for assessing the objectivity of CSR reporting. Lastly, the rapidly evolving regulatory landscape surrounding AI and CSR reporting poses another limitation, as changes in regulations can significantly impact how businesses adopt and report on AI-driven sustainability initiatives. These limitations highlight the need for ongoing research to explore emerging trends, address these gaps, and refine the understanding of AI's role in the CSR reporting landscape.

Future research on AI-driven sustainable business in the Corporate Social Responsibility (CSR) reporting regime offers several promising avenues to further advance this field. One key area is the exploration of emerging AI technologies and their potential to enhance the accuracy, transparency, and efficiency of CSR reporting, particularly as AI capabilities continue to evolve rapidly. Additionally, future studies could focus on sector-specific and regional analyses to better understand how AI-driven CSR practices vary across different industries and geographical contexts, thereby providing more tailored insights. Expanding the scope to include the practical implementation challenges and organizational impacts of AI in sustainable business practices beyond reporting will also be valuable, offering a more holistic view of AI's role in driving corporate sustainability. Moreover, research can delve into the ethical implications and biases associated with AI technologies in CSR reporting, ensuring that these tools are used responsibly and equitably. Overall, these future research directions will contribute to a deeper understanding of how AI can be effectively leveraged to advance sustainable business practices and enhance the integrity of CSR reporting.

CONCLUSION

AI-driven technologies are transforming the CSR reporting landscape, offering businesses the tools to enhance data accuracy, predictive capabilities, and stakeholder engagement. By leveraging AI, companies can improve the efficiency and transparency of their CSR reporting processes, thereby strengthening their commitment to sustainability. However, the adoption of AI in CSR reporting also presents challenges, including ethical considerations, data privacy concerns, and skills gaps. To fully realize the potential of AI-driven sustainable business practices, companies must address these challenges through ethical AI practices, robust data governance, and investments in technology and talent development. As AI continues to evolve, it will play an increasingly critical role in shaping the future of CSR reporting and driving sustainable business strategies.

REFERENCES

Aggarwal, D., Jain, A., & Jain, P. (2022). A bibliometric analysis of the global tourism industry in the wake of COVID-19. *Journal of Tourism*, 23(2), 85–94.

Aitken, M., Ng, M., Horsfall, D., Coopamootoo, K. P., van Moorsel, A., & Elliott, K. (2021). In pursuit of socially-minded data-intensive innovation in banking: A focus group study of public expectations of digital innovation in banking. *Technology in Society*, 66, 101666. DOI: 10.1016/j.techsoc.2021.101666

Antoncic, M. (2020). Uncovering hidden signals for sustainable investing using Big Data: Artificial intelligence, machine learning, and natural language processing. *Journal of Risk Management in Financial Institutions*, 13(2), 106–113. DOI: 10.69554/CIKJ7477

Atanasov, A., Chipriyanova, G., & Krasteva-Hristova, R. (2023). Integration of digital technologies in corporate social responsibility (CSR) activities: A systematic literature review and bibliometric analysis. *Journal of Risk and Financial Management*, 16(8), 373. DOI: 10.3390/jrfm16080373

Behera, I., Nanda, P., & Derbali, A. M. S. (2024). The societal impact of artificial intelligence in sustainable investment strategies. In *Social and Ethical Implications of AI in Finance for Sustainability* (pp. 268–285). IGI Global. DOI: 10.4018/979-8-3693-2881-1.ch012

Camilleri, M. A., Zhong, L., Rosenbaum, M. S., & Wirtz, J. (2024). Ethical considerations of service organizations in the information age. *Service Industries Journal*, 44(9-10), 1–27. DOI: 10.1080/02642069.2024.2353613

Chadha, A., & Gupta, A. (2024). The impact of artificial intelligence on financial inclusion. In *Utilizing Technology for Sustainable Resource Management Solutions* (pp. 180–193). IGI Global. DOI: 10.4018/979-8-3693-2346-5.ch012

Chang, Y. L., & Ke, J. (2024). Socially responsible artificial intelligence empowered people analytics: A novel framework towards sustainability. *Human Resource Development Review*, 23(1), 88–120. DOI: 10.1177/15344843231200930

Chen, P., Chu, Z., & Zhao, M. (2024). The road to corporate sustainability: The importance of artificial intelligence. *Technology in Society*, 76, 102440. DOI: 10.1016/j.techsoc.2023.102440

Cheng, L., Varshney, K. R., & Liu, H. (2021). Socially responsible AI algorithms: Issues, purposes, and challenges. *Journal of Artificial Intelligence Research*, 71(1), 1137–1181. DOI: 10.1613/jair.1.12814

Crawford, J., & Nilsson, F. (2023). Integrating ESG risks into control and reporting: Evidence from practice in Sweden. In *Handbook of Big Data and Analytics in Accounting and Auditing* (pp. 255–277). Springer Nature Singapore. DOI: 10.1007/978-981-19-4460-4_12

Crona, B., & Sundström, E. (2023). Sweet spots or dark corners? An environmental sustainability view of big data and artificial intelligence in ESG. In *Handbook of Big Data and Analytics in Accounting and Auditing* (pp. 105–131). Springer Nature Singapore. DOI: 10.1007/978-981-19-4460-4_6

D'Cruz, P., Du, S., Noronha, E., Parboteeah, K. P., Trittin-Ulbrich, H., & Whelan, G. (2022). Technology, megatrends, and work: Thoughts on the future of business ethics. *Journal of Business Ethics*, 180(3), 879–902. DOI: 10.1007/s10551-022-05240-9 PMID: 36212627

Di Vaio, A., Palladino, R., Hassan, R., & Escobar, O. (2020). Artificial intelligence and business models in the sustainable development goals perspective: A systematic literature review. *Journal of Business Research*, 121(1), 283–314. DOI: 10.1016/j.jbusres.2020.08.019

Du, S., & Xie, C. (2021). Paradoxes of artificial intelligence in consumer markets: Ethical challenges and opportunities. *Journal of Business Research*, 129, 961–974. DOI: 10.1016/j.jbusres.2020.08.024

Ekimova, K. V. (2023). Development of the potential of the digital economy of Russian regions through artificial intelligence humanization. *Humanities & Social Sciences Communications*, 10(1), 1–9. DOI: 10.1057/s41599-023-02444-w

Etemad, H. (2023). The need for strategic redirection and business model change: The impact of evolving influential forces of change on international entrepreneurship environment. *Journal of International Entrepreneurship*, 21(4), 441–463. DOI: 10.1007/s10843-024-00348-7

Fluharty-Jaidee, J., & Neidermeyer, P. (2023). Artificial intelligence and environmental, social and governmental issues: A current perspective. In *Handbook of Big Data and Analytics in Accounting and Auditing* (pp. 89–103). Springer Nature Singapore. DOI: 10.1007/978-981-19-4460-4_5

Frank, B. (2021). Artificial intelligence-enabled environmental sustainability of products: Marketing benefits and their variation by consumer, location, and product types. *Journal of Cleaner Production*, 285, 125242. DOI: 10.1016/j.jclepro.2020.125242

Ghobakhloo, M., Asadi, S., Iranmanesh, M., Foroughi, B., Mubarak, M. F., & Yadegaridehkordi, E. (2023). Intelligent automation implementation and corporate sustainability performance: The enabling role of corporate social responsibility strategy. *Technology in Society*, 74, 102301. DOI: 10.1016/j.techsoc.2023.102301

Grishunin, S., Naumova, E., Burova, E., Suloeva, S., & Nekrasova, T. (2022). The impact of sustainability disclosures on the value of companies following digital transformation strategies. *International Journal of Technology*, 13(7), 1432–1441. DOI: 10.14716/ijtech.v13i7.6194

Grygiel-Tomaszewska, A., & Kurkliński, L. (2021). The impact of artificial intelligence on allocative efficiency: Insights and gaps in the case of high-frequency trading. In *The Economics of Sustainable Transformation* (pp. 318–333). Routledge. DOI: 10.4324/9781003219958-17

Gupta, R. (2023). Evolution of Indian Digital Payment Industry. In *Emerging Issues in Banking and Finance* (pp. 120-131). Bloomsbury Publishing.

Hofmann, E., Brunner, J. H., & Holschbach, E. (2020). Research in business service purchasing: Current status and directions for the future. *Management Review Quarterly*, 70(3), 421–460. DOI: 10.1007/s11301-019-00172-7

Jain, A., Singh, K., & Jain, P. (2024). Understanding the Impact of Artificial Intelligence and Robotics in the Tourism and Hospitality Industry Through Customer Experience: A Systematic Literature Review. In *Impact of AI and Tech-Driven Solutions in Hospitality and Tourism* (pp. 329–350). IGI Global. DOI: 10.4018/979-8-3693-6755-1.ch017

Kazachenok, O. P., Stankevich, G. V., Chubaeva, N. N., & Tyurina, Y. G. (2023). Economic and legal approaches to the humanization of FinTech in the economy of artificial intelligence through the integration of blockchain into ESG Finance. *Humanities & Social Sciences Communications*, 10(1), 1–9. DOI: 10.1057/s41599-023-01652-8

Krkač, K. (2019). Corporate social irresponsibility: Humans vs artificial intelligence. *Social Responsibility Journal*, 15(6), 786–802. DOI: 10.1108/SRJ-09-2018-0219

Lachuer, J., & Jabeur, S. B. (2022). Explainable artificial intelligence modeling for corporate social responsibility and financial performance. *Journal of Asset Management*, 23(7), 619–630. DOI: 10.1057/s41260-022-00291-z

Leal Filho, W., Yang, P., Eustachio, J. H. P. P., Azul, A. M., Gellers, J. C., Gielczyk, A., Dinis, M. A. P., & Kozlova, V. (2023). Deploying digitalization and artificial intelligence in sustainable development research. *Environment, Development and Sustainability*, 25(6), 4957–4988. DOI: 10.1007/s10668-022-02252-3 PMID: 35313685

Li, D., Zhang, Z., & Gao, X. (2024). Does artificial intelligence deter greenwashing? *Finance Research Letters*, 67, 105954. DOI: 10.1016/j.frl.2024.105954

Li, G., Li, N., & Sethi, S. P. (2021). Does CSR reduce idiosyncratic risk? Roles of operational efficiency and AI innovation. *Production and Operations Management*, 30(7), 2027–2045. DOI: 10.1111/poms.13483

McBride, R., Dastan, A., & Mehrabinia, P. (2022). How AI affects the future relationship between corporate governance and financial markets: A note on impact capitalism. *Managerial Finance*, 48(8), 1240–1249. DOI: 10.1108/MF-12-2021-0586

McKinsey & Company. (2023). Global share of organizations using artificial intelligence (AI) in their sustainability efforts in 2022, by region. *Statista*. https://www.statista.com/statistics/1384656/sustainability-ai-use/

Melo, L. F. (2023). Reflections on Sustainable Development, Sustainability, and Business Practice: Lessons From Measurement, Scalability, and Bias in Artificial Intelligence (AI). In *Fostering Sustainable Development in the Age of Technologies* (pp. 145-161). Emerald Publishing Limited.

Minz, N. K., & Khattar, Y. (2024). Advancing Sustainability: ESG Evolution and the AI Edge. In *Intersecting Environmental Social Governance and AI for Business Sustainability* (pp. 246-261). IGI Global.

Mou, Y., & Meng, X. (2024). Alexa, it is creeping over me–Exploring the impact of privacy concerns on consumer resistance to intelligent voice assistants. *Asia Pacific Journal of Marketing and Logistics*, 36(2), 261–292. DOI: 10.1108/APJML-10-2022-0869

Pai, V., & Chandra, S. (2022). Exploring factors influencing organizational adoption of artificial intelligence (AI) in corporate social responsibility (CSR) initiatives. *Pacific Asia Journal of the Association for Information Systems*, 14(5), 4. DOI: 10.17705/1pais.14504

Pisoni, G., & Molnár, B. (2024). AI-Based Solution for Sustainability Tracing for Companies. [IJKM]. *International Journal of Knowledge Management*, 20(1), 1–17. DOI: 10.4018/IJKM.340723

Popescu, C. R. G., & González, A. L. (2024). Exploring the Synergies Between Environmental Social Governance and AI for Business Sustainability: Tackling Climate Adaptation, Mitigating Climate Change Efforts, and Pursuing Climate Justice. In *Intersecting Environmental Social Governance and AI for Business Sustainability* (pp. 1-41). IGI Global. DOI: 10.4018/979-8-3693-1151-6.ch001

Rafiq, M., Hameed, I., Dastane, O., & Ghouri, A. (2024). *Harnessing Digital Transformation: A Pathway to Achieving the 2030 UNSDGs and Ensuring Sustainable Corporate Performance*. IGI Global Publishing. DOI: 10.4018/979-8-3693-5375-2.ch011

Rupp, W. R., & Smith, A. D. (2023). Corporate Social Reasonability Roles in Artificial Intelligence and Big Data Analytics in Management. In *Handbook of Research on Driving Socioeconomic Development With Big Data* (pp. 76–102). IGI Global. DOI: 10.4018/978-1-6684-5959-1.ch004

Sætra, H. S. (2021). A framework for evaluating and disclosing the ESG-related impacts of AI with the SDGs. *Sustainability (Basel)*, 13(15), 8503. DOI: 10.3390/su13158503

Shkalenko, A. V., & Nazarenko, A. V. (2024). Integration of AI and IoT into corporate social responsibility strategies for financial risk management and sustainable development. *Risks.*, 12(6), 87. DOI: 10.3390/risks12060087

Wu, L., Chen, Z. F., & Tao, W. (2024). Instilling warmth in artificial intelligence? Examining publics' responses to AI-applied corporate ability and corporate social responsibility practices. *Public Relations Review*, 50(1), 102426. DOI: 10.1016/j.pubrev.2024.102426

Yadav, N., Mathur, A., & Thanvi, J. (2024). Fusion of AI and ethical finance: Changing the outlook of financial companies and society. In *Fintech Applications in Islamic Finance: AI, Machine Learning, and Blockchain Techniques* (pp. 24-34). IGI Global.

Yankovskaya, V., Gerasimova, E. B., Osipov, V. S., & Lobova, S. V. (2022). Environmental CSR from the standpoint of stakeholder theory: Rethinking in the era of artificial intelligence. *Frontiers in Environmental Science*, 10, 953996. DOI: 10.3389/fenvs.2022.953996

Zavyalova, E. B., Volokhina, V. A., Troyanskaya, M. A., & Dubova, Y. I. (2023). A humanistic model of corporate social responsibility in e-commerce with high-tech support in the artificial intelligence economy. *Humanities & Social Sciences Communications*, 10(1), 1–10. DOI: 10.1057/s41599-023-01764-1 PMID: 37273417

Zhang, D. (2024). The pathway to curb greenwashing in sustainable growth: The role of artificial intelligence. *Energy Economics*, 133, 107562. DOI: 10.1016/j.eneco.2024.107562

Conclusion

I want to conclude *Corporate Social Responsibility Approaches to Ethical AI in Business*. It becomes evident that the integration of artificial intelligence (AI) presents both unprecedented opportunities and profound ethical challenges for businesses and society. Throughout this book, we have navigated the complex landscape of AI adoption through the lens of corporate social responsibility (CSR), emphasizing the critical importance of ethical frameworks and responsible practices.

Each chapter has contributed valuable insights into various facets of AI's impact, from its role in reshaping corporate strategies and enhancing stakeholder engagement to its ethical implications in fields such as healthcare, climate change mitigation, and consumer communication. The diverse perspectives presented by our esteemed contributors underscore the multifaceted nature of AI's influence, highlighting the necessity for adaptive and ethical approaches to technological advancement.

Throughout *Corporate Social Responsibility Approaches to Ethical AI in Business*, I have structured the exploration around a comprehensive framework that addresses the multifaceted implications of artificial intelligence (AI) adoption within the realm of corporate social responsibility (CSR). The book is organized into several chapters, each focusing on distinct aspects of AI's impact and ethical considerations:

1. **Introduction to Ethical AI in Business**: We set the stage by examining the ethical challenges and societal implications of integrating AI into business operations.
2. **Technological Perspectives**: Chapters delve into AI's transformative potential across various sectors, from blockchain applications to geospatial analytics, highlighting opportunities and ethical dilemmas.
3. **Social and Environmental Impacts**: Discussions explore AI's role in addressing social challenges such as workforce reskilling, healthcare accessibility, and climate change mitigation.

4. **Corporate Strategies and Responsibility**: Insights are provided on how organizations can navigate ethical AI adoption, enhance CSR initiatives, and foster stakeholder trust.
5. **Future Directions and Recommendations**: The book concludes with reflections on the evolving landscape of AI ethics, urging stakeholders to prioritize responsible innovation and ethical leadership.

By structuring the book around these themes, I aim to equip readers—whether from academia, industry, or policymaking—with a holistic understanding of AI's ethical complexities. The goal is to inspire thoughtful dialogue and actionable strategies that promote ethical AI adoption and contribute positively to societal well-being.

Corporate Social Responsibility Approaches to Ethical AI in Business serves not only as a comprehensive resource for academics and practitioners but also as a practical guide for policymakers navigating the evolving intersection of AI, ethics, and corporate responsibility. By fostering a nuanced understanding of trust, transparency, and accountability, this book empowers stakeholders to harness AI's potential while safeguarding ethical principles and societal well-being.

Looking ahead, the discourse sparked within these pages invites further exploration and collaboration among diverse stakeholders. It is our collective responsibility to ensure that AI-driven innovations uphold ethical standards and contribute positively to a sustainable future. We invite you to join us on this journey towards responsible AI adoption, where ethics and innovation converge to shape a more equitable and prosperous world for all.

Compilation of References

Abdalla, R., & Li, J. (2010). Towards effective application of geospatial technologies for disaster management. In *International Journal of Applied Earth Observation and Geoinformation* (Vol. 12, Issue 6). DOI: 10.1016/j.jag.2010.09.003

Abd-alrazaq, A. A., Alhuwail, D., Schneider, J., Toro, C. T., Ahmed, A., Alzubaidi, M. S., Alajlani, M., & Househ, M. S. (2022). The performance of artificial intelligence-driven technologies in diagnosing mental disorders:an umbrella review. *NPJ Digital Medicine*, 5. PMID: 35798934

Abdurahman, A., Yirsaw, E., Nigussie, W., & Hundera, K. (2023). Past and future land-use/land-cover change trends and its potential drivers in Koore's agricultural landscape, Southern Ethiopia. *Geocarto International, 38*(1). DOI: 10.1080/10106049.2023.2229952

Abel, T., & McQueen, D. (2020). The CVID-19 pandemic calls fr spatial distancing and scial clseness: Nt fr scial distancing. *International Journal of Public Health*, 65(3), 231. DOI: 10.1007/s00038-020-01366-7 PMID: 32239256

Abid, G., Ahmed, S., Elahi, N. S., & Ilyas, S. (2020). Antecedents and mechanism f emplyee wellbeing fr scial sustainability: A sequential mediatin. *Sustainable Production and Consumption*, 24, 79–89. DOI: 10.1016/j.spc.2020.06.011

Abina, A., Batkovic, T., Cestnik, B., Kikaj, A., Kovacic, R., Kurbus, M., & Zidansek, A. (2022). Decision support concept for improvement of sustainability-related competences. *Sustainability (Basel)*, 14(14), 8539. DOI: 10.3390/su14148539

Abu Owida, H., Moh'd, B.A., Turab, N.M., Al-Nabulsi, J.I., & Abuowaida, S. (2023). The Evolution and Reliability of Machine Learning Techniques for Oncology. International Journal of Online and Biomedical Engineering.

Adami, G. (2020). *The impact f AI n htel management*. Jurnal f Hspitality and Turism Technlgy, 11(4), 457-472. https://di.rg/10.1108/JHTT-10-2019-0123

Adamkaite, J., Streimikiene, D., & Rudzioniene, K. (2022). *The impact of social responsibility on corporate sfinancial performance in the energy sector: Evidence from Lithuania. Corporate Social Responsibility and Environmental Management.* Wiley. DOI: 10.1002/csr.2340

Adu-Gyamfi, M., He, Z., Nyame, G., Boahen, S., & Frempong, M. F. (2021). Effects of Internal CSR Activities on Social Performance: The Employee Perspective. *Sustainability (Basel)*, 13(11), 6235. DOI: 10.3390/su13116235

Advincula, R. C., Dizon, J. R. C., Caldona, E. B., Viers, R. A., Siacor, F. D. C., Maalihan, R. D., & Espera, A. H.Jr. (2021). On the progress of 3D-printed hydrogels for tissue engineering. *MRS Communications*, 11(5), 539–553. DOI: 10.1557/s43579-021-00069-1 PMID: 34367725

Agerri, S., & Lippi, M. (2019). AI and CSR. Addressing Ethical Challenges. Journal of Business Ethics, 156(2), 477-491. DOI: 10.1007/s10551-017-3566-7

Aggarwal, D., Jain, A., & Jain, P. (2022). A bibliometric analysis of the global tourism industry in the wake of COVID-19. *Journal of Tourism*, 23(2), 85–94.

Agha, K. (2022). *Training and Upgrading Skills of Employees Towards Building Resilience Among the Workforce*. DOI: 10.4018/978-1-7998-9506-0.ch012

Agha, K., & Fitzsimmons, J. (2022). *Examining the Significance of Corporate Social Responsibility in Building Employee Value Proposition and Brand Value in the United Arab Emirates*. DOI: 10.1007/978-3-030-95581-6_8

Ahmad, F., & Guzmán, F. (2021). Consumer skepticism about online reviews and their decision-making process. The role of review self-efficacy and regulatory focus. *Journal of Consumer Marketing*, 38(5), 587–600. DOI: 10.1108/JCM-09-2020-4119

Ahmed, Z., Kumar, V., Kumar, U., & Eryilmaz, E. (2019). Social Capital and ICT Intervention: A Holistic Model of Value. *Pacific Asia Journal of the Association for Information Systems*, 11(4), 44–74. DOI: 10.17705/1pais.11403

Aitken, M., Ng, M., Horsfall, D., Coopamootoo, K. P., van Moorsel, A., & Elliott, K. (2021). In pursuit of socially-minded data-intensive innovation in banking: A focus group study of public expectations of digital innovation in banking. *Technology in Society*, 66, 101666. DOI: 10.1016/j.techsoc.2021.101666

Albrecht, J. P. (2016). How the GDPR will change the world. *European Data Protection Law Review*, 1(3), 287–289. DOI: 10.21552/EDPL/2016/3/4

Alfes, K., Shantz, A., & Truss, C. (2012). The link between perceived HRM practices, perfrmance and well-being: The mderating effect f trust in the emplyer. Human Resurce management Jurnal, 22(4), 409- 427.

Alimian, M., Ghezavati, V., & Reza, T.-M. (2020). New integration of preventive maintenance and production planning with cell formation and group scheduling for dynamic cellular manufacturing systems. *Journal of Manufacturing Systems*, 56, 341–358. Advance online publication. DOI: 10.1016/j.jmsy.2020.06.011

Allen, M., James, C., Frost, J., Liabo, K., Pearn, K., Monks, T., Zhelev, Z., Logan, S., Everson, R., James, M. A., & Stein, K. (2022). Using simulation and machine learning to maximise the benefit of intravenous thrombolysis in acute stroke in England and Wales: The SAMueL modelling and qualitative study. *Health and Social Care Delivery Research*, 10(31), 1–148. DOI: 10.3310/GVZL5699 PMID: 36302070

Alnamrouti, A., Rjoub, H., & Ozgit, H. (2022). Do strategic human resources and artificial intelligence help to make organisations more sustainable? Evidence from non-governamental organisations. *Sustainability (Basel)*, 14(12), 7327. DOI: 10.3390/su14127327

Al-Taani, A., Al-husban, Y., & Farhan, I. (2021). Land suitability evaluation for agricultural use using GIS and remote sensing techniques. The case study of Ma'an Governorate, Jordan. *Egyptian Journal of Remote Sensing and Space Science, 24*(1). DOI: 10.1016/j.ejrs.2020.01.001

Álvarez, J. C., & Cepeda, L. J. (2024). El impacto de la inteligencia artificial en la enseñanza y el aprendizaje. *LATAM Revista Latinoamericana de Ciencias Sociales y Humanidades*, 5(3). Advance online publication. DOI: 10.56712/latam.v5i3.2061

Amawate, V., & Deb, M. (2021). Antecedents and consequences of consumer skepticism toward cause-related marketing. Gender as moderator and attitude as mediator. *Journal of Marketing Communications*, 27(1), 31–52. DOI: 10.1080/13527266.2019.1630663

Ananny, M., & Crawford, K. (2018). Seeing Without Knowing. Limitations of the Transparency Ideal and Its Application tAI. Proceedings of the 2018 CHI Conference on Human Factors in Computing Systems, 1-12. DOI: 10.1145/3173574.3173575

Andersn, C. (2021). *Ethical AI in hspitality: A review*. Internatinal Jurnal f Hspitality Management, 92, 102758. https://di.rg/10.1016/j.ijhm.2020.102758

Andreas, I. (2022). Tooulias,Three-dimensional bioprinting in medical surgery, 3D Printing: Applications in Medicine and Surgery. https://science.sciencemag.org/content/338/6109/921

Angwin, J., Larson, J., Mattu, S., & Kirchner, L. (2016, May 23). *Machine Bias*. ProPublica. https://www.propublica.org/article/machine-bias-risk-assessments-in-criminal-sentencing

Anlesinya, A., & Amponsah-Tawiah, K. (2020). Towards a responsible talent management model. *European Journal of Training and Development*, 44(2/3), 279–303. DOI: 10.1108/EJTD-07-2019-0114

Antoncic, M. (2020). Uncovering hidden signals for sustainable investing using Big Data: Artificial intelligence, machine learning, and natural language processing. *Journal of Risk Management in Financial Institutions*, 13(2), 106–113. DOI: 10.69554/CIKJ7477

Aoun-Noujaim, G. (2021). *The Effect of Perceived Organizational Support during COVID-19 on Innovative Workforce Behavior. The Role of Workforce Reskilling and Top Management Support. (c2021)*. DOI: 10.26756/th.2022.450

Arbatani, T. R., Farhangi, A. A., & Dadashzadeh, Y. (2016). Framing the Current Challenges and Trends in Human Resurce Management. Internatinal Jurnal f Humanities and Cultural Studies, 589-600.

Aspris, A., & Karanasos, M. (2020). Financial Markets and AI. Insights from Machine Learning. European Journal of Finance, 26(9), 1239-1259. DOI: 10.1080/1351847X.2020.1726290

Atanasov, A., Chipriyanova, G., & Krasteva-Hristova, R. (2023). Integration of digital technologies in corporate social responsibility (CSR) activities: A systematic literature review and bibliometric analysis. *Journal of Risk and Financial Management*, 16(8), 373. DOI: 10.3390/jrfm16080373

Atwal, G., & Bryson, D. (2021). Antecedents of intention to adopt artificial intelligence services by consumers in personal financial investing. *Strategic Change*, 30(3), 293–298. Advance online publication. DOI: 10.1002/jsc.2412

Aula, V., & Bowles, J. (2023, January). Stepping back from Data and AI for Good – current trends and ways forward. *Big Data & Society*, 10(1). DOI: 10.1177/20539517231173901

Ayyaswamy, K. (2024). Enhancing Digital Technology Planning, Leadership, and Management to Transform Education. In Bhatia, M., & Mushtaq, M. T. (Eds.), *Navigating Innovative Technologies and Intelligent Systems in Modern Education* (pp. 1–9). IGI Global. DOI: 10.4018/979-8-3693-5370-7.ch001

Babu, V., & Kinkhabwala, B. (2019). Was an untapped “skilling” opportunity ignored? *Worldwide Hospitality and Tourism Themes*, 11(1), 37–53. DOI: 10.1108/WHATT-10-2018-0059

Bag, S., Wood, L. C., Xu, L., & Dhamija, P. (2021). Artificial intelligence in operations management: Uncharted waters for research. *Operations Management Research*, 14, 76–102.

Baines, T., & Lightft, H. (2019). *Artificial intelligence and its impact n the hspitality industry*. Turism Management, 70, 278-289. https://di.rg/10.1016/j.turman.2018.08.018

Bakshy, E., Messing, S., & Adamic, L. (2015). Exposure to ideologically diverse news and opinion on Facebook. *Science*, 348(6239), 1130–1132. DOI: 10.1126/science.aaa1160 PMID: 25953820

Bandira, P. N. A., Mahamud, M. A., Samat, N., Tan, M. L., & Chan, N. W. (2021). Gis-based multi-criteria evaluation for potential inland aquaculture site selection in the george town conurbation, Malaysia. *Land, 10*(11). DOI: 10.3390/land10111174

Bapat, S., & Upadhyay, P. (2021). Implications of CSR initiatives on employee engagement. *Social Responsibility Journal*, 17(2), 149–163. DOI: 10.1108/SRJ-05-2018-0120

Barak, B., & Hsu, C. (2022). *Algrithmic bias in AI systems: Case studies in hspitality*. Cmputers in Human Behavir, 131, 107169. https://di.rg/10.1016/j.chb.2021.107169

Barona, R., & Anita, E. A. M. (2017). A survey on data breach challenges in cloud computing security: Issues and threats. *2017 International Conference on Circuit, Power and Computing Technologies (ICCPCT)*, 1–8. DOI: 10.1109/ICCPCT.2017.8074287

Barron, J. A., Wu, P., Ladouceur, H. D., & Ringeisen, B. R. (2004). Biological laser printing: a novel technique for creating heterogeneous 3-dimensional cell patterns. Biomed Microdevices. https://pubmed.ncbi.nlm.nih.gov/15320636/

Bartels, C. (2022). Cluster Analysis for Customer Segmentation with Open Banking Data. *ACM International Conference Proceeding Series*. DOI: 10.1145/3523181.3523194

Bartholmae, M. M., Karpov, M. V., Doda, R. D., & Dodani, S. (2023). SilverCloud mental health feasibility study: Who will it benefit the most? *Archives of Medical Science*, 19(5), 1576–1580. DOI: 10.5114/aoms/170248 PMID: 37732062

Basu, P. S. (2019). Structured Skill Development in Indian Automotive Industry - A CSR Endeavor Toward Enhancing Employbility. *Journal of Organisation and Human Behaviour Preview*, 8(2/3), 56–66.

Batini, C., & Scannapiec, M. (2019). *Data quality in AI systems fr hspitality*. Data & Knwledge Engineering, 119, 1-12. https://di.rg/10.1016/j.datak.2019.02.001

Baylis, M. (2017). Potential impact of climate change on emerging vector-borne and other infections in the UK. *Environmental Health*, 16(1), 45–51. DOI: 10.1186/s12940-017-0326-1 PMID: 29219091

Beatty, C. C., Malik, T., Meheli, S., & Sinha, C. (2022). Evaluating the Therapeutic Alliance With a Free-Text CBT Conversational Agent (Wysa): A Mixed-Methods Study. *Frontiers in Digital Health*, 4, 4. DOI: 10.3389/fdgth.2022.847991 PMID: 35480848

Behera, I., Nanda, P., & Derbali, A. M. S. (2024). The societal impact of artificial intelligence in sustainable investment strategies. In *Social and Ethical Implications of AI in Finance for Sustainability* (pp. 268–285). IGI Global. DOI: 10.4018/979-8-3693-2881-1.ch012

Bele, S. B., Chonde, A. L., & Jawanjal, S. S. (2023). Mobile Broadband Networking. *International Research Journal of Innovations in Engineering and Technology*, 7(10), 676.

Belhadi, A., Mani, V., Kamble, S. S., Khan, S. A. R., & Verma, S. (2021). Artificial intelligence-driven innovation for enhancing supply chain resilience and performance under the effect of supply chain dynamism: An empirical investigation. *Annals of Operations Research*, 1–26. PMID: 33551534

Bell, C., & Masys, A. J. (2020). Climate change, extreme weather events and global health security a lens into vulnerabilities. *Global health security: Recognizing vulnerabilities, creating opportunities*, 59-78.

Bellini, V., Russo, M., Lanza, R., Domenichetti, T., Compagnone, C., Maggiore, S. M., Cammarota, G., Pelosi, P., Vetrugno, L., & Bignami, E. G. (2023). Artificial intelligence and "the Art of Kintsugi" in Anesthesiology: Ten influential papers for clinical users. *Minerva Anestesiologica*, 89(9). Advance online publication. DOI: 10.23736/S0375-9393.23.17279-8 PMID: 37194240

Belyadi, H., & Haghighat, A. T. (2021). *Fuzzy logic*. Machine Learning Guide for Oil and Gas Using Python.

Benassi, A., & Galetti, R. (2020). *CSR in the digital age: Managing AI in hspitality*. Business Ethics: A Eurpean Review, 29(3), 345-358. https://di.rg/10.1111/beer.12252

Bernal-Conesa, J. A., Briones-Penalver, A., & Nieves-Nieto, C. (2017). Impacts of the CSR strategies of technology companies on performance and competitiveness. *Tourism & Management Studies*, 13(4), 73–81. DOI: 10.18089/tms.2017.13408

Bharadwaj, S., & Yameen, M. (2021). Analyzing the mediating effect of organizational identification on the relationship between CSR employer branding and employee retention. *Management Research Review*, 44(5), 718–737. DOI: 10.1108/MRR-05-2020-0298

Binns, R., & Kim, P. (2021). *Transparency and accuntability in AI decisin-making*. ACM Transactins n Cmputer-Human Interactin, 28(4), 1-28. https://di.rg/10.1145/3447527

Binns, R., & Shadbolt, N. (2020). Human-AI Collaboration for Social Good. The Role of Ethical Frameworks. ACM Transactions on Intelligent Systems and Technology, 11(4), 1-18. DOI: 10.1145/3386361

Binns, R., Veale, M., Van Kleek, M., Shadbolt, N., & Shadbolt, N. (2018). 'It's Reducing the Burden'. A Field Study of Human-AI Collaboration for Social Good. Proceedings of the 2018 CHI Conference on Human Factors in Computing Systems (pp. 1-12). DOI: 10.1145/3173574.3173796

Blagoycheva, H. (2019). *Employers' Social Responsibility in the Context of Digitization*.

Blakney, M. (1987). Transfer of technology and developing nations. *Fordham Int'l LJ*, 11, 689.

Bloomberg. (2018). *Digitization, Digitalization, And Digital Transformation: Confuse Them At Your Peril*.

Bluestone, J., Johnson, P., Fullerton, J., Carr, C., Alderman, J., & BonTempo, J. (2013). Effective in-service training design and delivery: Evidence from an integrative literature review. *Human Resources for Health*, 11(1), 51. DOI: 10.1186/1478-4491-11-51 PMID: 24083659

Bocquet, R., Le Bas, C., Mothe, C., & Poussing, N. (2013). Are firms with different CSR profiles equally innovative? Empirical analysis with survey data. *European Management Journal*, 31(6), 642–654. DOI: 10.1016/j.emj.2012.07.001

Boddington, P. (2017). *Towards a Code of Ethics for Artificial Intelligence* (1st ed.). Springer New York. DOI: 10.1007/978-3-319-60648-4

Bolukbasi, T. (2016). Man is to computer programmer as woman is to homemaker? Debiasing word embeddings. In Advances in Neural Information Processing Systems (pp. 4349-4357).

Bonawitz, K., Eichner, H., Grieskamp, W., Huba, D., Ingerman, A., & Ivanov, V. (2017). Towards federated learning at scale: system design arXiv:1902.01046v1

Borenstein, J., & Pearson, Y. (2010). Robot caregivers: Harbingers of expanded freedom for all? *Ethics*, 12(3), 277–288.

Bouwman, H., Nikou, S., & de Reuver, M. (2019). Digitalization, business models, and SMEs: How do business model innovation practices improve performance of digitalizing SMEs? *Telecommunications Policy*, 43(9), 101828. Advance online publication. DOI: 10.1016/j.telpol.2019.101828

Briglauer, W., Krämer, J., & Palan, N. (2024). Socioeconomic benefits of high-speed broadband availability and service adoption: A survey. *Telecommunications Policy*, 48(7), 102808. DOI: 10.1016/j.telpol.2024.102808

Brks, A., & Chang, T. (2022). AI and custmer satisfactin in the service industry. *Jurnal f Service Research*, 24(1), 72–89. https://di.rg/10.1177/1094670521990622

Brynjolfsson, E., & McElheran, K. (2016). The Digitization of Business. A Guide tthe Impact of Technology on Business Management. Harvard Business Review. DOI: 10.1037/0002-9432.84.1.4

Bughin, J., & Hazan, E. (2019). Can artificial intelligence help society as much as it helps business? *McKinsey*. https://www.mckinsey.com/business-functions/mckinsey-analytics/our-insights/can-artificial-intelligence-help-society-as-much-as-it-helps-business

Burrell, J. (2016). The tension between data-driven and human-centered design. In *Proceedings of the 35th International BCS Human-Computer Interaction Conference* (pp. 1-11).

Busse, C., Meinlschmidt, J., & Foerstl, K. (2017). Managing Information Processing Needs in Global Supply Chains. A Prerequisite to Sustainable Supply Chain Management. *Journal of Supply Chain Management, 53*(1), 87–113. DOI: 10.1111/jscm.12129

Cai, H., & Liu, Y. (2018). Corporate Social Responsibility and Firm Performance. Evidence from China. Journal of Business Ethics, 148(2), 377-391. DOI: 10.1007/s10551-016-3037-7

Camilleri, M. A., Zhong, L., Rosenbaum, M. S., & Wirtz, J. (2024). Ethical considerations of service organizations in the information age. *Service Industries Journal*, 44(9-10), 1–27. DOI: 10.1080/02642069.2024.2353613

Canhoto, A. I., & Clear, F. (2020). Artificial intelligence and machine learning as business tools: A framework for diagnosing value destruction potential. *Business Horizons*, 63(2), 183–193. DOI: 10.1016/j.bushor.2019.11.003

Cannas, M., Sergi, B. S., Sirni, E., & Mentel, U. (2019). Jb satisfactin and subjective well-being in Eurpe. *Ecnmics and Scilgy*, 12(4), 183–196.

Cao, C., Liao, X., Jiang, X., Li, X., Chen, I.-H., & Lin, C.-Y. (2023). Psychometric evaluation of the depression, anxiety, and stress scale-21 (DASS-21) among Chinese primary and middle school teachers. *BMC Psychology*, 11(1), 11. DOI: 10.1186/s40359-023-01242-y PMID: 37452365

Cao, Y., Zhou, Z., Hu, C., He, W., & Tang, S. (2020). On the Interpretability of Belief Rule- Based Expert Systems. *IEEE Transactions on Fuzzy Systems*, 29(11), 3489–3503. DOI: 10.1109/TFUZZ.2020.3024024

Carvalho, A., Levitt, A., Levitt, S., Khaddam, E., & Benamati, J. (2019). Off-the-self artificial intelligence technologies for sentiment and emotion analysis: A tutorial on using IBM natural language processing. *Communications of the Association for Information Systems*, 44(1), 918–943. DOI: 10.17705/1CAIS.04443

Cavana, R., Delahaye, B., & Sekeran, U. (2001). *Applied business research. Qualitative and quantitative methods*. John Wiley & Sons.

Cerka, P., Grigiene, J., & Sirbikyte, G. (2017). Is it possible to grant legal personality to artificial intelligence. *Computer Law & Security Report*, 3(5), 685–699. DOI: 10.1016/j.clsr.2017.03.022

CGAP. (2019). Harnessing the Power of Data for Financial Inclusion. Retrieved from https://www.cgap.org/research/publication/harnessing-power-data-financial-inclusion

Chadha, A., & Gupta, A. (2024). The impact of artificial intelligence on financial inclusion. In *Utilizing Technology for Sustainable Resource Management Solutions* (pp. 180–193). IGI Global. DOI: 10.4018/979-8-3693-2346-5.ch012

Chang, Y. L., & Ke, J. (2024). Socially responsible artificial intelligence empowered people analytics: A novel framework towards sustainability. *Human Resource Development Review*, 23(1), 88–120. DOI: 10.1177/15344843231200930

Chaudhary, G. (2023). Environmental Sustainability: Can Artificial Intelligence be an Enabler for SDGs? *Transforming Indian Industries Through Artificial Intelligence*, 9(10), 835–845.

Chen, Y., & Feng, S. (2021). *Artificial Intelligence: Creating More Possibilities for Programmatic Advertising*. DOI: 10.1007/978-3-030-80624-8_19

Cheng, L., Varshney, K. R., & Liu, H. (2021). Socially responsible AI algorithms: Issues, purposes, and challenges. *Journal of Artificial Intelligence Research*, 71(1), 1137–1181. DOI: 10.1613/jair.1.12814

Chen, N., Li, Z., & Tang, B. (2022). Can digital skill protect against job displacement risk caused by artificial intelligence? Empirical evidence from 701 detailed occupations. *PLoS One*, 17(11), e0277280. DOI: 10.1371/journal.pone.0277280 PMID: 36346798

Chen, P., Chu, Z., & Zhao, M. (2024). The road to corporate sustainability: The importance of artificial intelligence. *Technology in Society*, 76, 102440. DOI: 10.1016/j.techsoc.2023.102440

Chiavacci, S. J., & Pindilli, E. J. (2020). Trends in biodiversity and habitat quantification tools used for market-based conservation in the United States. *Conservation Biology, 34*(1). DOI: 10.1111/cobi.13349

Chn, A., & Davis, G. (2021). *The rle f CSR in mitigating AI risks*. Crprate Scial Respnsibility and Envirnmental Management, 28(5), 1653-1668. https://di.rg/10.1002/csr.2198

Chung, J. J., Im, H., Kim, S. H., Park, J. W., & Jung, Y. (2020). Toward Biomimetic Scaffolds for Tissue Engineering: 3D Printing Techniques in Regenerative Medicine. Front. Bioeng. Biotechnol. https://www.frontiersin.org/articles/10.3389/fbioe.2020.586406/full

Chu, S. C., Kim, H., & Kim, Y. (2023). When brands get real. the role of authenticity and electronic word-of-mouth in shaping consumer response to brands taking a stand. *International Journal of Advertising*, 42(6), 1037–1064. DOI: 10.1080/02650487.2022.2138057

Cina, G., Rober, T.E., Goedhart, R., & Birbil, I. (2022). Why we do need Explainable AI for Healthcare. ArXiv, abs/2206.15363.

Cleveland, J. N., Byrne, Z. S., & Cavanagh, T. M. (2015). The future f HR is RH: Respect fr humanity at wrk. *Human Resource Management Review*, 25(2), 146–161. DOI: 10.1016/j.hrmr.2015.01.005

Collins, B., & Ntsika, V. (2019). Community Networks: Case Studies. Internet Society. Retrieved from https://www.internetsociety.org/resources/doc/2019/community-networks-case-studies/

Cordeiro, F., Epstein, D. A., Thomaz, E., Bales, E. S., Jagannathan, A. K., Abowd, G. D., & Fogarty, J. (2015). Barriers and Negative Nudges: Exploring Challenges in Food Journaling. *Proceedings of the 33rd Annual ACM Conference on Human Factors in Computing Systems*. DOI: 10.1145/2702123.2702155

Córdoba, B. U. (2018). Non-functional requirements orienting the development of socially responsible software. *Lecture Notes in Business Information Processing*, 387, 335–342. DOI: 10.1007/978-3-030-49418-6_23

Corvalan, C., Villalobos Prats, E., Sena, A., Campbell-Lendrum, D., Karliner, J., Risso, A., Wilburn, S., Slotterback, S., Rathi, M., Stringer, R., Berry, P., Edwards, S., Enright, P., Hayter, A., Howard, G., Lapitan, J., Montgomery, M., Prüss-Ustün, A., Varangu, L., & Vinci, S. (2020). Towards climate resilient and environmentally sustainable health care facilities. *International Journal of Environmental Research and Public Health*, 17(23), 8849. DOI: 10.3390/ijerph17238849 PMID: 33260752

Cosme, M., Hély, C., Pommereau, F., Pasquariello, P., Tiberi, C., Treydte, A. C., & Gaucherel, C. (2021). Qualitative Modeling for Bridging Expert-Knowledge and Social-Ecological Dynamics of an East African Savanna. *Land (Basel)*, 11(1), 42. DOI: 10.3390/land11010042

Council of Europe. (2001). Convention on Cybercrime. Retrieved from https://www.coe.int/en/web/conventions/full-list/-/conventions/treaty/185

Counselling, P. (2017). *KDU publications, Library copyright*. General Sir John Kotelawala Defence University. Retrieved from http://ir.kdu.ac.lk/bitstream/handle/345/1680/005.pdf?sequence=1&isAllowed=y

Crawford, J., & Nilsson, F. (2023). Integrating ESG risks into control and reporting: Evidence from practice in Sweden. In *Handbook of Big Data and Analytics in Accounting and Auditing* (pp. 255–277). Springer Nature Singapore. DOI: 10.1007/978-981-19-4460-4_12

Crawford, K., & Paglen, T. (2019). Exposing AI's "black box": How art can help. *Nature*, 565(7741), 422–424.

Cummings, M. L. (2017). Artificial Intelligence and the Future of Work. Implications for CSR. Journal of Business Ethics, 152(4), 1041-1054. DOI: 10.1007/s10551-016-3307-8

Currás-Pérez, R., Dolz-Dolz, C., Miquel-Romero, M. J., & Sánchez-García, I. (2018). How social, environmental, and economic CSR affects consumer-perceived value. Does perceived consumer effectiveness make a difference? *Corporate Social Responsibility and Environmental Management, 25*(5), 733–747. DOI: 10.1002/csr.1490

Cyrus, W. (2021). A fluid-supported 3D hydrogel bioprinting method. *Biomaterials*, 276, 121034. Advance online publication. DOI: 10.1016/j.biomaterials.2021.121034

D'Cruz, P., Du, S., Noronha, E., Parboteeah, K. P., Trittin-Ulbrich, H., & Whelan, G. (2022). Technology, megatrends and work: Thoughts on the future of business ethics. *Journal of Business Ethics*, 180(3), 879–902. DOI: 10.1007/s10551-022-05240-9 PMID: 36212627

Dalal, B. (2020). The antecedents and consequences of CSR skepticism. An integrated framwork. *Journal of Sustainable Marketing, 1*(1), 1–9. DOI: 10.51300/josm-2020-18

Damoah, I. S., Ayakwah, A., & Tingbani, I. (2021). Artificial intelligence (AI)-enhanced medical drones in the healthcare supply chain (HSC) for sustainability development: A case study. *Journal of Cleaner Production*, 328, 129598. DOI: 10.1016/j.jclepro.2021.129598

Darcy, A., Beaudette, A., Chiauzzi, E., Daniels, J., Goodwin, K., Mariano, T. Y., Wicks, P., & Robinson, A. (2023). Anatomy of a Woebot® (WB001): Agent guided CBT for women with postpartum depression. *Expert Review of Medical Devices*, 20(12), 1035–1049. DOI: 10.1080/17434440.2023.2280686 PMID: 37938145

Dastin, J. (2018). *Amazon scraps secret AI recruiting tool that showed bias against women*. Reuters. https://www.reuters.com/article/idUSKCN1MK0AG/

Dastin, J. (2019). Amazon Scraps Secret AI Recruiting Tool That Showed Bias Against Women. Reuters. DOI: 10.1080/17512786.2019.1646492

Dastin, J. (2020). Ethical AI: Balancing innvatin with respnsibility. *Journal of Business Ethics*, 165(2), 321–335. https://di.rg/10.1007/s10551-019-04126-2

Dauvergne, P. (2022). Is artificial intelligence greening global supply chains? Exposing the political economy of environmental costs. *Review of International Political Economy*, 29(3), 696–718. DOI: 10.1080/09692290.2020.1814381

Davidescu, A. A., Apstu, S. A., Paul, A., & Casuneanu, I. (2020). Wrk Flexibility, Jb Satisfactin, and Jb Perfrmance amng Rmanian Emplyees – Implicatins fr Sustainable Human Resurce Management. *Sustainability (Basel)*, 12(15), 6086. DOI: 10.3390/su12156086

De Baker, F. G. A., Groenewegen, P., & Den Hond, F. (2005). A bibliometric analysis of 30 years of research and theory on corporate social responsibility and corporate social performance. *Business & Society*, 44(3), 283–317. DOI: 10.1177/0007650305278086

De Bruin, B., & Heeley, J. (2017). The Role of CSR in Ethical AI Development. Challenges and Opportunities. Journal of Business Ethics, 143(3), 487-502. DOI: 10.1007/s10551-015-2827-6

de Jong, M. D. T., & van der Meer, M. (2017). How Does It Fit? Exploring the Congruence Between Organizations and Their Corporate Social Responsibility (CSR) Activities. *Journal of Business Ethics, 143*(1), 71–83. DOI: 10.1007/s10551-015-2782-2

De Mul, J. (2010). Moral machines: ICTs as mediators of human agency. *Research in Philosophy and Technology*, 3(14), 226–236. DOI: 10.5840/techne201014323

De Smet, M. M., Meganck, R., Truijens, F. L., De Geest, R., Cornelis, S., Norman, U. A., & Desmet, M. (2020). Change processes underlying "good outcome": A qualitative study on recovered and improved patients' experiences in psychotherapy for major depression. *Psychotherapy Research*, 30(7), 948–964. DOI: 10.1080/10503307.2020.1722329 PMID: 32022647

Dehghanian, P., Zhang, B., Dokic, T., & Kezunovic, M. (2019). Predictive Risk Analytics for Weather-Resilient Operation of Electric Power Systems. *IEEE Transactions on Sustainable Energy, 10*(1). DOI: 10.1109/TSTE.2018.2825780

del Mar García-De los Salmones, M., & Perez, A. (2018). Effectiveness of CSR Advertising. The Role of Reputation, Consumer Attributions, and Emotions. *Corporate Social Responsibility and Environmental Management, 25*(2), 194–208. DOI: 10.1002/csr.1453

Denner, S., Scherer, J., Kades, K., Bounias, D., Schader, P., Kausch, L., Bujotzek, M., Bucher, A.M., Penzkofer, T., & Maier-Hein, K.H. (2023). Efficient Large Scale Medical Image Dataset Preparation for Machine Learning Applications. DEMI@ MICCAI.

Desmond, L., & Salama, M. (2023). Integrating Blockchain and emerging technologies for sustainability assurance in the built environment. *IEEE International Conference on Artificial Intelligence, Blockchain, and Internet of Things, AIBThings Proceedings.* DOI: 10.1109/AIBThings58340.2023.10292472

Devaraj, S., & Khli, R. (2022). *AI applicatins and peratinal efficiency in htels.* Jurnal f peratins. *Management*, 68(3), 152–166. https://di.rg/10.1016/j.jm.2021.07.001

Di Vaio, A., Palladino, R., Hassan, R., & Escobar, O. (2020). Artificial intelligence and business models in the sustainable development goals perspective: A systematic literature review. *Journal of Business Research*, 121(1), 283–314. DOI: 10.1016/j.jbusres.2020.08.019

Diaz, J., & Halkias, D. (2021). Reskilling and Upskilling 4IR Leaders in Business Schools through an Innovative Executive Education Ecosystem: An Integrative Literature Review. SSRN *Electronic Journal*. DOI: 10.2139/ssrn.3897059

Diddi, S., & Niehm, L. S. (2016). Corporate Social Responsibility in the Retail Apparel Context. Exploring Consumers' Personal and Normative Influences on Patronage Intentions. *Journal of Marketing Channels, 23*(1–2), 60–76. DOI: 10.1080/1046669X.2016.1147892

DiSanto, N. (2023). Analyzing the Contextual Shortcomings of Artificial General Intelligence. ArXiv, abs/2304.00002.

Do Paço, A. M. F., & Reis, R. (2012). Factors affecting skepticism toward green advertising. *Journal of Advertising, 41*(4), 147–155. DOI: 10.1080/00913367.2012.10672463

Dobbe, R., & Verbeek, P. (2019). Ethical AI. The Importance of Designing AI Systems for Transparency. Technology and Society, 57, 101-110. DOI: 10.1016/j.techsoc.2018.11.001

Dosi, G., Piva, M., Virgillito, M. E., & Vivarelli, M. (2021). Embodied and disembodied technological change: The sectoral patterns of job-creation and job-destruction. *Research Policy*, 50(4), 104199. DOI: 10.1016/j.respol.2021.104199

Dubickis, M., & Gaile-Sarkane, E. (2021). Factors Influencing Technology Transfer in Companies at Emerging Economies. *Science, Technology & Society*, 26(2), 242–271. DOI: 10.1177/09717218211005615

Du, S., El Akremi, A., & Jia, M. (2023). Quantitative research on Corporate Social responsibility: A quest for relevance and rigor in a quickly evolving, turbulent world. *Journal of Business Ethics*, 187(1), 1–15. DOI: 10.1007/s10551-022-05297-6 PMID: 36465988

Du, S., & Xie, C. (2021). Paradoxes of artificial intelligence in consumer markets: Ethical challenges and opportunities. *Journal of Business Research*, 129, 961–974. DOI: 10.1016/j.jbusres.2020.08.024

Earnest, P. (2021). 3D Bioprinting of Vascularized Tissues for in vitro and in vivo Applications. Front Bioeng Biotechnol. https://www.ncbi.nlm.nih.gov/pmc/articles/PMC8158943/

Eckhardt, J., & Langenberg, C. (2020). *Algrithmic transparency and custmer trust.* Cmmunicatins f the ACM, 63(4), 22-25. https://di.rg/10.1145/3383916

Ekimova, K. V. (2023). Development of the potential of the digital economy of Russian regions through artificial intelligence humanization. *Humanities & Social Sciences Communications*, 10(1), 1–9. DOI: 10.1057/s41599-023-02444-w

El Ali, Z., & Siang, S. (2019). Corporate Social Responsibility and AI. Towards a Framework for Ethical Practice. Journal of Technology in Human Services, 37(2), 123-140. DOI: 10.1080/15228835.2018.1562969

El Medaker, R., Loukil, S., & McHich, R. (2024). Towards social responsibility 2.0 for Moroccan public establishments and enterprises: Artificial intelligence and new technologies at the service of sustainable development. *Journal of Autonomous Intelligence*, 7(3), 1385. DOI: 10.32629/jai.v7i3.1385

Ellen, P. S., Webb, D. J., & Mohr, L. A. (2006). Building corporate associations. Consumer attributions for corporate socially responsible programs. *Journal of the Academy of Marketing Science, 34*(2), 147–157. DOI: 10.1177/0092070305284976

Ernst-Linke, F., Enge, S., Viohl, L., Petzold, M. B., & Betzler, F. (2022). High five! – the big 5 personality traits, locus of control, and impulsivity and their relationship to substance use in a large cohort of university students in Berlin. *Addiction Research and Theory*, 31(2), 84–91. DOI: 10.1080/16066359.2022.2114075

Etemad, H. (2023). The need for strategic redirection and business model change: The impact of evolving influential forces of change on international entrepreneurship environment. *Journal of International Entrepreneurship*, 21(4), 441–463. DOI: 10.1007/s10843-024-00348-7

Eubanks, V. (2018). *Automating inequality: How high-tech tools profile, police, and punish the poor*. St. Martin's Press.

European Commission. (2015). *Digital Agenda for Europe*. European Commission.

European Commission. (2018). *Connectivity for a Competitive Digital Single Market*. European Commission.

European Commission. (2021). Digital Single Market Strategy. Retrieved from https://ec.europa.eu/digital-single-market/en/strategy

European Union. (2016). Regulation (EU) 2016/679 of the European Parliament and of the Council of 27 April 2016 on the protection of natural persons with regard to the processing of personal data and on the free movement of such data, and repealing Directive 95/46/EC (General Data Protection Regulation). Official Journal of the European Union. Retrieved from https://eur-lex.europa.eu/legal-content/EN/TXT/?uri=CELEX%3A32016R0679

Evans, O., Hardacre, S., Rubin, M., & Tran, M. (2023). Content appraisal and age moderate the relationship between passive social media use and mental ill-being. *Frontiers in Psychology*, 14, 14. DOI: 10.3389/fpsyg.2023.1181233 PMID: 37529318

Faeq, D., Ali, B., & Akoi, S. (2022). The Impact of People Related TQM and CSR on Employees Job Satisfaction. *UKH Journal of Social Sciences*, 6(1), 1–9. DOI: 10.25079/ukhjss.v6n1y2022.pp1-9

Fang, Guo, Liu, Xu, Mao, Mo, Zhang, Ouyang, Xiong, & Sun. (2022). Advances in 3D Bioprinting. Chinese Journal of Mechanical Engineering: Additive Manufacturing Frontiers. DOI: 10.1016/j.cjmeam.2022.100011

Farooq, Y., & Wicaksono, H. (2021). Advancing on the analysis of causes and consequences of green skepticism. *Journal of Cleaner Production*, 320, 128927. DOI: 10.1016/j.jclepro.2021.128927

Farrelly, C.T. (2021). Toleration, "Mindsight" and the Epistemic Virtues.

Federal Communications Commission. (2015). Protecting and Promoting the Open Internet. Retrieved from https://www.fcc.gov/restoring-internet-freedom

Federal Communications Commission. (2020). *Broadband Deployment Report*. Federal Communications Commission.

Federal Communications Commission. (2021). Bridging the Digital Divide for All Americans. Retrieved from https://www.fcc.gov/Broadband-Deployment-Initiative

Feng, Y., Zhu, Q., & Lai, K. H. (2017). Corporate social responsibility for supply chain management: A literature review and bibliometric analysis. *Journal of Cleaner Production*, 158, 296–307. DOI: 10.1016/j.jclepro.2017.05.018

Fernandes, K. (2018, September 20). Companies In India Funding CSR In Education. Medium.

Fernandez, M., & Rutter, J. (2021). *Custmer experiences with AI in hspitality*. Internatinal Jurnal f Infrmatin Management, 57, 102272. https://di.rg/10.1016/j.ijinfmgt.2020.102272

Fernandez, D., Dastane, O., Omar, H., & Aman, A. (2024). Robotic process automation: Bibliometric reflection and future opportunities. *European Journal of Innovation Management*, 27(2), 692–712. DOI: 10.1108/EJIM-10-2022-0570

Floridi, L., & Cowls, J. (2019). Telling Right from Wrong in AI. The Role of Corporate Responsibility. Nature Machine Intelligence, 1(6), 285-287. DOI: 10.1038/s42256-019-0030-6

Floridi, L., & Cowls, J. (2022). A unified framework of five principles for AI in society. Machine Learning and the City: Applications in Architecture and Urban Design, 535–545. DOI: 10.1002/9781119815075.ch45

Floridi, L., Cowls, J., Beltrametti, M., Chatila, R., Chazerand, P., Dignum, V., Luetge, C., Madelin, R., Pagallo, U., Rossi, F., Schafer, B., Valcke, P., & Vayena, E. (2018). AI4People—An Ethical Framework for a Good AI Society: Opportunities, Risks, Principles, and Recommendations. *Minds and Machines*, 28(4), 689–707. DOI: 10.1007/s11023-018-9482-5 PMID: 30930541

Floridi, L., Cowls, J., King, T. C., & Taddeo, M. (2020). How AI can be a force for good. [Link]. *Science*, 361(6404), 751–752. PMID: 30139858

Flückiger, C., Del Re, A. C., Wampold, B. E., & Horvath, A. O. (2018). The Alliance in Adult Psychotherapy: A Meta-Analytic Synthesis. *Psychotherapy (Chicago, Ill.)*, 55(4), 316–340. DOI: 10.1037/pst0000172 PMID: 29792475

Ford, M. (2019). *Architects of Intelligence: The Truth About AI from the People Building It*. Packt Publishing.

Forehand, M. R., & Grier, S. (2003). When Is Honesty the Best Policy? The Effect of Stated Company Intent on Consumer Skepticism. *Journal of Consumer Psychology, 13*(3), 349–356. DOI: 10.1207/S15327663JCP1303_15

Formosa, P., Wilson, M., & Richards, D. (2021). A principlist framework for cybersecurity ethics. *Computers & Security*, 109, 102382. DOI: 10.1016/j.cose.2021.102382

Frank, B. (2021). Artificial intelligence-enabled environmental sustainability of products: Marketing benefits and their variation by consumer, location, and product types. *Journal of Cleaner Production*, 285, 125242. DOI: 10.1016/j.jclepro.2020.125242

Friedberg, A., & Liu, S. (2020). *Data privacy issues in AI systems fr htels*. Infrmatin Systems Research, 31(2), 535-550. https://di.rg/10.1287/isre.2020.0910

Frontino, G., Meschi, F., Rigamonti, A., Favalli, V., Bonura, C., & Bonfanti, R. (2016). Opportunities and Challenges of Telemedicine. Diabetes Technology & Therapeutics, 18(6), 404.

Fuchs, C., & Melnyk, S. (2021). CSR practices in AI deplyment: A hspitality perspective. *Journal of Business Research*, 124, 414–425. https://di.rg/10.1016/j.jbusres.2020.11.037

G, M. (2021). Mega Bot – The Healthcare Chatbot. 2021 Second International Conference on Electronics and Sustainable Communication Systems (ICESC), 1386-1395.

Gadzhiev, G. A. (2018). Whether robot-agent is a person? *Journal of Russian Law*, 1(29).

Galbraith, J. R. (1974). Organization Design. An Information Processing View. *Interfaces, 4*(3), 28–36. DOI: 10.1287/inte.4.3.28

Galport, N., & Azzam, T. (2017). Evaluator Training Needs and Competencies. *The American Journal of Evaluation*, 38(1), 80–100. DOI: 10.1177/1098214016643183

Gao, J., Peng, P., Lu, F., Wang, S., Xie, X., & Claramunt, C. (2024). Knowledge-driven spatial competitive intelligence for tourism. *Transactions in GIS*. DOI: 10.1111/tgis.13145

Gao, Q., Liu, Z., Lin, Z., Qiu, J., Liu, Y., Liu, A., Wang, Y., Xiang, M., Chen, B., Fu, J., & He, Y. (2017). 3D Bioprinting of Vessel-like Structures with Multilevel Fluidic. *ACS Biomaterials Science & Engineering*, 3(3), 399–408. Advance online publication. DOI: 10.1021/acsbiomaterials.6b00643 PMID: 33465937

Gartner. (2021). Gartner Forecasts Worldwide Public Cloud Revenue to Grow 23% in 2021. Retrieved from https://www.gartner.com/en/newsroom/press-releases/2021-04-13-gartner-forecasts-worldwide-public-cloud-revenue-to-grow-23-percent-in-2021

Gekara, V., & Snell, D. (2018). Designing and delivering skills transferability and employment mobility: The challenges of a market-driven vocational education and training system. *Journal of Vocational Education and Training*, 70(1), 107–129. DOI: 10.1080/13636820.2017.1392996

Gerger, H., Nascimento, A. F., Locher, C., Gaab, J., & Trachsel, M. (2020). What are the Key Characteristics of a 'Good' Psychotherapy? Calling for Ethical Patient Involvement. *Frontiers in Psychiatry*, 11, 11. DOI: 10.3389/fpsyt.2020.00406 PMID: 32581856

Ghasemaghaei, M., & Calic, G. (2020). Assessing the impact of big data on firm innovation performance: Big data is not always better data. *Journal of Business Research*, 108, 147–162. DOI: 10.1016/j.jbusres.2019.09.062

Ghobakhloo, M., Asadi, S., Iranmanesh, M., Foroughi, B., Mubarak, M. F., & Yadegaridehkordi, E. (2023). Intelligent automation implementation and corporate sustainability performance: The enabling role of corporate social responsibility strategy. *Technology in Society*, 74, 102301. DOI: 10.1016/j.techsoc.2023.102301

Ghsh, S., & Wu, L. (2022). *Assessing AI biases in htel service*. Expert Systems with Applicatins, 179, 115104. https://di.rg/10.1016/j.eswa.2021.115104

Gillett, S. E. (2019). *A History of Telecommunications and Networks: From the ARPANET to the Internet*. Cambridge University Press.

Giovanola, B., & Tiribelli, S. (2023). Beyond bias and discrimination. redefining the AI ethics principle of fairness in healthcare machine-learning algorithms. *AI and Society, 38*(2). DOI: 10.1007/s00146-022-01455-6

Gobinath, V. M., Kathirvel, A., Rajesh Kanna, S. K., & Annamalai, K. (2024). Smart Technology in Management Industries: A Useful Perspective. Artificial Intelligence Applied to Industry 4.0. Wiley. https://www.wiley.com/en-us/Topics+in+Artificial+Intelligence+Applied+to+Industry+4+0-p-9781394216116DOI: 10.1002/9781394216147.ch5

Gobinath, V., Ayyaswamy, K., & Kathirvel, N. (2024). Information Communication Technology and Intelligent Manufacturing Industries Perspective: An Insight. *Asian Science Bulletin*, 2(1), 36–45. DOI: 10.3923/asb.2024.36.45

Golembiewski, R. T., & Murlis, H. (2018). Implementing Effective CSR Strategies. International Journal of Management Reviews, 20(1), 55-73. DOI: 10.1111/ijmr.12143

Goniewicz, K., Goniewicz, M., Włoszczak-Szubzda, A., Burkle, F. M., Hertelendy, A. J., Al-Wathinani, A., Molloy, M. S., & Khorram-Manesh, A. (2021). The importance of pre-training gap analyses and the identification of competencies and skill requirements of medical personnel for mass casualty incidents and disaster training. *BMC Public Health*, 21(1), 114. DOI: 10.1186/s12889-021-10165-5 PMID: 33422033

Goodell, J. W., Kumar, S., Lim, W. M., & Pattnaik, D. (2021). Artificial intelligence and machine learning in finance: Identifying foundations, themes, and research cluster from bibliometric analysis. *Journal of Behavioral and Experimental Finance*, 32, 100577. DOI: 10.1016/j.jbef.2021.100577

Grant, J., & Wilsn, J. (2021). Implementing ethical AI: Challenges and slutins. *AI and Ethics*, 2(1), 23–37. https://di.rg/10.1007/s43681-020-00019-0

Greenough, G., McGeehin, M., Bernard, S. M., Trtanj, J., Riad, J., & Engelberg, D. (2001). The potential impacts of climate variability and change on health impacts of extreme weather events in the United States. *Environmental Health Perspectives*, 109(suppl 2), 191–198. PMID: 11359686

Gregg Greenough, P., & Nelson, E. L. (2019). Beyond mapping. A case for geospatial analytics in humanitarian health. In *Conflict and Health* (Vol. 13, Issue 1). DOI: 10.1186/s13031-019-0234-9

Grill, J., Strub, F., Altch'e, F., Tallec, C., Richemond, P.H., Buchatskaya, E., Doersch, C., Pires, B.Á., Guo, Z.D., Azar, M.G., Piot, B., Kavukcuoglu, K., Munos, R., & Valko, M. (2020). Bootstrap Your Own Latent: A New Approach to Self-Supervised Learning. ArXiv, abs/2006.07733.

Grishunin, S., Naumova, E., Burova, E., Suloeva, S., & Nekrasova, T. (2022). The impact of sustainability disclosures on the value of companies following digital transformation strategies. *International Journal of Technology*, 13(7), 1432–1441. DOI: 10.14716/ijtech.v13i7.6194

Gruetzemacher, R., Paradice, D., & Lee, K. B. (2020). Forecasting extreme labor displacement: A survey of AI practitioners. *Technological Forecasting and Social Change*, 161, 120323. DOI: 10.1016/j.techfore.2020.120323

Grygiel-Tomaszewska, A., & Kurkliński, L. (2021). The impact of artificial intelligence on allocative efficiency: Insights and gaps in the case of high-frequency trading. In *The Economics of Sustainable Transformation* (pp. 318–333). Routledge. DOI: 10.4324/9781003219958-17

GSMA. (2020). State of Mobile Internet Connectivity 2020. Retrieved from https://www.gsma.com/mobilefordevelopment/resources/state-of-mobile-internet-connectivity-2020/

Guest, D. E. (2017). Human resurce management and emplyee well-being: Twards a new analytic framewrk. Human resurce management jurnal, 27(1), 22-38.

Gupta, K., Sadana, S. K., & Gupta, B. (2020). Geospatial data preprocessing and visualization for the logistics industry. *Journal of Discrete Mathematical Sciences and Cryptography, 23*(1). DOI: 10.1080/09720529.2020.1721859

Gupta, R. (2023). Evolution of Indian Digital Payment Industry. In *Emerging Issues in Banking and Finance* (pp. 120-131). Bloomsbury Publishing.

Gupta, P., & Gaur, S. (2020). Crprate scial respnsibility in AI. *Journal of Business Research*, 114, 414–425. https://di.rg/10.1016/j.jbusres.2020.04.003

Gürhan-Canli, Z., & Maheswaran, D. (2000). Determinants of country-of-origin evaluations. *Journal of Consumer Research, 27*(1), 96–108. DOI: 10.1086/314311

Gurney, J. K. (2016). Crashing into the unknown: An examination of crash-optimization algorithms. *Albany Law Review*, 183, 79.

Haenlein, M., & Kaplan, A. (2019). A Brief History of Artificial Intelligence: On the Past, Present, and Future of Artificial Intelligence. *California Management Review*, 61(4), 5–14. Advance online publication. DOI: 10.1177/0008125619864925

Haggerty, K. D., & Ericson, R. V. (2019). Transparency and Accountability in AI. The Role of CSR. Surveillance & Society, 17(3), 274-288. DOI: 10.24908/ss.v17i3.6757

Hahn, T., Sharma, G., & Glavas, A. (2023). Employee-CSR Tensions: Drivers of Employee (Dis)Engagement with Contested CSR Initiatives. *Journal of Management Studies*. Advance online publication. DOI: 10.1111/joms.12923

Haines, A., Kovats, R. S., Campbell-Lendrum, D., & Corvalán, C. (2006). Climate change and human health: Impacts, vulnerability and public health. *Public Health*, 120(7), 585–596. DOI: 10.1016/j.puhe.2006.01.002 PMID: 16542689

Ham, C. D., & Kim, J. (2020). The effects of CSR communication in corporate crises. Examining the role of dispositional and situational CSR skepticism in context. *Public Relations Review, 46*(2). DOI: 10.1016/j.pubrev.2019.05.013

Haque, A. B., Islam, A. K. M. N., Hyrynsalmi, S., Naqvi, B., & Smolander, K. (2021). GDPR compliant blockchains-a systematic literature review. In *IEEE Access* (Vol. 9). DOI: 10.1109/ACCESS.2021.3069877

Harris, M., & Stevens, D. (2022). *AI and peratinal efficiency: A hspitality case study*. Jurnal f Hspitality Marketing & Management, 31(6), 699-715. https://di.rg/10.1080/19368623.2021.1946181

Hart, D. L. (2023, September 18). *IBM Commits to Train 2 Million in Artificial Intelligence in Three Years, with a Focus on Underrepresented Communities*. IBM.

Haynes, S. H., Lene, M. C., Keena, L. D., May, D. C., Ricciardelli, R., & Lambert, E. G. (2020). The assciatin between different frms f rganizatinal trust and crrectinal staff jb stress. *Journal of Crime and Justice*, 43(5), 623–639. DOI: 10.1080/0735648X.2020.1734056

Heisenberg, D. (2005). *Negotiating privacy: the European union. The United States and Personal Data*. Lynn Rienner Publishers. DOI: 10.1515/9781626370074

He, K., Fan, H., Wu, Y., Xie, S., & Girshick, R. B. (2019). Momentum Contrast for Unsupervised Visual Representation Learning. *2020 IEEE/CVF Conference on Computer Vision and Pattern Recognition (CVPR)*, 9726-9735.

He, L., & Shin, K. G. (2023). Rethink Physical Security: Protecting Vehicles via Battery-Enabled Sensing and Control. *Proceedings of the IEEE*, 111(8), 921–927. DOI: 10.1109/JPROC.2023.3285166

Helliwell, J. F., & Huang, H. (2011). Well-being and trust in the wrkplace. *Journal of Happiness Studies*, 12(5), 747–767. DOI: 10.1007/s10902-010-9225-7

Henderson, L. H., Wersun, A., Wilson, J., Mo-ching, S., & Zhang, K. (2019). Principles of responsible management education in 2068. *Futures*, 111, 81–89. DOI: 10.1016/j.futures.2019.05.005

Hesamifard, E., Takabi, H., Ghasemi, M., & Jones, C. (2017). Privacy-preserving Machine Learning in Cloud. *Proceedings of the 2017 on Cloud Computing Security Workshop - CCSW '17*. DOI: 10.1145/3140649.3140655

Heyns, M., & Rthmann, S. (2018). Vlitinal trust, autnmy satisfactin, and engagement at wrk. Psychlgical reprts, 121(1), 112-134.

Hines, P., Butterworth, C., Greenlee, C., & Jekiel, C. (2023). The mental and physical wellbeing flow within the People Value Stream. *Human Resources Management and Services*.

Hofmann, E., Brunner, J. H., & Holschbach, E. (2020). Research in business service purchasing: Current status and directions for the future. *Management Review Quarterly*, 70(3), 421–460. DOI: 10.1007/s11301-019-00172-7

Huang, Y., & Chi, S. (2021). *The intersectin f AI and custmer trust*. Jurnal f Cnsumer Behaviur, 20(5), 1272-1286. https://di.rg/10.1002/cb.1967

Hudson, C. C., Bowers, E. M., Björgvinsson, T., & Beard, C. (2023). Changes in Perspective-Taking During Cognitive Behavioral Therapy in a Partial Hospital Setting. *Cognitive Therapy and Research*, 47(6), 909–918. DOI: 10.1007/s10608-023-10422-4

Hur, W. M., Kim, H., & Jang, J. H. (2016). The Role of Gender Differences in the Impact of CSR Perceptions on Corporate Marketing Outcomes. *Corporate Social Responsibility and Environmental Management, 23*(6), 345–357. DOI: 10.1002/csr.1380

Hüttl-Maack, V., Sedghi, T. M., & Daume, J. M. (2024). Through rose-tinted glasses. how inducing and resolving curiosity makes consumers less skeptical and improves their product evaluations. *Journal of Consumer Psychology*, 34(1), 92–100. DOI: 10.1002/jcpy.1369

Huynh, Q. L., Hoque, M. E., Susanto, P., Watto, W. A., & Ashraf, M. (2022). Does financial leverage mediates corporate governance and firm performance? *Sustainability (Basel)*, 14(20), 13545. DOI: 10.3390/su142013545

Infosys. (2023). *Flagship Platform to accelerate 21st Century Digital Learning*. Infosys.

International Telecommunication Union. (2020). *Measuring Digital Development: Facts and Figures 2020*. ITU.

ITU. (2019). Measuring the Information Society Report 2019. Retrieved from https://www.itu.int/en/ITU /Statistics/Documents/publications/misr2019/MISR2019_Volume1.pdf

Jacques, P. (2005). How Should Corporations Deal with Environmental Scepticism? *Corporate Social Responsibility and Environmental Management, 13*(1), 25–36. DOI: 10.1002/csr.089

Jadhav, S. B., & Kodavade, D. V. (2023). Enhancing Flight Delay Prediction through Feature Engineering in Machine Learning Classifiers: A Real Time Data Streams Case Study. *International Journal on Recent and Innovation Trends in Computing and Communication*, 11(2s), 212–218. DOI: 10.17762/ijritcc.v11i2s.6064

Jain, A., Singh, K., & Jain, P. (2024). Understanding the Impact of Artificial Intelligence and Robotics in the Tourism and Hospitality Industry Through Customer Experience: A Systematic Literature Review. In *Impact of AI and Tech-Driven Solutions in Hospitality and Tourism* (pp. 329–350). IGI Global. DOI: 10.4018/979-8-3693-6755-1.ch017

Jamali, D. R., El Dirani, A. M., & Harwood, I. A. (2015). Exploring human resource management roles in corporate social responsibility: The CSR-HRM co-creation model. *Business Ethics (Oxford, England)*, 24(2), 125–143. Advance online publication. DOI: 10.1111/beer.12085

Jardine, D. S. (2007). Heat illness and heat stroke. *Pediatrics*, 28(7), 249–258. PMID: 17601937

Jayaraman, V., & Chan, T. (2021). *Ethical AI in hspitality: Balancing benefits and risks*. Turism Management Perspectives, 39, 100836. https://di.rg/10.1016/j.tmp .2021.100836

Jena, L. K., Pradhan, S., & Panigrahy, N. P. (2018). Pursuit f rganisatinal trust: Rle f emplyee engagement, psychlgical well-being and transfrmatinal leadership. *Asia Pacific Management Review*, 23(3), 227–234. DOI: 10.1016/j.apmrv.2017.11.001

Jobin, A., Ienca, M., & Vayena, E. (2019). Artificial Intelligence: the global landscape of ethics guidelines.

Jobin, A., Ienca, M., & Vayena, E. (2019). The global landscape of AI ethics guidelines. *Nature Machine Intelligence*, 1(9), 389–399. DOI: 10.1038/s42256-019-0088-2

Johnson, K. B., Wei, W., Weeraratne, D., Frisse, M. E., Misulis, K., Rhee, K., Zhao, J., & Snowdon, J. L. (2021). Precision Medicine, AI, and the Future of Personalized Health Care. DOI: 10.1111/cts.12884

Jorge, C. F. B., & De Araujo, A. S. (2019). Spatial analysis in the process of competitive intelligence as a strategy for the construction of intelligence products and services aimed at organizations. *Ciência da Informação*, 48(1).

Jung, M., Eom, M. T., & Yayla, A. (2022). Investigating the interaction effect between IT-enabled innovation and corporate social responsibility on firm performance. *Information Systems Management*, 1–20.

Kalhor, E., Horn, B. P., Valentin, V., & Berrens, R. P. (2018). Investigating the Effects of both Historical Wildfire Damage and Future Wildfire Risk on Housing Values. *International Journal of Ecological Economics & Statistics, 39*(1).

Kang, E. Y., & Atkinson, L. (2021). Effects of message objectivity and focus on green CSR communication. The strategy development for a hotel's green CSR message. *Journal of Marketing Communications*, 27(3), 229–249. DOI: 10.1080/13527266.2019.1640270

Kang, H. W., Lee, S., Ko, I., Kengla, C., Yoo, J. J., & Atala, A. (2016). A 3D bioprinting system to produce human-scale tissue constructs with structural integrity. *Nature Biotechnology*, 34(3), 312–319. Advance online publication. DOI: 10.1038/nbt.3413 PMID: 26878319

Kathirvel, A., & Gobinath, V. M. (2004). A Review on Additive Manufactuing in Industrial. Modern Hybird Machince and Super Finishing Process: Technology and Application. CRC. https://books.google.co.in/books/about/Modern_Hybrid_Machining_and_Super_Finish.html?id=I_VW0AEACAAJ&source=kp_book_description&redir_esc=y

Kathirvel, A., & Maheswaran, C. P. (2023). Enhanced AI-Based Intrusion Detection and Response System for WSN. Artificial Intelligence for Intrusion Detection Systems. CRC. https://www.taylorfrancis.com/chapters/edit/10.1201/9781003346340-8/enhanced-ai-based-intrusion-detection-response-system-wsn-kathirvel-maheswaranDOI: 10.1201/9781003346340-8

Kathirvel, A., Maheswaran, C. P., Subramaniam, M., & Naren, A. K. (2023). Quantum Computers Based on Distributed Computing Systems for the Next Generation: Overview and Applications. Quantum Computers Based on Distributed Computing Systems for the Next Generation, Handbook of Research on Quantum Computing for Smart Environments. IGI Global. DOI: 10.4018/978-1-6684-6697-1.ch025

Kathirvel, A., Rithik, G., & Naren, A. K. (2024). Automation of IOT Robotics. In *Predicting Natural Disasters With AI and Machine Learning*. IGI Global. DOI: 10.4018/979-8-3693-2280-2.ch011

Kathirvel, A., Subramaniam, M., Navaneethan, S., & Sabarinath, C. (2021). Improved IDR Response System for Sensor Network. Journal of Web Engineering, 20(1), 53–88. DOI: 10.13052/jwe1540-9589.2013

Kathirvel, A., Sudha, D., Naveneethan, S., Subramaniam, M., Das, D. & Kirubakaran, S. (2022). AI Based Mobile Bill Payment System using Biometric Fingerprint. American Journal of Engineering and Applied Sciences, 15(1), 23-31. DOI: 10.3844/ajeassp.2022.23.31

Kathirvel, A. (2024). Applications of Serverless Computing: Systematic Overview. In Aluvalu, R., & Maheswari, U. (Eds.), *Serverless Computing Concepts, Technology and Architecture*. IGI Global. DOI: 10.4018/979-8-3693-1682-5.ch014

Kathirvel, A. (2024). Innovation and Industry Application: IoT-Based Robotics Frontier of Automation in Industry Application. In Satishkumar, D., & Sivaraja, M. (Eds.), *Internet of Things and AI for Natural Disaster Management and Prediction* (pp. 83–105). IGI Global. DOI: 10.4018/979-8-3693-4284-8.ch004

Kathirvel, A., Gopinath, V. M., Naren, K., Nithyanand, D., & Nirmaladevi, K. (2024). Manufacturing Smart Industry Perspective an Overview. *American Journal of Engineering and Applied Sciences*, 17(1), 33–39. DOI: 10.3844/ajeassp.2024.33.39

Kathirvel, A., & Naren, A. K. (2024). Critical Approaches to Data Engineering Systems Innovation and Industry Application Using IoT. In *Critical Approaches to Data Engineering Systems and Analysis*. IGI Global. DOI: 10.4018/979-8-3693-2260-4.ch005

Kathirvel, A., & Naren, A. K. (2024). Diabetes and Pre-Diabetes Prediction by AI Using Tuned XGB Classifier. In Khang, A. (Ed.), *Medical Robotics and AI-Assisted Diagnostics for a High-Tech Healthcare Industry* (pp. 52–64). IGI Global. DOI: 10.4018/979-8-3693-2105-8.ch004

Kathirvel, A., Naren, K., Nithyanand, D., & Santhoshi, B. (2024). Overview of 5G Technology: Streamlined Virtual Event Experiences. *Advances of Robotic Technology*, 2(1), 1–8. DOI: 10.23880/art-16000109

Kazachenok, O. P., Stankevich, G. V., Chubaeva, N. N., & Tyurina, Y. G. (2023). Economic and legal approaches to the humanization of FinTech in the economy of artificial intelligence through the integration of blockchain into ESG Finance. *Humanities & Social Sciences Communications*, 10(1), 1–9. DOI: 10.1057/s41599-023-01652-8

Kelly, J. T., Campbell, K. L., Gong, E., & Scuffham, P. (2020). The Internet of Things: Impact and implications for health care delivery. *Journal of Medical Internet Research*, 22(11), e20135. DOI: 10.2196/20135 PMID: 33170132

Kempton, A. M., & Vassilakopoulou, P. (2021). *Accountability*. Transparency and Explainability in AI for Healthcare.

Kessler, A., & Lee, M. (2020). *Algrithmic bias and transparency in htel AI*. ACM Transactins n Internet Technlgy, 20(3), 1-21. https://di.rg/10.1145/3393047

Khalaf, A. T., Wei, Y., Wan, J., Zhu, J., Peng, Y., Abdul Kadir, S. Y., Zainol, J., Oglah, Z., Cheng, L., & Shi, Z. (2022). Bone Tissue Engineering through 3D Bioprinting of Bioceramic Scaffolds: A Review and Update. *Life (Chicago, Ill.)*, 12(6), 903. Advance online publication. DOI: 10.3390/life12060903 PMID: 35743934

Khare, S., Uniyal, V., Kathuria, S., Chauhan, A. S., Akram, S. V., & Aluvala, S. (2023, December). Transformation of Corporate Social Responsibility Practices: Adapting Artificial Intelligence and Internet of Things. In *International Conference on Recent Trends in Image Processing and Pattern Recognition* (pp. 165-177). Cham: Springer Nature Switzerland.

Khnaisser, C., Lavoie, L., Fraikin, B., Barton, A., Dussault, S., Burgun, A., & Éthier, J. (2022). Using an Ontology to Derive a Sharable and Interoperable Relational Data Model for Heterogeneous Healthcare Data and Various Applications. *Methods of Information in Medicine*, 61(S 02), e73–e88. DOI: 10.1055/a-1877-9498 PMID: 35709746

Khreva, V., & Wechtler, H. (2018). HR practices and emplyee perfrmance: The mediating rle f wellbeing. *Employee Relations*, 40(2), 227–243. DOI: 10.1108/ER-08-2017-0191

Khuong, M. N., Truong an, N. K., & Thanh Hang, T. T. (2021). Stakeholders and Corporate Social Responsibility (CSR) programme as key sustainable development strategies to promote corporate reputation—Evidence from vietnam. *Cogent Business & Management*, 8(1), 1917333. Advance online publication. DOI: 10.1080/23311975.2021.1917333

Kim, S. (2019). The Process Model of Corporate Social Responsibility (CSR) Communication. CSR Communication and its Relationship with Consumers' CSR Knowledge, Trust, and Corporate Reputation Perception. *Journal of Business Ethics, 154*(4), 1143–1159. DOI: 10.1007/s10551-017-3433-6

Kim, S., & Ferguson, M. A. T. (2018). Dimensions of effective CSR communication based on public expectations. *Journal of Marketing Communications, 24*(6), 549–567. DOI: 10.1080/13527266.2015.1118143

Kim, M.-J., & Kim, B.-J. (2020). Analysis of the Importance of Job Insecurity, Psychological Safety and Job Satisfaction in the CSR-Performance Link. *Sustainability (Basel)*, 12(9), 3514. DOI: 10.3390/su12093514

Kim, S., & Rim, H. (2024). The role of public skepticism and distrust in the process of CSR communication. *International Journal of Business Communication*, 61(2), 198–218. DOI: 10.1177/2329488419866888

Kleine, A., Kokje, E., Lermer, E., & Gaube, S. (2023). Attitudes Toward the Adoption of 2 Artificial Intelligence–Enabled Mental Health Tools Among Prospective Psychotherapists: Cross-sectional Study. *JMIR Human Factors*, 10, 10. DOI: 10.2196/46859 PMID: 37436801

Knapp, J. R., Diehl, M. R., & Dugan, W. (2020). Twards a scial-cgnitive thery f multiple psychlgical cntracts. Eurpean Jurnal f Wrk and rganizatinal Psychlgy, 29(2), 200-214.

Koch, C., & Riek, L. D. (2021). The Intersection of Corporate Responsibility and AI Ethics. A Review of the Literature. IEEE Transactions on Technology and Society, 2(1), 45-55. DOI: 10.1109/TTS.2020.3034720

Kodavati, B., & Ramarakula, M. (2021). Latency based Re-Enforcement Learning over Cognitive Software Defined 5G Networks. 2021 7th International Conference on Advanced Computing and Communication Systems (ICACCS), 1, 1848-1853.

Kofas, J. (2017). Artificial intelligence: socioeconomic, political and ethical dimensions. https://countercurrents.org/2017/04/artificial-intelligence-socioeconomic-politicaland-ethicaldimensions

Kolding, M., Sundblad, M., Alexa, J., Stone, M., Aravopoulou, E., & Evans, G. (2018). Information management – a skills gap? *The Bottom Line (New York, N.Y.)*, 31(3/4), 170–190. DOI: 10.1108/BL-09-2018-0037

Königstorfer, F., & Thalmann, S. (2020). Applications of Artificial Intelligence in commercial banks – A research agenda for behavioral finance. *Journal of Behavioral and Experimental Finance*, 27, 100352. Advance online publication. DOI: 10.1016/j.jbef.2020.100352

Krac, K. (2019). Corporate social responsibility: Humans vs artificial intelligence. *Social Responsibility Journal*, 6(6), 786–802. DOI: 10.1108/SRJ-09-2018-0219

Kroll, J. A., & Raji, I. D. (2020). The Ethical Implications of AI. A Corporate Social Responsibility Perspective. Proceedings of the 2020 AAAI/ACM Conference on AI, Ethics, and Society, 135-143. DOI: 10.1145/3375627.3375826

Kroll, J. A., Hurlburt, H., & Roth, P. (2017). Accountable Algorithms. University of Pennsylvania Law Review, 165(3), 633-701. DOI: 10.2139/ssrn.2932348

Księzak, P. (2016). The Benefits from CSR for a Company and Society. *Journal of Corporate Responsibility and Leadership*, 3(4), 53–65. DOI: 10.12775/JCRL.2016.023

Kulhavy, R. W., & Schwartz, N. H. (2015). Tone of Communication and Climate Perceptions. *Journal of Business Communication*, 18(1), 17–24. DOI: 10.1177/002194368101800103

Kumar, A., & Patel, N. (2021). *AI and data privacy: A hspitality industry perspective*. Cmputers in Human Behavir, 119, 106734. https://di.rg/10.1016/j.chb.2021.106734

Kumar, S. (2021). *The digital frontier: Infrastructures of control on the global web*. Indiana University Press. DOI: 10.2307/j.ctv21hrjv1

Kumar, V. V., & Tankha, G. (2023). Association Between the Big Five and Trait Emotional Intelligence Among College Students. *Psychology Research and Behavior Management*, 16, 915–925. DOI: 10.2147/PRBM.S400058 PMID: 36974037

Kurakin, A. (2018). The impact of AI on society. *Nature*, 551(7681), 429–431.

Labadie, C., & Legner, C. (2023). Building data management capabilities to address data protection regulations. Learnings from EU-GDPR. *Journal of Information Technology, 38*(1). DOI: 10.1177/02683962221141456

Lacerenza, C. N., Reyes, D. L., Marlow, S. L., Joseph, D. L., & Salas, E. (2017). Leadership training design, delivery, and implementation: A meta-analysis. *The Journal of Applied Psychology*, 102(12), 1686–1718. DOI: 10.1037/apl0000241 PMID: 28749153

Lachuer, J., & Jabeur, S. B. (2022). Explainable artificial intelligence modeling for corporate social responsibility and financial performance. *Journal of Asset Management*, 23(7), 619–630. DOI: 10.1057/s41260-022-00291-z

Lalejini, A., Dolson, E., Vostinar, A. E., & Zaman, L. (2022). Artificial selection methods from evolutionary computing show promise for directed evolution of microbes. *eLife*, 11. PMID: 35916365

Lary, D. J., Lary, T., & Sattler, B. (2016). Using machine learning to estimate global PM2.5 for environmental health studies. *Environmental Health Insights*, 10, EHI-S38448.

Le Gat, Y., Curt, C., Werey, C., Caillaud, K., Rulleau, B., & Taillandier, F. (2023). Water infrastructure asset management. state of the art and emerging research themes. *Structure and Infrastructure Engineering*. DOI: 10.1080/15732479.2023.2222030

Leal Filho, W., Yang, P., Eustachio, J. H. P. P., Azul, A. M., Gellers, J. C., Gielczyk, A., Dinis, M. A. P., & Kozlova, V. (2023). Deploying digitalization and artificial intelligence in sustainable development research. *Environment, Development and Sustainability*, 25(6), 4957–4988. DOI: 10.1007/s10668-022-02252-3 PMID: 35313685

Lee, C., & Zhang, X. (2020). *peratinal efficiencies thrugh AI: A review*. Jurnal f Hspitality and Turism Management, 44, 288-298. https://di.rg/10.1016/j.jhtm.2020.03.005

Lee, J., & Kim, K. (2021). The Role of Corporate Social Responsibility in Artificial Intelligence Adoption. Journal of Corporate Finance, 69, 102066. DOI: 10.1016/j.jcorpfin.2020.102066

Lee, S. Y., Zhang, W., & Abitbol, A. (2019). What Makes CSR Communication Lead to CSR Participation? Testing the Mediating Effects of CSR Associations, CSR Credibility, and Organization–Public Relationships. *Journal of Business Ethics, 157*(2), 413–429. DOI: 10.1007/s10551-017-3609-0

Lee, C., Lai, H., Lee, C., & Chen, M. (2022). Medical Dispute Cases Caused by Errors in Clinical Reasoning: An Investigation and Analysis. *Health Care*, 10. PMID: 36360564

Lee, J., Davari, H., Singh, J., & Pandhare, V. (2018). Industrial Artificial Intelligence for industry 4.0-based manufacturing systems. *Manufacturing Letters*, 18, 20–23. Advance online publication. DOI: 10.1016/j.mfglet.2018.09.002

Lee, J., Suh, T., Roy, D., & Baucus, M. (2019). Emerging technology and business model innovation: The case of artificial intelligence. *Journal of Open Innovation*, 5(3), 44–56. DOI: 10.3390/joitmc5030044

Lee, M. D. P. (2008). A review of the theories of corporate social responsibility: Its evolutionary path and the road ahead. *International Journal of Management Reviews*, 10(1), 53–73. DOI: 10.1111/j.1468-2370.2007.00226.x

Leenes, R., Palmerini, E., Koops, B., Bertolini, A., Lucivero, F., Leenes, R., Palmerini, E., Koops, B., & Bertolini, A. (2017). Regulatory challenges of robotics: some guidelines for addressing legal and ethical issues. DOI: 10.1080/17579961.2017.1304921

Lee, P., Bubeck, S., & Petro, J. (2023). Benefits, Limits, and Risks of GPT-4 as an AI Chatbot for Medicine. *The New England Journal of Medicine*, 388(13), 1233–1239. DOI: 10.1056/NEJMsr2214184 PMID: 36988602

Lee, Y. (2021). Linking internal CSR with the positive communicative behaviors of employees: The role of social exchange relationships and employee engagement. *Social Responsibility Journal*. Advance online publication. DOI: 10.1108/SRJ-04-2020-0121

Lewis, T. (1998). The new economics of information. *IEEE Internet Computing*, 2(5), 93–94. DOI: 10.1109/4236.722237

Li, H., Yu, L., & He, W. (2019). The Impact of GDPR on Global Technology Development. In *Journal of Global Information Technology Management* (Vol. 22, Issue 1). DOI: 10.1080/1097198X.2019.1569186

Li, S., & Yang, S. (2019). The Impact of CSR on AI Transparency and Fairness. Journal of Business Research, 104, 110-118. DOI: 10.1016/j.jbusres.2019.07.022

Li, Y., & Zha, L. (2021). *Transparency and ethical cnsideratins in AI deplyment.* Business & Sciety, 60(6), 1447-1473. https://di.rg/10.1177/0007650320904849

Lia, C., & Wang, J. (2020). *CSR and AI ethics: The rle f htels.* Jurnal f Crprate Finance, 64, 101-117. https://di.rg/10.1016/j.jcrpfin.2020.101118

Li, D., Zhang, Z., & Gao, X. (2024). Does artificial intelligence deter greenwashing? *Finance Research Letters*, 67, 105954. DOI: 10.1016/j.frl.2024.105954

Li, G., Li, N., & Sethi, S. (2021). Does CSR reduce idiosyncratic risk? Roles of operational efficiency and AI innovation. *Production and Operations Management*, 30(7), 2027–2045. DOI: 10.1111/poms.13483

Li, H. (2019). Special Section Introduction: Artificial Intelligence and Advertising. *Journal of Advertising*, 48(4), 333–337. DOI: 10.1080/00913367.2019.1654947

Lii, Y. S., Wu, K. W., & Ding, M. C. (2013). Doing Good Does Good? Sustainable Marketing of CSR and Consumer Evaluations. *Corporate Social Responsibility and Environmental Management, 20*(1), 15–28. DOI: 10.1002/csr.294

Lim, R. E., & Lee, W. N. (2023). Communicating corporate social responsibility. How fit, specificity, and cognitive fluency drive consumer skepticism and response. *Corporate Social Responsibility and Environmental Management*, 30(2), 955–967. DOI: 10.1002/csr.2399

Lim, W. M. (2023). The workforce revolution: Reimagining work, workers, and workplaces for the future. *Global Business and Organizational Excellence*, 42(4), 5–10. DOI: 10.1002/joe.22218

Lin, B., Zecevic, S., Bouneffouf, D., & Cecchi, G.A. (2023). TherapyView: Visualizing Therapy Sessions with Temporal Topic Modeling and AI-Generated Arts. ArXiv, abs/2302.10845.

Line, N. D., Hanks, L., & Zhang, L. (2016). Sustainability communication. The effect of message construals on consumers' attitudes towards green restaurants. *International Journal of Hospitality Management, 57*, 143–151. DOI: 10.1016/j.ijhm.2016.07.001

Lins, S., Greulich, M., Löbbers, J., Benlian, A., & Sunyaev, A. (2024). Why so skeptical? Investigating the emergence and consequences of consumer skepticism toward web seals. *Information & Management*, 61(2), 103920. DOI: 10.1016/j.im.2024.103920

Liu, P., Zhao, R., Li, H., Zhu, T., Li, Y., Wang, H., & Zhang, X.-D. (2022). Near-infrared-II deep tissue fluorescence microscopy and application. Nano Research. DOI: 10.1007/s12274-022-4836-y

Liu, P., Zhao, R., Li, H., Zhu, T., Li, Y., Wang, H., & Zhang, X.-D. (2022). Near-infrared-II deep tissue fluorescence microscopy and application. Nano Research. https://www.ncbi.nlm.nih.gov/pmc/articles/PMC8126817/

Liu, S., & Murphy, R. (2021). *Algrithmic fairness in hspitality AI*. Infrmatin Prcessing & Management, 58(2), 102427. https://di.rg/10.1016/j.ipm.2020.102427

Li, X., & Guo, Z. (2021). *The Belt and Road Initiative: Connectivity, Cooperation, and Development.* World Scientific Publishing.

Lombardi, M., Leal, C., & Basso, L. (2010). The activity of Natura from the perspective of sustainable development and of corporate social responsibility. *Management Research*, 8(3), 165–182.

Loor-Zambrano, H. Y., Santos-Roldán, L., & Palacios-Florencio, B. (2022). Relationship CSR and employee commitment: Mediating effects of internal motivation and trust. *European Research on Management and Business Economics*, 28(2), 100185. DOI: 10.1016/j.iedeen.2021.100185

Low, M. P., & Bu, M. (2022). Examining the impetus for internal CSR Practices with digitalization strategy in the service industry during COVID-19 pandemic. *Business Ethics, the Environment & Responsibility*, 31(1), 209–223. DOI: 10.1111/beer.12408

Luo, R., Xing, J., Chen, L., Pan, Z., Cai, X., Li, Z., Wang, J., & Ford, A. (2021). Glassboxing Deep Learning to Enhance Aircraft Detection from SAR Imagery. *Remote Sensing (Basel)*, 13(18), 3650. DOI: 10.3390/rs13183650

Luo, Y., Jiang, H., & Zeng, L. (2023). Linking informative and factual CSR communication to reputation. an understanding of CSR motives and organizational identification. *Sustainability (Basel)*, 15(6), 5136. DOI: 10.3390/su15065136

Lu, X., Zhu, W., & Tsai, F. S. (2019). Social responsibility toward the employees and career development sustainability during manufacturing transformation in China. *Sustainability (Basel)*, 11(17), 4778. DOI: 10.3390/su11174778

Machado, R. N., Mello, R., Pinna, C., Nunes, R. M., Magalhães, A. S., & Féres-Carneiro, T. (2022). Family Psychotherapy in the Context of Adoption: Parental Suppression of Adopted Children's Epistemophilic Drive in the Pursuit of Their Origins. *Psychology (Irvine, Calif.)*, 13(8), 1286–1298. DOI: 10.4236/psych.2022.138083

Madry, A., Markelov, A., Schmidt, L., Tsipras, D., & Vladu, A. (2018). Towards deep learning models resistant to adversarial attacks. 6th International Conference on Learning Representations, ICLR 2018 - Conference Track Proceedings, 1–28.

Mai, J. E. (2016). Big data privacy: The datafication of personal information. *The Information Society*, 32(3), 192–199. DOI: 10.1080/01972243.2016.1153010

Ma, L., & Bentley, J. M. (2022). Can strategic message framing mitigate the negative effects of skeptical comments against corporate-social-responsibility communication on social networking sites? *Public Relations Review*, 48(4), 102222. DOI: 10.1016/j.pubrev.2022.102222

Manjarrez-Domínguez, C., Uc-Campos, M. I., Esparza-Vela, M. E., Baray-Guerrero, M. del R., Giner-Chávez, O., & Santellano-Estrada, E. (2023). Geospatial-Temporal Dynamics of Land Use in the Juárez Valley. Urbanization and Displacement of Agriculture. *Sustainability (Switzerland), 15*(11). DOI: 10.3390/su15118499

Marin, L., Rubio, A., & De-Maya, S. R. (2012). Competitiveness as a strategic outcome of corporate social responsibility. *Corporate Social Responsibility and Environmental Management*, 19(6), 364–376. DOI: 10.1002/csr.1288

Martin, K. (2019). Ethical implications and accountability of algorithms. [Link]. *Journal of Business Ethics*, 160(4), 835–850. DOI: 10.1007/s10551-018-3921-3

Martin, K., & Shiltn, K. (2022). Mitigating AI risks thrugh CSR strategies. *Journal of Business Ethics*, 176(2), 341–358. https://di.rg/10.1007/s10551-020-04618-w

Matsuura, H., & Liu, B. (2020). AI and Ethical Practices. The Role of Corporate Governance. Journal of Corporate Governance, 22(3), 55-73. DOI: 10.1108/JCG-03-2019-0056

Matytsin, D. E., Dzedik, V. A., Makeeva, G. A., & Boldyreva, S. B. (2023). "Smart" outsourcing in support of the humanization of entrepreneurship in the artificial intelligence economy. *Humanities & Social Sciences Communications*, 10(1), 13. DOI: 10.1057/s41599-022-01493-x PMID: 36644399

Mayer-Schönberger, V., & Cukier, K. (2019). Big Data. A Revolution That Will Transform How We Live, Work, and Think. Houghton Mifflin Harcourt. DOI: 10.1080/08985626.2015.1022747

Mazurek Melnyk, B., Hoying, J., & Tan, A. (2020). Effects of the MINDSTRONG© CBT-based program on depression, anxiety and healthy lifestyle behaviors in graduate health sciences students. *Journal of American College Health*, 70(4), 1001–1009. DOI: 10.1080/07448481.2020.1782922 PMID: 32672515

McBarnet, D. (2007). Corporate social responsibility beyond law, through law, for law: the new corporate accountability. In McBarnet, D., Voiculescu, A., & Campbell, T. (Eds.), *The new corporate accountability: corporate social responsibility and the law* (pp. 9–57). Cambridge University Press.

McBride, R., Dastan, A., & Mehrabinia, P. (2022, July 07). How AI affects the future relationship between corporate governance and financial markets: A note on impact capitalism. *Managerial Finance*, 48(8), 1240–1249. DOI: 10.1108/MF-12-2021-0586

McCormick, J., & Fitzgerald, L. (2020). Ethical AI and CSR. Understanding the Links. Business Ethics Quarterly, 30(1), 55-72. DOI: 10.1017/beq.2019.28

McGuinness, S., & Ortiz, L. (2016). Skill gaps in the workplace: Measurement, determinants and impacts. *Industrial Relations Journal*, 47(3), 253–278. DOI: 10.1111/irj.12136

McKinsey & Company. (2019). AI and the Future of Corporate Social Responsibility. McKinsey & Company Reports. DOI: 10.2139/ssrn.3442050

McKinsey & Company. (2023). Global share of organizations using artificial intelligence (AI) in their sustainability efforts in 2022, by region. *Statista*. https://www.statista.com/statistics/1384656/sustainability-ai-use/

McLachlan, C. J. (2022). Developing a framework for responsible downsizing through best fit: The importance of regulatory, procedural, communication and employment responsibilities. *International Journal of Human Resource Management*, 33(1), 16–44. DOI: 10.1080/09585192.2021.1958248

McMichael, A. J., Woodruff, R. E., & Hales, S. (2006). Climate change and human health: Present and future risks. *Lancet*, 367(9513), 859–869. DOI: 10.1016/S0140-6736(06)68079-3 PMID: 16530580

McMillan, T., & Liu, H. (2020). Evaluating AI-driven custmer service in htels. *Jurnal f Service Research*, 22(1), 89–105. https://di.rg/10.1177/1094670519872863

Meena, M. E., & Geng, J. (2022). Dynamic competition in telecommunications: A systematic literature review. *SAGE Open*, 12(2). DOI: 10.1177/21582440221094609

Mehta, CA. S. (2024, January 20). India's Digital Workforce Revolution: Reskilling and Upskilling for Growth. *Bharat Buzz*.

Mehta, A., Niles, A. N., Vargas, J. H., Marafon, T., Couto, D. D., & Gross, J. J. (2020). Acceptability and Effectiveness of Artificial Intelligence Therapy for Anxiety and Depression (Youper): Longitudinal Observational Study. *Journal of Medical Internet Research*, 23. PMID: 34155984

Melo, L. F. (2023). Reflections on Sustainable Development, Sustainability, and Business Practice: Lessons From Measurement, Scalability, and Bias in Artificial Intelligence (AI). In *Fostering Sustainable Development in the Age of Technologies* (pp. 145-161). Emerald Publishing Limited.

Meng, F., Zhou, J., Kong, D., Yao, M., Wu, K., Liu, X., Wang, X., & Guo, Y. (2022). The Design and Implementation of Geospatial Information Verification Middle Platform for Natural Resources Government Affairs. *ISPRS International Journal of Geo-Information, 11*(10). DOI: 10.3390/ijgi11100496

Merino-Soto, C., Angulo-Ramos, M., Rovira-Millán, L. V., & Rosario-Hernández, E. (2023). Psychometric properties of the generalized anxiety disorder-7 (GAD-7) in a sample of workers. *Frontiers in Psychiatry*, 14, 14. DOI: 10.3389/fpsyt.2023.999242 PMID: 37051164

Meschini, S., Pellegrini, L., Locatelli, M., Accardo, D., Tagliabue, L. C., Di Giuda, G. M., & Avena, M. (2022). Toward cognitive digital twins using a BIM-GIS asset management system for a diffused university. *Frontiers in Built Environment, 8*. DOI: 10.3389/fbuil.2022.959475

Mhlanga, D. (2020). Industry 4.0 in Finance: The Impact of Artificial Intelligence (AI) on Digital Financial Inclusion. *International Journal of Financial Studies*, 8(3), 45. Advance online publication. DOI: 10.3390/ijfs8030045

Michael, Pramanik, Basak, Prakash, & Shankar. (2022). Progress and challenges on extrusion based three dimensional (3D) printing of biomaterials. DOI: 10.1016/j.bprint.2022.e00223

Michaels, A., & Grüning, M. (2017). Relationship of corporate social responsibility disclosure on information asymmetry and the cost of capital. *Journal of Management Control*, 28(3), 251–274. DOI: 10.1007/s00187-017-0251-z

Miethlich, B., & Šlahor, Ľ. (2018). Creating shared value through implementing vocational rehabilitation in the corporate social responsibility strategy: A literature review. *Vision 2020: Sustainable Economic Development and Application of Innovation Management,32nd International Business Information Management Association Conference (IBIMA).*

Miller, G. A. (1994). The Magical Number Seven, Plus or Minus Two Some Limits on Our Capacity for Processing Information. *Psychological Review, 101*(2), 343–352. spider.apa.org/ftdocs/rev/1994/april/rev1012343.html

Miller, G. A. (1956). The magical number seven, plus or minus two. Some limits on our capacity for processing information. *Psychological Review*, 63(2), 81–97. DOI: 10.1037/h0043158 PMID: 13310704

Miller, K. E., & Akdere, M. (2019). Advancing organizational corporate social responsibility (CSR) agenda. *European Journal of Training and Development*, 43(9), 860–872. DOI: 10.1108/EJTD-10-2018-0107

Min, J., Kim, J., & Yang, K. (2023). CSR attributions and the moderating effect of perceived CSR fit on consumer trust, identification, and loyalty. *Journal of Retailing and Consumer Services*, 72, 103274. DOI: 10.1016/j.jretconser.2023.103274

Minkkinen, M., Niukkanen, A., & Mantymaki, M. (2022). What about investors? ESG analyses as tools for ethics-based AI auditing. *AI & Society*. Advance online publication. DOI: 10.1007/s00146-022-01415-0

Minz, N. K., & Khattar, Y. (2024). Advancing Sustainability: ESG Evolution and the AI Edge. In *Intersecting Environmental Social Governance and AI for Business Sustainability* (pp. 246-261). IGI Global.

Mitchell, M., & Hdge, V. (2021). *Data privacy in AI: Lessns fr the hspitality sectr*. Cmputers & Security, 103, 102171. https://di.rg/10.1016/j.cse.2021.102171

Mittelstadt, B. D., & Floridi, L. (2018). The Ethics of Big Data. Current and Future Directions. Computer Science Review, 35, 7-14. DOI: 10.1016/j.cosrev.2019.03.002

Mohammad Amini, M., Jesus, M., Fanaei Sheikholeslami, D., Alves, P., Hassanzadeh Benam, A., & Hariri, F. (2023). Artificial Intelligence Ethics and Challenges in Healthcare Applications. A Comprehensive Review in the Context of the European GDPR Mandate. In *Machine Learning and Knowledge Extraction* (Vol. 5, Issue 3). DOI: 10.3390/make5030053

Moher, D., Liberati, A., Tetzlaff, J., & Altman, D. G. (2009). Preferred Reporting Items for Systematic Reviews and Meta-Analyses: The PRISMA Statement. *PLoS Medicine*, 6(7), e1000097. DOI: 10.1371/journal.pmed.1000097 PMID: 19621072

Mohr, L. A., & Ellen, P. S. (1998). The Development and Testing of a Measure of Skepticism Toward Environmental Claims in Marketers' Communications. *The Journal of Consumer Affairs*, 32(1), 30–55. DOI: 10.1111/j.1745-6606.1998.tb00399.x

Moreno, F., & Kang, J. (2020). How to alleviate consumer skepticism concerning corporate responsibility. The role of content and delivery in CSR communications. *Corporate Social Responsibility and Environmental Management, 27*(6), 2477–2490. DOI: 10.1002/csr.1969

Morkhat, P. M. (2018). Concerning the question about the legal personality of electronic person. *Legal Studies*, 4(1).

Mor, S., & Gupta, G. (2021). Artificial intelligence and technical efficiency: The case of Indian commercial banks. *Strategic Change*, 30(3), 235–245. Advance online publication. DOI: 10.1002/jsc.2406

Mou, Y., & Meng, X. (2024). Alexa, it is creeping over me–Exploring the impact of privacy concerns on consumer resistance to intelligent voice assistants. *Asia Pacific Journal of Marketing and Logistics*, 36(2), 261–292. DOI: 10.1108/APJML-10-2022-0869

Moyo, T., Crafford, G. J., & Emuze, F. (2019). *Assessing Strategies For Improving The Social Security Of Construction Workers In Zimbabwe.*

Mughal, A. A. (2017). Artificial Intelligence in Information Security: Exploring the Advantages, Challenges, and Future Directions.

Mukhuty, S., Upadhyay, A., & Rothwell, H. (2022). Strategic sustainable development of Industry 4.0 through the lens of social responsibility: The role of human resource practices. *Business Strategy and the Environment*, 31(5), 2068–2081. DOI: 10.1002/bse.3008

Mulansky, L. (2020). Untersuchung der Geodaten von Benutzern der Moodpath mHealth App mithilfe von Methoden des Maschinellen Lernens.

Munirathinam, S. (2020). Industry 4.0: Industrial internet of things (IIOT). *Advances in Computers*, 117(1), 129–164. DOI: 10.1016/bs.adcom.2019.10.010

Muravyov, S. V., Antipov, D., Buzdalova, A., & Filchenkov, A. (2019). *Efficient Computation of Fitness Function for Evolutionary Clustering*. MENDEL. DOI: 10.13164/mendel.2019.1.087

Murphy, S., & Atala, A. (2014). 3D bioprinting of tissues and organs. *Nature Biotechnology*, 32(8), 773–785. DOI: 10.1038/nbt.2958 PMID: 25093879

Musa, G. J., Chiang, P. H., Sylk, T., Bavley, R., Keating, W., Lakew, B., ... Hoven, C. W. (2013). Use of GIS mapping as a public health tool--from cholera to cancer. *Health Services Insights, 6*, HSI-S10471.

Nadimpalli, M. (2017). Artificial Intelligence – Consumers and Industry Impact. *International Journal of Economics & Management Sciences*, 06(03). Advance online publication. DOI: 10.4172/2162-6359.1000429

Nagendra, N. P., Narayanamurthy, G., & Moser, R. (2022). Management of humanitarian relief operations using satellite big data analytics. the case of Kerala floods. *Annals of Operations Research, 319*(1). DOI: 10.1007/s10479-020-03593-w

Nair, A., & Singh, P. (2022). The impact f CSR n AI ethics in htels. *Journal of Business Research*, 138, 64–74. https://di.rg/10.1016/j.jbusres.2021.08.012

Naqvi, A. (2018). How AI and robotics can transform CSR. *Ethical Corporation*. http://www.ethicalcorp.com/how-ai-and-robotics-can-transform-csr

Narayanan, A., & Binns, R. (2018). The Role of Ethical AI in Corporate Social Responsibility. AI & Society, 33(4), 509-519. DOI: 10.1007/s00146-017-0752-2

Narayanan, A., & Shadbolt, N. (2018). Understanding AI and the Impact of Data Bias. Journal of AI Research, 63, 467-496. DOI: 10.1613/jair.1.11944

Naveneethan, S., Madhan, E.S., & Kathirvel, A. (2022). Identifying and Eliminating the Misbehavior Nodes in the Wireless Sensor Network. In Soft Computing and Signal Processing. ICSCSP 2021. Advances in Intelligent Systems and Computing, vol 1413. Springer International Publishing. DOI: 10.1007/978-981-16-7088-6_36

Ngo, V. M. (2024). Does ChatGPT change artificial intelligence-enabled marketing capability? Social media investigation of public sentiment and usage. *Global Media and China*, 9(1), 101–125. DOI: 10.1177/20594364241228880

Nguyen, N., Priporas, C. V., McPherson, M., & Manyiwa, S. (2023). CSR-related consumer scepticism. A review of the literature and future research directions. *Journal of Business Research*, 169, 114294. DOI: 10.1016/j.jbusres.2023.114294

Nigatu, A. S., Asamoah, B. O., & Kloos, H. (2014). Knowledge and perceptions about the health impact of climate change among health sciences students in Ethiopia: A cross-sectional study. *BMC Public Health*, 14(1), 1–10. DOI: 10.1186/1471-2458-14-587 PMID: 24916631

Ni, Y., Ding, R., Chen, Y., Hou, H., & Ni, S. (2023). Focusing on Needs: A Chatbot-Based Emotion Regulation Tool for Adolescents. *2023 IEEE International Conference on Systems, Man, and Cybernetics (SMC)*, 2295-2300. DOI: 10.1109/SMC53992.2023.10394600

Noorman, M., & Johnson, D. G. (2014). Negotiating autonomy and responsibility in military robots. *Ethics and Information Technology*, 16(1), 51–62. DOI: 10.1007/s10676-013-9335-0

O'Brien, G., O'keefe, P., Rose, J., & Wisner, B. (2006). Climate change and disaster management. *Disasters*, 30(1), 64–80. DOI: 10.1111/j.1467-9523.2006.00307.x PMID: 16512862

O'Heigeartaigh, S. (2013). Would you hand over a moral decision to a machine? Why not? Moral outsourcing and artificial. http://blog.practicalethics.ox.ac.uk/2013/08/would-youhand-over-a-moral-decision-to-a-machine-why-not-moral-outsourcing-and-artificial-intelligence

O'neil, C. (2016). *Weapons of math destruction: how big data increases inequality and threatens democracy*. Crown.

O'Neil, C. (2016). Weapons of Math Destruction. How Big Data Increases Inequality and Threatens Democracy. Crown Publishing Group. DOI: 10.1177/0276146716654008

Organisation for Economic Co-operation and Development. (2019). *OECD Digital Economy Outlook 2019*. OECD Publishing.

Osburg, T., & Lohrmann, C. (2017). *Sustainability in a digital world*. Springer International. DOI: 10.1007/978-3-319-54603-2

Pacchiardi, L., Chan, A.J., Mindermann, S., Moscovitz, I., Pan, A.Y., Gal, Y., Evans, O., & Brauner, J.M. (2023). How to Catch an AI Liar: Lie Detection in Black-Box LLMs by Asking Unrelated Questions. ArXiv, abs/2309.15840.

Packard, N. (2023). Internet prehistory: ARPANET chronology. *Cogent Social Sciences*, 9(2), 2245237. DOI: 10.1080/23311886.2023.2245237

Pai, V., & Chandra, S. (2022). Exploring factors influencing organizational adoption of artificial intelligence (AI) in corporate social responsibility (CSR) initiatives. *Pacific Asia Journal of the Association for Information Systems*, 14(5), 4. DOI: 10.17705/1pais.14504

Palinkas, L. A., & Wong, M. (2020). Global climate change and mental health. *Current Opinion in Psychology*, 32, 12–16. DOI: 10.1016/j.copsyc.2019.06.023 PMID: 31349129

Pallathadka, H., Ramirez-Asis, E. H., Loli-Poma, T. P., Kaliyaperumal, K., Ventayen, R. J. M., & Naved, M. (2021). Applications of artificial intelligence in business management, e-commerce and finance. *Materials Today: Proceedings*. Advance online publication. DOI: 10.1016/j.matpr.2021.06.419

Pandya, J. (2021). The Role of CSR in providing Employment opportunity to Persons with Disabilities. SSRN *Electronic Journal*. DOI: 10.2139/ssrn.3992351

Pantano, E., & Pizzi, G. (2020). Forecasting artificial intelligence on online customer assistance: Evidence from chatbot patents analysis. *Journal of Retailing and Consumer Services*, 55, 102096. Advance online publication. DOI: 10.1016/j.jretconser.2020.102096

Park, E., & Kim, K. J. (2019). What drives “customer loyalty”? The role of corporate social responsibility. *Sustainable Development, 27*(3), 304–311. DOI: 10.1002/sd.1901

Park, S. B., Kim, J., Lee, Y. K., & Ok, C. M. (2020). Visualizing theme park visitors’ emotions using social media analytics and geospatial analytics. *Tourism Management, 80*. DOI: 10.1016/j.tourman.2020.104127

Park, K. (2022). The mediating role of skepticism. How corporate social advocacy builds quality relationships with publics. *Journal of Marketing Communications*, 28(8), 821–839. DOI: 10.1080/13527266.2021.1964580

Pasquale, F. (2019). The Black Box Society. The Secret Algorithms That Control Money and Information. Harvard University Press. DOI: 10.1145/2772951

Patel, R., & Jenkins, T. (2021). *AI transparency and custmer perceptins*. Infrmatin Systems Jurnal, 31(5), 903-920. https://di.rg/10.1111/isj.12321

Patel, N., Dahman, B., & Bajaj, J. S. (2022). Development of New Mental and Physical Health Sequelae among US Veterans after COVID-19. *Journal of Clinical Medicine*, 11(12), 11. DOI: 10.3390/jcm11123390 PMID: 35743461

Patra, A. K., Praharaj, A., Sudarshan, D., & Chhatoi, B. P. (2024). AI and business management: Tracking future research agenda through bibliometric network analysis. *Heliyon*, 10(1), e23902. DOI: 10.1016/j.heliyon.2023.e23902 PMID: 38230239

Patrawala, R. (2019). The Artificial Intelligence Era its Seismic Potential to Create a Job Displacement Conundrum. *IIBM'S Journal of Management*, 112–129. DOI: 10.33771/iibm.v4i1-2.1074

Patre, S., Chakraborty, D., Kar, A. K., Singu, H. B., & Tiwari, D. A. (2023). The Role of Enablers and Barriers in the Upskilling and Reskilling of Users Through Professional Skilling Programs on EdTech Platforms. *IEEE Transactions on Engineering Management*, 1–15. DOI: 10.1109/TEM.2023.3328261

Pavaloiu, A., & Kose, U. (2017). Ethical artificial Intelligence – an open question. *Journal of Multidisciplinary Developments*, 2, 15–27.

Pavlou, P. A. (2018). Internet of Things–Will Humans be Replaced or Augmented? *Marketing Intelligence Review*, 10(2), 43–48. DOI: 10.2478/gfkmir-2018-0017

Peixoto, J. P. J., Costa, D. G., Portugal, P., & Vasques, F. (2023). A geospatial dataset of urban infrastructure for emergency response in Portugal. *Data in Brief, 50*. DOI: 10.1016/j.dib.2023.109593

Pérez, A., & Rodríguez del Bosque, I. (2015). How customer novelty seeking influences customer CSR perceptions. *Marketing Intelligence and Planning, 33*(4), 486–507. DOI: 10.1108/MIP-07-2014-0140

Petrin, M. (2019). Corporate management in the age of AI. *Columbia Business Law Review*, 2019(3), 965–1030.

Pfajfar, G., Shoham, A., Małecka, A., & Zalaznik, M. (2022). Value of corporate social responsibility for multiple stakeholders and social impact – Relationship marketing perspective. *Journal of Business Research*, 143, 46–61. DOI: 10.1016/j.jbusres.2022.01.051

Pinto-López, I. N., & Montaudon-Tomas, C. M. (2021). *Distance Learning: A bibliometric – Based Review in Handbook of Research on Determining the Reliability of Online Assessment and Distance Learning*. IGI Global. DOI: 10.4018/978-1-7998-4769-4.ch003

Pisoni, G., & Molnár, B. (2024). AI-Based Solution for Sustainability Tracing for Companies. [IJKM]. *International Journal of Knowledge Management*, 20(1), 1–17. DOI: 10.4018/IJKM.340723

Plikas, J. H., Trakadas, P., & Kenourgios, D. (2024). *Assessing the Ethical Implications of Artificial Intelligence (AI) and Machine Learning (ML) on Job Displacement Through Automation: A Critical Analysis of Their Impact on Society* (pp. 313–325). DOI: 10.1007/978-981-99-9836-4_24

Popescu, C. R. G., & González, A. L. (2024). Exploring the Synergies Between Environmental Social Governance and AI for Business Sustainability: Tackling Climate Adaptation, Mitigating Climate Change Efforts, and Pursuing Climate Justice. In *Intersecting Environmental Social Governance and AI for Business Sustainability* (pp. 1-41). IGI Global. DOI: 10.4018/979-8-3693-1151-6.ch001

Rab-Kettler, K., & Lehnervp, B. (2019). Recruitment in the times of Machine Learning. *Management Systems in Production Engineering*, 27(2), 105–109. DOI: 10.1515/mspe-2019-0018

Rafiq, M., Hameed, I., Dastane, O., & Ghouri, A. (2024). *Harnessing Digital Transformation: A Pathway to Achieving the 2030 UNSDGs and Ensuring Sustainable Corporate Performance*. IGI Global Publishing. DOI: 10.4018/979-8-3693-5375-2.ch011

Rai, A., & Selander, L. (2018). Can Corporate Social Responsibility Influence AI Ethics? IEEE Transactions on Engineering Management, 65(1), 113-126. DOI: 10.1109/TEM.2017.2787907

Raji, I. D., & Buolamwini, J. (2019). Actionable Auditing. Investigating the Impact of Publicly Naming Biased Performance Results of Commercial AI Products. Proceedings of the 2019 CHI Conference on Human Factors in Computing Systems, 1-15. DOI: 10.1145/3306618.3314244

Ramesh, K., Saha, R., Goswami, S., Sekar, & Dahiya, R. (2019). Consumer's response to CSR activities. Mediating role of brand image and brand attitude. *Corporate Social Responsibility and Environmental Management, 26*(2), 377–387. DOI: 10.1002/csr.1689

Ramirez, M. A., Kim, S.-K., Al Hamadi, H., Damiani, E., Byon, Y.-J., Kim, T.-Y., Cho, C.-S., & Yeun, C. Y. (2022). Poisoning Attacks and Defenses on Artificial Intelligence: A Survey. http://arxiv.org/abs/2202.10276

Rawashdeh, A. (2023). The consequences of artificial intelligence: an investigation into the impact of AI on job displacement in accounting. *Journal of Science and Technology Policy Management*. DOI: 10.1108/JSTPM-02-2023-0030

Rawshdeh, Z. A., Makhbul, Z. K. M., Rawshdeh, M., & Sinniah, S. (2023). Perceived socially responsible-HRM on talent retention: The mediating effect of trust and motivation and the moderating effect of other-regarding value orientation. *Frontiers in Psychology*, 13, 1087065. Advance online publication. DOI: 10.3389/fpsyg.2022.1087065 PMID: 36726518

Rim, H., & Kim, S. (2016). Dimensions of corporate social responsibility (CSR) skepticism and their impacts on public evaluations toward CSR. *Journal of Public Relations Research, 28*(5–6), 248–267. DOI: 10.1080/1062726X.2016.1261702

Rim, H., Dong, C., & Zhang, Y. (2024). Cross-National Study of Transparency in CSR Communication and Corporate Trust. Mediating Roles of Perceived Altruism and Perceived Skepticism. *International Journal of Business Communication*. DOI: 10.1177/23294884231223181

Rixom, J. M., & Rixom, B. A. (2023). Perceived brand authenticity. Examining the effects of inferred dedication and anticipated quality on consumers' purchase intentions and actual choices. *Journal of Consumer Behaviour*, 22(3), 721–737. DOI: 10.1002/cb.2156

Robbins Schug, G., Buikstra, J. E., DeWitte, S. N., Baker, B. J., Berger, E., Buzon, M. R., Davies-Barrett, A. M., Goldstein, L., Grauer, A. L., Gregoricka, L. A., Halcrow, S. E., Knudson, K. J., Larsen, C. S., Martin, D. L., Nystrom, K. C., Perry, M. A., Roberts, C. A., Santos, A. L., Stojanowski, C. M., & Zakrzewski, S. R. (2023). Climate change, human health, and resilience in the Holocene. *Proceedings of the National Academy of Sciences of the United States of America*, 120(4), e2209472120. DOI: 10.1073/pnas.2209472120 PMID: 36649426

Rolnick, D., Donti, P. L., Kaack, L. H., Kochanski, K., Lacoste, A., Sankaran, K., Ross, A. S., Nikola, D. M., Natasha, J., Brown, A. W., Luccioni, A. L., Maharaj, T., Sherwin, E. D., & Mukkavilli, S. (2022). Tackling Climate Change with Machine Learning. *ACM Computing Surveys*, 55(2), 1–96. DOI: 10.1145/3485128

Rossi, C., & Rivetti, F. (2023). Young consumers' purchase behaviour of sustainably-labelled food products. What is the role of scepticism? *Food Quality and Preference*, 105, 104772. DOI: 10.1016/j.foodqual.2022.104772

Rupp, W. R., & Smith, A. D. (2023). Corporate Social Reasonability Roles in Artificial Intelligence and Big Data Analytics in Management. In *Handbook of Research on Driving Socioeconomic Development With Big Data* (pp. 76–102). IGI Global. DOI: 10.4018/978-1-6684-5959-1.ch004

Rust, R. T., & Huang, M. H. (2018). The Service Revolution and the Impact of AI. Journal of Service Research, 21(1), 3-10. DOI: 10.1177/1094670517752401

Ryan, M. (2020). In AI We Trust: Ethics, Artificial Intelligence, and Reliability. *Science and Engineering Ethics*, 26(5), 2749–2767. DOI: 10.1007/s11948-020-00228-y PMID: 32524425

Ryška, P. (2017). Deflation anD economic Growth: the Great Depression as the Great outlier.

Sadasivan, A. (2018). Expanding the Scope of Corporate Social Responsibility (CSR): Strategizing Skill Development in the Indian Scenario. *The Arab Journal of the Social Sciences*, 17(2), 21–38. DOI: 10.12724/ajss.45.2

Saetra, H. S. (2021). A framework for evaluating and disclosing the ESG-related impacts of AI with the SDGs. *Sustainability (Basel)*, 13(15), 8503. DOI: 10.3390/su13158503

Sandel, M. J. (2020). The Tyranny of Merit. What's Become of the Common Good? Farrar, Straus and Giroux. DOI: 10.1111/j.1468-0327.2009.00160.x

Saraswati, K. D. H., & Lie, D. (2020). Psychlgical Well-Being: The Impact f Wrk-Life Balance and Wrk Pressure. Advances in Scial Science, Educatin and Humanities Research. Internatinal Jurnal f Research in Management. *Ecnmics and Cmmerce*, 7(11), 40–47.

Sari, R. E., Min, S., Purwoko, H., Furinto, A., & Tamara, D. (2020). Artificial Intelligence for a Better Employee Engagement. *International Research Journal of Business Studies*, 13(2), 173–188. DOI: 10.21632/irjbs.13.2.173-188

Sarkar, S., Shukla, S., & Mishra, R. K. (2023). *Enabling Skill Development in the Pandemic – The CSR Perspective*. DOI: 10.1108/S2043-905920230000016006

Saurabh, K., Arora, R., Rani, N., Mishra, D., & Ramkumar, M. (2022). AI led ethical digital transformation: Framework, research, and managerial implications. *Journal of Information. Communication and Ethics in Society*, 20(2), 229–256. DOI: 10.1108/JICES-02-2021-0020

Schlenoff, C.I. (2015). IEEE standard ontologies for robotics and automation. IEEE std, 1-60.

Schmeltz, L. (2012). Consumer-oriented CSR communication. Focusing on ability or morality? *Corporate Communications, 17*(1), 29–49. DOI: 10.1108/13563281211196344

Schmeltz, L. (2014). Introducing value-based framing as a strategy for communicating CSR. *Social Responsibility Journal, 10*(1), 184–206. DOI: 10.1108/SRJ-06-2012-0065

Schmeltz, L. (2017). Getting CSR communication fit. A study of strategically fitting cause, consumers and company in corporate CSR communication. *Public Relations Inquiry, 6*(1), 47–72. DOI: 10.1177/2046147X16666731

Selvarajan, S., Mohamed, A., White, T., & Boodram, N. (2009). Assessment of geospatial technologies for natural resource management in Florida. *Journal of Forestry*, 107(5), 242–249. DOI: 10.1093/jof/107.5.242

Sewada, R., Jangid, A., Kumar, P., & Mishra, N. (2023). Explainable Artificial Intelligence (XAI). international journal of food and nutritional sciences.

Shadbolt, N., & Harnad, S. (2017). Ethical AI. The Role of Transparency and Accountability. Artificial Intelligence Review, 50(1), 1-16. DOI: 10.1007/s10462-016-9501-3

Shaikh, E., Brahmi, M., Thang, P. C., Watto, W. A., Trang, T. T. N., & Loan, N. T. (2022). Should I stay or should I go? explaining the turnover intentions with corporate social responsibility (CSR), organizational identification and organizational commitment. *Sustainability (Basel)*, 14(10), 6030. DOI: 10.3390/su14106030

Sharma, A., & Dey, A. (2021). The Influence of CSR on Ethical AI. An Empirical Study. Journal of Strategic and International Studies, 12(2), 89-104. DOI: 10.1142/S1793823321500120

Shinde, N. V., Akhade, A., Bagad, P., Bhavsar, H., Wagh, S. K., & Kamble, A. (2021, June 3). Healthcare Chatbot System using Artificial Intelligence. *2021 5th International Conference on Trends in Electronics and Informatics (ICOEI)*. DOI: 10.1109/ICOEI51242.2021.9452902

Shkalenko, A. V., & Nazarenko, A. V. (2024). Integration of AI and IoT into corporate social responsibility strategies for financial risk management and sustainable development. *Risks.*, 12(6), 87. DOI: 10.3390/risks12060087

Shukla, A. K., Gao, G., & Kim, B. S. (2022). Applications of 3D Bioprinting Technology in Induced Pluripotent Stem Cells-Based Tissue Engineering. Micromachines. https://www.ncbi.nlm.nih.gov/pmc/articles/PMC8876961/

Singh, M., & Sharma, A. (2020). *Custmer trust and AI in the hspitality industry.* Internatinal Jurnal f Hspitality Management, 88, 102518. https://di.rg/10.1016/j.ijhm.2020.102518

Singh, B., Kashyap, S., & Grover, A. (2019). Artificial intelligence and dichotomy on benefits and challenges: What do healthcare providers say? International Journal of Research in Medical Sciences.

Singh, S. V., Jha, R., Singh, A. K., Ranjan, R., & Pandey, S. (2024). Sustainable Tourism Perspective in the Sustainable Development Goals. A Case Study of Heritage Sites in Uttarakhand. In *Implementing Sustainable Development Goals in the Service Sector* (pp. 91–107). IGI Global.

Skarmeas, D., & Leonidou, C. N. (2013). When consumers doubt, Watch out! The role of CSR skepticism. *Journal of Business Research, 66*(10), 1831–1838. DOI: 10.1016/j.jbusres.2013.02.004

Smith, A. (2020). The Role of Digital Infrastructure in Economic Development. *The Journal of Economic Perspectives*, 34(3), 202–219.

Song, B., & Choi, M. (2023). Testing Publics' Perceptions of Corporate Social Advocacy Messaging. Linking Organizational and Social Outcomes. *International Journal of Strategic Communication*, 17(4), 325–344. DOI: 10.1080/1553118X.2023.2228293

Srivetbodee, S., & Igel, B. (2021). Digital technology adoption in agriculture: Success factors, obstacles and impact on corporate social responsibility performance in Thailand's smart farming projects. *Thammasat Review,* 24(2), 149-170. DOI: DOI: 10.14456/tureview.2021.22

Stahl, B. C., & Wright, D. (2018). Ethics and Privacy in AI and Big Data: Implementing Responsible Research and Innovation. *IEEE Security and Privacy*, 16(3), 26–33. DOI: 10.1109/MSP.2018.2701164

Staniškienė, E., & Stankevičiūtė, Ž. (2018). Social sustainability measurement framework: The case of employee perspective in a CSR-committed organisation. *Journal of Cleaner Production*, 188, 708–719. DOI: 10.1016/j.jclepro.2018.03.269

Stankevičiūtė, Z., & Kalvaitienė, J. (2023). Human resource business partner role in respect to internal corporate social responsibility: The case of banking sector. *Human Systems Management*, 1–17. DOI: 10.3233/HSM-230113

Statz, K. M., Bogina, A. C., Schmult, J. L., & Gordon, B. S. (2023). Salute to service or salute to skepticism? An empirical analysis of military members' perceptions of the NFL's military campaign. *International Journal of Sports Marketing & Sponsorship*, 24(4), 661–681. DOI: 10.1108/IJSMS-05-2022-0102

Stephens, T. N., Joerin, A., Rauws, M., & Werk, L. N. (2019). Feasibility of pediatric obesity and prediabetes treatment support through Tess, the AI behavioral coaching chatbot. *Translational Behavioral Medicine*, 9(3), 440–447. DOI: 10.1093/tbm/ibz043 PMID: 31094445

Subramaniam, M., Kathirvel, A., Sabitha, E., & Anwar Basha, H. (2021). Modified Firefly Algorithm and Fuzzy C-Mean Clustering Based Semantic Information Retrieval. Journal of Web Engineering, 20(1), 33–52. DOI: 10.13052/jwe1540-9589.2012

Sudha, D., & Kathirvel, A. (2022). An Intrusion Detection System to Detect and Mitigating Attacks Using Hidden Markov Model (HMM) Energy Monitoring Technique. Stochastic Modeling an Applications, 26(3), 467-476.

Sudha, D., & Kathirvel, A. (2022). The effect of ETUS in various generic attacks in mobile ad hoc networks to improve the performance of Aodv protocol. International Journal of Humanities, Law, and Social Sciences, 9(1), 467-476.

Sudha, D., & Kathirvel, A. (2023). The performance enhancement of Aodv protocol using GETUS. International Journal of Early Childhood Special Education, 15(2), 115-125. DOI:DOI: 10.48047/INTJECSE/V15I2.11

Sudha, D., & Kathirvel, A. (2022). The Effect of ETUS in Various Generic Attacks in Mobile Ad hoc Networks to Improve the Performance of AODV Protocol. International Journal of Humanities. *Law and Social Sciences*, 9(1), 23–31.

Sullins, J. P. (2006). When is a robot a moral agent? *International Journal of Information Ethics*, 6(12), 23–30. DOI: 10.29173/irie136

Sun, W., Nasraoui, O., & Shafto, P. (2020). Evolution and impact of bias in human and machine learning algorithm interaction. *PLoS ONE, 15*(8). DOI: 10.1371/journal.pone.0235502

Sun, Y., Kong, Z., Song, Y., Liu, J., & Wang, X. (2022). The validity and reliability of the PHQ-9 on screening of depression in neurology: A cross sectional study. *BMC Psychiatry*, 22(1), 22. DOI: 10.1186/s12888-021-03661-w PMID: 35139810

Sunyaev, A., & Sunyaev, A. (2020). Cloud computing. *Internet computing: Principles of distributed systems and emerging internet-based technologies*, 195-236.

Talwar, S., Talwar, M., Tarjanne, V., & Dhir, A. (2021). Why retail investors traded equity during the pandemic? An application of artificial neural networks to examine behavioral biases. *Psychology and Marketing*, 38(11), 2142–2163. DOI: 10.1002/mar.21550

Taylor, W., & Hollenbeck, B. (2021). Leveraging loyalty programs using competitor based targeting. *Quantitative Marketing and Economics, 19*(3–4). DOI: 10.1007/s11129-021-09237-y

Teah, K., Sung, B., & Phau, I. (2023). Examining the moderating role of principle-based entity of luxury brands and its effects on perceived CSR motives, consumer situational scepticism and brand resonance. *Journal of Fashion Marketing and Management*, 27(5), 784–809. DOI: 10.1108/JFMM-03-2022-0066

Temple, P., Acher, M., Jézéquel, J., & Barais, O. (2017). Learning Contextual-Variability Models. *IEEE Software*, 34(6), 64–70. DOI: 10.1109/MS.2017.4121211

Tenkanen, H., Pereira, R. H. M., Arcaute, E., & Gonzalez, M. C. (2023). Advances in geospatial approaches to transport networks and sustainable mobility. In *Environment and Planning B. Urban Analytics and City Science* (Vol. 50, Issue 8). DOI: 10.1177/23998083231207768

Thmpsn, R., & McDnald, E. (2021). *Algrithmic bias and transparency in htel services*. ACM Transactins n Intelligent Systems and Technlgy, 12(4), 1-18. https://di .rg/10.1145/3460606

Thomas, S., Bhatt, V., & Patel, R. (2024). Impact of skepticism on CRM luxury campaign participation intention of Generation Z. *International Journal of Emerging Markets*, 19(4), 964–988. DOI: 10.1108/IJOEM-10-2021-1568

Thormundsson, B. (2024, January 10). Artificial intelligence (AI) in productivity and labor - statistics & facts. Statista.

Timmermans, S., & Berg, M. (2018). The Gold Standard. The Challenge of Evidence-Based Medicine. Temple University Press. DOI: 10.1080/0952813X.2017.1388037

Ting, C. Y., Zakariah, H., Kamaludin, F., Cheng, D. L. W., Tan, N. Y. Z., & Yee, H. J. (2021). Geospatial analytics for COVID-19 active case detection. *Computers, Materials and Continua, 67*(1). DOI: 10.32604/cmc.2021.013327

Tlili, A., Huang, R., Shehata, B., Liu, D., Zhao, J., Metwally, A. H. S., Wang, H., Denden, M., Bozkurt, A., Lee, L. H., Beyoglu, D., Altinay, F., Sharma, R. C., Altinay, Z., Li, Z., Liu, J., Ahmad, F., Hu, Y., Salha, S., & Burgos, D. (2022). Is Metaverse in education a blessing or a curse: A combined content and bibliometric analysis. *Smart Learning Environments*, 9(1), 24. DOI: 10.1186/s40561-022-00205-x

Torrance, S. (2013). Artificial agents and the expanding ethical circle. DOI: 10.1007/s00146-012-0422-2

Torres, P., & Augusto, M. (2020). Digitalisation, social entrepreneurship and national well-being. *Technological Forecasting and Social Change*, 161, 120279. DOI: 10.1016/j.techfore.2020.120279

Townsend, B. A., Sihlahla, I., Naidoo, M., Naidoo, S., Donnelly, D., & Thaldar, D. W. (2023). Mapping the regulatory landscape of AI in healthcare in Africa. *Frontiers in Pharmacology*, 14, 14. DOI: 10.3389/fphar.2023.1214422 PMID: 37693916

Tran, B. X., Vu, G. T., Ha, G. H., Vuong, Q. H., Ho, M. T., Vuong, T. T., La, V. P., Ho, M. T., Nghiem, K. C. P., Nguyen, H. L. T., Latkin, C. A., Tam, W. W. S., Cheung, N. M., Nguyen, H. K. T., Ho, C. S. H., & Ho, R. C. M. (2019). Global evolution of research in artificial intelligence in health and medicine: A bibliometric study. *Journal of Clinical Medicine*, 8(3), 360. DOI: 10.3390/jcm8030360 PMID: 30875745

Truong, N. B., Sun, K., Lee, G. M., & Guo, Y. (2020). GDPR-Compliant Personal Data Management. A Blockchain-Based Solution. *IEEE Transactions on Information Forensics and Security, 15*. DOI: 10.1109/TIFS.2019.2948287

Tschumi, E., & Zscheischler, J. (2020). Countrywide climate features during recorded climate-related disasters. *Climatic Change*, 158(3-4), 593–609. DOI: 10.1007/s10584-019-02556-w PMID: 32165774

Turker, D., Can, O., & Aras-Beger, G. (2023). How authenticity of corporate social responsibility affects organizational attractiveness. Stakeholder perceptions of organizational ideology. *Corporate Social Responsibility and Environmental Management*, 30(4), 1680–1697. DOI: 10.1002/csr.2444

Tybout, A., Calder, B. J., & Sternthal, B. (1981). Using Information Processing Theory to Design Marketing Strategies. *JMR, Journal of Marketing Research*, 18(1), 73–79. DOI: 10.1177/002224378101800107

Tyssen, R. (2019). Wrk and mental health in dctrs: A shrt review. *Prt Bimedical Jurnal*, 4(5), 1–3.

United Nations Development Programme. (2018). Climate change and human development. Retrieved from https://www.undp.org/content/undp/en/home/librarypage/climate-and-disaster-resilience-/climate-change-and-human-development.html

United Nations. (2019). Financing for Development Report 2019. United Nations. Retrieved from https://developmentfinance.un.org/sites/developmentfinance

Valentín-Sívico, J., Canfield, C., Low, S. A., & Gollnick, C. (2023). Evaluating the impact of broadband access and internet use in a small underserved rural community. *Telecommunications Policy*, 47(4), 102499. DOI: 10.1016/j.telpol.2023.102499 PMID: 36685614

Van den Hoven, J., & Weckert, J. (2019). The Ethical Implications of AI in CSR. A Theoretical Framework. Ethics and Information Technology, 21(4), 289-303. DOI: 10.1007/s10676-019-09550-7

van Giffen, B., Herhausen, D., & Fahse, T. (2022). Overcoming the pitfalls and perils of algorithms. A classification of machine learning biases and mitigation methods. *Journal of Business Research, 144*. DOI: 10.1016/j.jbusres.2022.01.076

Van Prooijen, A. M., Bartels, J., & Meester, T. (2021). Communicated and attributed motives for sustainability initiatives in the energy industry. The role of regulatory compliance. *Journal of Consumer Behaviour*, 20(5), 1015–1024. DOI: 10.1002/cb.1907

Vega, B., & Varona, F. L. (2024). Impacto de la Responsabilidad Social Corporativa en la Gestión ambiental y la Sostenibilidad en los destinos turísticos: Análisis bibliométrico del 2007-2022. *Compendium: Cuadernos de Economía y Administración*, 11(1), 89. Advance online publication. DOI: 10.46677/compendium.v11i1.1227

Verma, S., Sharma, R., Deb, S., & Maitra, D. (2021). Artificial intelligence in Marketing: Systematic review and future research direction. *International Journal of Information Management Data Insights*, 1(1), 100002. DOI: 10.1016/j.jjimei.2020.100002

Vidanage, K., & Jayaratne, K. (2016). Ontology And Expert System Based Intervention, For Psychological Consultation. *European Journal of Computer Science and Information Technology, 4*. https://www.eajournals.org/wp-content/uploads/Ontology-and-Expert- System-Based-Intervention-for-Psychological-Consultation.pdf

Vidanage, K., Mohamad, N. M., & Mohemad, R. (2019). Upper–Level Task Ontology for Generic Ontology Verbalization. 2019 2nd International Conference of Intelligent Robotic and Control Engineering (IRCE), 148-155. DOI: 10.1109/IRCE.2019.00037

Vidanage, K., & Jayaratne, L. (2015). Machine Learning and Natural Language Processing Usage for Psychological Consultation. *GSTF International Journal on Computing*, 4(3), 17. DOI: 10.7603/s40601-014-0017-5

Vidanage, K., Noor, N. M. M., Mohemad, R., & Bakar, Z. A. (2020). Semantic Web-Based Knowledge Extraction: Upper Ontology Guided Crime Knowledge Discovery. In Vasudevan, H., Michalas, A., Shekokar, N., & Narvekar, M. (Eds.), *Advanced Computing Technologies and Applications. Algorithms for Intelligent Systems*. Springer. DOI: 10.1007/978-981-15-3242-9_30

Vlachos, P. A., Tsamakos, A., Vrechopoulos, A. P., & Avramidis, P. K. (2009). Corporate social responsibility. Attributions, loyalty, and the mediating role of trust. *Journal of the Academy of Marketing Science, 37*(2), 170–180. DOI: 10.1007/s11747-008-0117-x

Walke, S., & Khillare, S. (2023). Vulnerabilities And Ethical Implications. In *Machine Learning*. International Journal For Multidisciplinary Research.

Wamba, S. F., Gunasekaran, A., Akter, S., Ren, S. J., Dubey, R., & Childe, S. J. (2017). Big data analytics and firm performance: Effects of dynamic capabilities. *Journal of Business Research*, 70, 356–365. DOI: 10.1016/j.jbusres.2016.08.009

Wang, C., Zhang, L., Qin, T., Xi, Z., Sun, L., Wu, H., & Li, D. (2020). 3D printing in adult cardiovascular surgery and interventions: a systematic review. J Thorac Dis. https://www.ncbi.nlm.nih.gov/pmc/articles/PMC7330795/

Wang, L., Fan, H., & Wang, Y. (2018). Site selection of retail shops based on spatial accessibility and hybrid BP neural network. *ISPRS International Journal of Geo-Information, 7*(6). DOI: 10.3390/ijgi7060202

Wang, K. (2021). Unified distributed robust regression and variable selection framework for massive data. *Expert Systems with Applications*, 186, 115701. Advance online publication. DOI: 10.1016/j.eswa.2021.115701

Wang, L., Wang, X., Hawbani, A., Xiong, Y., & Zhang, X. (2020). Convolution Encoders for End-to-End Action Tracking With Space-Time Cubic Kernels. *IEEE Access : Practical Innovations, Open Solutions*, 8, 139023–139032. DOI: 10.1109/ACCESS.2020.3012154

Wang, Q., Dou, J., & Jia, S. (2015). A Meta-Analytic Review of Corporate Social Responsibility and Financial Performance: The Moderating Effect of Contextual Factors. *Business & Society*, 1–39. DOI: 10.1177/0007650315584317

Wang, Y., & Bouroncle, L. (2023). To trust or not to trust. Consumer perceptions of corporate sociopolitical activism. *Business and Professional Communication Quarterly*.

Wang, Y., Deng, L., Zheng, L., & Robert, X. (2021). Gao, Temporal convolutional network with soft thresholding and attention mechanism for machinery prognostics. *Journal of Manufacturing Systems*, 60, 512–526. Advance online publication. DOI: 10.1016/j.jmsy.2021.07.008

Wang, Y., Xiong, M., & Olya, H. (2020). Toward an understanding of responsible artificial intelligence practices. *Proceedings of the 53rd Hawaii International Conference on System Sciences*. DOI: 10.24251/HICSS.2020.610

Watto, W. A., Manurung, D. T., Saputra, K. A. K., & Mustafa, S. G. (2020). Corporate social responsibility and firm financial performance: A case of SME's sector in Pakistan. *International Journal of Environmental, Sustainability, and Social Science*, 1(2), 62–74. DOI: 10.38142/ijesss.v1i2.30

Weiss, J. N. (2023). The Health Insurance Portability and Accountability Act (HIPAA). In *Physician Crisis*. DOI: 10.1007/978-3-031-27979-9_15

Weller, A., & Raji, I. D. (2020). The Role of AI in Advancing CSR. Opportunities and Challenges. Journal of Technology Management & Innovation, 15(2), 26-37. DOI: 10.4067/S0718-27242020000200026

Werfel, S., Witko, C., & Heinrich, T. (2022). Public support for assistance for workers displaced by technology. *Research & Politics*, 9(2), 205316802210934. DOI: 10.1177/20531680221093440

Wichmann, J. R. K., Scholdra, T. P., & Reinartz, W. J. (2023). Propelling International Marketing Research with Geospatial Data. *Journal of International Marketing, 31*(2), 82–102. DOI: 10.1177/1069031X221149951

Willmen, T., Völkel, L., Ronicke, S., Hirsch, M. C., Kaufeld, J., Rychlik, R. P., & Wagner, A. D. (2021). Health economic benefits through the use of diagnostic support systems and expert knowledge. *BMC Health Services Research*, 21(1), 21. DOI: 10.1186/s12913-021-06926-y PMID: 34503507

Wong, R. T. (2021). Telecommunications network design: Technology impacts and future directions. *Networks*, 77(2), 205–224. DOI: 10.1002/net.21997

World Bank. (2016). Shock waves: Managing the impacts of climate change on poverty. Retrieved from https://openknowledge.worldbank.org/handle/10986/22787

World Bank. (2018). The Global Findex Database 2017: Measuring Financial Inclusion and the Fintech Revolution. Retrieved from https://globalfindex.worldbank.org/sites/globalfindex/files /2018-04/2017%20Findex%20full%20report_0.pdf

World Bank. (2019). *Digital Infrastructure for the 21st Century*. World Bank Publications.

World Economic Forum. (2021). Inclusive Growth and Development Report 2017. Retrieved from http://www3.weforum.org/docs/WEF_Forum_IncGrwth_2017.pdf

World Health Organization. (2018). Climate change and health. Retrieved from https://www.who.int/news-room/fact-sheets/detail/climate-change-and-health

Wu, L., Chen, Z. F., & Tao, W. (2024). Instilling warmth in artificial intelligence? Examining publics' responses to AI-applied corporate ability and corporate social responsibility practices. *Public Relations Review*, 50(1), 102426. DOI: 10.1016/j.pubrev.2024.102426

Xiang, H., Shaikh, E., Tunio, M. N., Watto, W. A., & Lyu, Y. (2022). Impact of corporate governance and CEO remuneration on bank capitalization strategies and payout decision in income shocks period. *Frontiers in Psychology*, 13, 901868. DOI: 10.3389/fpsyg.2022.901868 PMID: 36106037

Xie, T., & Pentina, I. (2022). Attachment Theory as a Framework to Understand Relationships with Social Chatbots: A Case Study of Replika. *Hawaii International Conference on System Sciences*. DOI: 10.24251/HICSS.2022.258

Xie, Y., Ma, W., Ma, Y., Ren, Z., Tong, Z., & Wang, Y. (2023). A counterfactual thinking perspective of moral licensing effect in machine-driven communication: An example of natural language processing chatbot developed based on WeChat API. *Technological Forecasting and Social Change*, 197, 122926. DOI: 10.1016/j.techfore.2023.122926

Xue, Z., Jin, T., Xu, S., Bai, K., He, Q., Zhang, F., Cheng, X., Ji, Z., Pang, W., Shen, Z., Song, H., Shuai, Y., & Zhang, Y. (2022). Assembly of complex 3D structures and electronics on curved surfaces. *Science Advances*, 8(32), 32. DOI: 10.1126/sciadv.abm6922 PMID: 35947653

Xu, S., Jiang, M., Lu, Q., Gao, S., Feng, J., Wang, X., He, X., Chen, K., Li, Y., & Ouyang, P. (2020). Properties of Polyvinyl Alcohol Films Composited With Hemicellulose and Nanocellulose Extracted From Artemisia selengensis Straw. *Frontiers in Bioengineering and Biotechnology*, 8, 980. Advance online publication. DOI: 10.3389/fbioe.2020.00980 PMID: 32984277

Yadav, A., Chandel, S., Chatufale, S., & Bandhakavi, A. (2023). LAHM: Large Annotated Dataset for Multilingual & Multi-Domain Hate Speech Identification. ArXiv, abs/2304.00913.

Yadav, N., Mathur, A., & Thanvi, J. (2024). Fusion of AI and ethical finance: Changing the outlook of financial companies and society. In *Fintech Applications in Islamic Finance: AI, Machine Learning, and Blockchain Techniques* (pp. 24-34). IGI Global.

Yang, G., Wang, L., Xu, X., & Xia, J. (2021). Footballer Action Tracking and Intervention Using Deep Learning Algorithm. *Journal of Healthcare Engineering*, 2021, 2021. DOI: 10.1155/2021/5518806 PMID: 33815728

Yang, J., & Mundel, J. (2021). "Are we all in this together?". Brand opportunism in covid-19 cause related marketing and the moderating role of consumer skepticism. *Journal of Promotion Management*, 27(6), 877–899. DOI: 10.1080/10496491.2021.1888181

Yan, H., Fu, L., & Hu, X. (2022). Harnessing service robots to increase frontline service employees' safety and health: The critical role of CSR. *Safety Science*, 151, 105731. DOI: 10.1016/j.ssci.2022.105731

Yankovskaya, V., Gerasimova, E. B., Osipov, V. S., & Lobova, S. V. (2022). Environmental CSR from the standpoint of stakeholder theory: Rethinking in the era of artificial intelligence. *Frontiers in Environmental Science*, 10, 953996. DOI: 10.3389/fenvs.2022.953996

Yao, X., & Lin, Y. (2020). Ethical implications of artificial intelligence (AI) in supply chain management: A systematic review. *Supply Chain Management*, 25(5), 569–588.

Yoo, D., & Lee, J. (2018). The effects of corporate social responsibility (CSR) Fit and CSR consistency on company evaluation. The role of CSR support. *Sustainability (Switzerland), 10*(8). DOI: 10.3390/su10082956

Yu. (2020). A Perspective on Using Machine Learning in 3D Bioprinting. *International Journal of Bioprinting*, 253. https://www.ncbi.nlm.nih.gov/pmc/articles/PMC7415853/

Zaidi, H., & Azmi, F. T. (2024). Workplace pro-environmental behaviour: A review and bibliometric analysis. *International Journal of Productivity and Performance Management*, 73(1), 158–185. DOI: 10.1108/IJPPM-09-2021-0507

Zainee, I. A., & Puteh, F. (2020). Corporate social responsibility impact on talent retention among Generation Y. *Revista de Gestão*, 27(4), 369–392. DOI: 10.1108/REGE-06-2019-0070

Zárate-Torres, R. A., & Correa, J. (2023). How good is the Myers-Briggs Type Indicator for predicting leadership-related behaviors? *Frontiers in Psychology*, 14, 14. DOI: 10.3389/fpsyg.2023.940961 PMID: 36936015

Zavyalova, E. B., Volokhina, V. A., Troyanskaya, M. A., & Dubova, Y. I. (2023). A humanistic model of corporate social responsibility in e-commerce with high-tech support in the artificial intelligence economy. *Humanities & Social Sciences Communications*, 10(1), 1–10. DOI: 10.1057/s41599-023-01764-1 PMID: 37273417

Zeng, Y., & Lu, X. (2018). Corporate Social Responsibility and AI. The Role of Stakeholders. Journal of Business Ethics, 152(2), 269-285. DOI: 10.1007/s10551-017-3417-3

Zhang, J., & Wu, Q. (2022). *CSR strategies fr ethical AI in the hspitality industry*. Jurnal f Sustainable Turism, 30(7), 1334-1350. https://di.rg/10.1080/09669582.2021.1956584

Zhang, Y., & Jiang, W. (2019). Corporate Social Responsibility and Ethical AI. A New Paradigm. Business Ethics Quarterly, 29(2), 345-368. DOI: 10.1017/beq.2018.52

Zhang, D. (2024). The pathway to curb greenwashing in sustainable growth: The role of artificial intelligence. *Energy Economics*, 133, 107562. DOI: 10.1016/j.eneco.2024.107562

Zhao, J., & Gomez Farinas, B. (2022). Artificial Intelligence and Sustainable Decisions. *European Business Organization Law Review*, 24(1), 1–39. DOI: 10.1007/s40804-022-00262-2

Zhao, L., Dai, T., Qiao, Z., Sun, P., Hao, J., & Yang, Y. (2020). Application of artificial intelligence to wastewater treatment: A bibliometric analysis and systematic review of technology, economy, management, and wastewater reuse. *Process Safety and Environmental Protection*, 133, 169–182. DOI: 10.1016/j.psep.2019.11.014

Zhao, W. W. (2018). How to improve corporate social responsibility in the era of artificial intelligence? *IOP Conference Series. Earth and Environmental Science*, 186(6), 012036. DOI: 10.1088/1755-1315/186/6/012036

Zhao, Y., & Jakkampudi, K. (2023). Assessing Policy Measures Safeguarding Workers from Artificial Intelligence in the United States. *Journal of Computer and Communications*, 11(11), 149–166. DOI: 10.4236/jcc.2023.1111008

Zheng, L., Chiang, W., Sheng, Y., Zhuang, S., Wu, Z., Zhuang, Y., Lin, Z., Li, Z., Li, D., Xing, E.P., Zhang, H., Gonzalez, J., & Stoica, I. (2023). Judging LLM-as-a-judge with MT- Bench and Chatbot Arena. ArXiv, abs/2306.05685.

Zhou, W., Li, X., Duan, H., & Pengyu, L. (2021). Multi-Material Integrated Three-Dimensional Printing of Cylindrical Li-Ion Battery. Journal of Manufacturing Science and Engineering. https://www.sciencedirect.com/science/article/pii/S1226086X17301559

About the Contributors

Erum Shaikh has a PhD from the Institute of Business Administration, University of Sindh, Jamshoro, Pakistan. She is an assistant professor and head of the Department of Business Administration at Shaheed Benazir Bhutto University, Sanghar Campus. Her research interests are Corporate Social Responsibility, Finance, Entrepreneurship, Sustainability, Corporate Governance, Management and Entrepreneurial Finance. She has authored over 40 publications (research papers, conference papers and book chapters) in top-notch research journals. She has edited seven books and is the editor of five research journals. She has wide experience in teaching and administration and has served more than ten years in academics. She has organized and participated in several research conferences and workshops as a keynote speaker, session Chair and guest speaker. She is a good teacher, researcher, speaker and trainer.

* * *

Munir Ahmad is a seasoned professional in the realm of Spatial Data Infrastructure (SDI), Geo-Information Productions, Information Systems, and Information Governance, boasting over 25 years of dedicated experience in the field. With a PhD in Computer Science, Dr. Ahmad's expertise spans Spatial Data Production, Management, Processing, Analysis, Visualization, and Quality Control. Throughout his career, Dr. Ahmad has been deeply involved in the development and deployment of SDI systems specially in the context of Pakistan, leveraging his proficiency in Spatial Database Design, Web, Mobile & Desktop GIS, and Geo Web Services Architecture. His contributions to Volunteered Geographic Information (VGI) and Open Source Geoportal & Metadata Portal have significantly enriched the geospatial community. As a trainer and researcher, Dr. Ahmad has authored over 50 publications, advancing the industry's knowledge base and fostering innovation in Geo-Tech, Data Governance, and Information Infrastructure, and Emerging

Technologies. His commitment to Research and Development (R&D) is evident in his role as a dedicated educator and mentor in the field.

Kathirvel Ayyaswamy acquired B.E.(CSE), M.E. (CSE) from Crescent Engineering College affiliated to University of Madras and Ph. D (CSE.) from Anna University. He is currently working as Professor, Dept of Computer Science and Engineering, Karunya Institute of Technology and Sciences, Coimbatore. He is a studious researcher by himself, completed 18 sponsored research projects worth of Rs 103 lakhs and published more than 110 articles in journals and conferences. 4 research scholars have completed Ph. D and 3 under progress under his guidance. He is working as scientific and editorial board member of many journals. He has reviewed dozens of papers in many journals. He has author of 13 books. His research interests are protocol development for wireless ad hoc networks, security in ad hoc network, data communication and networks, mobile computing, wireless networks, WSN and DTN. He is a Life member of the ISTE (India), IACSIT (Singapore), Life Member IAENG (Hong Kong), Member ICST (Europe), IAES, etc. He has given a number of guest lecturers/expert talks and seminars, workshops and symposiums.

Himanshi Bhatia is an Assistant Professor at School of Law, Graphic Era Hill University.

Indraneel Bose is currently working as Associate professor at Swami Vivekanand Subharti University Meerut UP in Hotel Management Department. Also He has PhD in Hotel Management from Swami Vivekanand Subharti University He has 3 patents published and also published research papers in various national and international journals. He has also presented research papers in many national and international conferences.

Maheswaran C. P. has more than 17 years of expertise in teaching. He completed his under graduation in Manonmaniam Sundaranar University and post graduation in Anna University. Dr. Maheswaran C. P. obtained his Doctorate of Philosophy in Faculty of Information and Communication Engineering at 2017 from Noorul Islam Centre for Higher Education. He started his career in 2006 and worked in few institutions. His areas of interest constitute the study of wireless networks, cloud computing, mobile networks, and information security. He has published 62 research papers in SCI-indexed journals, UGC and Scopus-indexed journals. He has written four book chapters and two books. He filed five patents to demonstrate the potential of his studies and four of them were published and a few patents under examination. He has extensive experience in guiding students in a variety of national and international activities. He was also influential in industry academic collaboration.

Aarti Chopra is a seasoned academician with over 18 years of teaching and administrative experience in higher education. Besides doctorate, she also holds a professional law degree. She is an active member of an NGO working for the promotion of sustainable fashion and saving environment. She is a member of many professional bodies and also in the executive committee of few of them. Dr Chopra is a certified corporate trainer and has been invited by number of PSUs and banks for conducting management trainings.

Abdul Dahri, PhD, is an assistant professor of human resource management in the Department of Management Science of Muhammad Ali Jinnah University in Karachi, Pakistan. He holds a PhD degree in human resource management conferred by University Utara Malaysia in 2019. He is also serving as a program advisor for the Management Sciences program of the university and a member of key committees in the university. With the research interest in waste area of social and management science, the author enjoys an edge in a variety of publications of international repute in the field of human resource management.

Asela Gunasekara had been acquired his bachelor's degree in Computing and Information Systems from London metropolitan University in UK with a 1st Class Honors, and his masters from the University of Colombo. Dr. Gunasekara has secured a full scholarship from the People's Republic of China for his PhD in Management Science & Engineering and there, he was awarded with the Honorary International Graduate and Academic Excellence awards from Huazhong University of Science & Technlogy, China. He was a regional higher achiever of UK National Computing Center programmes in the south Asian region and awarded with the Role of Honor award at the Global Examinations of National Computing Center of UK. He has held many administrative positions in General Sir John Kotelawala Defence University including the Headship of the Department of Computer Science, the In charge of MBA in E-Governance programme and the Coordination of International relations of Faculty of Computing. He pursued his PhD research in Usability Heuristics in Human Computer Interaction and he is interested in Brain Machine Interfacing, E-Health and E-Learning research. He has secured several Indexed journal conference publication at international level. He is a Senior member of Institute of Electrical and Electronics Engineering, Professional Member of BCS and CSSL. At present Dr. Gunasekara is holding the Deanship of Faculty of Computing in General Sir John Kotelawala Defence University.

Reeti Gupta is working as assistant professor of commerce in Government College, Israna (Panipat), which is a constituent college of a prestigious state university, Kurukshetra university, Kurukshetra, Haryana. She has research and teaching experience of more than fifteen years in 'commerce and management'. Given her keen interest in academics and research activities, she has presented research papers in more than fifty national/international conferences/ seminars and has published fifteen research papers in refereed journals of national/international repute. Her research interests include entrepreneurship, artificial intelligence in business, international trade, social media, and strategy. ORCID ID: https://orcid.org/0009-0008-8341-8096.

Aastha Jain is an Assistant Professor in the Department of Management Studies at Vaish College of Engineering, Rohtak, affiliated with Maharshi Dayanand University, Rohtak, Haryana, India. With a solid academic foundation in Commerce and Management, Dr. Jain has made significant contributions to the field through numerous studies published in various reputed academic journals and edited books. Her research interests include Investment Behaviour, Artificial Intelligence in business, Women Entrepreneurship, Tourism and Sustainability.

Nikhilesh Jain is associated with ROTTO and SOTTO premier organ transplant organizations in India and instrumental in assisting brain death guidelines and part of intensivist subcommittee on the same. Teaching Faculty for DNB (Critical Care), Program director Fellowship in Neuro Critical Care, FCCCM fellowship course in Critical Care/guideline faculty, abstract reviewer and nursing leadership section for Neurocritical care society along with multiple teaching lectures on platform of Indian Society of Critical Care Medicine and Mohan Foundation.

Shenson Joseph is a distinguished AI researcher and data science expert. With expertise in Data Science, Analytics, and Artificial Intelligence, he has authored 2 books and authored more than 6 research papers. Shenson has judged over many national and international events and actively contributes to editorial boards and conferences. He has earned a master's degree in Data Science and second masters degree in Electrical & Computer Engineering.

Jagbir Singh Kadyan is a post graduate in Commerce, Management, Economics and Social Work from the Savitribai Phule Pune University (Erstwhile University of Pune), Bharti Vidyapeeth Pune, Tilak Maharashtra University Pune and IGNOU Indira Gandhi National Open University, New Delhi respectively. He has also been awarded Ph.D in the field of CSR – Corporate Social Responsibility from the Department of Commerce, Maharishi Dayanand University, Rohtak, Haryana. His research interest includes Business Management (Marketing; OB & HRM; Accounting, Finance and Taxation); Corporate Governance & CSR-Corporate Social Responsibility. He is a reviewer for igi-global; GSI Journals; The Common Ground Research Networks; American Journal of Information Technology and

Management Science; World Academy of Science, Engineering and Technology, (WASET), USA; Integration of Education, Russia. Presently, he is working as Assist. Professor, Dept. of Commerce, Shri Ram College of Commerce, University of Delhi and is also Honorary Associate Director, - Research with Centre for Socio-economic and Sustainability Research,, New Delhi, India.

Muhammad Khan is an accomplished professional in the field of business administration, holding a Master's degree in Business Administration with a specialization in International Management from Ballarat University, Australia. His academic journey has provided him with a profound understanding of international business practices, leadership, and management strategies. Throughout his career, Muhammad has garnered extensive experience as a Program Director and Coordinator, skillfully overseeing and developing academic programs to align with industry trends and meet student needs. Currently, he serves as a Senior Lecturer and MBA Program Coordinator in the Business Management Department at Villa College in the Maldives, where he continues to impart his knowledge and expertise to the next generation of business leaders.

Pankaj Kumar is currently working as an Assistant Professor in Faculty of Commerce and Management, United University, Prayagraj, Uttar Pradesh. He has completed his Ph.D. in Finance from Faculty of Commerce, Banaras Hindu University and published number of research papers in ABDC and Care listed journals.

Crishelen Kurezyn Díaz is a Full-time Professor-Researcher at Universidad Popular Autónoma del Estado de Puebla (UPAEP) in Puebla, Mexico. She holds a PhD in Organization Management, a Master in Work and Organizational Psychology and a Bachelor in Psychology. Her work focuses on the development and behavior of the person. She has been an active member of the Group of Leaders of the Future of Mexico at the Business Summit since 2016, and a member of Academia B México belonging to B Corp. She has served as a speaker at international companies such as Volkswagen, and the United Nations Fourth Global Forum at Case Western Reserve University and B Corp Academic Roundtable at the University of Toronto. Dr. Kurezyn serves as a Latin American Ambassador Professor at AIM2Flourish. She was awarded the Flourish Prizes for her collaborative work with the United Nations in 2017, 2018, 2019 and 2020.

Cynthia Montaudon-Tomas is a full-time professor and a business consultant at the Business School at UPAEP. Since September 2018, she became head of the Observatory on Competitiveness and New Ways of Working, which deals with numerous issues related to social problems and creates awareness about current and future social needs. She has obtained a Post Doctorate Certificate In Organizational Leadership from Regent University in Virginia, USA; a Ph.D. in Strategic Planning and Technology Management from UPAEP, in Puebla, Mexico; a Ph.D. in Business from the University of Lincoln in Lincolnshire, UK, and three masters degrees: one in Quality Engineering from the Universidad Iberoamericana in Puebla, Mexico, another in Communication and media from the Jean Moulin, Lyon II University in Lyon, France, and the last one in Business Administration from the Tec de Monterrey in Mexico.

Kumari Neelam is currently pursuing her Ph.D in Finance from from Department of Commerce, Mahatma Gandhi Kashi Vidyapith, Varanasi, Uttar Pradesh. She has published number of research papers in ABDC and Peer reviewed journals.

Ankit Pathania is working as an Assistant Professor (Management) at Akal College of Economics, Commerce & Management, Eternal University, Baru Sahib, Distt.-Sirmaur (HP), India. He did his MBA and doctorate in the discipline of Agri-Business Management from Dr YS Parmar University of Horticulture and Forestry, Nauni, Solan, HP, India and qualified ICAR-NET.

Ingrid Pinto López is a university professor, researcher and consultor at Business School of UPAEP University, recognized by the National System of Researchers (SNI Conacyt). Ph.D. in Strategic Planning and Technology Management. Currently coordinator of the competitiveness observatory and new forms of work, coordinator of the international arbitration of the Latin American Association of Accounting and Administration Schools ALAFEC, member of Barcelona Economics Network and the Illustrious Latin American Academy of doctors.

Ankit Prakash is currently working in RKDF University Ranchi Jharkhand.

Sabyasachi Pramanik is a professional IEEE member. He obtained a PhD in Computer Science and Engineering from Sri Satya Sai University of Technology and Medical Sciences, Bhopal, India. Presently, he is an Associate Professor, Department of Computer Science and Engineering, Haldia Institute of Technology, India. He has many publications in various reputed international conferences, journals, and book chapters (Indexed by SCIE, Scopus, ESCI, etc). He is doing research in the fields of Artificial Intelligence, Data Privacy, Cybersecurity, Network Security, and Machine Learning. He also serves on the editorial boards of several international journals. He is a reviewer of journal articles from IEEE, Springer, Elsevier, Inderscience, IET and IGI Global. He has reviewed many conference papers, has been a keynote speaker, session chair, and technical program committee member at many international conferences. He has authored a book on Wireless Sensor Network. He has edited 8 books from IGI Global, CRC Press, Springer and Wiley Publications.

Karun Sanjaya is an Assistant Professor at Symbiosis Law School, Nagpur, Symbiosis International (Deemed University), Pune, India. He is specialised in Intellectual Property Laws and is currently the Faculty-in-charge of the Centre for Intellectual Property Rights and Advocacy at SLS, Nagpur. His areas of interest include Tort Laws, Contract Laws, Cyber Laws, Intellectual Property Laws, Artificial Intelligence and allied laws. He is a recipient of the Justice Krishna Iyer Memorial Merit Award, 2019, Adv. P.F., Thomas Memorial Gold Medal, 2019, Dr. K.N. Chandrashekharan Pillai Gold Medal 2022 and Justice Krishna Iyer Memorial Merit Award, 2022. He was formerly the executive editor of IILS Law Review and has authored over twenty book chapters and fourteen research articles in diverse areas of law. Karun had also qualified UGC NET with JRF (Law) and is presently pursuing his PhD from VIT School of Law, Vellore Institute of Technology, Chennai, Tamil Nadu, India.

Vikas Sharma is an alumnus of IHM Gwalior. He has 8 years of experience, including teaching and industry experience in luxury brands like ITC grand Bharat Gurugram, The Leela Ambience Hotel and Residences Gurugram and Le Meridian Gurugram. Currently he is associated with Swami Vivekanand Subharti University, Bhikaji Cama Subharti college of Hotel Management as Assistant Professor. Also He is currently pursuing PhD in Hotel Management from Swami Vivekanand Subharti University and has completed Masters in Travel and Tourism Management. He has 7 patents published and also published 8 research papers in various national and international journals. He has attended 15 FDPs and workshops. He has also presented research papers in many national and international conferences.

Kuldeep Singh currently serves as Assistant Professor in Amity School of Hospitality, Amity University, Manesar, Haryana, India. He completed his Ph.D. in tourism from Maharishi Dayanand University(Rohtak) in India in the year 2020. He is also a UGC (Net- JRF qualified). Dr. Singh has also served the tourism industry for couple of years and three years in academics. Dr. Singh has so far published more than 30 research articles in both international and national referred journals as well as in edited books in the field of Tourism. Currently, He is serving as an editor of book series in various reputed publications (Emerald, IIP series). Dr. Singh is passionate about the academic areas of Service Quality Management, Rural tourism, Ecotourism, and Sustainable tourism. He also won aspiring researchers welcome award from Indian Hospitality Congress. His credential may be verified on various research platforms like Google Scholar, SSRN, LinkedIn, Academia, and Research Gate.

Pravin Chandra Singh is currently working as an Assistant Professor at MSMSR, Mats University, Raipur. Prior to Mats University he was associated with Raffles University, Rajasthan. He has done his Doctorate from IM-BHU in Marketing and published a number of research paper in the journal and publisher of repute Like IIM-S, IGI-Global, PBRI.

Sujay Vikram Singh, a Senior Research Fellow currently pursuing a doctoral degree at Banaras Hindu University, completed his graduation and post-graduation from IHM Lucknow. His research interests encompass Hospitality, CRM, Service Marketing, Service Quality, and Systematic Literature reviews. He has authored papers featured in diverse handbooks and journals, with recent publications in reputable outlets such as the International Journal of Market Research (Sage publishing), ABDC-A, Scopus, and the Journal of Global Information Management (IGI Publishing), indexed in Scopus and ABDC-A. Additionally, he has presented papers at numerous conferences and seminars, earning recognition for the best papers at events like IHM Bhopal and Subharati University, with special mentions at Shaheed Bhagat Singh College, DU, and achieving the highest marks in special tracks at Wosxen University and AMU.

Yajvendra Singh is currently associated with Swami Vivekanand Subharti University, Bhikaji Cama Subharti college of Hotel Management as Assistant Professor.

C. Sinha is a veteran in the field of Hotel & Tourism, who has served the hospitality sector for more than two decades in Taj grp. of Hotels & Ashok grp. of Hotels. Then moved to the Hospitality educational institutions to facilitate the knowledge of gourmet and other required subjects to the buddies of Hotel & Tourism sector since 2007 in the capacity of Principal/Director. Also enlightened the Pro poor stakeholders of hospitality sector in Agra & Braj region under the banner of World Bank & UP Tourism.

Pradeep Soni has over 16 years of experience teaching UG and PG students. He is the program officer of NSS and Scouts wing of the college. He is awarded at the state level for his contribution to the National Service Scheme. His core areas are Income Tax, Cost Accounting and Management. He is a keen observer and persistent learner. He conducts many educational tours and seminars for the students.

Ambar Srivastava is a faculty in School of Commerce, Finance & Accountancy at Christ (Deemed to be University), Delhi NCR, Ghaziabad, India. He qualified for the NET (Commerce) conducted by UGC in 2013.

Ankit Srivastava is currently associated with Swami Vivekanand Subharti University, Bhikaji Cama Subharti College of Hotel Management as Assistant Professor.

Usha Srivastava is an associate member of the Institute of Company Secretaries of India (ICSI), an academician, and a keen researcher. She has over 15 years of experience in academics and corporate. She has published more than 12 Research papers in UGC CARE, Scopus, and other reputed Journals and 2 edited book chapters. She has contributed to Professional publication of ICSI titeld "company law exploring procedural dimensions". Her areas of interest include capital market, microfinance, SME, and corporate Governance. Currently she is working as an associate professor in School of Management Studies and Research, at MATS University.

Saurabh Tripathi is currently associated with Swami Vivekanand Subharti University, Bhikaji Cama Subharti College of Hotel Management as Assistant Professor.

Index

D

E

G

H

I

J

M

O

P

Q

R

S

T

W

www.ingramcontent.com/pod-product-compliance
Lightning Source LLC
LaVergne TN
LVHW080602300926
849162LV00005B/1027